Strategies of Compliance with the European Court of Human Rights

PENNSYLVANIA STUDIES IN HUMAN RIGHTS

Bert B. Lockwood, Jr., Series Editor

A complete list of books in the series
is available from the publisher.

Strategies of Compliance with the European Court of Human Rights

Rational Choice Within Normative Constraints

Andreas von Staden

PENN

UNIVERSITY OF PENNSYLVANIA PRESS

PHILADELPHIA

Published by
University of Pennsylvania Press
Philadelphia, Pennsylvania 19104-4112
www.upenn.edu/pennpress

Printed in the United States of America on acid-free paper
1 3 5 7 9 10 8 6 4 2

Library of Congress Cataloging-in-Publication Data
Names: Von Staden, Andreas, author.
Title: Strategies of compliance with the European Court of Human Rights: rational choice within
    normative constraints / Andreas von Staden.
Description: 1st edition. | Philadelphia: University of Pennsylvania Press, [2018] | Series:
    Pennsylvania studies in human rights | Includes bibliographical references and index.
Identifiers: LCCN 2017056089 | ISBN 9780812250282 (hardcover: alk. paper)
Subjects: LCSH: European Court of Human Rights. | Compliance. | Human rights—Government
    policy—Germany. | Human rights—Government policy—Great Britain. | Effectiveness and
    validity of law—European Union countries. | International law and human rights—European
    Union countries.
Classification: LCC KJC5138 .S725 2018 | DDC 342.4108—dc23
LC record available at https://lccn.loc.gov/2017056089

CONTENTS

PART II. GERMANY

The Convention, the Court,
and Second-Order Compliance

During the last two decades, the system of human rights protection set up under the European Convention on Human Rights (ECHR, or the "Convention"), with the European Court of Human Rights (ECtHR, or the "Court")—frequently heralded as being one of the most effective international courts in existence[1]—at its center, has come under stress. One source of that stress has been the rapid growth of the number of individual applications lodged since the late 1990s, which have vastly increased the workload of the Court. While the resources allocated to the Court from among the Council of Europe's budget also increased, they did so at a disproportionately lower rate that proved insufficient to process the mounting number of applications in a timely manner,[2] resulting in a massive backlog of pending cases that at its peak exceeded 150,000 applications.[3] Several factors interacted to produce this development, among them the doubling of the number of states party to the ECHR as part of the enlargement of the Council of Europe (COE)—the ECtHR's parent organization—following the end of the Cold War, direct access to the Court after the 1998 institutional reforms under Protocol No. 11, certain jurisprudential developments that made applying to Strasbourg appear attractive to potential litigants, as well as the very mundane fact that it had simply become more widely and better known among potential beneficiaries of rights litigation and their lawyers in the member states. To reduce the backlog, further institutional reforms were initiated with Protocol No. 14 which, inter alia, tightened admissibility requirements and provided for inadmissibility decisions by single-judge formations. These reforms contributed to reducing the number of applications pending before a judicial formation to 64,850 at the end of 2015.[4]

A second source of stress for the ECHR system arose as a growing number of member states began to challenge the boundaries of the Court's authority more vocally and persistently than in previous instances of disagreement with the Court's judgments. This "diffusion of critical discourse"[5] may find its most prominent manifestations in the debates within the United Kingdom of adopting a domestic bill of rights to shield against the influence of the ECtHR[6] and in the Russian Constitutional Court's 2015 judgment that the execution of ECtHR judgments could be refused when they are seen to contradict the Russian constitution,[7] but criticisms have been voiced in many other countries as well.[8] At the multilateral level, efforts to "rebalance the system [. . .] between law and politics and between the international and the national"[9] have resulted in the 2012 Brighton and 2015 Brussels Declarations' foregrounding of the principle of subsidiarity,[10] the future inclusion of an express reference to the national margin of appreciation in the Convention's preamble,[11] and the Court's competence to give advisory opinions at the request of the member state's "highest courts and tribunals."[12]

A third source of strain, in part correlated with the first two, concerns the problem of insufficient, delayed, or outright noncompliance with the Court's judgments. With the most recent institutional reforms after Protocol No. 14 now implemented, the 2015 Brussels Declaration pointed out that "emphasis must now be placed on the current challenges, in particular the repetitive applications resulting from the non-execution of Court judgments [. . .] and the difficulties of States Parties in executing certain judgments due to the scale, nature or cost of the problems raised."[13] The COE's Steering Committee for Human Rights (CDDH) has similarly noted that while "the overwhelming majority of Court judgments are executed without any particular difficulty [. . .] the execution of some cases is problematic for reasons of a more political nature, while the execution of some other cases is problematic for reasons of a more technical nature due notably to the complexity of the execution measures or the financial implications of the judgment" and stressed "that the execution of Court judgments raising structural or systemic problems is key to alleviating the Court's burden and to preventing future similar violations."[14] In 2015 the Parliamentary Assembly of the Council of Europe (PACE) which selectively monitors compliance with the Court's judgments of its own accord[15] "note[d] with concern that the main challenges facing the Court, most notably the high number of repetitive applications and persistent human rights violations of a particularly serious nature, reveal a failure by certain High Contracting Parties to discharge their obligations under the Convention."[16]

The COE's Committee of Ministers is charged with supervising the execution of the Court's judgments by respondent states (Article 46 (2) ECHR) and has had to deal with its own backlog of unexecuted cases, with the number of judgments pending execution at year's end hovering around 10,000 since 2010.[17] The Committee's most recent report on supervising the execution of judgments classifies 89 percent of the 9,941 cases pending before it at the end of 2016 as "repetitive cases," that is, those relating to a convention violation found in an earlier judgment that has not yet been adequately remedied.[18] This development of delayed and insufficient compliance is problematic not least because of the self-reinforcing effects it may have in that it "risks generating a vicious circle in which government officials point to public criticisms of the Court and compliance delays in other States to justify non-compliance in their own jurisdictions and to legitimize criticism of those who advocate adherence to the Court's rulings."[19]

What is clear is that earlier claims that the Court's judgments "have [. . .] not only generally but always been complied with by the Contracting States concerned,"[20] with "no exceptions" and "without the need for 'enforcement,'"[21] so that they could be considered "as effective as those of any domestic court,"[22] are no longer sustainable in an unqualified manner in the face of the mounting empirical evidence that at a minimum challenges, and at worst contradicts, such claims. Furthermore, the earlier assertions of perfect compliance have long suffered from a lack of systematic empirical verification. While there have been a good number of (usually legal) analyses of compliance with select individual judgments, or sets of judgments, as well as occasional country-wide studies,[23] comprehensive assessments covering all judgments across all years and respondent states, or at least a representative sample thereof, and methodologically well-grounded inquiries into the causal factors producing the observable patterns of implementation and compliance have long been a desideratum in the literature.[24]

More recently, this lacuna is beginning to be filled,[25] not least due to the growing interest in studying the ECtHR among social scientists[26] and an emerging focus on researching specifically the issues of compliance with the Court's judgments (what Roger Fisher had labeled "second-order" compliance),[27] as well as with the Convention as such ("first-order compliance").[28] In a 2006 book on the ECHR's "achievements, problems and prospects," Steven Greer discusses certain problems especially of first-order (non)compliance from an aggregate as well as comparative point of view, without, however, subjecting any of the emerging hypotheses to systematic testing.[29] Similarly, the 2008 edited volume *A Europe of Rights*[30] examines the impact of the Convention and of the Court's jurisprudence on national legal systems through focusing on the ECHR's domestic "reception," with "reception" being understood as "how— that is, through what mechanisms—national officials confront, make use of, and resist or give agency to Convention rights."[31] Rich in descriptive detail, the study's country reports "chart cross-national variance in the impact of the ECHR on national legal systems, and they provide materials for generating hypotheses that might explain this variance," without again, however, testing these hypotheses in other cases.[32] In any event, while compliance with individual judgments is addressed as part of the country studies, neither its systematic assessment nor its causal explanation is the study's principal focus. The same holds true for a recent volume, authored by ECtHR and national judges as well as by some other legal practitioners, on the impact of the Convention and Court on the democratization process in Central and Eastern Europe.[33]

In other work, Darren Hawkins and Wade Jacoby have mined Council of Europe data on compliance trends in support of their argument that "partial compliance" is a significant outcome with respect to a nontrivial number of ECtHR judgments,[34] but they do not test any causal hypotheses to explain why such partial compliance obtains. A 2013 edited volume expressly foregrounds the causal questions concerning the implementation of ECtHR judgments, but in order to canvass possibilities rather than to "advanc[e] a consistent causal argument or a theory about the factors promoting and obstructing the domestic impact of and compliance with ECtHR case law."[35] In a separately published article, two of the contributors to that volume found, on the basis of a sample of judgments and violations of Articles 8–11 ECHR against nine respondent states, that "the greater the legal infrastructure capacity and government effectiveness, the more expeditious the implementation of the ECtHR's rulings is likely to be."[36]

In the first book-length study of compliance with human rights judgments by the ECtHR and its counterpart in the Americas, the Inter-American Court of Human Rights (IACtHR), Courtney Hillebrecht has foregrounded three causal pathways that might be expected to affect compliance with adverse judgments. Such compliance may occur, Hillebrecht argues, (1) because it enables states to credibly signal their commitment to human rights and build a reputation for compliance with human rights in particular and international law more generally; (2) because it allows domestic actors to set and advance their own human rights agendas in contexts where they face political or institutional constraints; or (3) because a democratic commitment to human rights and the rule of law makes states comply "begrudgingly," despite diverging substantive preferences.[37] Empirically, Hillebrecht finds, inter alia, that compliance varies across remedial measures, with financial obligations being more readily complied with than, for example, the requirement to implement legislative reforms, and that compliance is positively correlated with the strength of domestic institutional constraints on the executive.[38] Most recently, Sharanbir Grewal and Erik Voeten have found that new democracies tend to be quicker than established democracies in achieving compliance with comparable types of judgments.[39]

This book adds to this emerging literature on compliance with ECtHR judgments. It makes two main contributions. First, it provides the first comprehensive assessment of the current state of compliance, as of March 2017, with all of the Court's judgments rendered up to the end of 2015, making use of the Committee of Ministers' own accumulated data on the execution of judgments. While raising certain questions as to the validity of the Committee's data as reliable indicators of compliance—which I address later on—the data set constructed for this assessment allows identifying actual compliance rates for countries, years, and types of violations across all judgments rendered through 2015. The quantitative evidence shows that 43.3 percent of the ECtHR's compliance-relevant judgments had not been sufficiently complied with as of March 10, 2017, and therefore remained under supervision with the Committee of Ministers, with some of them dating back all the way to 1996. While these aggregate statistics are significant in their own right, they remain limited with respect to the information they convey. Being concerned solely with the final outcome of the process of executing the Court's judgments, they do not say anything about whether the lack of compliance equates to outright noncompliance, partial compliance, or (so far) insufficient attempts to achieve full compliance, nor do they allow any inference as to the causal factors at work.

The second—and larger—part of this study tackles some of these issues. It examines both what may be called the "depth of compliance" issue as well as the question of how the observable compliance patterns can best be explained. Both compliance and noncompliance with the Court's judgments may be said to present puzzles from the vantage point of the two main theoretical orientations in international relations: rationalism and constructivism. As concerns compliance and rationalist theories, why would the governments of sovereign states comply with human rights judgments they disagree with, especially if they have popular majorities behind them, given that the Court and the Council of Europe (of whose institutional architecture the Court forms a part) have no means of enforcement nor any material incentives at their disposal, and that other states, in light of the largely domestically limited impact of international human rights regulation, for the most part have no incentive to enforce such judgments either?[40] Even if we accept that European democracies created the Convention system to lock in a particular from of liberal democracy,[41] this does not automatically translate into a preference in favor of complying with each and every of the Court's substantive decisions, not least because the governmental actors that initiated ratification of the Convention and those that have to implement adverse judgments are usually not the same (except occasionally with respect to countries that only recently joined the Convention system). From a rationalist perspective, then, this leaves certain domestic channels of influence as the principal pathways of exerting influence on decision-makers to comply with the ECtHR's judgments.[42] These pathways, I argue, may explain some, but by no means all, instances of compliance and thus remain only partially satisfactory in the ECHR context.

Constructivists, by contrast, might argue that widespread compliance should not be surprising, given that the parties to the ECHR are, for the most part, liberal democracies (or at least endeavor to be so), and that it is implicit in the identity of a liberal democracy that it accept the authority of a duly constituted court and comply with human rights judgments rendered against it; indeed, it is precisely through such compliance with human rights norms, among other behavioral expectations, that the very identity of a liberal democracy is reaffirmed and recreated. While such a norm- and identity-based approach may help illuminate compliance in the face of conflicting policy preferences on the part of the governmental actors that have to implement a given judgment, it runs into its own difficulties when faced with the phenomenon of judgments that fail to be complied with for many years. Furthermore, even if compliance occurs as a formal legal matter, a purely norm-based approach is underspecified in that it remains silent on the specific manner in which states implement ECtHR's judgments. As will become clear in the course of this study, these specific choices can matter a great deal for the actual impact of a given compliance decision on domestic law or policy and those affected by them—a differential impact that is not captured by merely postulating norm-following as such.

In light of these challenges for each position taken separately, I argue that the best explanation of the empirically observable patterns of compliance with the judgments of the European Court of Human Rights requires *combining* rationalist and constructivist logics of action into a joint model that takes both positions seriously. Specifically, I argue that to understand the compliance behavior of European liberal democracies, the reason *why* states comply with ECtHR judgments should be considered separately from the question of *how* they comply with them, at least analytically. Whereas the former is best explained, in the specific context here under consideration, by what may be thought of as a normative compliance pull exerted on European liberal democracies by the obligation to comply with the judgments of a duly constituted international court (the constructivist element), the decision of how to comply remains generally subject to a consequentialist logic based on political preferences and cost-benefit calculations (the rationalist element). In other words, governments will generally choose rationally among the available options within the normative constraint of having to comply formally with the judgment(s) rendered against them. Because there is no reason to expect that ECtHR judgments will trigger immediate preference reversals on the part of respondent governments, and because the issues decided by the ECtHR in its judgments against liberal democracies are, for the most part and with some notable exceptions, not of such a nature as to elicit widespread political or even electoral pressures to implement a judgment broadly, the standard course of action pursued by respondent states will be to execute judgments narrowly, guided by the preferences held prior to the judgment. These considerations result in the expectation that liberal democracies will generally comply with ECtHR judgments rendered against them, even without any meaningful enforcement beyond peer pressure, but that they will frequently do so in a restrictive, minimalist, or otherwise evasive manner and not infrequently with some delay.

These theoretical expectations are tested in the context of two case studies of two established democracies and longtime parties to the ECHR: the United Kingdom and Germany. With respect to each of these two countries, I examine the manner in which they have complied with all of the ECtHR's judgments rendered against them until the end of 2010.[43] Two considerations guided the case selection. First, established democracies are commonly expected to perform better with respect to complying with human rights—not least because human rights protection is a defining characteristic of most conceptions of democracy—and I was particularly interested in the manner in which they live up to that expectation. Second, the feasibility of conducting comprehensive case studies of all judgments rendered against a country required limiting the number of countries studied. Comprehensiveness is desirable to be able to observe remedial responses to all types of judgments in which violations have been found against a particular country, not just those deemed most important (by whatever standard) or a sample that might miss observations from the quite varied spectrum of issue areas and types of violations that can provide important insights for the present inquiry.

In this study, I take seriously both the internal logic of international law generally, and of the ECHR specifically, as well as the political forces that affect how law operates within a given political community and historical context. The work is placed squarely at the intersection of research strands on human rights, on compliance, and on judicial politics. The focus on the European Court of Human Rights and the particular sociopolitical context within which it operates gives rise to some distinct themes and issues. First, the countries subject to the Court's jurisdiction are, or aspire to be, for the most part, liberal democracies, which leads to a change in focus both in terms of the human rights issues that arise within the system as well as with respect to the institutional mechanisms through which remedies may be sought and adopted. So far, much of the human rights literature in international relations has predominantly addressed physical integrity rights: the right to life, freedom from torture, and liberty and security of the person.[44] Given the fundamental nature of these rights as well as the still-widespread violations thereof that can be witnessed the globe over, this is justifiable because it is here that human rights improvements are most urgently needed.

The issues addressed by the ECtHR, by contrast, go well beyond the important but limited set of physical integrity rights and include the full panoply of civil and political rights protected by the Convention and its protocols. While violations of the right to life and of freedom from torture are unfortunately not absent in contemporary Europe, they are, at least in the established liberal democracies, comparatively rare. Many cases instead concern what may be qualified as policy disputes that revolve around different interpretations of what a given right requires in specific circumstances, including such issue areas as the protection of private property, privacy rights, and procedural fairness. In many of these cases the stark language of human rights "abuses" or "crimes" in the form of intentional violations of clear treaty standards that suffuses the literature on physical integrity rights[45] is inapposite. Rather, many of these cases are better characterized as disputes concerning rival interpretations as to what implications a particular norm has for law and policy in a given issue area, and it is only after the Court's judgment that what is to count as a violation is authoritatively established. Still, the fact that many of these decisions may be qualified as "fine-tuning sophisticated national democratic engines that [are], on the whole, working well"[46] should not diminish the significance of these judgments. To the claimants and to others in similar circumstances in the respondent state and beyond, possible changes in policies on such issues as parental visitation rights, compensation for infringements of property rights, access to personal data, protection of privacy, or length of proceedings, and so forth, are of key importance. With physical integrity largely assured, other rights and their exercise move to the foreground and become the legally and politically relevant criteria according to which one's ability to live a "good life" as one sees fit is assessed.

In addition to greater clarity and precision that comes with the specificity of judicial decisions, exploring second-order compliance with judgments, rather than first-order compliance with the Convention, involves a shift in focus "from rights to remedies,"[47] that is, away from the scope of a right and the reason for its violation to the willingness of respondent states to adopt appropriate remedial measures to end that violation, prevent its recurrence, and compensate the victims, as necessary. The question of why state authorities chose a particular course of action that was subsequently found to be in breach of the Convention naturally remains relevant to the question of second-order compliance because it will likely affect the state's response; the implementation of the ECtHR's judgments, after all, frequently takes place in the same political and institutional environment that previously sustained the policy, action, or situation later found to constitute a violation. Because most of the Convention parties are democracies that have their own domestic systems of human rights protection in place, possess a modicum of bureaucratic infrastructure, and are by comparison with many of the human rights trouble spots in the world comparatively well-off economically, we should expect different opportunities for compliance with the Court's judgments— as well as different obstacles—than in the case of many developing countries that often lack some of the elements of a fully functioning state apparatus and political system. The state, after all, is not only the violator of human rights but also their most important protector.

Finally, in terms of research on judicial politics beyond the state, propelled particularly by interest in the Court of Justice of the European Union (CJEU, formerly known as the European Court of Justice [ECJ]) as a motor of European integration[48] and by the global expansion of adjudication and other forms of institutionalized dispute settlement,[49] the strategic environments within which international courts operate are partly similar, partly distinct. On the one hand, all courts share certain functional features that underpin their "court-ness," structurally, as dispute settlement institutions generally,[50] and in contrast to other forms of third-party dispute settlers specifically.[51] On the other hand, they also differ with respect to their specific institutional designs and procedures, with some differences being more consequential than others. Most important, the specific strategic environment within which courts operate—defined by the legal regime of which they are part, interactions with state and non-state users, and the relationship with other international institutions—is different for each court. Because the ECtHR is part of the intergovernmental COE, not the European Union (EU), it does not benefit from the direct effect and supremacy of EU law as does the CJEU. It remains formally an international court whose judgments do not have direct effect in domestic law, except to the extent that states themselves provide for it. Also, in terms of the states that fall under its jurisdiction, the post–Cold War enlargement of the COE and the increase in the number of ECHR parties has significantly diversified the range of issues the Court faces as well as the types of domestic institutional and political contexts within which its judgments have to be executed.[52]

While it is not required for understanding the compliance dynamics discussed in this book to have specialist knowledge of the historical origins and development of the European Convention on Human Rights and of the procedures before its supervisory machinery,[53] a basic understanding of how the Convention and Court have evolved and operate is useful. The next section provides such an overview.

The European Court and Convention of Human Rights: A Brief Overview

When the Convention for the Protection of Human Rights and Fundamental Freedoms—the ECHR's official name—was signed on November 4, 1950, assessments of its supervisory mechanism in particular were mixed.[54] While the call for a "Charter of Human Rights" and for a "Court of Justice with adequate sanctions for the implementation of this Charter" included in the 1948 Congress of Europe's "Message to Europeans"[55] found resonance in some of the Convention drafts coming out of the Consultative (later renamed Parliamentary) Assembly of the newly founded COE, the governments of the member states could not agree on a mandatory supervisory mechanism with a strong court at its center. Instead, the original Convention provided for a more cautious, tripartite supervisory mechanism comprising a commission, a court, and the Committee of Ministers, the COE's executive decision-making body composed of government representatives. Incoming complaints were first to be screened for admissibility and assessed as to their merits by the European Commission of Human Rights (the "Commission"), whose reports, however, were not legally binding. Moreover, both the right of the Commission to receive complaints from individuals and the jurisdiction of the Court were made optional, each requiring separate declarations of acceptance, in addition to ratification, by the states party to the Convention (cf. Articles 25 and 46 ECHR [1950]).[56]

In the absence of a state's declaration accepting the individual complaints procedure, the Commission could deal only with interstate complaints against that state,[57] while any complaints against states that had not accepted the jurisdiction of the Court were instead decided by the Committee of Ministers (Article 32 ECHR [1950]). The Committee's decisions required a two-thirds majority of the members entitled to sit on the Committee (not only of those actually present and voting) and were legally binding. While this requirement denied veto power to the respondent state, the specific supermajority requirement also resulted in a few "nondecisions" where the votes for or against the finding of a violation failed to reach the required two-thirds threshold.[58] Even when the Court's jurisdiction had been accepted by a respondent state, cases still needed to be actively referred to it, or else they would also be decided by the Committee of Ministers.[59] Notably, under the original design, such referrals to the ECtHR could be initiated by the Commission or by a state party to the Convention with a stake in the case (see Article 48 ECHR [1950]) within three months after the Commission had issued its report, but not by individual applicants themselves.[60]

From 1959, when the (then part-time) Court was first set up after eight states had accepted its jurisdiction (as required by Article 56 ECHR [1950]), until November 1998, when Protocol No. 11 entered into force, the Convention's control mechanism essentially operated under this original design. While many states accepted the right of individual petition and the jurisdiction of the Court at the time of ratification of the Convention or shortly thereafter,[61] some states did so only with some delay. The United Kingdom, for example, was the first state to ratify the ECHR in 1951 but accepted the optional elements only in 1966; for Italy, the gap was eighteen years; for

Turkey thirty-three years (acceptance of individual petitions) and thirty-six years (acceptance of the Court's jurisdiction). France ratified the Convention in 1974 and while accepting the jurisdiction of the Court at the same time, it submitted to the individual complaints procedure only in 1981. These delays, among other factors, explain why judgments involving some ECHR parties only appear later on in the Court's history. Only in 1990 was there identity for the first time between the number of Convention parties and those subject to individual complaints and the Court's jurisdiction. In the subsequent post–Cold War enlargement of the COE, it became a political expectation of all new member states—met without exception—to ratify the Convention and accept both optional clauses.

With the entry into force of reform Protocol No. 11 on November 1, 1998, the optional clauses were eliminated. Henceforth, individual complaints (Article 34 ECHR) and the Court's jurisdiction (Article 32 ECHR) became part and parcel of a fully judicialized Convention control system: the European Commission of Human Rights was abolished, as was the Committee of Minister's quasi-judicial function of deciding cases under Article 32 ECHR [1950]. From then on, the now full-time Court became the sole Convention body to decide on the admissibility and merits of complaints. Because some states had valued the opportunity to reargue their case before the Court or Committee in light of the Commission's report, the post–Protocol No. 11 system provides for the possibility of a request—by the applicant, the respondent state, or both—within three months of the date of a judgment by a chamber, composed of seven judges, for a rehearing of that case by the Grand Chamber (GC), consisting of seventeen judges, at the latter's discretion.[62] When such a request is rejected, or none is submitted, the chamber judgment becomes final; when the request is accepted, the Grand Chamber's judgment will be the final decision in the case (Article 44 ECHR). This is significant because only final judgments trigger the obligation of having to abide by them (Article 46 (1) ECHR).

While Protocol No. 11 reformed key institutional and procedural aspects of the ECHR system, many elements also stayed the same. Most important, the Committee of Ministers continued to be responsible for supervising the execution of the ECtHR's judgments (Article 46 (2) ECHR) and for determining whether execution has been satisfactory in light of applicable compliance standards. This is a significant feature of the ECHR's institutional architecture, and I argue below that the Committee's assessments have become an acceptable proxy for determining compliance with the Court's judgments. Furthermore, at least in formal terms and in contrast to EU law and the output of the

CJEU,[63] the Court's judgments continue to have legal effects only at the international level (unless national law provides otherwise); that is, they do not directly invalidate, displace, or modify national laws and policies found to be in violation of the Convention. A proposal prepared by the European Movement had still included a provision that would have provided the Court with prescriptive powers, including the power to demand the "repeal, cancellation or amendment of the [domestic] act" found to be in violation of the Convention,[64] but this provision had been rejected at the Convention's drafting stage[65] and was not revived in the lead-up to Protocol No. 11. Instead, as under the original design, the Court can only award just satisfaction (effectively meaning financial compensation) for pecuniary and nonpecuniary damages (as well as costs and expenses) that result from a Convention violation "if the internal law of the High Contracting Party concerned allows only partial reparation to be made" (Article 41 ECHR, previously Article 50 ECHR [1950]).[66] Although in most cases awarded together with the decision on the merits, the Court sometimes finds the question of just satisfaction not yet ripe for decision and reserves it for a separate judgment.

In terms of substance, the ECHR protects the principal civil and political rights of the Western liberal tradition, with some additions and changes included in subsequent protocols (for quick reference, see Table 1). These rights are guaranteed to "everyone" within the Convention parties' "jurisdiction" (Article 1 ECHR), that is, independent, for the most part,[67] of citizenship and not necessarily, even if usually, ending at a state's territorial borders. While merely suffering adverse consequences of a Convention party's actions abroad has been deemed insufficient to establish the Court's jurisdiction,[68] when a Convention party exercises powers extraterritorially that are normally exercised by, or tantamount to, governmental authority, that party will be subject to the ECHR and responsible for violations.[69] Article 15 ECHR provides for the possibility to derogate from Convention obligations "in time of war or other public emergency threatening the life of the nation," with the exception of a few rights, including the prohibition of torture under Article 3 ECHR.

All beneficiaries of a right can, in principle, submit applications charging violations to the ECtHR. Before the merits of an application can be considered, however, the complaint has to satisfy a number of admissibility criteria, which are laid down in Articles 34 and 35 of the Convention.[70] Among these is the requirement that the applicant has been an actual victim of the alleged Convention violation or is at least a closely related person with a justifiable interest in the case (e.g., parents, caretakers) in situations where the rights holder

Table 1. Rights and Freedoms Protected Under the European Convention on Human Rights and Its Protocols

	Article	Content
European Convention on Human Rights (1950)	2	Right to life
	3	Prohibition of torture, inhuman, and degrading treatment or punishment
	4	Prohibition of slavery, servitude, and forced labor
	5 (1)	Right to liberty and security; deprivation of liberty only in accordance with law
	5 (2)	Right to be promptly informed of reasons of arrest and of any charges
	5 (3)	Right to habeas corpus; entitlement to trial within reasonable time
	5 (4)	Right to speedy review of legality of arrest or detention by a court of law
	5 (5)	Right to compensation in case of violation of these rights
	6 (1)	Right to fair, public hearing within reasonable time by independent, impartial tribunal
	6 (2)	Right to presumption of innocence until proven guilty
	6 (3)	Minimum rights in case of criminal offenses
	lit. a	Right to be informed promptly of details of accusation
	lit. b	Right to adequate time and facilities for defense
	lit. c	Right to defense and support for legal assistance if interests of justice so require
	lit. d	Right to cross-examination and to call witnesses
	lit. e	Right to an interpreter
	7	*Nullum crimen, nulla poena sine lege*
	8	Right to privacy, protection of family life, home, and correspondence
	9	Freedom of thought, conscience, and religion
	10	Freedom of expression and right to disseminate and obtain information
	11	Freedom of assembly and association, including the joining of trade unions
	12	Right to marry and to found a family
	13	Right to an effective domestic remedy against Convention violations
	14	Prohibition of discrimination with respect to Convention rights
P-1 (1952)	1	Right to peaceful enjoyment of possessions
	2	Right to education
	3	Right to free elections

	Article	Content
P-4 (1963)	1	Prohibition of imprisonment for debt
	2	Freedom of movement
	3	Prohibition of expulsion of nationals
	4	Prohibition of collective expulsion of aliens
P-6 (1983)	1	Abolition of the death penalty
	2	Permissibility of death penalty in war time in accordance with law
P-7 (1984)	1	Procedural safeguards relating to the expulsion of aliens
	2	Right of appeal in criminal matters
	3	Right to compensation for wrongful convictions
	4	Right not to be tried or punished twice (prohibition of double jeopardy)
	5	Equality of rights and obligations among spouses in all civil law matters
P-12 (2000)	1	Prohibition of discrimination with respect to legal rights in general
P-13 (2002)	1	Abolition of the death penalty in all circumstances

Note: "P-1" refers to Protocol No. 1, "P-4" to Protocol No. 4, and so forth. The years in parentheses reference the year in which the protocol was adopted and opened for signature.

is unable (deceased, disappeared, or otherwise incapacitated) to submit the complaint him- or herself (Article 34 ECHR). This victim requirement thus excludes both abstract assessments of the compatibility of domestic law and policy with the Convention as well as *actio popularis* suits on behalf of others.[71] Further key requirements are that all available and reasonably effective domestic remedies must have been exhausted (with exceptions in cases of demonstrable ineffectiveness or intolerable hardships) and that the application must have been lodged within six months of the final domestic decision (Article 35 (1) ECHR). Furthermore, the complaint must not be manifestly ill-founded or incompatible with the Convention; that is, it must concern conduct legally attributable to a state party that has occurred (or has ongoing effects) after the Convention entered into force for that state, and it must implicate a right actually protected by the Convention (Article 35 (3) lit. a ECHR).

Protocol No. 14, in force since June 1, 2010, added a controversial new admissibility criterion that enables the Court to declare inadmissible applications if it finds that "the applicant has not suffered a significant disadvantage"

(Article 35 (3) lit. b ECHR), subject to certain safeguards. This new criterion was seen as a necessary response to the Court's caseload crisis to enable it to focus on graver human rights violations.[72] The combined significance of the admissibility criteria—with further restrictions on the horizon as part of Protocol No. 15[73]—becomes evident when one considers that most applications fail to meet them. Over the period from 1959 through 2015, of the 674,155 applications decided by the Court, 28,674 applications were disposed of by way of a judgment, whereas 645,481 (95.7 percent) were declared inadmissible or struck out of the Court's list.[74] While the latter category includes cases that may already have passed the admissibility hurdle but were discontinued as a result of a friendly settlement or unilateral declaration by the respondent state recognizing a Convention violation, a much larger share is due to inadmissibility issues. In 2015, of the 43,135 applications declared inadmissible or struck out, 4,628 were based on a friendly settlement or unilateral declaration, whereas most of the remainder (38,507, or 89.3 percent) failed to clear at least one of the admissibility hurdles.[75]

The lack of speedy and broad compliance with the ECtHR's judgments contributes its own share to the Court's caseload. When legal or factual situations resulting in Convention violations are not tackled expeditiously and broadly, they will often result in many, sometimes thousands of, clone cases that further clog up the Court's docket. Indeed, this problem was the key motivation for including in Protocol No. 14 two new competences for the Committee of Ministers: the first intended to remove interpretive differences hindering supervision by allowing the Committee to ask the Court for an interpretation of the judgment concerned (Article 46 (3) ECHR), and the second enabling it to initiate "infringement proceedings" by asking the Court for its view on whether the state party in question has breached its obligation to comply with the judgments of the Court (Article 46 (4) ECHR). As the protocol's explanatory report noted, "Execution of the Court's judgments is an integral part of the Convention system. [...] The Court's authority and the system's credibility both depend to a large extent on the effectiveness of this process. Rapid and adequate execution has, of course, an effect on the influx of new cases: the more rapidly general measures are taken by States Parties to execute judgments which point to a structural problem, the fewer repetitive applications there will be."[76] As one commentator has noted, it is "the slothfulness, or even recalcitrance, of states which have been the sources of hundreds or thousands of clone cases which have been plaguing the Court."[77] Even though the Court has begun to join clone cases and to stay their consideration pending the execution of remedial measures as part of the pilot judgment procedure,[78] they still, at a minimum, consume administrative resources. So far, however, the Committee of Ministers has refrained from making use of the new infringement procedure which its own rules see as apposite only in "exceptional circumstances"[79] (despite calls by nongovernmental organizations [NGOs] to begin using it in cases that appear to meet this criterion[80]).

The State of Compliance: A Quantitative Assessment

So how good—or bad—is the state of compliance with the Court's judgments? While most of the relevant raw data is publicly available, no comprehensive data set that could be readily used for descriptive or inductive statistical analysis has been previously assembled. Earlier assessments have either taken findings of violations by the Court as an indicator, with qualifications, of first-order noncompliance without researching second-order compliance rates;[81] or have made inferences from the cases whose supervision was still pending before the Committee of Ministers during select years, without connecting that data back to the overall number of compliance-relevant judgments to calculate an actual compliance rate;[82] or have limited their assessment to lead cases that reveal a new type of violation;[83] or have looked at only a subset of states and violations of select articles.[84] In this section, by contrast, while also using the Committee's final resolutions as a proxy for compliance, I present descriptive statistics based on just such a comprehensive data set that addresses the compliance status of all 16,368 compliance-relevant judgments issued by the Court until December 31, 2015.

The Value of Resolutions of the Committee of Ministers as Proxies for Compliance

As a matter of formal legal obligation, the duty to comply with adverse judgments and with the terms of friendly settlements, as well as the principal elements of that duty, are not (or in any event, no longer) contentious. The extent to which the Committee of Ministers' supervision of the "execution" of judgments can be taken as a suitable proxy for the existence and quality of compliance may be less so.[85] The answer to the question of whether it is has to be provided by examining the manner in which the Committee has come to understand and exercise its supervisory function in practice.[86] That practice has evolved over time. In the beginning, the Committee, as far as can be gleaned from the publicly available documents, discharged its duty in a rather restrained and "timorous"[87] fashion and did little more than acknowledge the information submitted to it by the respondent state.[88] This restrained approach was enshrined in the formal (and very few) rules for the application of former Article 54 ECHR [1950] that the Committee adopted for the first time in 1976.[89] During this early phase, there were a number of cases in which "the Committee appears not to have been especially strict with the state concerned, and where it might have been expected that more severe measures would have been appropriate."[90] On several occasions, the Committee accepted as sufficient to end its supervision a state's promise not to repeat the impugned conduct or its announcement that legislation was currently being prepared and to be put before parliament when ready.[91]

Over time, however, the Committee has strengthened the standards it applies during the supervision of the execution of judgments. Beginning in the early 1980s, the Committee made clear that its competence to review a judgment's execution extended to the adoption of general measures beyond the individual case, where relevant, and that such general measures were not merely welcomed when adopted, but were indeed required to end the Committee's supervision, a practice followed ever since.[92] Furthermore, since the mid-1980s, the Committee stopped the practice of adopting final resolutions on the basis of promised or pending legislative projects and instead demanded evidence that the latter had actually been enacted before the former would be adopted.[93] Similarly, when a state argued that the status of the Convention in domestic law would assure judgment-compliant interpretations and applications of relevant legal provisions by domestic courts, the Committee began requesting proof in the form of actual case-law to that effect.[94] Moreover, in 1988 the Committee introduced a new instrument, the interim resolution, which it uses to address publicly—sometimes simply noting, sometimes criticizing—the current status of a judgment's execution without yet ending the supervisory process.[95] What these changes make clear is that the Committee has stopped acting merely as the passive recipient of government information and now assesses with some thoroughness the information submitted against increasingly demanding standards.[96] Supervision as a substantive compliance-control function has thus been in evidence since relatively shortly after the Committee began exercising its supervisory function, and this substantive understanding has been repeatedly reaffirmed politically, most recently in the 2012 Brighton and the 2015 Brussels Declarations.[97]

The increased level of scrutiny exercised by the Committee is also reflected in the revised rules for the application of Article 46 (2) ECHR adopted in 2001, expanded in 2006, and most recently amended in January 2017, which state more expressly the requirements for compliance than the rather cursory 1976 rules did:

> When supervising the execution of a judgment by the High Contracting Party concerned [. . .] the Committee of Ministers shall examine:
> a. whether any just satisfaction awarded by the Court has been paid, including as the case may be, default interest; and
> b. if required, and taking into account the discretion of the High Contracting Party concerned to choose the means necessary to comply with the judgment, whether:
>   i. individual measures have been taken to ensure that the violation has ceased and that the injured party is put, as far as possible, in the same situation as that party enjoyed prior to the violation of the Convention;
>   ii. general measures have been adopted, preventing new violations similar to that or those found or putting an end to continuing violations.[98]

The Committee, it is true, is first and foremost a political body composed of state representatives who are neither necessarily lawyers nor otherwise experts in human rights issues; what is more, because they are political delegates under direction of their state's government, there is the concern that as peer reviewers they "either lack incentives or have the wrong incentives when it comes to reviewing"[99] the compliance behavior of other ECHR parties. The dangers of diplomatic logrolling and horse-trading are considerably mitigated, although not entirely eliminated, by the fact that the Committee has been assisted in its supervisory task by what is today the COE's Directorate General of Human Rights and Rule of Law, and, since the late 1990s, by the specialized Department for the Execution of Judgments of the ECtHR within it, both of which are staffed with legally trained personnel. It is the Department that undertakes the first evaluation of any compliance-relevant information, both as to requirements and measures adopted, and on the basis of those assessments then makes recommendations to the Committee of Ministers.[100] The Committee does retain the formal authority to decide on ending or continuing supervision of a judgment's execution, and while it has happened that it has decided to close a case despite the Department's doubts as to whether full compliance had been achieved, such occurrences are reportedly very rare.[101] In any event, the participation of the Secretariat's legal staff assures that the execution of judgments receives principled legal evaluation before the Committee decides whether to end or continue supervision[102] and "reinforces the removal of peer review activities from a political to a rulebound domain,"[103] thus assuring the integrity and reliability of the Committee's compliance assessments. The political space for what might be thought of as "post-judgment compliance bargaining" is thereby being reined in.[104]

In conclusion, while issues with respect to determining the normative requirements and assessing the actual measures adopted in achieving compliance continue to exist, it is fair to say that supervision by the Committee has "become quite rigorous"[105] and that is has worked reasonably well for the most part.[106] The standards that the Committee has come to apply set thresholds sufficiently high so as to make the Committee's final resolutions a reasonably reliable indicator of compliance with the ECtHR's judgments. With regard to the obligation to pay just satisfaction awards, a final resolution establishes full compliance. With regard to individual and general measures, while different views as to requirements under the Convention may arise, a final resolution establishes compliance at a reasonably high level,[107] a level that has also been affirmed as sufficiently compliant by the Secretariat, even if broader, more extensive or additional measures might have been conceivable.

The Compliance Data Set

Using the Committee's resolutions as an indicator of compliance, it is possible to assess the state of compliance with the Court's judgments. To do so, I created a data set of all compliance-relevant judgments issued by the court between 1960 and 2015 and linked each entry with its current compliance status as of March 10, 2017.

I first generated a list of all judgments issued by the Court from its own chronological list of judgments as well as from HUDOC, the Court's online judgment database.[108] Pieces of information collected include the core case identifiers (applicant name[s], respondent state, application number[s], date of judgment); the type of judgment (merits, just satisfaction, admissibility/

preliminary objections, revision, interpretation, or striking-out judgments); the formation by which it was issued (committee, chamber, grand chamber); the judgment's finding (violation, no violation, friendly settlement, etc.); and the Convention article(s) violated (or, in the cases of striking-out judgments and findings of no violation, alleged to have been violated). In thirty-six instances, judgments involved more than one respondent state. Because the relevant unit of analysis is individual state responses, I split these up as if judgments had been issued against each state individually and only included the finding specifically for that state (generating additional observations in the data set).[109] Next, I grouped together as a single observation those judgments that concerned separate aspects of the same case, as identified by application number. This concerns separate judgments on just satisfaction, subsequent revision judgments, and chamber judgments that had been successfully referred to the Grand Chamber under Article 43 ECHR (reducing the number of observations).[110] I also removed thirty-one cases that had been successfully referred to the GC for a rehearing, but which were either still pending before the GC as of March 2017 or in which the GC issued its judgments only in 2016 and 2017, that is after, the cut-off year for this study. This cleaned-up data set for the years 1960–2015 comprises a total of 17,891 observations.

As the next step, I dropped from the data set all judgments that did not require any execution measures. This includes merits judgments that did not find a violation of the Convention and judgments addressing various procedural issues, such as those declaring an application inadmissible, addressing preliminary objections, or striking out an application from the Court's list due to reasons other than a friendly settlement or unilateral declaration and without making an award for costs and expenses. After eliminating all judgments that do not require any remedial response from respondent states, the data set includes 16,368 compliance-relevant observations: 15,441 judgments on the merits finding at least one violation of the Convention; 905 judgments recognizing friendly settlements between the parties in accordance with Article 39 ECHR (entailing the obligation of paying any agreed sums and sometimes of adopting substantive individual or general measures); 14 judgments ending proceedings in response to unilateral declarations by respondent states (and the promised undertakings therein); and 8 judgments that were struck off the Court's list for reasons other than a friendly settlement or unilateral declaration but that contained a financial award for costs and expenses.[111]

Finally, I matched all judgments requiring some remedial response from states with their current compliance status, as determined by the Committee of Ministers.[112] If a final resolution was adopted in a case, that case is considered sufficiently complied with and closed, and the date and number of the final resolution has been recorded in the data set. If supervision of the execution of a given judgment is still continuing, it is considered not yet fully complied with and has been coded as "pending." The data set includes all final resolutions adopted as of March 10, 2017 (that is, up to and including those adopted at the Committee of Ministers' first human rights meeting in 2017, held March 7–10).

Aggregate Compliance Status by Year of Judgment

Figure 1 depicts the aggregate compliance status of all judgments in the data set by year of judgment and as of March 10, 2017. It clearly shows the stark increase in the Court's workload and output after the COE's enlargement in the 1990s and the reforms that instituted the full-time Court when Protocol No. 11 entered into force in 1999. Several aspects are worth mentioning. First, as revealed by the source data, viewed cumulatively across the entire time period, 9,279 judgments (56.7 percent) had been satisfactorily complied with, while 7,087 judgments (43.3 percent) were still pending before the Committee of Ministers due to insufficient compliance or lack of information as to the measures taken.[113] Second, the compliance rate decreases when less time has passed between the year in which judgments have been issued and the present. This is generally in line with what one should expect: achieving and then assessing compliance are processes that take time, especially when general measures have to be adopted, implemented, and evaluated. Third, except for 2003, the rate of compliance with striking-out judgments has been slightly higher than for merits judgments (implied by the fact that the rate for merits judgments is below the overall rate for all judgments); this also is in line with expectations, given that such judgments require mostly only payment of compensation and, in the case of friendly settlements, reflect—ideally at least—mutually agreeable terms.

Fourth, and particularly important with respect to the assertions about compliance with the Court's judgments, is the observation that one has to go back all the way to 1995 to find a perfect compliance rate.[114] Beginning with 1996, we find the first judgments that have remained under the supervision of the Committee of Ministers for over twenty years. While it is true that many of these judgments concern so-called clone cases that originate from the same systemic shortcomings—concerning, for example, actions of the Turkish[115]

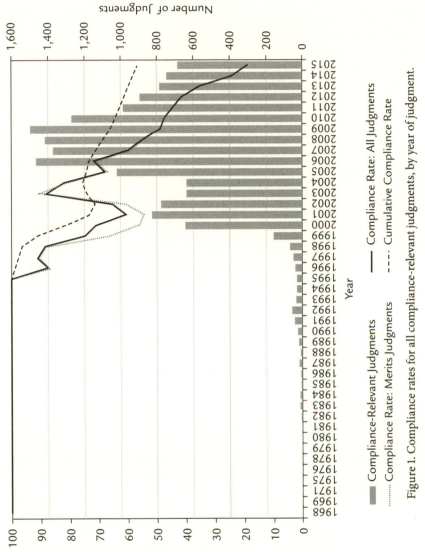

Figure 1. Compliance rates for all compliance-relevant judgments, by year of judgment.

and Russian[116] security forces, Italy's problems with respect to the efficient administration of justice,[117] or the failure of Ukrainian authorities to execute judgments of domestic courts rendered against the state[118]—so that they overstate the number of distinct problems when viewed discretely (clone cases are individual, but not independent, observations),[119] the fact remains that appropriate general measures that successfully remedy these systemic problems have either not yet been adopted or, when some such measures have been adopted, have not yet been (or shown to be) effective.[120] As discussed in the country case studies below, even long periods of formal noncompliance do not necessarily mean that a respondent state has failed to take any remedial measures whatsoever. The more time passes between a judgment and compliance with it, however, the more this gap invites scrutiny of the government's commitment to bringing about compliance within a reasonable time and to devoting sufficient resources to that objective. While there are no strictly defined time periods within which compliance of particular types of violations that require individual or general remedial measures need to be accomplished—just satisfaction awards, by contrast, need to be paid within the time limit set by the Court (normally three months) or else incur default interest[121]—the nontrivial number of judgments that have remained under the Committee's supervision in excess of five, ten, and even more years indicates serious issues with respect to some states' commitment to ensuring, or their ability to achieve, effective and swift compliance with the Court's judgments.

Compliance Status by Respondent State

Compliance patterns are crucially determined by national characteristics and, as the theory advanced in this book assumes, in the human rights domain, especially by a country's democratic credentials. To check the relationship between democracy and compliance, Figure 2 maps countries' aggregate compliance rates against their Polity IV polity scores,[122] with the latter averaged across the number of years the state has been subject to the ECtHR's jurisdiction, that is, from the year of the acceptance of the Court's jurisdiction until 2015. The polity score is derived by subtracting a country's autocracy score from its democracy score, each of which ranges from 0 to 10; the resulting polity score can thus assume values between +10 (strongly democratic) to −10 (strongly autocratic). Both autocracy and democracy scores measure institutional regime aspects and do not include substantive compliance with human rights or civil liberties.[123] In addition, the total number of compliance-relevant judgments involving a country as respondent is indicated by the size of its bubble, ranging from 20 for Montenegro, 144 for Finland, 387 for Hungary, and 802 for Greece, to 1,603 for Russia, 2,088 for Italy, and 2,986 for Turkey. Seven countries, accounting for 122 judgments, are not depicted due to lack of inclusion in the Polity IV data set,[124] and the outlier Azerbaijan (average polity score of −7, 102 judgments, compliance rate of 1 percent) has been omitted for reasons of better graphic representation.

Overall, the results shown in Figure 2 show a positive correlation between polity score and compliance rate: the trend-line (not shown) slopes upward, but its R^2 value is modest, at .336, meaning that only about a third of the variation in compliance rates can be explained by a state's polity score. The graph also reveals that, with the exception of Italy, all states with compliance rates below 70 percent are states that became subject to the ECtHR's jurisdiction only after the end of the Cold War, and of these all except for Turkey (which accepted the jurisdiction of the Court in 1990) are formerly communist or socialist countries. This history is clearly not determinative, however, because several former Eastern Bloc countries—Slovenia, Poland, Lithuania, and the Czech and Slovak Republics—score high on both the polity variable and compliance rates. Three countries shown have perfect compliance rates of 100 percent: Denmark, Sweden, and Norway.[125] Because the bulk of the judgments were rendered by the post–Protocol-11 Court, limiting the analysis to the period from November 1999 onward does not change the overall picture (only 3.7 percent of the judgments in the data set originated with the pre-reform Court).

The fact that quite a number of countries with high polity scores and compliance rates cluster together in the upper right-hand corner of the graph provides suggestive support for the expected positive impact of democracy on compliance. At the same time, the graph also shows that there is great variance in terms of compliance rates even among those countries that have consistently scored a perfect 10 on the polity variable while subject to the ECtHR's jurisdiction. In the end, this variance and the modest explanatory power of the polity score in a simple bivariate relationship is not surprising when one recalls that this score measures only a small set of institutional aspects that may be said to define a regime as more or less democratic, but that the modalities of the execution of adverse judgments are conditioned by many other potential factors, such as the specifics of domestic institutional arrangements and procedures, bureaucratic efficiency, resources, aspects of the legal system, prevailing political and cultural preferences, and so forth.

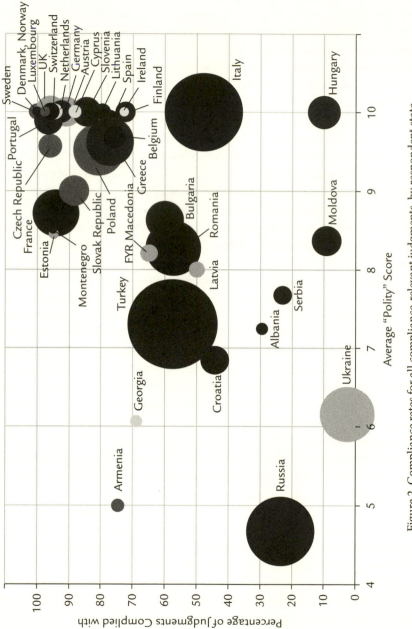

Figure 2. Compliance rates for all compliance-relevant judgments, by respondent state.

Plan of the Book

While the quantitative data presented above provide a good sense of the aggregate state of compliance with the Court's judgments, they necessarily offer only a snapshot of the compliance status at a particular point in time. By itself, that snapshot is incapable of revealing the underlying legal and political dynamics that have resulted in either compliance or the continuing absence thereof, and, just as important, whether noncompliance results from the intentional disregard of the Court's judgments and the absence of any remedial measures, or whether relevant measures have already been adopted that have, however, (so far) failed to remedy effectively (all of) the violations found by the Court. The compliance data set could be exploited further and be used for additional quantitative analysis by adding variables that can be expected to affect the speed and depth of compliance, such as the type of violation involved, the remedial measures required, various country-specific control variables, and a time dimension. For the purpose of providing empirical evidence for the main argument in this book, however, which is primarily qualitative in nature, additional cross-sectional and time-series analyses are not the most auspicious strategy.

Instead, in the pages that follow I employ a case-study approach to investigate the particular behavioral logic guiding compliance decisions by liberal democracies. To avoid charges of selection bias with respect to the judgments covered, I opt for a comprehensive approach that examines all ECtHR judgments issued against two liberal democracies—the United Kingdom and Germany—until the cut-off year 2010. The next chapter presents the hybrid constructivist-rationalist theory of compliance that I argue best explains the empirically observable patterns of compliance by liberal democracies with the judgments of the ECtHR. In the two main parts that follow, I then examine the resulting hypotheses against the empirical evidence of the remedial responses adopted by the United Kingdom (Part I) and by Germany (Part II), organized along the lines of the principal types of remedial measures required to comply with a given judgment and the issue area in which the violation falls. The conclusion summarizes and provides a final assessment of the sustainability of the theory in light of the empirical evidence.

CHAPTER 1

Compliance Theory: Rational Choice Within Normative Constraints

Much research on compliance with international law remains either predominantly rationalist or constructivist in orientation. For those adopting a rational choice lens,[1] the focus is on the balance of the expected costs and benefits that are associated with the alternative choices of compliance and noncompliance, as well as on how and through what mechanisms such cost-benefit calculations can be manipulated by other actors. The three factors that Andrew Guzman has summarized as the "Three Rs of Compliance"—reputation, reciprocity, and retaliation—are a recurrent concern, each theorized as being able to "increase the costs of violation and, therefore, promote cooperation."[2] Because reciprocity, retaliation, and reputation (at least in its instrumentalist version) have much less purchase to explain compliance in the human rights domain than in other international issue areas, researchers have turned to domestic politics instead as the realm in which relevant causal mechanisms operate.

In one of the most prominent studies on the domestic effects of international human rights law, Beth Simmons recognizes human rights as "one of the most powerful *normative* concepts of the past half century" but does not explore the extent to which that normative quality as such affects domestic politics and compliance.[3] Instead, in Simmons' story, human rights treaties "are causally meaningful to the extent that they empower individuals, groups, or parts of the state with different rights preferences that were not empowered to the same extent in the absence of the treaties."[4] Such empowerment may occur through the impact of human rights norms on agenda-setting within the policy- and law-making branches of government; through the facilitation of human rights litigation in domestic courts; and by increasing the probability of successful mobilization and related political pressures on decision-makers.[5] The normativity of international human rights law presumably continues to lurk in the background—for example, in providing legitimacy for agenda-setting or by giving special weight to human rights in adjudication due to their character as normatively elevated, fundamental values—but the three mechanisms, with their emphasis on empowerment as a way to accomplish actor preferences, reflect primarily a logic of consequences, not one of appropriateness.

If approaches focusing on rational choice mechanisms can be faulted for sidelining, if not eliminating, recognition of normative effects beyond those that can be linked to mechanisms that tangibly affect actors' cost-benefit calculations, constructivist approaches focusing on norm- and identity-driven behavior as a result of processes of socialization, persuasion, and learning too often seek to demonstrate that normative considerations may trump and fully supersede instrumentalist ones.[6] Jeffrey Checkel, for example, in work on socialization in Europe, has argued that "[i]n adopting community rules, socialization implies that an agent switches from following a logic of consequences to a logic of appropriateness," resulting in "sustained compliance based on the internalization of these new norms . . . quite independent from a particular structure of material incentives or sanctions."[7] A similar "replacement logic" is at work in the spiral model in the human rights domain which conceives of the relationship between rationalist and constructivist logics as a sequential one. While a rational-instrumentalist mode of action is posited as dominant during the early phases of the model, it is expected to give way eventually to "institutionalization and habitualization processes" that result in "rule-consistent behavior" guided by normative considerations of appropriateness.[8]

While rationalist and constructivist approaches at times offer rival explanations of observable behavior, it has been recognized for some time that the two logics more often than not provide complementary, rather than mutually exclusive, explanations of observable behavior.[9] The research question, then, is not whether it is rational choice *or* norms that explain a given outcome, but rather "the nature of the link between rationality and norm-based behavior,"[10] with several relationships between them being conceivable.[11] Which relationship pertains in a concrete context or issue area needs "to be established theoretically and empirically, rather than assumed."[12] While some studies addressing especially second-order compliance with judgments of international courts have theorized compliance in predominantly rationalist terms, foregrounding cost-benefit considerations and the availability and use of enforcement mechanisms,[13] others have begun to explore the interaction of normative and rationalist causes of action,[14] have proceeded on the expectation of a general inclination on the part of states towards some form of compliance,[15] or have remained open to the possibility that some states may be motivated by instrumentalist reasons while others are driven by normative considerations.[16]

In this chapter, I argue that, by themselves, neither rationalist nor constructivist approaches to compliance are sufficient to explain the observable patterns of responses by liberal democracies to ECtHR judgments. Instead, what is needed is a hybrid model that combines the two underlying logics of action. One the one hand, given the absence in most instances of meaningful domestic or international enforcement to tweak actors' cost-benefit calculations and the fact that the impugned laws and policies are frequently supported by political majorities, a rational choice approach should predict a far greater number of instances of outright noncompliance even by liberal democracies than we actually observe. On the other hand, while a constructivist, norm-based approach might explain why liberal democracies cannot disregard adverse human rights judgments, even if against the preferences of the current government, it remains underspecified with regard to explaining the actual measures a state adopts in order to live up formally to the obligation to comply. Successful socialization into norm-abiding behavior does not *replace* rational choice in making compliance decisions so much as *constrain* it: the obligation to comply with adverse judgments by the ECtHR restricts the spectrum of legally permissible choices available to states, without, however, in many cases eliminating choice altogether. Explaining the selection of the specific measures adopted to comply with a given judgment, or set of judgments, among available alternatives requires a theory of choice that needs to complement the mere prediction of norm-following, and I argue that these choices are best understood in terms of rational choice theory.

Compliance, Law, and Interpretation

Before turning to an elaboration of the behavioral hypotheses, it is necessary to engage briefly in conceptual clarification of the study's key term, compliance. For purposes of the subsequent analysis, I adopt a standard definition of compliance as the *conformity of an actor's observed behavior with the behavioral requirements of a normative pre- or proscription applicable to that actor*[17]—in the present context, the behavioral requirements following from the norms enshrined in the ECHR, as interpreted by the Court. Understood this way, compliance is a descriptive concept that makes no claim to identify the causes of compliance or noncompliance.[18] I also continue to conceptualize compliance, for assessment purposes, as a binary outcome variable: at any given time, a state either complies or does not (yet fully) comply with a given judgment or set of judgments. (Viewed this way, the concept of partial compliance[19] is a subcategory of noncompliance whose significance depends in part on whether it is merely a way station to full compliance or remains an end state).[20] The point is well taken that the various measures that states may take in response to a particular legal norm, and the resulting degree of conformity with that norm, argue in favor of conceptualizing compliance as a continuous variable.[21] Indeed, I fully agree that it is precisely the behavioral variance both above as well as below the threshold which separates compliance from noncompliance that invites scrutiny and explanation in its own right. In the context of regulatory regimes, legal compliance provides one particular yardstick to assess behavioral effects of law and institutions, and, depending on the research question, it need not be the most appropriate or meaningful one.[22]

Still, in the context of adverse judgments by an international court (or any court, for that matter), the key question that cannot (and, for normative reasons, should not) be skirted remains whether the response chosen along that continuum meets the minimal *legal* requirements, as understood and determined by the participants within the system, of fulfilling the respondent states' obligation to "abide by the final judgment of the Court in any case to which they are parties" (the language of Article 46 (1) ECHR). Such an assessment requires drawing a line between what is seen as a sufficiently remedial (i.e., compliant) and an insufficient (i.e., noncompliant) response. To take a straightforward example, individual complainants that have been awarded a specific amount of financial compensation for a past violation will not be satisfied if the respondent state pays them only half that amount, even if the state does so directly in response to the judgment, thus attesting to the latter's causal force. Instead, such applicants will want (and deserve) the full amount and thus full compliance. A social science inquiry into a legalized system such as the ECHR will therefore have to address not only whether the ECtHR's judgments cause a behavioral response as such, but more specifically whether they trigger behavior that meets the requirements of legal compliance (not least because the status of legal noncompliance carries consequences of its own, such as the continuing supervision by the Committee of Ministers and possible follow-up litigation). That the requirements for legal compliance are often less clear-cut when it comes to individual and general measures beyond the payment of financial compensation, and that the compliance standards applicable in these cases are more often than not subject to contention[23] and malleable across time, raises important issues of its own. Rather than doing away with the binary character of compliance as a descriptive outcome variable, though, it points to the necessity of investigating the determinants of the threshold that is applied, its politicization, and the consequences that follow from it.[24]

Studies of the behavioral effects of international norms and institutions frequently invoke two other analytical concepts in addition to compliance: implementation and effectiveness. Implementation, a concept borrowed from public policy studies,[25] and in the specific context of responses to ECtHR judgments proxied by the term "execution," usually refers to the process through which international obligations are being put into operation ("implemented") domestically and, as an analytic concept, aims at describing and inventorying the measures adopted.[26] As has been pointed out, while implementation often marks the first step toward compliance, it is "neither a necessary nor sufficient condition for compliance."[27] Rather, the need of first having to engage in implementation to achieve compliance depends crucially on the gap between current behavior and the behavioral requirement(s) of the prescription in question: "If an international commitment matches current practice in a given state, for instance, implementation is unnecessary and compliance is automatic."[28]

The concept of effectiveness—often also implied by the notion of "impact"[29]—has been used in different ways, but its prevalent thrust in political science in the context of research on the role of norms is as an indicator of the causal influence of norms—social, legal, and otherwise—on behavior: "An effective rule is simply a rule that leads to observable, desired behavioral change. Effectiveness is the measure of that change."[30] In this definition, then, effectiveness implicates causality, as opposed to the descriptive nature of the concepts of compliance and implementation. As Raustiala notes, "[T]o speak of compliance is to be agnostic about causality: compliance as a concept draws no causal linkage between a legal rule and behavior, but simply identifies conformity between the rule and behavior. To speak of effectiveness is to speak directly of causality: to claim that a rule is 'effective' is to claim that it led to certain behaviors or outcomes, which may or may not meet the legal standard of compliance."[31] Oran Young and Marc Levy concur, noting that "effectiveness in a political sense means spurring action toward achieving [certain] objectives. [...] Activities that move the system in the right direction, even if they fall short of full compliance, are signs of effectiveness."[32]

In contrast to cases where the behavioral requirements of a primary international legal rule may coincide with actual or already intended state behavior, and compliance is thus automatic and effectiveness absent or at best "shallow,"[33] in most cases of adverse judgments that are being complied with, compliance and effectiveness coincide. In the present context, because ECtHR judgments finding one or more violation(s) of the Convention require the respondent state to end the violation, prevent its recurrence, and provide reparation,[34] the state's government will almost always have to implement appropriate measures to achieve these objectives, measures that in most cases would not have been adopted in the absence of the judgment, thus meeting the counterfactual test for assessing causality.[35] If measures remedying the violation are adopted only after an adverse judgment has been issued, it is then not unreasonable to expect, subject to empirical refutation, that the judgment causally contributed to that outcome.[36] This expectation of the coincidence of compliance and effectiveness is rebuttable in some circumstances—for instance, where the domestic change that resulted in compliance preceded not only the judgment, but even the submission of the related application to Strasbourg,[37] with complainants essentially seeking only recognition of, and usually financial compensation for, an earlier Convention-violating situation that has already been remedied. In this case, only the subsequent payment of financial compensation, if awarded, can be causally linked to the judgment (in a small number of judgments that concern past violations and in which no individual or general measures are indicated, the Court has not awarded any financial compensation, so that not even payment is required of the respondent state).[38]

In the context of his goal-based approach to studying international judicial effectiveness, Yuval Shany has reminded researchers that an institution's effectiveness cannot be defined in terms of some general or abstract metric, but instead has to be gauged with respect to the specific objectives that a particular institution is intended to pursue: "[I]n order to measure the effectiveness of an organization according to the goal-based approach, we must identify the organization's aims or goals, i.e., the desired outcomes it ought to generate, and ascertain the time-frame over which it is reasonable to expect that some or all of these goals could be met."[39] While courts may serve functions other than inducing compliance with their judgments,[40] providing redress in cases of human rights violations by compelling national actors to execute judgments domestically must be among the goals of judicial (as well as quasi-judicial)[41] human rights institutions that have jurisdiction over individual human rights complaints.[42] This is so not least because their institutional design as dispute settlement mechanisms will necessarily generate legitimate expectations as to the fulfillment of this function among the prospective users of the institution, independent of whether the institution's mandate providers—the states that created a particular court—designed it with a view to pursuing, and achieving, this objective in good faith or not. Compliance with the judgments that a human rights court issues against respondent states through the provision of individual and/or general remedial measures is thus at the core of what Laurence Helfer has called "case-specific effectiveness."[43] Such judgments may have effects beyond the decided case, for example, in states not party to the dispute decided by the court,[44] but a human rights court will arguably have only limited overall effectiveness if the core objective of providing redress in the specific cases it decides through compliance with its judgments is not achieved.

In practical terms, assessing compliance with international legal norms requires a three-step analysis. First, the concrete behavioral requirements that follow from a given norm, or set of norms, need to be specified. Second, the facts of actual state behavior that comes within the purview of the norm at issue needs to be empirically ascertained. The last step is the evaluation of actual conduct against the normative yardstick of required behavior: where the former is in line with the latter, behavior is compliant; where it is not, noncompliance results. Of course, what appears deceptively straightforward in theory raises significant challenges in practice. Regarding the first step, the identification of the concrete behavioral requirements is complicated by the fact that these usually do not follow unambiguously and directly from the legal text as such, but need first to be "constructed" by way of interpretation. The underlying problem here is the "indeterminacy" of legal norms, that is, the fact that "the content and nature of a legal provision cannot be read off the provision."[45] Legal language, like all language, is often capable of accommodating more than one specific meaning, with the consequence that defensible "just disagreements"[46] may arise as to which one of the feasible meanings included in the set of semantic possibilities is to be controlling.[47]

As a consequence, all legal norms require interpretation, that is, a process through which "to choose its legal meaning from among a number of semantic possibilities—to decide which of the text's semantic meanings constitutes its proper legal meaning."[48] Note that this is not the same as searching for a legal text's "true" meaning. As the former chief justice of the Israeli Supreme Court Aharon Barak aptly notes, "A text has no 'true' meaning. We have no ability to compare the meaning of a text before and after its interpretation by focusing on its 'true' meaning. All understanding results from interpretation, because we can access a text only after it has been interpreted. There is no pre-exegetic understanding. At best, we can compare different interpretations of a text."[49] As a corollary, any text (such as a legal rule) that appears to have a clear, unambiguous meaning only does so because the terms it employs have already been interpreted, and that interpretation has become widely accepted as conventional and remains, at least for the time being, uncontested.[50] In the absence of a stable, settled meaning, interpretation can be expected to be colored by the views and value judgments that an interpreter brings to the task. The "practice of legal interpretation," as Ingo Venzke has aptly put it, can then best be understood as "semantic struggles in which actors craft legal interpretations in an attempt to implement meanings of legal expressions that are aligned with their convictions or interests."[51]

It is one of the central functions of third-party dispute settlement mechanisms, such as the ECtHR, to determine what interpretation of a given norm is to be controlling in the case before it. To borrow Ronald Dworkin's terminology, the ECHR lays down certain abstract legal concepts ("independence," "fairness," "promptness," "reasonableness," etc.), but to make these concepts operational in judicial practice requires the judge (or another interpreter) to fill them with a specific conception of what "independence," "fairness," "promptness," or "reasonableness" are to mean in concrete circumstances.[52] Rules of interpretation provide argumentative devices that can be invoked to support such conceptions, but they do not, by themselves, unequivocally determine the outcome of the interpretive process by unambiguously reducing the possible spectrum of interpretations to a single one;[53] to the contrary, the same rules of interpretation are often relied upon in support of alternative interpretations. In such cases, the determinative last step falls to judicial discretion: "[W]here there is judicial discretion ... there comes a point at which the decision is not dictated by the legal system" but instead by "judicial subjectivity."[54] Judicial subjectivity here does not equate with personal whim, but is a function, inter alia, of different views as to the appropriate role of the judge in public decision-making, the relative weight and persuasiveness of arguments and evidence, and the specific object and purpose of a given legal regime that judges may legitimately hold.[55] It is the interpretation of the ECHR—that is, the infusion of the Convention's general concepts with concrete, authoritative conceptions—that is the ECtHR's specific contribu-tion to human rights policy- and law-making under the ECHR.[56]

While the Court thus establishes the behavioral reference points for first-order compliance by interpreting the text of the ECHR provision(s) relevant to a case, assessing second-order compliance in turn generally raises the self-same need to interpret the Court's pronouncement to identify the concrete measures that are necessary to achieve it.[57] While it is clear that, as a matter of results, any ongoing Convention violation must be ended, the language of the Court's judgments often permits different takes on what results a judg-ment specifically requires in light of the particular facts of the case and the reasoning and findings of the Court,[58] with different stakeholders often hav-ing different views on these. As Marc Galanter has emphasized in a related context, "[T]he messages disseminated by courts do not carry endowments or produce effects *except as they are received, interpreted, and used by (poten-tial) actors. Therefore the meaning of judicial signals is dependent on the information, experience, skill, and resources that disputants bring to them.*"[59] By the same token, the dividing line between compliance and noncompliance with an adverse judgment generally has no exogenously given, "objective" answer;[60] rather, it must first be established through interpretation and agree-ment between the relevant stakeholders involved. In the case of the ECtHR's judgments, that compliance threshold is set by the Committee of Ministers, aided by the COE Secretariat, with the Court playing only an incidental role in supervising the execution of its own judgments.[61]

Adding to the need to interpret the Court's judgments arising from semantic ambiguities, further interpretive leeway is provided by the fact that the ECtHR's judgments have been, with few exceptions,[62] and "as a matter of judicial policy,"[63] declaratory only; that is, its judgments pronounce certain state behavior to be incompatible with the requirements of the Convention without prescribing concrete remedies, except for just satisfaction, or offering guidance on how to change it. While states are subject, in most cases,[64] to an "obligation of result" in that they need to remove the Convention violation found in the Court's judgment, prevent its recurrence, and provide restitu-tion, as far as possible, the choice of remedial means—again, save for the payment of just satisfaction—is at the state's discretion, subject to supervi-sion by the Committee of Ministers.[65] As the empirical chapters will show, however, different means may have quite different implications and conse-quences in terms of both general policies as well as for individual applicants, and their choice can thus not be dismissed as merely a technical issue. There are indications that this practice may be undergoing some changes, with the Court (and especially some of its judges) being more frequently inclined to take an explicit stance on the prescription of specific remedies;[66] but so far this practice has remained erratic,[67] with the majority of judgments continuing to remain silent on the issue of remedies.[68]

Last not but least, it is important to recognize that whether a state has complied with a judgment of the Court needs to be assessed not only against the background of a decision's particular finding and reasoning, but also in light of the Convention as a whole. The ECHR, like many international agreements, includes as part of its institutional design certain "impact mitigation" features that enable states to avoid potential consequences that might otherwise be stipulated to follow from an isolated reading of a judgment.[69] Article 41, on just satisfaction, for example, was included at the time of the Convention's drafting (then Article 50 ECHR [1950]) as a sort of "sovereignty shield" in order to make clear that any restitution was to be owed only to the extent that it could be provided within the possibilities afforded by the domestic legal system.[70] The provision was thus meant to protect structural features of the domestic legal system, especially the res judicata authority of final domestic judgments. As a result, even though the reopening of domestic proceedings will often be the most appropriate remedy where such proceedings have been found to fall short of the guarantees of the Convention, states are not legally obligated to provide for it,[71] and it would thus be formally sufficient for compliance to pay compensatory just satisfaction as awarded by the Court, notwithstanding that the domestic (faulty) judgment remains on record. Similarly, a state may be able to escape the obligation to change its legislation in response to an adverse judgment—though not the adoption of individual remedial measures—if it subsequently lodges a valid derogation under Article 15 ECHR (if only for the duration of that derogation).[72] This might be unsatisfactory to the applicants and other stakeholders, but it would comply with the rules of the Convention as a whole.

Challenges in the study of compliance can also concern the empirical side of the assessment of compliance, with some actions and changes easier to verify empirically than others.[73] The payment of monetary compensation, where awarded, for example, is comparatively easy to ascertain; so are, usually, formal changes to legislation and other legal and policy documents that are publicly available. By contrast, the extent to which required changes in jurisprudence are adopted across a country's judicial system may already be more difficult to establish, if only because the potentially relevant actors and cases are becoming more numerous. The same holds true of the extent to which formal changes to domestic policy and legislation find reflection in actual behavioral changes of the various governmental actors that apply them. The best one can often do is to rely on the absence of follow-up complaints and litigation as evidence that a formal legal change is also "lived" in practice, but this remains imperfect evidence because other reasons may keep (alleged) victims from pursuing formal complaints, thus keeping potential violations from appearing on the noncompliance radar screen.[74]

In short, then, assessing compliance encounters normative and empirical challenges. Research on compliance must grapple with both. Because the indeterminacy of law and legal language, if only minimally and residually, and the attendant necessity to engage in interpretation preclude an "objective" identification of the specific behavioral requirements that follow from a Convention norm or from a judgment of the Court (save for financial just satisfaction awards), compliance research must specify these and how they have been arrived at (and their source, if the interpretations of other actors are adopted). Doing so permits placing the applied behavioral standard(s) in the context of feasible alternatives that were, however, discarded. As concerns empirical evidence, assessments of compliance are always only as good as the available data. Here as well, then, it is important to describe the data on the basis of which compliance-relevant behavior is being assessed (e.g., formal statutory amendments as one indicator of behavioral change versus data on how such statutory changes are being applied in practice). Given that the collection of full behavioral data is often impracticable and/or too costly, findings of formal legal and policy changes are significant in their own right, even if subject to the caveat that their implementation may still suffer from deficiencies. In any event, the level, or "depth," of compliance must be properly identified.

The Causal Model: Rational Choice within Normative Constraints

In this section I defend the theoretical argument that governments of liberal European democracies, while generally responding rationally and in line with their preferences to adverse judgments rendered against them by the ECtHR, do so in light of a choice set from which noncompliance has effectively been removed as an available option for a large set of cases, even if in terms of expected material and political costs and benefits it might otherwise have been the preferred course of action yielding the highest utility. In other words, compliance with the ECtHR's judgments is pursued, in most cases, despite the net costs that this course of action yields for the government. The source of that general inclination to comply with adverse human rights judgments is, I argue, ultimately normative in character and linked to the prevailing, self-professed identity of most of the relevant states as liberal rule-of-law democracies. Such states cannot disregard the final judgments of the ECtHR, not because they would be sanctioned for noncompliance either internationally or domestically, but because noncompliance jars with, and undermines, key elements of that identity, to wit, the safeguarding of human rights and the recognition of the legitimate role of courts in their protection. This is not a naïve claim that European states are "do-gooders"—there is much to be criticized in the human rights practices of contemporary Europe and, as I will also argue below, the very same states that comply with the ECtHR's judgments will also in most cases seek to minimize the latter's concrete impact as much as possible. Neither is it a claim that what I identify as the currently prevailing identity is necessarily a given and here for eternity; in fact, having been under stress from different political corners for some time, that clearly is not a foregone conclusion. My more modest assertion is that the idea of liberal democracy in Europe as it has developed and been embraced by a significant number of states since the end of World War II has resulted in a situation where noncompliance with the judgments of the European Court has, for the most part, not been a politically viable option, because compliance has become the norm, both in the descriptive and the normative senses of the term.

It merits emphasizing that I say noncompliance has not been an option for "the most part." Norms can exert a powerful influence on human behavior, but rarely do they operate in isolation as a sole cause of action, nor do they do so unconditionally; rather, I expect norms to have effects within a (bounded) range of (expected) costs of compliance, but when these costs— real or perceived, material or political—become too large in the eyes of the relevant decision-makers, other considerations, such as conflicting demands of rival norms or instrumental cost-benefit considerations, may trump the pro-compliance norm. At what specific level of costs this threshold is located cannot theoretically be determined ex ante, but, rather, needs to be explored empirically and inductively, affected as it will be by (the interaction of) a variety of country-, context-, and issue-specific factors. The key point here is that depending on the cues that a particular compliance situation generates, logics of action different from habitual judgment compliance may be foregrounded and result in intentional norm violation even for states with an otherwise fairly established and entrenched liberal-democratic identity.

Even when a state routinely seeks to comply with adverse judgments by the ECtHR, this does not predetermine the details in terms of changes to domestic laws, policies, or practices that remedial action will take, due to the interpretive permissiveness that is part and parcel of most legal and judicial signals, as noted above. And while governmental actors in liberal democracies may feel obliged to give effect to the human rights judgments of a Court that they have freely accepted, despite the net costs of compliance, this does not necessarily imply that such actors are indifferent to the extent of these costs. Rather, in the face of usually limited material and political resources, it is reasonable to expect that governments, like other actors facing comparable constraints, will seek to achieve the desired outcome—here, compliance—in the least costly manner. If that is indeed the case, then we should expect that in the face of two or more alternatives that can be reasonably argued to produce compliance with a judgment, the government will choose the option that minimizes the expected costs, both materially and politically. If these two theoretical expectations hold, then what we should observe is widespread compliance by liberal democracies with the judgments of the ECtHR, but in a systematically minimalist way. The following sections explore in some greater depth the two prongs of this argument.

The Normative Constraint Element

According to the constructivist logic of appropriateness, norms motivate action and move states toward compliance with them because they define the standards for the collectively expected "proper behavior of actors with a given identity."[75] In the present context, we could label the relevant identity "(European) liberal democracy."[76] And democracy, in most contemporary understandings—certainly in its liberal variant[77]—can hardly be thought of without human rights protection; indeed, it is seen as a key feature that sets democracy apart from other regime types, to the point that human rights and democracy are "mutually constitutive."[78] As Juan Linz has written, "A democracy, in order to be a democracy, has to recognize a wide range of human rights, especially a series of political rights, denied or limited severely by other regimes."[79] Similarly, Robert Dahl has pointed out that "extensive political rights and liberties are integral to democracy: they are necessary to the functioning of the institutions that distinguish modern democracy from other kinds of political orders. The rights and liberties are therefore an element in what we often mean by democracy or the democratic process, or a democratic country."[80] Emily Hafner-Burton has put this view succinctly: "[P]rotecting human rights is an essential feature of liberal democracy."[81]

This core feature has also been foregrounded in the Statute of the Council of Europe, whose preamble highlights "individual freedom, political liberty and the rule of law [as] principles which form the basis of all genuine democracy."[82] Accordingly, the Statute stipulates as requirements for membership in the Council the acceptance by each member of "the principles of the rule of law and of the enjoyment by all persons within its jurisdiction of human rights and fundamental freedoms" as well as the willingness to "collaborate sincerely and effectively in the realization of the aim of the Council,"[83] which is identified as the achievement of "greater unity between its members for the purpose of safeguarding and realizing the ideals and principles which are their common heritage and facilitating their economic and social progress."[84] Ratification of the ECHR and acceptance of the jurisdiction of the ECtHR have over time come to be seen as a required signal by prospective or recently added member states that they are willing to live up to these requirements.

Of course, democracy and its rights-related elements are only one aspect of a state's identity (or, rather, of one of its many identities, the relevance of each one varying with the specific contexts in which a state acts).[85] Also in certain cases, notably for states in transition from other, more autocratic types of regimes to liberal democracy, the effective protection of democratic principles and of human rights may be an aspiration rather than a description of the status quo. In either case, whether aspiration or achievement, we can identify a liberal democracy only through the performance of the actions that are intersubjectively associated with that type of state identity—here, protection of human rights and adherence to the rule of law—and should expect states that want to maintain or acquire that specific identity to act accordingly. A state's identity as a liberal democracy is thus both a dependent variable in that the degree to which it is recognizable (and recognized) as such is in good part the outcome of the state's actions in the human rights field, as well as an independent variable in that it causes the state to act in a particular way.[86] Although these two are intertwined in practice, analytically it is the causal role of the interaction of a state's identity as a liberal democracy with concrete human rights requirements that is of concern here.

Even if we adopt only a "thin" procedural definition that brackets domestic rights protection as a definitional element, that democracies can be expected to be more inclined to comply with international human rights obligations than autocracies is of course not a novel claim, and there is empirical evidence to support that expectation,[87] with some variation to be expected according to the level of development and pedigree of national democracy.[88] The same holds for the effects of human rights treaties with respect to which "treaty ratification often becomes more beneficial to human rights the more democratic a country is."[89] In a study covering the twenty-five-year period between 1976 and 2000, Todd Landman has found that "the difference between rights in principle and rights in practice is most positive [i.e., smallest] for the old democracies, where rights violations remain low, whereas ratification [of human rights treaties] increases over the period."[90] Central among the aspects that appear to contribute to the better performance of democracies vis-à-vis nondemocracies are the existence of genuine political contestation and accountability mechanisms, of stable multiparty systems, and of the institutional and procedural wherewithal to implement their international legal obligations.[91]

An important element of the institutional makeup of contemporary democracies intended to foster accountability and peaceful dispute settlement is an independent judiciary. Whether the judiciary is an indispensable element for democracy to survive and flourish may be debatable empirically,[92] but it does figure "axiomatically"[93] in many definitions of democracy and the closely related concept of the rule of law.[94] In any event, all of the liberal democracies relevant to this book provide, as part of their institutional architecture, for independent courts whose powers also comprise the review of individual complaints against governmental acts (though not necessarily the power to invalidate them); indeed, every person's right to have, "[i]n the determination of his civil rights and obligations or of any criminal charge against him, . . . a fair and public hearing within a reasonable time by an independent and impartial tribunal established by law" is itself guaranteed by Article 6 (1) ECHR.

Against this backdrop, it is not unreasonable to expect that liberal democracies that habitually employ courts domestically and generally comply with their judgments will also do so with respect to the judgments of a duly constituted international court whose authority they have freely accepted. Joseph Weiler's dictum made in the context of the CJEU's preliminary questions procedure that the advantage of involving the domestic judiciary was that "[a] state, in our Western democracies, cannot disobey its own courts,"[95] can, I submit, be extended to the ECtHR as well. Modeled on the national courts of the founding members of the COE, the ECtHR generally partakes of the legitimacy that judicial third-party dispute settlement tends to enjoy domestically within liberal democracies, and there is no compelling a priori reason not to expect a comparable record of cooperation and compliance with regard to the ECtHR, the CJEU,[96] or other such judicial institutions. More broadly, as Andrew MacMullen has argued, "[t]he discourse of liberal democracy, rule of law and human rights is strongly embedded both at the national and European level, and provides both a set of justifying principles for policy proposals and a set of constraints on those states which might be tempted to break the rules."[97]

This is in line with the constructivist prediction that socialization into a liberal democratic identity results in state compliance as a matter of course when "norm compliance becomes a habitual practice of actors and is enforced by the rule of law."[98] Such socialization does not necessarily require deep persuasion and the complete internalization of the relevant norms. The mechanism of acculturation, as discussed by Ryan Goodman and Derek Jinks, whereby "varying degrees of identification with a reference group generate varying degrees of cognitive and social pressures to conform" with key norms associated with that group,[99] may suffice to bring about habitual compliance. Compliance with the judgments of the ECtHR can thus be understood as an outcome through which states reproduce their identity as liberal democracies committed to the rule of law by following "taken-for-granted scripts of how 'liberal' or 'modern' states behave."[100] In Ronald Mitchell's words, "A democratic state will tend to value an identity as a country that is subject to the 'rule of law'—behaving in conformance with international commitments represents one social 'marker' of such an identity."[101]

If these considerations are correct, then such a democratic "culture of compliance" should have empirically observable implications.[102] While it would not require that a liberal democracy rushes to action to execute and comply with adverse judgments as speedily as possible—not only is achieving compliance a process that always takes some time, especially in democracies where prescribed procedures and formalities need to be followed, every new task also has to compete for time and resources with other items already on a government's agenda and will not necessarily be prioritized, especially if the government is unhappy with the judgment—what should be observable is evidence that a respondent state accepts the legally binding obligation to comply with the judgments rendered against it and is taking, or is demonstrably preparing to take, good-faith steps aimed at eventually achieving compliance with the judgments at issue.[103] While some delay or slowness in the execution of judgments will not by itself undermine the "culture of compliance" assumption (states may, after all, as Courtney Hillebrecht notes, only "begrudgingly" comply and then not necessarily rush to do so[104]), a difficult task will be to distinguish sluggish or delayed implementation that does not question the obligation as such from merely rhetorical lip service to formal obligations or the adoption of intentionally perfunctory measures that are only intended to mask a government's true intention not to comply with a decision by the Court.

Expressed as a hypothesis (H_{NORM}), the basic behavioral expectation flowing from the "general propensity . . . to comply"[105] can then be put as follows: "For normative reasons, liberal democracies will not disregard ECtHR judgments rendered against them and will take remedial measures that address the violations identified in those judgments and can be reasonable expected to achieve compliance with them." For H_{NORM} to hold empirically, we need to observe, first, that the respondent state acknowledges its obligation to abide by a given judgment; second, that it is undertaking good-faith efforts, even if slowly or reluctantly, at executing the judgment in question through the adoption of appropriate legislative, executive, judicial, or practical measures, as the case may be; and, third, that such action is indeed normatively motivated. Because normative motivations operate actor-internally and cannot be observed directly, at a minimum it would need to be shown that the major alternative explanations, based on rational choice, do not have any traction or greater explanatory power.[106] The behavioral expectation will be contradicted if a liberal democracy refuses to comply with an ECtHR judgment and/or fails to take any implementing measures. Causally, the hypothesis will suffer if it can be shown that liberal democracies only take remedial measures on the basis of cost-benefit calculations and in particular when they are subject to credible threats of enforcement or actual domestic and/or international sanctions.

H_{NORM} states the behavioral expectation in categorical terms, but as noted above, identities and norms, like other causal variables in the social realm, operate probabilistically, not deterministically.[107] Occasional instances even of outright noncompliance by liberal democracies would thus not deny as such the existence of a normative constraint effect, but would weaken its strength by pointing to the conditions under which that effect no longer operates as expected. I already surmised that the compliance pull is subject to certain scope conditions in terms of the material and/or political costs that are entailed by full compliance. When that threshold is crossed and the expected costs of compliance exceed what may be called the respondent state's "reservation costs"—that is, the highest costs an actor is willing to bear to comply with a judgment[108]—the normative compliance pull might no longer be able to counter other, interest-based considerations, however, and intentional noncompliance or partial compliance could obtain. Abram Chayes and Antonia Handler Chayes argue along the same lines when they note that "[t]he existence of a legal obligation, for most actors in most situations, translates into a presumption of compliance, *in the absence of strong countervailing circumstances.*"[109] Where they exist, such countervailing circumstances may result in a shift in the dominant motivation and displace the normative logic of action with one that is consequentialist.[110] The greater the incidence of noncompliance and the lower the reservation costs among liberal democracies, the lower will be the threshold for such displacement of the hypothesized normative constraint effect.

Due to the manner in which normative causes of action operate, the strength of the hypothesis H_{NORM} depends on the demonstrable absence of rationalist cost-benefit calculations to explain a state's decision against considering and pursuing noncompliance, and here especially, the absence of external pressure applied to the decision-maker in question. While I address domestic mechanisms below, it is worthwhile to briefly consider the reasons that undermine the traction of rational choice explanations at the international level. The first of Andrew Guzman's "Three Rs of Compliance," reciprocity, which is credited with making agreements in other issue areas such as trade and investment self-enforcing, is the easiest to discard as a factor in the human rights domain,[111] where reaping the benefits of human rights protection is, with the exception of a few special constellations that can generate negative externalities,[112] not dependent on the reciprocal behavior of other states.[113] With cooperation not being necessary, the instrumental value of reciprocity drops out.

Enforcement of ECtHR judgments ("retaliation" in Guzman's terminology) through material or political sanctions or positive incentives in the form of the conditional granting or withholding of benefits,[114] though not precluded as a possibility, is empirically largely absent. For one, the COE—the immediate institutional context within which the Court operates—does not provide for any direct material incentives or sanctions that its executive organ, the Committee of Ministers, could offer or impose; the strongest possible sanction that exists is expulsion from the Council under Article 8 of its Statute.[115] Apart from that, the Committee has only naming and shaming at its disposal. Some tangible enforcement may take place through admission conditionalities with regard to EU applicant countries such as Turkey,[116] but this instrument is no longer available for the countries that are already EU members or with respect to those that have no intention of joining the EU in the first place. Furthermore, while EU members cannot as a matter of EU law unilaterally impose economic sanctions on other members for noncompliance with an ECtHR judgment, there are few cases that sufficiently touch upon the interests of other states that would make them want to choose such a course of action in the first place,[117] be it against other EU or non-EU countries (such as Russia). The scarcity of interstate complaints under the ECHR—in more than sixty years, only twenty-eight such applications have been lodged[118]—is mirrored by the rarely observable instances of interstate enforcement beyond diplomatic reproof.

In the absence, largely, of reciprocity and enforcement as plausible causal drivers of compliance with human rights judgments, the burden to explain such compliance in rational choice terms falls on the third of Guzman's "Three Rs," reputation. According to the standard account, in environments of incomplete information state actors seek to develop (usually domain-specific) reputations through their actions as a means to send information regarding their behavioral type to those with whom they interact, while the latter use such reputations—beliefs about what type the other actor represents—to infer their most likely future behavior.[119] In the context of international agreements states may thus "keep commitments, even those that produce a lower level of returns than expected, [. . .] because they fear that any evidence of unreliability will damage their current cooperative relationships and lead other states to reduce their willingness to enter into future agreements. Since the opportunity costs associated with this foregone cooperation are substantial, the vast majority of states possess a strong incentive to behave cooperatively."[120] Compliance with ECtHR judgments, then, might be due to such reputation-based and forward-looking cost-benefit considerations.

The instrumentalist logic that underpins such reputational arguments is convincing in some issue areas, but it does not travel well to the human rights domain in general, and to the ECHR and ECtHR specifically, because the nature of the opportunity costs incurred by a reputation damaged by non-compliance with human rights norms and judgments is not clear.[121] This is so for two related reasons. First, because the benefits of human rights agreements—and, by extension, of judicial decisions interpreting and applying them—does (again, for the most part) not require cooperation with other states, a state's reputation as a complier or non-complier has little meaningful instrumentalist role to play as a signal of reliable future cooperation within that same domain. Second, whether and to what extent a state's reputation for compliance or noncompliance in one domain is transferable to other issue areas is unclear. Shai Dothan suggests that such transferability exists when he argues that by complying with ECtHR judgments, states not only increase their "judgment-compliance reputation," but also their reputation for complying with international law more broadly.[122] Some such "bundling" of reputation across issue areas would have to occur if reputation is to have effects beyond the individual agreement in the context of which it was generated and to yield sufficiently high reputational benefits to offset the costs of compliance.[123] According to Dothan, this is, after all, the key factor driving compliance with the ECtHR's judgments: "A state will comply if the reputational payoff (the reputational gain for compliance plus the avoided reputational loss the state would have incurred for noncompliance) is higher than the material costs of complying with the judgment."[124]

Neither Dothan nor Guzman tests his reputational claims systematically, and without the ability to estimate or measure reputational costs and to distinguish them from other influences, it is impossible to assess their truth value empirically.[125] In any event, the assertion that "compliance *proves* that the reputational payoff is higher than the material cost of compliance" is,[126] by itself and without controlling for other factors, a non sequitur. This is not to say that reputation, even if generated in the field of human rights, cannot, or does not, have effects on state behavior, but rather that its effects are both contingent and likely smaller than made out to be.[127] George Downs and Michael Jones have convincingly argued that states are best seen as having "multiple or segmented reputations" that signal "different levels of reliability in connection with different agreements."[128] The role that such reputations play and the significance ascribed to them will vary with "the utility of the cooperation that an agreement represents or the opportunity cost of defecting from it," and whether they have effects beyond the immediate agreement will depend on whether "the stochastic cost function that leads to defection from it is correlated with those connected with other regimes."[129] In other words, will the reasons that lead to noncompliance in one issue area also affect compliance in other issue areas? Where this can be expected to be the case, as with respect to shocks in the areas of the economy and security, reputational implications will travel; where correlation is low, as with human rights, they will not, or not much.[130]

While the instrumentalist signaling function of a reputation for compliance with human rights in general, and human rights judgments in particular, as conveying a state's reliability with respect to present and future cooperative arrangements in the same or other domains is thus arguably rather low—and, as a consequence, insufficient to carry the major weight of explaining compliance with ECtHR judgments—the rationalist variant is only one way to conceptualize the role of reputation. An alternative way is to think of reputation for compliance with human rights judgments not so much as a functionalist signal, but rather as signaling a state's identity as a law-abiding, human-rights-observing liberal democracy. Alex Geisinger and Michael Stein have explained such reputational concerns as an effect of esteem-seeking on the part of states.[131] A state's esteem-seeking is said not to be fueled by "a preference for direct material or economic benefits" but rather "affects state behavior [. . .] to the extent that a state is concerned about the regard it receives from other states to which it is attracted."[132] Such esteem may of course also result in future cooperative opportunities and benefits, but the ability to enter into such cooperative arrangements is, from this perspective on reputation, not due to the state being seen as a cooperative actor, but because of the appeal of its identity (often because of its similarity with one's own); its proximate significance (in other words, the functioning of this conception of reputation) is value based and normative in character and resonates much more with the logic of appropriateness than with the logic of consequences.

Above I noted that enforcement, when understood as the imposition of costly material or political sanctions, is employed quite rarely internationally to promote compliance with human rights, and certainly too rarely to explain compliance in the particular institutional context of the European Convention and Court of Human Rights. If we broaden the concept of enforcement, however, to include intangible sanctions in the form of social disapproval,[133] transmitted by way of naming and shaming, and its effects on esteem-seeking states, then some such enforcement of ECtHR judgments does take place at the COE as part of the compliance monitoring by the Committee of Ministers, which publicly identifies the state of (non)compliance and sometimes voices express criticism of state conduct in its decisions and interim resolutions. Andrea Huneeus' comment that "supervision mechanisms are not, strictly speaking, forms of enforcement" since "they could be just as easily eluded by states as the ruling itself"[134] is correct insofar as the Committee of Ministers, just like the Court, cannot coerce respondent states against their will to execute judgments; but as long as those states remain members of the COE and continue to interact with the other member states, they cannot escape social sanctioning through the expression of disapproval. State pursuit of compliance in order to avoid being "disesteemed" for noncompliance could be characterized as essentially a rational choice mechanism in which the preferred outcome is the prevention of a loss of esteem, but note that in this case the key driver here is still a normative concern, not a materialist one; that is, states are willing to accept material costs in exchange for nonmaterial benefits with uncertain consequences.

Some critics might more generally question the necessity of the stipulation of a normative constraint effect when compliance could also possibly be explained as fully rational by assuming a *preference* for (if begrudging) compliance with ECtHR's judgments among the states party to the ECHR.[135] The Convention, after all, was brought into being by governments with an apparent preference for locking in central aspects of liberal democracy—the protection of basic civil and political rights[136]—and a preference for judgment compliance might simply be a logical extension of it. There are at least two principal reasons that make such a reformulation of the compliance decision in rational choice terms less compelling than the norm-based alternative. First, the preference-based approach mixes, or rather confuses, a preference for an institutional arrangement with preferences for concrete substantive legal and policy outcomes. Actors may agree that the courts serve useful monitoring and dispute-settlement functions and may thus prefer a governance arrangement that provides for judicial institutions, without, however, necessarily preferring the substance of each and every judicial decision over other feasible alternatives. When actors comply with an adverse decision by the ECtHR despite substantive disagreement with the Court's ruling, they likely do so, despite their original preference for winning the case, because they accept the Court, whose jurisdiction they have freely consented to, as legitimate. Legitimacy, however, is, in the terminology of Joseph Raz,[137] precisely a second-order reason for compliance and is based on normative considerations, not a first-order reason relating to the substance of a decision and one's agreement with, or a preference for, that outcome.

Second, and relatedly, assuming a preference for compliance with adverse judgments raises issues of time inconsistency. When a state defends itself in court, the plausible assumption in most cases is that it would like to win the case and not lose it, suggesting that it has a preference for maintaining the impugned domestic laws or policies intact. Once the court rules against the state, that preference would then have to change to favoring compliance with the judgment, that is, a preference that requires, in most cases, precisely a change of the status quo. In terms of substance, these preferences are contradictory. What accounts for this preference change from the pre- to post-judgment phase? As noted, the standard rationalist mechanisms of tweaking preference orders by manipulating costs and benefits are mostly not available or applicable in the ECHR context, and it is not apparent how the issuing of the judgment, by itself, changes the costs and benefits attaching to the originally preferred course of action so that it would no longer be pursuable—except that it is now no longer possible to claim that that course of action is in conformity with the Convention. So it seems we are ultimately thrust back to a normative explanation. The preference for compliance replaces the previously highest-ranked preference for the status quo ante because maintaining the latter would result in noncompliance, which, as I have posited here, is normatively inappropriate for European liberal democracies, at least in the majority of cases. Relatedly, the question arises as to where the preference for compliance comes from in the first place. Since the immediate material or political payoffs of compliance (or costs in case of noncompliance) with ECtHR judgments are in most cases not obvious, it remains unclear why governmental actors should maintain such a preference, *unless* of course the compliance decision is, after all, not motivated by the immediate costs and benefits of that decision, but rather by its normative appropriateness. Thus, even when rephrased in terms of a preference for compliance, these arguments ultimately again point toward normative factors as the underlying motivation for most observable compliance behavior.

The Rational Choice Element

The expectation that liberal democracies are subject to a normative constraint effect that for the most part eliminates noncompliance from the politically feasible choice set with respect to executing adverse judgments remains insufficient, however, to explain concrete outcomes of compliance. In light of the above-noted fuzziness of legal and juridical language and the possibility of different interpretations of one and the same legal text that may come with different behavioral implications, the expectation of habitual compliance remains underspecified. The fact that the precise requirements for second-order compliance cannot be directly read off the judgments in a quasi-objective and self-evident way gives rise both to the *need* as well as the *opportunity* to interpret the obligations that are entailed by the finding of a Convention violation, allowing decision-makers to take advantage of alternative interpretations with different consequences, and to adopt specific remedial measures accordingly. In light of the "difficulty of determining what constitutes compliance with a judgment by the Court," commentators have pointed out that "there is a spectrum of [. . .] 'general compliance': At one end, literal compliance may occur when a State takes the narrowest interpretation of the decision against it. Extended compliance takes place when a State considers the broader implications of the decisions and the reasons given for it. It could be said that it looks to the spirit of the decision, thereby forestalling future complaints and adverse decisions."[138] While the constructivist expectation of the elimination of noncompliance as a feasible option predicts compliance as the standard behavioral outcome for liberal democracies, it does not by itself provide a compelling explanation as to *how* states will choose to comply when different options are available that may all arguably result in achieving compliance.

Rational choice theory, by contrast, does. Within the legal constraint of having to comply with any adverse judgment to which a state is a party (cf. Article 46 (1) ECHR), I expect governments to choose rationally among the feasible options in line with their preferences and argue that these preferences will generally privilege narrow, restrictive, or otherwise minimal compliance. Underlying this expectation is the assumption that respondent governments have a relatively stable preference for the status quo ante, at least in the short to medium term, and that an ECtHR judgment will not by itself trigger an immediate preference change.[139] This assumption is justified by the fact that had the government been persuaded by the arguments of the opposing side to the extent that its own preference in the matter had changed, it could have adjusted its position and made (or at least pledged) the required changes to domestic law and policy at several stages prior to the final ruling in the case. Doing so would have been possible either during domestic proceedings on the issue (which need to be exhausted prior to applying to the ECtHR, see Article 35 (1) ECHR), or at any time while the case was pending before the Court—by concluding a friendly settlement with the applicant (Article 39 ECHR) or by making a unilateral declaration in which the respondent state affirms the alleged violation and accepts the obligation to remedy it.[140] While it is true that friendly settlements and unilateral declarations need not imply a preference change—they might also be motivated by strategic-instrumental reasons[141]—the nonpursuit of this option can, in most cases (possible exceptions are discussed below) be interpreted as an unwillingness to make changes and as revealing a preference in favor of the status quo.

The strategy of responding to adverse judicial decisions not with outright noncompliance, but rather with efforts to minimize their impact has been repeatedly recognized and documented in the context of the ECtHR's sister institution, the CJEU.[142] Lisa Conant in particular has argued that in the absence of the mobilization of pressure, "EU Member States typically limit ECJ interference with the content of European rights and obligations by *containing* their *compliance*: national administrations obey individual ECJ judgments and simultaneously ignore the implication that unwelcome judicial interpretation has for the universe of parallel situations."[143] Even if pressure can be mobilized to trigger broader policy changes, the result will still often remain reflective of "contained justice," with the "ultimate policy outcome usually restrict[ing] the application of judicial principles by specifying the scope and conditions of particular rights and obligations."[144] Relatedly, investigating the impact of the CJEU's output on EU-level secondary legislation, Dorte Martinsen has argued that while "override" of unwelcome CJEU positions occurs, it is quite rare as a tool of "political correction," not least because successful override requires broad agreement among the member states (as does its unadulterated codification); the much more common legislative response to CJEU jurisprudence is its "modification" with a view to limiting its impact.[145] "Law depends on politics to execute its decisions,"[146] and execution is thus often subject to divergent or even conflicting preferences that will be reflected in the eventual outcome. Interviews of members of different stakeholder groups in five COE countries has shown that such preferences in favor of domestic policy positions, or the maintenance of the integrity of the domestic rule of law more generally, which work against unquestioning obedient compliance, figure prominently in the human rights domain as well.[147]

Against the background of these considerations, I hypothesize that remedial behavior will generally seek to minimize any changes that are necessary to bring the state into compliance with a judgment. Expressed as hypothesis H_{RC-1}, when there is some choice in executing an adverse judgment by the Court, governmental actors will seek to limit the impact of the judgment by opting for narrow, restrictive, or otherwise minimal compliance. When no justifiable choice exists, however—for example, when the issue is so specific that only one remedy is available to end the violation[148]—states would be expected to act in accordance with the normative compliance-pull hypothesis as articulated above and adopt all required measures.

In the presence of feasible alternatives, H_{RC-1} is supported by empirical evidence that shows that in light of the available choices, the governmental actors charged with executing an adverse judgment opt for those that are least costly either in material terms and/or in terms of changes that have to be made to domestic policy, legislation, and administrative practices.

Evidence to the contrary (broad compliance, despite the availability of narrower options) does not necessarily imply nonrational behavior but weakens the reasonableness of the assumed preference in favor of minimal compliance (circumstances where this may be the case are addressed below). Depending on the nature of the violation found by the Court, respondent states may have to take one, two, or all of the following types of measures: they have to pay any financial compensation awarded by the Court (just satisfaction, Article 41 ECHR), take individual measures that end the violation and remove its effects in the applicant's case to the extent possible, and adopt general measures (e.g., legislative or administrative reforms, change in jurisprudence, etc.) to prevent their recurrence.[149] Whereas just satisfaction needs to be paid as awarded and without any margin of appreciation on the part of the respondent state,[150] the adoption of individual and general measures often provides governments with some choices from which to select.

Figure 3 illustrates the notion of this option space. Conceptualizing human rights as protecting the enjoyment of certain material and/or non-material goods (e.g., physical integrity, fairness of proceedings, property, privacy, etc.), we can classify state action that touches upon rights in terms of the degree to which they enable or restrict enjoyment of them, with the

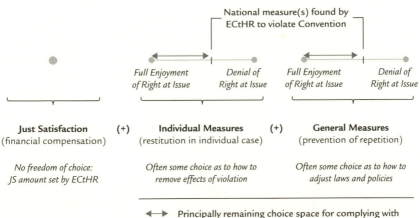

Figure 3. Remedial measures and choice space following ECtHR judgments.

possibilities ranging from enabling full, unimpeded enjoyment to complete denial of enjoyment. A finding of a Convention violation by the Court means that the ECtHR views the domestic measure(s) at issue as too restrictive, intrusive, or not sufficiently effective (especially in the case of positive obligations). While measures of equal or greater restrictiveness are thus no longer available to comply with the Convention and the judgment, all less restrictive measures are in principle still on the table. Clearly, however, it makes a difference *where* within the remaining range the measure chosen to comply with the judgment is located.

The hypothesis advanced here predicts that governments even in liberal democracies generally committed to rights protection will choose measures, whenever possible, that are positioned closer to the ones impugned by the Court (and the policy preferences they represent) than to the full enjoyment pole. Similarly, given the different material and sovereignty costs implied, governments will prefer to pay just satisfaction over the adoption of substantive measures and will prefer to take individual measures rather than general measures. While the overall "wiggle room" in this respect has become smaller over the years under the Court's and the Committee's evolving supervisory practices,[151] both of which have been pushing especially for the adoption of effective general measures to stop the inflow of repeat clone cases originating from the same domestic structural situations, some margin of appreciation with respect to the design of individual and/or general measures that can be exploited by states often remains.

There are two types of circumstances in which the expectation of minimalist compliance as expressed in H_{RC-1} will not hold. The first exception concerns situations in which the governmental actor that is in charge of executing a given judgment actually has a preference for deep(er) and/or broad(er) compliance. This may occur if a change in the composition of the relevant governmental actor—the administration/government, parliamentary majorities, composition of high courts or of other execution-relevant public agencies—has taken place between the lodging of the complaint and the final judgment (or takes place shortly thereafter). The Court's judgment could then enter a political environment more sympathetic to its findings, and speedier and broader execution could obtain than would have been expected under the previous actors that had initiated, or defended, the impugned policy or law in question.[152] The possibility of an intervening change of the composition of government while a case is pending before the ECtHR is not all that unlikely, given that the average length of time that cases remained pending before the original, three-tier control system had been five to six years,[153] and that this situation has not improved for a significant number of cases despite the changes made to the operating procedures of the Court.[154] With many electoral systems providing for elections every four to six years, a change of government during a pending case's lifetime is thus a real possibility as are changes in the personal makeup of other state organs and public offices.

An alternative scenario in which one may detect a counterintuitive willingness to push for broad compliance may occur when a governmental actor with pro-compliance preferences seeks to use the Court's judgment strategically either to overcome resistance by another domestic decision-maker whose cooperation is needed (especially if that actor has veto power) to bring about the preferred changes, or to deflect domestic political backlash of unpopular decisions by pointing to the requirement of complying with the Court's decision.[155] The actor whose preferences are aligned with those of the ECtHR would then be playing a judicialized version of a two-level game in which the outcome at the international level (here, the Court's judgment) is used domestically to further that actor's agenda against domestic (popular or institutional) opposition by restricting its available set of policy choices to those that meet the requirements of the Court's finding.[156] The legal constraints following from the ECtHR's decision would, in other words, be used to tie the relevant decision-makers' hands domestically.[157]

The strategy of using international legal-dispute settlement mechanisms to provide political cover in situations where freely pursued choices might have higher expected political costs (because they are directly attributable to the relevant decision-makers) or where a negotiated settlement is blocked by domestic political or institutional opposition has been shown to play a role in the international settlement of territorial disputes,[158] and there is no reason why the same logic should not also apply elsewhere. Indeed, Courtney Hillebrecht has located part of the force of human rights judgments in "provid[ing] political cover for difficult or divisive policy reforms,"[159] and empirical evidence adduced by Laurence Helfer and Eric Voeten on the *erga omnes* effects of ECtHR jurisprudence on lesbian, gay, bisexual, and transgender (LGBT) rights suggests that such judgments have their biggest effects when relied on to overcome opposing domestic preferences.[160] The underlying domestic disagreements need not necessarily manifest themselves as outright and intense political conflict; they may also take more subtle forms of substantive policy debates about what is permissible (or required) in terms of human rights protection, with the judgment of the Court being seen, or proffered, as providing a legitimate focal point for the desired changes. Importantly, effectively using ECtHR judgments to overcome domestic opposition or to generate political cover requires that those with diverging preferences also accept the Court's output as legitimate and binding, and hence to be followed. If they do not, then ECtHR judgments will fail to have the desired effect. If they do, then those in charge of executing them may be able to implement them more broadly than is required.

Phrased as hypothesis H_{RC-2}, we can state this expectation as follows: Deeper, broader or speedier compliance with an adverse ECtHR judgment occurs when the governmental actor in charge of executing a given judgment holds a preference *in favor of* the policy position articulated or implied in the judgment in question. Empirical proof of this hypothesis would need to show the existence of such a pro-judgment preference, in addition to evidence of broad over-compliance. Because such preferences may not be openly voiced, they may have to be inferred from the available empirical evidence. In any event, while offering a possible explanation for some instances of broad compliance, assuming pro-compliance preferences on the part of domestic actors does not offer a compelling account of compliance across the board because governmental actors often need to change their own preferred laws and policies in response to an adverse judgment.

The second exception that allows for broad compliance involves the possibility of enforcement. The rational choice assumption with respect to the design of remedial measures adopted by governmental actors in order to execute adverse judgments implies as its corollary that such actors should in principle also be susceptible to manipulations of their cost-benefit calculations through threatened or imposed material and/or political costs or through the conditional withholding of benefits by stakeholders in favor of broad compliance.[161] Such costs or withheld benefits would need to be sizable enough to affect decision-makers' calculations in a way that makes swifter and/or broader compliance their preferred course of action in light of them (if the imposition of costs or withholding of benefits are only threatened, such threats or promises would need to be credible). The depth of compliance, in other words, is expected to vary with the intensity of enforcement.[162] Where enforcement is absent or negligible, decision-makers will be able to comply in accordance with their own substantive preference; where enforcement is sufficiently strong, they will opt to accommodate the enforcer's preferences and comply more broadly than they otherwise would have. Because interstate enforcement, as noted above, is very rare in the human rights domain in general and even more so at the level of specificity involved with respect to ECtHR judgments, any such enforcement and pressure will have to be generated domestically.

In her "contained justice" approach, which deals with the impact of CJEU jurisprudence, Lisa Conant has similarly argued that "broader policy effects from ECJ rulings are a function of the reaction of organized societal actors and public institutional actors that support legal claims. Only organizational and institutional actors can sustain the persistent legal and political pressure that will compel governments to abandon evasive strategies and align policy with evolving legal obligations."[163] The mobilization necessary to mount such pressure, Conant argues, is conditioned by the distribution and magnitude of the consequences associated with a particular ruling: where high-magnitude consequences are concentrated among only comparatively few actors with an intense interest in them, they will tend to give rise to "collective political and legal mobilization by organized actors" where such high-magnitude consequences are more widely diffused, well-known collective action challenges arise and they will be more likely to trigger "individual legal mobilization" instead or possibly become an electoral issue.[164] By contrast, if consequences are of a low magnitude to begin with, giving rise only to weak interest in them, there will be little, if any, mobilization, irrespective of whether these consequences are concentrated or more widely distributed.[165] For the mobilization of pressure to be successful, Conant emphasizes, being endowed with sufficient political and economic resources to sustain pressure on decision-makers in support of one's preferred implementation of CJEU jurisprudence and against opposition is key, with the consequence that those who might benefit from a broad implementation of CJEU decisions but are politically and/or economically disadvantaged will have a much harder time succeeding.[166]

In addition, information may also be crucial in tilting compliance decisions in one's favor. As Xinyuan Dai has pointed out in the context of domestic interest groups, a government's compliance decision need not always tilt toward the numerically larger group but may instead favor the better informed one:

[A] government's compliance is determined not only by the electoral leverage of domestic constituencies but also by how much information they have—their informational endowment. On the one hand, compliance decisions tend to be biased toward large interest groups which have a large electoral influence. On the other hand, interestingly, compliance decisions can also be biased toward special interests, if these groups are much better informed about the policy process. This is because, facing an inference problem, the relatively better-informed group is more likely to base its approval of the government on the actual policy rather than exogenous disturbances in the policy process. Accordingly, the policymaker would lose more support by fooling the well-informed than by fooling the ill-informed.[167]

Dai uses electoral influence broadly as "a shorthand for public support," where votes "can be replaced by dollars, acquiescence, and so on, as a form of political support" that affects "a government's survival or more generally its welfare."[168] The key in either case is that, for Dai, political influence on compliance decisions is the result of the combined effect of numbers and information, not just one or the other.

In light of these theoretical considerations, a further hypothesis ($H_{RC\text{-}2}$), then, is that broad compliance will be accomplished in situations where interest groups can exert sufficient pressure on decision-makers to implement a judgment swiftly and broadly despite the latter's preferences prior to such enforcement. What type of pressure, and on what scale, is necessary to have such effects is difficult to specify ex ante for the wide range of compliance issues and different institutional and political settings in which execution takes place, but empirically we should be able to observe some manifestations of collective action—political marches and demonstrations, direct engagements with decision-makers, repeat public criticism of the governmental actor's course by interest group organizations, etc.—or a demonstrable issue salience for electoral politics—through surveys, repeat coverage in the new media, etc.—to make a plausible case that broad compliance, where we find it despite assumed preferences to the contrary on the part of the relevant decision-makers, has been due to enforcement. (One difficulty here is that some adverse reactions may have been threatened only in private; this will have to be noted when broad compliance occurs in the absence of observable enforcement).

While domestic enforcement is a possibility, we should expect its actual incidence in liberal democracies to be quite rare because the magnitude of costs and benefits implied by many ECtHR judgments is comparatively small and often limited to an individual's situation or a small number of similarly situated cases and, if Conant is correct, will thus not be suited to trigger any sizable mobilization. This expectation is also in line with Beth Simmons' argument that for there to be meaningful mobilization, two factors need to come together: first, a sufficiently high value attached to improvements in the right in question; and second, a reasonable probability of being successful with one's demands.[169] While institutional arrangements and the political culture in liberal democracies tend to make governments generally responsive to citizen demands, relative improvements in the human rights situation, although important for those affected, are often modest in light of already high standards of human rights protection and, as noted, will tend to be limited to comparatively small numbers of stakeholders. As a result, without additional factors giving the issues at stake political salience, most adverse ECtHR judgments will fail to generate significant mobilization beyond the group of those immediately affected by them.[170] Even more important, the government's policy preference will often be reflective of, and be shared by, domestic political majorities, so that if there is mobilization, it will more likely be *against* change.[171]

Rather than enforcement through social mobilization, what will more likely be observable in liberal democracies is enforcement by hierarchically higher positioned actors with pro-compliance preferences (e.g., supreme vs. lower courts, federal vs. state governments). Policy preferences are rarely uniformly distributed across domestic institutions and officeholders, and where hierarchically superior institutional actors have a preference for broader or swifter compliance, in certain circumstances they might be able to impose their preference on subordinate, less inclined actors that are charged with executing a given judgment. This type of compliance action effectively combines a preference-based explanation with an institutionalized enforcement mechanism based on the hierarchical organization of the state apparatus.

Due to the expected scarcity of domestic enforcement, it is relatively clear that enforcement is not a viable alternative explanation to the normative constraint hypothesis, which seeks to explain the *if* of compliance, not the *how*. If enforcement were the principal driver of compliance, then those judgments that do not reverberate beyond the individual claimant's case should for the most part remain unexecuted. Alternatively, where there is popular support for a judgment by the Court, it will frequently be the case that domestic contestation of the issue in question already preceded Strasbourg's decision. Indeed, it is not rare that individual applications are lodged strategically as part of larger campaigns by social movements,[172] with such cases being reflective of societal preferences for general reform beyond the individual decided case.[173] Still, even if a social movement exerts pressure on decision-makers in order to achieve broad and speedy compliance with a given judgment, the question remains why such pressure should succeed. After all, the mobilization of pressure, if already triggered previously, had apparently failed to bring about the desired changes prior to obtaining the ECtHR's judgment, and it is not clear why the governmental actors that resisted such pressure prior to the judgment should now respond positively to it[174]—*unless*, of course, the judgment does indeed change the dynamics of the game, by increasing the size and/or composition of the movement, by providing the movement's cause with enhanced legitimacy, or simply by being a legal judgment that cannot be disregarded. The latter two effects, however, would be normative in character and thus strengthen hypothesis H_{NORM} rather than an alternative enforcement hypothesis.

Compliance with Friendly Settlements

The theoretical expectations above have been developed in the context of adverse judgments in the case of which it can be reasonably inferred that the finding of a Convention violation goes against the legal and/or policy preferences of the respondent government. A nontrivial number of judgments that contain obligations for the respondent state, however, are not based on decisions on the merits of the complaints, but instead represent judicial acknowledgements of friendly settlements reached between the parties which can occur at any stage of the proceedings (Article 39 (1) ECHR).[175] The judgments (and, since the entry into force of Protocol No. 14, decisions)[176] in which the Court recognizes friendly settlements and at the same time strikes the cases from its list of pending applications are, like merits judgments, subject to the supervision of their execution by the Committee of Ministers (Article 39 (4) ECHR).[177] Proceedings aiming at the conclusion of a friendly settlement are confidential (Article 39 (2) ECHR).

Important for present purposes is the fact that the respondent state, in contrast to a judgment on the merits, has expressly agreed to the terms of the settlement. Although financial compensation is the predominant and often sole obligation included in friendly settlements, pledges of substantive individual, and occasionally even general, measures on the government's part are not uncommon either.[178] The possible reasons for concluding friendly settlements are varied.[179] While the amount of compensation proposed by and acceptable to the Court tends to be 10–20 percent higher than in a comparable just satisfaction award to provide an additional incentive to settle,[180] the costs incurred by the state for the overall proceedings should generally be lower than in proceedings leading up to a merits judgment, due to the shorter duration of friendly settlement proceedings. In addition, states may prefer to settle because friendly settlements are not counted as Convention violations, attract less publicity than judgments finding a violation, and leave more present and future "room to maneuver"[181] if a precedent-setting judgment can be avoided and especially if the remedy can be limited to financial compensation. Moreover, in contrast to striking out applications on the basis of a unilateral declaration by the respondent state, which generally requires an acknowledgement of the alleged Convention violation,[182] in the case of friendly settlements remedial measures are normally pledged ex gratia without such an acknowledgment.[183]

Whatever the specific motives in a given case, the assumption that the obligations agreed upon in a friendly settlement go against the preferences of the government cannot be upheld unqualifiedly. Rather, while compelled to take action that the state would have had no reason to engage in absent the complaint before the Court, the settlement and the specific obligations included therein must be taken as reflecting the government's preference, at least with regard to the remedial consequences in the concrete circumstances of the case;[184] at the same time, it is reasonable to assume that the government will have attempted to minimize the overall costs imposed on it as part of the settlement negotiations. In most settled cases there will be little remaining discretion. The amount of compensation is always, and the substantive measures to be taken are usually, expressly stated—as opposed to declaratory merits judgments, which do not indicate the substantive measures to be taken—and these terms of the settlement need to be executed as pledged. Only occasionally, for example, when legislative reforms are promised but not specified in terms of concrete provisions should we observe meaningful maneuvering space for the respondent government. All in all, given both the scope and depth of the remedial measures promised and the state's involvement in actively negotiating or offering them, compliance with friendly settlements should raise much fewer interpretive issues and thus be more straightforward and occur faster than compliance with judgments on the merits.

Testing the Theory: Methodological Approach

To test the hypotheses articulated above, I conducted two comprehensive qualitative country case studies that examine the remedial measures adopted by the respondent states with respect to all compliance-relevant judgments issue by the Court until the end of 2010. If the theoretical claims I advance here are correct, then we should be able to observe the expected behavior particularly in the context of those countries that are indubitably liberal democracies. As a convenient shortcut, these should include the sixteen countries that have scored a perfect ten on the polity variable (most democratic) of the most recent Polity IV data set during the years that these countries have been party to the ECHR and subject to the ECtHR's jurisdiction.[185] If the two principal hypotheses fail with these countries, they can be expected to fail with less strongly established democracies as well.

For presentation in this book I selected two countries from this set—the United Kingdom and Germany[186]—that, while sharing some characteristics, also differ in other respects that may be expected to affect whether and how states comply (see Table 2). Both states ratified the Convention early on, and although the UK lagged Germany in the acceptance of the Court's jurisdiction, acceptance still occurred well before the Court's "activation" phase in the 1980s, thus exposing both countries to the Convention's control mechanism in a comparable fashion. Furthermore, both countries are institutionally enmeshed to a similar extent, sharing membership in many regional and global organizations, including the COE, the European Union, the North Atlantic Treaty Organization, the United Nations, the World Trade Organization, the International Monetary Fund, the World Bank, and the Organization for Economic Cooperation and Development, among many others.

While comparable along some dimensions, the two countries also differ in ways that may be consequential regarding both the number and the types of cases that reach the Court and their subsequent compliance behavior. Probably most important, while Germany, a civil law country, has a constitutional bill of rights and a constitutional court with the power to quash public acts, including legislation, if found to be in violation of the constitution, the United Kingdom, a common law country, has no homegrown bill of rights and incorporated the ECHR only in 2000 by way of the 1998 Human Rights Act. While enabling the courts to review legislation for its conformity with the Convention, the UK continues to adhere to the principle of parliamentary sovereignty, with the consequence that the courts can declare the incompatibility of legislation with the ECHR but cannot strike it down.

The units of analysis in the case studies are the remedial responses to the violations found in specific judgments (or sets of related judgments). In order to reveal that governments tend to execute judgments restrictively, it is necessary first to identify the range of feasible options available to a

Table 2. Comparison of Select Characteristics of the United Kingdom
and Germany

	United Kingdom	Germany
Polity Score (Polity IV v. 2015)	10 (1922–)	10 (1949–)
Year of ECHR Ratification	1951	1952
Subject to Court's Jurisdiction since	1966	1959
Form of Government	Constitutional Monarchy	Federal Republic
System of Government	Parliamentary	Parliamentary
Domestic Bill of Rights	No	Yes (constitutional)
(Strong Form of) Judicial Review	No	Yes
Domestic Status of ECHR	Act of Parliament (since 2000)	Federal Statute (since 1952)
Type of Legal System	Common Law	Civil Law
Compliance-Relevant Judgments	317 (through 2010) 351 (through 2015)	130 (through 2010) 184 (through 2015)

respondent government and then to show that the chosen option is narrower
or more restrictive than its alternatives. Where no such spectrum exists, the
only alternative to execution is defection, that is, outright noncompliance.
Given that the Court's judgments address issues that vary widely in terms of
issues, scope, and implications for domestic law and policy, the analysis of
the available options must necessarily be context specific. On the one hand,
the execution of cases that require individual measures only are by definition
different in scope than those that require general measures (change of legislation, policies, or practices). On the other hand, depending on issue area
and specificity of the violation, general measures will also present a narrower
or wider spectrum of available remedial responses to rectify the impugned
situation. To identify available remedial alternatives, I take into account all
available materials surrounding a case in which possible forms of execution
are being suggested and discussed, including government documents, press
reports, and academic commentary. On occasion, I construct plausible alternatives from the information available on a case and its circumstances.

This study is an exercise in descriptive inference: I seek to understand
the likely causal factors motivating the compliance decisions of governmental
actors from the analytic description of observable courses of events.[187] The
hypothesized normative force motivating governments of liberal states to
comply with the ECtHR's judgments in particular remains unobservable in
positivist terms but is deduced from the absence of concrete and meaningful

enforcement through "sticks" or the conditional granting or withholding of "carrots." Proving such absence empirically, however, runs into the problem captured by the well-known reminder that "absence of evidence is not evidence of absence." The lack of evidence in the sources consulted as to actions arguably qualifying as enforcement of the Court's judgments does not definitively preclude the possibility that there may be such evidence elsewhere, including in nonpublic sources, or that the occurrence of such action has simply not been (sufficiently) recorded. In light of this, the following chapters will not be able to deliver a hard-and-fast proof of the theory of compliance here articulated but should be taken as a substantial "plausibility probe"[188] into the reasonableness and validity of the proposed causal logic of action.

PART I

The United Kingdom

CHAPTER 2

The Uneasy Place of the ECHR and ECtHR in UK Law and Politics

Fortunate to never have suffered an extremist national government on either the right or the left, the United Kingdom has, among the European countries, the longest uninterrupted democratic history. The UK was also a main sponsor of the Convention and was the first state to ratify it, although the prevailing view at the time was that this was done "as an example for others, and not with the expectation that it would be found in violation itself, at least not regularly."[1] This confident view was based on the belief that the UK's constitutional design already provided sufficient protection of civil and political rights and that its domestic laws were largely in conformity with the Convention.[2] As a result, it came as an irritating surprise to subsequent UK governments that the country was regularly brought before the Convention organs and, to boot, regularly found to be in violation of its substantive provisions. As early as the mid-1980s, some observers detected a shift in British public opinion toward "growing resentment" that Parliament and the domestic judiciary were being "replaced" by "mainly foreign judges or jurists,"[3] a sentiment that would develop into the "sometimes intense hostility in UK public discourse towards [. . .] the European Court of Human Rights" observable in recent times,[4] fueled by a string of controversial judgments, such as those on prisoner voting rights and the imposition of restrictions on the deportation of the terrorist suspect known as Abu Qatada. The debates about the future relationship with the ECtHR have become entangled with similar criticisms directed at the European Union that resulted in the 2016 Brexit referendum (with the well-known result of the UK leaving the EU as of March 29, 2019), and while the two (sets of) institutions are often confused and lumped together,[5] a core criticism is the same: their presumably

illegitimate meddling with UK self-governance and the constitutional principle of parliamentary sovereignty.

Against this backdrop of an often less-than-enthusiastic engagement with
the Convention system, the UK should be an easy case for showing the logic
of minimalist compliance in action, and even for finding repeated instances of
noncompliance by UK governments vexed by Strasbourg's allegedly activist
jurisprudence. Reviewing remedial action with respect to all judgments issued
against the UK until 2010 (the descriptive tables cover judgments until 2015),
I show in this chapter that save for the judgments dealing with prisoner voting
rights, the UK has in fact complied with nearly all adverse judgments in this
set, if often only "begrudgingly"[6] so, or has at least taken meaningful steps
toward such compliance in the remaining cases whose supervision is still continuing. At the same time, it has over and over again exploited the available
options to strive for compliance on minimalist terms. This chapter addresses
the role of the Convention in the UK legal system and describes the universe of
judgments involving the United Kingdom. I then turn to discussing the depth
of compliance with judgments that required remedial responses from the UK
in the following chapters.[7] Due to length constraints, not all judgments can
be discussed in full in the text.[8] Instead, I present substantive discussions of a
large number of significant adverse judgments that have been formally complied with, as well as of judgments still under supervision by the Committee of
Ministers, in order to illustrate the full range of "minimization" strategies that
different UK governments have employed in adopting remedial measures. The
legal issues and remedial measures adopted with respect to all remaining judgments are presented in summary form in an appendix at the end of this book.

The United Kingdom and the Convention

The prominent role played by the United Kingdom in promoting and drafting
the Convention has been well documented.[9] Although the UK quickly ratified
the ECHR on March 8, 1951, a mere four months after it had been signed,[10]
it was not until January 14, 1966, under the recently elected government of
the Labour prime minister Harold Wilson, that the UK accepted, on the basis
of renewable declarations valid for three years, the then-optional right of
individual petition and the equally optional jurisdiction of the Court.[11] Prior
to that date, the UK was thus subject only to interstate complaints and the
decision-making authority of the Committee of Ministers, and the prevailing

opinion had been that, in line with Albert Venn Dicey's highly influential constitutional theory,[12] human rights were sufficiently protected by Parliament and the common law,[13] obviating the need to submit to external control bodies. Probably as weighty a reason, if not more so and notwithstanding the UK's successful lobbying to include a colonial application clause in the Convention,[14] was the concern that a good number of regulations relating to the British colonies might not stand muster under the Convention and that acceptance of individual petitions and the jurisdiction of the Court would interfere with London's governing of the UK's dominions.[15] By 1966, however, this concern had vanished, together with the British Empire.

At the same time, the Convention remained unincorporated into domestic law, with the result that it could not be directly invoked before UK courts.[16] From the beginning, incorporation had been a contentious issue, with majorities in both the Labour and the Conservative Parties opposed to it for a good forty years.[17] It was only after the 1992 general elections that Labour began to change its position in favor of supporting the idea of incorporation, against continued Tory opposition. In doing so, Labour picked up on growing popular sentiments in favor of a domestic bill of rights that was fueled, inter alia, by perceptions that civil liberties had been significantly eroded under the Thatcher government,[18] as well as by growing support from inside the judiciary.[19] Campaigning on the promise, inter alia, of "bringing rights home" in the 1997 general election,[20] the new Labour government under Prime Minister Tony Blair promptly delivered on its promise and incorporated the Convention into UK law through the enactment of the Human Rights Act 1998 (HRA).[21] The (ultimately non-entrenched[22]) HRA received Royal Assent on November 9, 1998, and entered into force on October 2, 2000.[23]

Under section 6 of the HRA, it is unlawful for any public authority (including the courts) to act in contravention of the Convention (with some exceptions). Section 7 provides for recourse to the courts for any individual who can claim to be adversely affected by such an act, and section 8 empowers the courts, if they find such act to be unlawful, to "grant such relief or remedy, or make such order, within its powers as it considers just and appropriate" (section 8.1). While the court-made common law—even in its horizontal, private-law dimensions—is generally seen to fall under the obligation to interpret and apply domestic law in line with the Convention,[24] the supremacy of Parliament—which is expressly excluded from the definition of "public authority" in section 6.3 of the HRA and thus not bound by it[25]— has formally remained untouched. When a sufficiently senior court finds that primary legislation violates the Convention, the most it can do is issue a "dec-laration of incompatibility" (section 4) to put Parliament on notice.[26] Such a declaration, however, neither invalidates the relevant piece of legislation—that is, it is still to be enforced—nor is it binding on the parties to the current dispute in which it is made (section 4.6). In response to such a declaration, a minister of the Crown can, but does not have to, seek to amend the legisla-tion in question (section 10.2). The Human Rights Act specifically obliges any domestic court or tribunal faced with the adjudication of an issue under the Convention to "take into account"—that is, not necessarily strictly follow—any relevant judgments, advisory opinions, reports, or other decisions issued by the Strasbourg control bodies (section 2.1)[27] and to interpret all parlia-mentary statutes, to the extent possible, in a Convention-compliant manner (section 3.1). As David Feldman has noted, the fact that the case law of the Strasbourg institutions is "persuasive but not binding" on UK courts has been justified by the fact that the Strasbourg court itself does not recognize the doctrine of stare decisis and that it would have been odd "had the Strasbourg case-law been more authoritative in the UK than it is in Strasbourg."[28]

A specialty of the UK situation is that the United Kingdom is interna-tionally responsible for several national jurisdictions with different legal sys-tems, namely for England, Wales, Scotland, and Northern Ireland, as well as for those dependent territories to which it has extended the coverage of the Convention under Article 56 (1) ECHR. As Churchill and Young have pointed out, although a violation found by the European Court will usually relate to only one of these jurisdictions, "broad compliance would require corrective action in other jurisdictions where the law is the same or similar."[29] Contemporaneous with the passage of the HRA, the Labour government also adopted the Scotland Act 1998, the Northern Ireland Act 1998, and the Gov-ernment of Wales Acts 1998, which resulted in the devolution of certain legis-lative powers previously held by Westminster to the regional parliaments and executives. Under the HRA, legislative acts in devolved areas of competence are considered secondary, or subordinate, legislation (section 21.1), with the consequence that the courts can invalidate such acts, if it is not possible to interpret them in line with the Convention and *unless* the impossibility of that removal results directly from primary legislation (section 3.2.c),[30] in which case subordinate legislation remains enforceable.

A further development initiated by the Labour government in 2003 con-cerned the institutional reorganization of the branches of government in the UK, resulting in the Constitutional Reform Act 2005. One key element of this reform was the creation of a Supreme Court of the United Kingdom, which began operating on October 1, 2009. Prior to that date, since 1876, the highest court in the country was the Appellate Committee of the House of Lords, the second chamber of Parliament, composed of up to twelve Lords of Appeal in Ordinary. Although Law Lords were expected (though not legally required) to refrain from commenting on party political policy or controversy,[31] this allocation of judicial power still sat oddly with orthodox theories of the separation of powers. The new Supreme Court's jurisdiction covers all types of cases that could previously be appealed to the House of Lords, including those raising issues under the HRA 1998, plus jurisdiction over devolution disputes that had until then been subject to the jurisdiction of the Judicial Committee of the Privy Council (the latter remains the highest court of appeal for several Commonwealth countries, British overseas territories, and Crown dependencies, i.e., Guernsey, Jersey, and the Isle of Man).[32]

Although only in its second decade, it remains to be seen for how long the Human Rights Act will continue to perform its function as the UK's bill of rights. In some political quarters, discontent with the practical effects of the HRA has fueled debates about scrapping the act and replacing it with an "indigenous" British bill of rights.[33] Building on then prime minister Gordon Brown's 2007 proposal of national consultations on the creation of a Bill of Rights and Duties as part of an overhaul of Britain's constitutional settlement,[34] David Cameron's coalition government in 2011 followed up on its promise to "establish a Commission to investigate the creation of a British Bill of Rights that incorporates and builds on all our obligations under the European Convention on Human Rights, ensures that these rights continue to be enshrined in British law, and protects and extends British liberties."[35] The commission issued its report in December 2012, with the majority supporting the idea of a domestic bill of rights to remedy the perceived lack of public ownership of the currently existing human rights instruments, the HRA and ECHR.[36] More recently, in the run-up to the 2015 general elections, a Conservative policy document reiterated the intention to replace the HRA with a homegrown bill of rights to curtail the powers of the ECtHR, and, as a potential last resort, to withdraw from the ECHR.[37] While ECHR withdrawal did not make it into the 2015 election manifesto, the plan to replace the HRA and to limit the domestic impact of the ECtHR did.[38] More recently, with Brexit preparations moving center stage, the 2017 election manifesto stipulated that the repeal or replacement of the HRA would be considered only after the conclusion of the Brexit process and that the UK would remain party to the

ECHR for the duration of at least the next parliament (the Labour Party, by contrast, expressly vowed to keep the HRA in place).[39]

The disenchantment with the HRA goes hand in hand with occasionally vociferous criticism of the ECtHR, which has intensified in recent years.[40] The "strained relationship" between the UK and the ECHR/ECtHR is multidimensional and has a number of sources, central among which is the charge that the ECtHR is illegitimately interfering in areas that should be more appropriately left to national decision-makers and their margin of appreciation. In the case of the UK, this sovereignty concern in fact has two distinct elements: interference with state sovereignty—that is, meddling with what are regarded as domestic concerns—and interference specifically with parliamentary sovereignty as the cornerstone of the UK's constitutional arrangement.[41] In the words of one UK parliamentarian critical of the ECtHR, the tendency of the latter to usurp the role of lawmaker forces "democratic parliaments [. . .] across Europe [. . .] to choose between the will of their people and the views of foreign judges."[42] Critics see the Court as not paying sufficient tribute to the subsidiary nature of the ECHR control mechanism: "Where two views might reasonably be taken of a human rights problem, and the Member State in question has opted for one, it should not be for Strasbourg to opt for the other."[43]

The process of exiting the European Union, prompted by the thin majority in favor of leaving the EU in the June 2016 referendum and begun in earnest when the UK triggered Article 50 of the Treaty on European Union on March 30, 2017, is formally independent of the question of ECHR membership and the HRA, but it is politically intertwined with both of them since it foregrounds the question of independent British self-governance free from intervention by multilateral governance institutions. If it is true that "[t]he British are . . . 'peculiarly averse to, and particularly suspicious of, being told what they can and can't do by pan-European bodies,'"[44] then it is reasonable to expect that this will be reflected in the modalities of responding to the judicial stimuli coming from the ECtHR and enhance the inclination to seek compliance on minimalist terms.

The Universe of Judgments Involving the United Kingdom

Until the end of 2015, the Court issued a total of 488 judgments involving the UK as respondent state (see Table 3).[45] Of these, 67 (13.7%) were judgments striking out applications from the Court's list that did not result in a decision

Table 3. Judgments Involving the UK and their Compliance Status as of March 10, 2017

Year	Number of Judgments	At Least One Violation	No Violation	Struck Out/ Inadmissible	Executed	Pending
1975	1	1	—	—	1	—
1976	1	—	1	—	—	—
1978	2	2	—	—	2	—
1979	1	1	—	—	1	—
1981	3	3	—	—	3	—
1982	1	1	—	—	1	—
1983	1	1	—	—	1	—
1984	2	2	—	—	2	—
1985	2	1	1	—	1	—
1986	5	1	4	—	1	—
1987	7	6	1	—	6	—
1988	2	2	—	—	2	—
1989	3	2	1	—	2	—
1990	6	4	2	—	4	—
1991	3	2	1	—	2	—
1992	3	1	1	1	2	—
1993	6	1	3	2	3	—
1994	7	2	4	1	3	—
1995	8	4	4	—	4	—
1996	11	7	4	—	7	—
1997	10	6	4	—	6	—
1998	10	6	4	—	6	—
1999	14	12	—	2	14	—
2000	26	15	3	8	21	—
2001	31	18	11	2	15	4
2002	39	29	4	6	34	1
2003	24	19	2	3	21	1
2004	22	18	—	4	22	—
2005	17	14	—	3	16	1

(*continued*)

Table 3. Judgments Involving the UK and their Compliance Status as
of March 10, 2017 (*Continued*)

Year	Number of Judgments	At Least One Violation	No Violation	Struck Out/ Inadmissible	Executed	Pending
2006	19	9	5	5	14	—
2007	50	19	7	24	37	—
2008	35	26	6	3	27	1
2009	17	13	3	1	14	—
2010	21	14	7	0	13	1
2011	18	7	9	2	7	1
2012	22	10	12	—	10	—
2013	13	8	5	—	5	3
2014	13	4	9	—	3	1
2015	12	4	8	—	3	1
Total	**488**	**295**	**126**	**67**	**336**	**15**

Source: Extracted from author's own compliance data set.

on the merits (56 of these still required some type of execution as a result of a friendly settlement or unilateral declaration). Of those decided on the merits, 126 (25.8 percent of the total) resulted in a finding of no violation. This leaves 295 judgments (60.5 percent) that found infringements of one or more ECHR provisions.[46] Of the resulting total of 351 compliance-relevant judgments, 336 (95.7 percent) had been complied with as of March 10, 2017, while 15 judgments (4.3 percent), some dating back to 2001, remained under supervision.

In its adverse judgments against the UK, the Court has found a total of 376 violations of particular Convention rights. Table 4 shows their distribution across the principal articles and issue areas involved. The most frequently violated articles are Article 6 (guaranteeing certain procedural and fairness rights, 27.7 percent), Article 5 (right to liberty and security, 17.3 percent), and Article 8 (right to respect for private and family life, 17.0 percent). Notably, in contrast to many other Convention parties, the majority of violations involving Article 6 do not concern the length of proceedings but, rather, various substantive fairness issues, well over a dozen of them in the context of the military justice system. The majority of right-to-life violations concerned mostly infringements of its procedural aspect due to the lack of effective investigations into responsibility for the death of the deceased,

Table 4. Violations Found in 295 Merits Judgments against the UK (through 2015)

Type of Violation	Count	Percent (rounded)
Physical Integrity Rights (Articles 2 and 3)	**36**	**9.6**
thereof: right to life (including right to effective investigation)	17	
thereof: related to Northern Ireland	*13*	
freedom from torture and inhuman and degrading treatment	19	
thereof: conditional on deportation/extradition	*8*	
Right to Liberty and Security of the Person (Article 5)	**65**	**17.3**
thereof: right to review of lawfulness of detention	26	
right to compensation for unlawful deprivation of liberty	18	
Right to Fair and Speedy Proceedings (Article 6)	**104**	**27.7**
thereof: unfair civil or criminal proceedings	53	
unfair military/court-martial proceedings	17	
excessive length of proceedings	25	
lack of access to a court	9	
Right to Respect for Private and Family Life (Article 8)	**64**	**17.0**
thereof: issues related to (covert) surveillance practices	16	
interference with correspondence	9	
issues related to homo- and transsexuals	9	
Freedom of Expression and of the Press (Article 10)	**11**	**2.9**
Right to an Effective Remedy (Article 13)	**33**	**8.8**
Freedom from Discrimination (Article 14)	**42**	**11.2**
thereof: different social security entitlements for widows and widowers	36	
Right to Vote (Article 3 of Protocol No. 1)	**5**	**1.3**
Violations of Miscellaneous Other Rights	**16**	**4.3**
Total	**376**	**100**

Source: Author's own compliance data set; HUDOC.

especially in the context of the conflict in Northern Ireland, and as regards Article 3, eight of the nineteen violations were conditional on the applicant being actually extradited or deported without appropriate safeguards to prevent such violation.

Most of the friendly settlements concluded by the UK and recognized in a judgment deal with issues that are also addressed elsewhere in merits judgments or that are of a minor nature. For example, more than half of the friendly settlements (thirty-three) concerned disputes arising out of the differential treatment of widows and widowers with respect to social security benefits, an issue also subject to an even larger number of merits judgments. The terms of friendly settlements and unilateral declarations are mostly limited to financial compensation, but in three instances the UK specifically promised individual or general measures.[47]

Having sketched the UK's overall compliance record and the general range of issues involved, I will now turn to examining in greater detail the specifics of a sizable share of judgments rendered against the UK and of the UK's remedial responses to them, beginning, in Chapter 3, with the assessment of the UK's compliance with just satisfaction awards and the obligation to adopt individual measures with respect to the applicant's case.

CHAPTER 3

Compliance with Just Satisfaction Awards and Individual Measures

The sovereignty and material costs of complying with adverse judgments can generally be expected to increase with the scope and complexity of the remedial measures required, being lowest in the case of simple payments of just satisfaction, higher when additional individual measures have to be adopted, and highest when general measures such as changes in legislation, are needed as well. Given the assumption of a preference on the part of governmental actors for minimizing these costs and the expectation that the range of feasible options will be different for different types of remedial responses, I consider the execution of the Court's judgments from the vantage point of the principal measures required to abide by them. In this chapter, I begin with the assessment of the United Kingdom's responses to those judgments rendered until 2010 and considered sufficiently complied with by the Committee of Ministers as of March 2017 that required, as the principal remedial measure, only the payment of just satisfaction or the adoption of individual measures in the applicant's case.

Just Satisfaction

Most of the Court's judgments include the award of just satisfaction together with the decision on the merits. The Court may award compensation for pecuniary and/or nonpecuniary damages and for costs and expenses. While payment has on occasion been late—that is, after the three-month deadline usually set by the Court, thus triggering the need to add default interest—there is no indication for any judgment in the data set that the UK has ever

failed to abide by this obligation, even with respect to politically highly contentious cases such as the *McCann* judgment (1995), which involved counter-
terrorism operations, or the judgments in *Hirst (no. 2)* (2005) and *Greens and
M.T.* (2010) on prisoners' voting rights.

In some types of cases, payment of just satisfaction is the only conceivable
remedial measure necessary to comply with a judgment. This applies arguably
to the twenty-three judgments against the UK involving the excessive length
of domestic proceedings in violation of Article 6 (1) ECHR.[1] As the Court
itself has noted, "[W]hen proceedings are continued beyond the 'reasonable
time' [. . .] the intrinsic nature of the wrong prevents complete reparation
(restitutio in integrum). This being so, the only claim the applicant can make
is for just satisfaction."[2] Time lost, after all, cannot be regained.[3] Given that
all domestic proceedings had been concluded by the time the ECtHR issued
its judgments and that no structural problems which might have required
additional general measures had been identified, the only remedy owed was
financial compensation for any damage caused by the delays. The Committee of Ministers accordingly closed the supervision of the execution of these
judgments upon proof of payment.[4]

In addition to the set of length of proceedings judgments, just satisfaction was also the only required remedy—other than the rote dissemination
and publication of the Court's judgments—in a number of cases in which
the violation resulted from isolated (mis)applications of domestic law, rather
than from the laws as such, or when the outcome of the impugned domestic
decisions no longer made other forms of reparation possible or meaningful.
In *Gillow*, the Guernsey Housing Authority's refusal to grant the applicants
licenses to occupy a home owned by them and its fining them for living there
without a license was considered disproportionate by the Court and a violation of Article 8 ECHR, but because the Gillows had subsequently sold the
house, financial compensation remained the only remedy for the violation.[5]
In *McLeod*, the unwarranted police intrusion into the home of a post-divorce
couple to prevent a breach of the peace when at the material time there was
no reasonable risk of such breach ran afoul not only of Article 8 ECHR, but
also of domestic law, and thus did not require any further individual or general measures.[6]

In a set of five cases concerning the lack of independence of the Royal
Ulster Constabulary (RUC) when conducting investigations in 1999 into
possible collusion in the death of the applicants' next of kin in Northern
Ireland in the mid-1970s that implicated the RUC itself (a violation of the

procedural aspect of Article 2 ECHR), the investigations had, by the time of the judgments in 2007—and indeed prior to the lodging of the complaints in 2004—already been transferred to new investigative bodies the independence of which was not doubted even by the applicants.[7] Further violations in which domestic law without obvious compliance issues of its own was applied in a Convention-violating manner include, inter alia,[8] the unjustified stopping of a prisoner's letter to the Scottish minister of state (Article 8 ECHR),[9] the violation of right to effective legal representation due to proximity, within hearing, of a police officer during the applicant's first consultation with his solicitor (Article 6 (1) in conjunction with Article 6 (3) lit. c ECHR),[10] and the unlawful detention ordered by magistrates' courts for failure to pay local taxes or court-imposed fines due to the erroneous application of domestic legislation and case-law (Article 5 (1) ECHR).[11] In all of these cases—isolated violations in the past that had no continuing effects in the present and were not due to Convention-infringing general aspects of domestic law or policy—financial compensation was considered sufficient for compliance.

The fact that the UK has never skirted its payment obligations is not insignificant since it is with respect to just satisfaction awards that the causal role of the Court's judgments is most obvious. Not only are amounts and conditions of payment set by the Court, in the counterfactual absence of the Court's award there would simply be no legal or other ground to disburse any funds to the applicants beyond what they may have been awarded previously at the national level. To the extent that payment occurs, the judgments are causally significant, if only partially so. They are a necessary but not sufficient cause— after all, not all countries honor their obligation to make payment[12]—which requires interaction with the normative pull effect. There is no evidence in the publicly available materials that any meaningful domestic political pressure was applied, less any sanctions threatened, to compel the UK to comply with just satisfaction awards. Nor has the UK—unlike Greece[13] or Turkey[14]—been subject to any naming and shaming specifically concerning the failure to pay just satisfaction in the form of interim resolutions by the Committee of Minsters. Rather, just satisfaction awards have been fully complied with in the absence of enforcement. In most cases, just satisfaction awards involve small to modest amounts and will generally be politically the least controversial remedy. While thus a comparatively easy case for the normative constraint hypothesis—the same holds even more strongly for the fifty-three striking-out judgments that were limited to financial compensation—it does provide empirical proof of the causally significant role of the Court's judgments in triggering state behavior that would not have occurred in their absence.

Individual Measures

Compliance with judgments concerning violations that are either ongoing or have continuing effects, or that might result from impending state action, will often require—in addition to payment of just satisfaction, if awarded— substantive individual measures to end (or prevent) the violation in the applicant's case. When the violation results from conduct that is required by domestic law or policy, general measures will also have to be adopted, usu- ally before appropriate remedial individual measures can be taken (discussed, where relevant, together with the general measures in the next chapters). Fre- quently, however, violations result from disproportionate or otherwise defec- tive decisions, or actions, by public authorities that affect, or have affected, only the applicant. In such cases, just satisfaction and individual measures suffice to comply with the relevant judgment.

One type of judgment that falls within this category concerns cases involv- ing extradition or deportation proceedings in which the applicant can make a credible claim that he or she will likely be subject to torture or inhuman or degrading treatment or punishment in the target country (Article 3 ECHR) or that the removal would be a disproportionate infringement of the right to respect for family life (Article 8 ECHR). Notably, while most cases before the Court concern violations that have occurred in the past or are ongoing, the majority of removal cases involve expected future human rights violations that would, or would likely, occur as a result of extraditing or deporting the appli- cant to a particular target country so that the finding of a breach of the Conven- tion in these cases is conditional on the actual implementation of that course of action and can thus still be avoided by the respondent country. The UK has been subject to a number of such findings, plus one judgment that concerns a related friendly settlement. In six of these, including the friendly settlement, the UK quashed the deportation orders and granted (or reinstated) indefinite leave to stay for the applicants;[15] in two others it complied by extending temporally limited leave to remain.[16]

These latter two responses show that there is no "compliance automatism" when it comes to the substance of remedial measures. Instead, the govern- ment took into account the specific circumstances of the cases as well as the reasoning of the Court and designed the remedies accordingly. In the case of *NA.*, the Court expressly noted that "*at the present time* there would be a violation of Article 3 ECHR if the applicant were to be returned" to his native Sri Lanka.[17] In the case of *S.H.*, the finding of the Court appears in large part motivated by the paucity of evidence as to the human rights situation in the applicant's home country, Bhutan,[18] suggesting, by implication, that more information as to the actual probability of treatment contrary to Article 3 ECHR might result in a different conclusion. In the five cases in which indefinite leave to stay was granted, the finding of a violation was, by comparison, stated in much more categorical terms that effectively eliminated the possibility to be able to comply with them with time-limited leaves to stay. Rather than consistently responding with the most beneficial (for the applicants) response of indefinite leave to stay, the UK took a differential response based on the specific reasoning in the *NA.* and *S.H.* judgments, availing itself of the option to reassess the threat of maltreatment in light of possible changes in the relevant countries when the temporary leaves to stay came would come up for renewal.

In two further cases concerning the removal of the applicant from British territory, the extent of compliance was arguably less than broadly sympathetic to the applicants. The first of these is the well-known *Soering* case, in which the Court found that Article 3 ECHR would be violated should the applicant be extradited to the United States to stand trial for murder in Virginia and, if convicted and sentenced to capital punishment, be subjected to the "death row syndrome."[19] To comply with the judgment, the UK extradited Soering only after receiving diplomatic assurances that he would not be charged with a crime that might entail the death penalty. While this promise was eventually honored—Soering received two consecutive life sentences—it remains unclear to what extent it can be considered legally sufficient. After all, the sworn affidavit made earlier by the competent state attorney in Virginia to make representations to the judge at the sentencing stage that it was the wish of the United Kingdom that the death penalty be neither imposed nor carried out was earlier considered insufficient by the Court. It further noted that "the offence charged, being a State and not a Federal offence, comes within the jurisdiction of the Commonwealth of Virginia; it appears as a consequence that no direction could or can be given to the Commonwealth's Attorney by any State or Federal authority to promise more; the Virginia courts as judicial bodies cannot bind themselves in advance as to what decisions they may arrive at on the evidence; and the Governor of Virginia does not, as a matter of policy, promise that he will later exercise his executive power to commute a death penalty."[20] The Committee of Ministers' final resolution, on the other hand, notes that the US government "confirmed [. . .] that, in light of the applicable provisions of the 1972 extradition treaty, United States *law* would *prohibit* the applicant's prosecution in Virginia for the offence of capital murder."[21] Since no material legal changes had occurred in the meantime, it is unclear how to square the different assessments of the legal situation; the extradition treaty itself, however, does not bestow any legally binding effect on the requested assurance.[22]

How is the depth of compliance in this case to be evaluated? Two conceivable alternatives existed: the United Kingdom could have prosecuted Soering domestically, in accordance with the principle *aut dedere aut iudicare*, or it could have extradited him to his country of nationality, Germany, which had also requested his extradition. The first alternative, however, was practically barred because UK law at the time did not provide for the trial of foreigners for acts of murder committed abroad. The second alternative, however, while presenting problems of evidence and of compelling witnesses to testify in a German court,[23] would have legally removed the threat of the death row syndrome since the death penalty did not exist in Germany.[24] So from the vantage point of the threatened violation of Article 3 ECHR, extradition to Germany would have provided absolute protection against the death row syndrome whereas extradition to the United States retained an element of insecurity with respect to whether the assurances that had been made would be viewed as legally binding on the state of Virginia. The latter can thus arguably be qualified as a lesser form of compliance, even if such assurances deserve, as the Court more recently held, a "presumption of good faith."[25] Except for Amnesty International's submission of comments to the Court, there is no evidence of any civil society or other political pressure on the UK not to extradite Soering to the United States, and so the UK government did not face any meaningful political constraints that might have kept it from proceeding on the basis of its preference for what it viewed as the stronger of the two extradition requests.[26]

With respect to the *Al-Saadoon and Mufdhi* judgment, the assessment of the depth of compliance is made difficult by the fact that the threefold violation of Articles 3, 13, and 34 of the Convention found in the judgment followed from the UK's failure to comply with interim measures requested by the Court. The case concerned two Iraqi nationals who had been captured by British forces in Iraq in 2003 and were subsequently detained as suspects in the murder of two UK soldiers. When the Iraqi authorities began to take over the case in 2005, the applicants became exposed to the risk of the death penalty, which had been reintroduced in Iraq in 2004. On December 30, 2008, one day before the end of the UK's authority to detain people in Iraq, the ECtHR requested that the UK, as an interim measure under Rule 39 of the Rules of Court, refrain from handing over the two applicants to the Iraqi authorities while their case was pending before the Court. Despite the request, however, the following day they were transferred into the custody of the Iraqi authorities. While both were ultimately released in mid-2011 because of insufficient evidence,[27] until then the Damoclean sword of the death penalty hung over their heads while proceedings before Iraqi courts were ongoing.

The UK argued that there had been an "objective impediment" to complying with the interim measure since it was acting on foreign territory and had "no lawful option other than transfer to the Iraqi authorities,"[28] so that continuing to detain the two applicants would have violated "the law and sovereignty of a non-Contracting state," namely Iraq.[29] But the UK of course did have a choice: a choice between violating either one or the other of two applicable norms, and it chose not to comply with the Court's request to retain the applicants in UK custody, rather than to infringe Iraqi sovereignty. This was a conscious, not a fortuitous, choice. Indeed, the issue of the applicants' fate after December 31, 2008, had already been raised during judicial review proceedings before a domestic court. In light of the ongoing negotiations between the UK and Iraqi governments on the conditions under which UK troops could and would remain in Iraq, one of the UK chief negotiators had frankly remarked that "the judgment was made that to introduce the issue of UK forces continuing to hold detainees, whether generally or specifically in relation to the two Claimants, risked adversely affecting the conduct and outcome of these important and urgent negotiations"; there was, in any event, "no likelihood [. . .] of the UK being able to secure any agreement from the Iraqi authorities that we may continue to hold the Claimants either indefinitely or pending the outcome of this litigation."[30]

Strictly speaking, this is not an instance of noncompliance with a *judgment* of the Court because none had been rendered yet; indeed, the failure to comply with the requested interim measures resulted in the finding of violations of Articles 13 and 34 ECHR and thus belongs more properly to the realm of first-order (non)compliance. Once the judgment had been rendered, one could argue that the United Kingdom, given its by-then seriously constrained options, did what it could do to comply with the Court's decision in the case, in light of the explicit admonishment that "compliance with [the] obligations under Article 3 ECHR requires the Government to seek to put an end to the applicants' suffering as soon as possible, by taking all possible steps to obtain an assurance from the Iraqi authorities that they will not be subjected to the death penalty."[31] The UK accordingly sought guarantees from Iraq's prime minister, president, and the president of the Iraqi High Tribunal that the death penalty would not be imposed on the applicants, and in the absence of such guarantees, declined to cooperate with the tribunal in the applicants' cases.[32]

Still, looking at the overall set of rules that govern the relationship between the Court and respondent states, noncompliance with an interim measures request in pending proceedings that triggers violations of its own casts a shadow of any subsequent claims to compliance with the judgment proper. Seen as a whole, the UK's response to the decisions of the Court is a mix of noncompliance and compliance that is akin to overall minimalist compliance in other situations. Faced with the dilemma of conflicting obligations and an interest in negotiating a satisfactory agreement with Iraq on the status of UK forces in the country after 2008, the UK chose the path of lesser political inconvenience. Instead of risking friction and conflict with Iraq by keeping Al-Saadoon and Mufdhi in UK detention, or by pressing hard for a mutually agreed-upon temporary arrangement (which would have constituted a broader approach to compliance with the Convention in this case), the government apparently preferred a subsequent admonishment by the Court and the politically less costly obligation to make representations to the Iraqi authorities after the handover of the applicants. This course of action constitutes a rational choice in light of the government's higher-ranked preference concerning Iraq-UK relations, but at the same time it represents an only minimally acceptable response to the rules of the Convention system as a whole.

Other judgments with isolated violations requiring the adoption of individual measures include a case concerning a violation of the prohibition of the retroactive imposition of criminal penalties—*nulla poena sine lege*, enshrined in Article 7 ECHR—due to a confiscation order that was imposed on the applicant on the basis of legislation that had entered into force only after the events in question and that had resulted in the applicant's conviction for drug trafficking.[33] In executing the judgment, the UK chose not to enforce the confiscation order and lifted restrictions on the applicant's assets, providing for *restitutio in integrum*.[34] In another case, the failure to conduct a fair trial by an independent and impartial tribunal due to racist comments allegedly having been made by some of the jurors was closed on the basis of the applicant's option to ask for a quashing of the domestic judgment in light of the ECtHR's decision.[35] No broader, or narrower, alternatives are readily apparent in these two cases.

If we look only at the responses to final judgments, then the UK did take remedial measures in all cases that required individual measures in addition to any payment of just satisfaction. At the same time, in response to *Soering* and *Al-Saadoon and Mufdhi*, the UK chose courses of action that resulted in lower levels of human rights protection than would have been afforded by feasible alternatives (extradition to Germany in *Soering*, a negotiated agreement in *Al-Saadoon and Mufdhi* allowing the UK to continue to detain the applicants while the case was pending before the ECtHR, or legally binding assurances ruling out the death penalty). The same can be said of the two cases in which the UK granted temporal, rather than indefinite, leave to stay, preserving its ability to reevaluate the cases again in the future. In none of these cases has there been any discernible civil society, less any international, pressure on the government to opt for broader compliance in favor of the applicants. As unfortunate as this may be for the affected individuals, this is in line with expectations. Not only are cases that require individual but not general measures limited in scope to the applicant's case, extradition and deportation cases also often concern individuals that have been charged with, or convicted of, serious crimes, so that sympathy for their situation and willingness to mobilize for them tends to be scarce. While the absence of any discernible domestic or international enforcement did not result in the UK opting for outright noncompliance, the absence of such pressure also meant that there was no compelling reason to go beyond what was strictly necessary to achieve compliance, even if broader options were in principle available.

CHAPTER 4

Compliance with General Measures I:
Sociopolitical Issues

Having to adopt general measures in order to comply with an adverse judgment—that is, having to change the law (including, if need be, a country's constitution), to modify administrative or judicial policies, or to take practical measures such as overhauling aspects of infrastructure—generally yields the highest sovereignty costs, understood as "the surrender of national discretion,"[1] among the three types of remedial measures that may have to be taken in response to an ECtHR judgment. Just satisfaction and individual measures may be objectionable on substantive grounds to respondent governments, but their immediate consequences are usually limited to the applicants' individual cases. The obligation to adopt general measures in line with the judgment's finding and reasoning, by contrast, circumscribes a polity's ability to set law and policy as its elected government sees fit—in short, its ability to engage in domestic self-government. Of course, submitting to the Court's jurisdiction is also a voluntary exercise of self-government; but at the level of concrete judgments, the findings of the Court frequently require changes in law or policy that the government would not have contemplated in the absence of such judgments and whose implications often jar with its own substantive legal or policy preferences.

A False Negative: Broad Compliance by Way of the Human Rights Act 1998

The incorporation of the ECHR into UK domestic law through the Human Rights Act directly remedied certain shortcomings in domestic law that had repeatedly resulted in the finding of two particular Convention violations, often jointly with infringements of other ECHR provisions (as well as occasional other ones).[2] The lack of an effective domestic remedy to complain about Convention violations before a national authority (Article 13 ECHR, 32 instances)[3] and the absence of an enforceable right to compensation for arrests and detentions in violation of the requirements of Article 5 (Article 5 (5) ECHR, eighteen instances).[4] The HRA remedied the first violation by providing legal recourse for any person claiming to have been the victim of a public authority acting, or proposing to act, in contravention of the ECHR (section 7 HRA)—excluding, however, as pointed out above, Parliament and primary legislation—and by providing judicial remedies should a court find that the Convention had been breached (section 8 HRA). By including among the remedies the power to award damages (cf. sections 8.2–8.4 HRA), the HRA removed the source of the second violation. Prior to the HRA, the previous (Conservative) governments had repeatedly rejected compensation for deprivations of liberty in violation of Article 5 (1) through (4) ECHR on the basis of the restrictive interpretation of Article 5 (5) ECHR as applying only where domestic law resulted in arbitrary arrests and detention, not automatically whenever other provisions of Article 5 had been violated, as well as the argument that, since the Convention had not been part of UK law prior to the HRA, such violations could in any event not give rise to a domestic claim for compensation.[5]

Ostensibly, the adoption of the HRA might be considered an instance of counterintuitive broad compliance because the act provides for incorporation of the ECHR and judicial remedies with respect to *all* future Convention violations, not only for those at issue in the judgments in which violations of Articles 13 and 5 (5) ECHR were found; a minimalist approach to compliance would have provided remedies only for the latter. Yet while the elimination of two recurrent sources of Convention violations may have been a welcome side effect of the HRA, its adoption of course cannot be reduced to being solely a remedial response, but rather a more general one to the UK's experience under the Convention since ratification. Indeed, as noted earlier, debates about the benefits and drawbacks of incorporating the ECHR into domestic law had been on and off the political-legal agenda for some time, with the tide beginning to turn in the 1990s in favor of incorporation among some parts of the political elites. When the new Labour government followed up on its campaign promise to incorporate the Convention into domestic law, it presented several general justifications. These included practical considerations as to the expected greater speed and lower costs of litigating Convention complaints in domestic courts; the normative desirability that individuals claiming to have been the victims of a human rights violation by the state should be able to argue their cases before courts within that state; and the strategic consideration that enabling British courts to adjudicate complaints under the Convention, and using its specific concepts and language, would likely give their decisions and reasoning greater influence in Strasbourg, helping them "to influence the development of case law on the Convention by the European Court of Human Rights on the basis of familiarity with our laws and customs and of sensitivity to practices and procedures in the United Kingdom."[6]

So while reducing the number of ECtHR judgments by addressing sources of Convention violations at home was part of the raison d'être of the HRA, it was not conceived as a remedial instrument as such. The HRA is thus best seen as a general response to the perceived problems of an unincorporated Convention, and to the human rights situation in Britain overall, promoted by a newly elected government with preferences different from its predecessor, not as an instance of broad compliance in direct response to, and directly triggered by, the judgments finding violations in particular of Article 13 and 5 (5) ECHR. Nor can the adoption of the Human Rights Act be explained by mounting public pressure to provide for a written domestic bill of rights. As Frederica Klug has written, "[T]here was no groundswell of enthusiasm for incorporation"; the issue "did not even attract the level of grass-roots support which existed in Scotland (and to a lesser degree in Wales) for devolution or in London for a new assembly."[7]

Corporal Punishment and Chastisement

The implementation of the judgments against the UK dealing with the issue of corporal punishment met with some resistance. The 1978 *Tyrer* judgment, which had held that the judicially imposed punishment of "birching" as practiced on the Isle of Man (a UK Crown dependency), constituted degrading treatment in breach of Article 3 ECHR,[8] met with open refusal to execute it by the Manx government,[9] much to the UK's embarrassment.[10] Although birching was no longer imposed in practice, it remained technically available as a punishment until its eventual abolition in 1993;[11] strictly speaking, only then was there full compliance; but in line with its early, less stringent practice, the Committee of Ministers had ended supervision of the case already in light of the judgment's dissemination to the relevant Manx officials.[12] In part motivated by the Manx government's recalcitrance and to spare it additional future humiliation, the United Kingdom stopped extending the right of individual petition to the Isle of Man shortly after the *Tyrer* judgment.[13] While this may be seen as a "rather unsatisfactory" outcome from the vantage point of increasing effective human rights adjudication and protection,[14] it was in conformity with ECHR rules under which extending the coverage of the Convention and the right to individual petition to "territories for whose international relations [a state] is responsible" (Article 56 (4) ECHR) is a voluntary act that the Convention parties can also decide not to renew once it expires.

When the Court ruled that the threat of corporal punishment in public schools, while not as such rising to the level of a violation of Article 3 ECHR nonetheless infringed parents' right to an education of their children "in conformity with their own religious and philosophical convictions" (Article 2 of Protocol No. 1),[15] the initial solution proposed, with many teachers and the education ministers in favor of the retention of corporal punishment, was to opt for narrow compliance by permitting parents, if they so desired, to exempt their children from such punishment.[16] The bill, however, was torpedoed in the House of Lords by an amendment that would have eliminated corporal punishment in state schools altogether, forcing the government to withdraw it.[17] Ultimately, however, the House of Lords had its way, and upon a new initiative that the government failed to defeat in the House of Commons by a single vote, corporal punishment was abolished in schools receiving public funds as of November 1986, resulting in compliance with respect to public schools—but not private ones[18]—albeit with a substantial delay of five and a half years after the Court's judgment.[19] The abolition of corporal punishment in all schools, public and private, and including nursery schools, occurred only under the new Labour government in 1998,[20] which had made educational reform one of its top priorities, against vocal Tory opposition.[21]

That same year the Court issued its judgment in the case *A.*,[22] which extended its jurisprudence on corporal punishment into the private domain of parents' homes. In this case the Court found that the centuries-old defense of reasonable chastisement that A.'s stepfather had successfully raised in justifying beating A. several times with a garden cane, "did not provide adequate protection to the applicant against treatment or punishment contrary to Article 3."[23] The supervision of the execution of this case became surprisingly contentious. After domestic consultations and apparent incentives for the government to appear supportive of parental rights,[24] the Blair government sought to have the case closed on the basis of domestic case law that recognized the judgment in *A.* and without intending to legislate,[25] but this case law was deemed insufficient by the Committee, not least because the defendant in it had actually been acquitted after having hit his son with a belt across the back for refusing to write his name.[26] In part due to the pressure of children advocacy groups,[27] and after contentious debates in both Houses of Parliament—with the Blair government being opposed to a full ban[28]—the Children Act 2004, while not eliminating the right to parental corporal punishment altogether, replaced the reasonable chastisement defense in England and Wales with one of "reasonable punishment," whose availability was limited to charges of common assault, that is, instances where the injury suffered is considered "transient or trifling."[29] The UK saw its obligation fulfilled, but the Committee, in line with earlier practice, required evidence of legislative change in the other jurisdictions for which the UK is responsible (Scotland and Northern Ireland).[30] Subsequently, some remedial measures were prepared or adopted in these two jurisdictions, but, unusual for a subject matter that does not directly implicate the affairs of other member states, a wide spectrum of opinions was voiced by a number of delegations as to their conformity with the Convention, with several of them expressing doubts.[31]

Supervision of the case thus continued while the outcome of domestic proceedings that challenged the conformity of existing legislation with the Convention was being awaited,[32] much to the dissatisfaction of the UK government. Only in mid-2009 was the supervision of the case eventually considered ready for closure.[33] While no new legal developments had occurred, the UK had submitted evidence of various awareness-raising measures to prove that the new standard was sufficiently publicized and known by the public, and the Committee and Secretariat had resolved that the question of whether the current solution of allowing the defense only with respect to common assault charges stayed below the "minimum level of severity of treatment of children" still in conformity with Article 3 ECHR was eventually for the Court to decide.[34]

It is worth noting that the public debate on the limits of physical discipline revolved not so much around the graver forms of physical discipline, but rather around the issue of whether parental "smacking" would still be permissible or not, and the question has remained quite visible domestically. Although the government has repeatedly rejected calls for a total ban on smacking[35]—a position in line with the majority of public opinion[36] as well as corresponding practices[37]—parliamentary challenges have periodically reemerged, but so far without any tangible results.[38] In any event, the fact that the remedial response to the *A.* judgment chose to retain the legality of at least some forms of the physical disciplining of children, rather than outlawing them altogether as the fullest protection of the physical integrity rights of children, as is the case in most other Council of Europe states,[39] is indicative of restrictive compliance. What is also clear is that issue remains politically salient domestically and will likely remain so, given the Council of Europe's campaign to ban smacking in all member states;[40] the string of decisions by the European Committee of Social Rights finding several states in violation of the European Social Charter (ESC) for failure to "prohibit and penalize all forms of violence against children;"[41] and direct admonishment by the Human Rights Committee "to put an end to corporal punishment in all settings, including the home, throughout United Kingdom and all Crown dependencies and overseas territories, and should repeal all existing legal defenses across the State party's jurisdiction."[42] Indeed, the government of Wales has announced that it would seek to outlaw the practice once it receives the authority to legislate on parenting and parental responsibilities under new devolution legislation,[43] a move that would put the issue on the agenda again in the other UK jurisdictions as well.

Gender and Sexual Orientation Issues

Demands for equal protection and nondiscrimination of homosexuals had resulted in the prominent 1981 *Dudgeon* judgment,[44] in which the Court found that the continuing penalization in Northern Ireland of homosexual acts between two consenting adults in the privacy of their homes violated the Convention's protection of the right to respect for one's private life (Article 8 ECHR).[45] The UK responded promptly, with large majorities in favor in both Houses of Parliament and despite "vociferous objection in Northern Ireland,"[46] by removing criminal liability for such acts,[47] probably eased by the fact that private homosexual practices had already been decriminalized in England and Wales in 1967[48] and in Scotland in 1980[49] and that draft legislation to that effect for Northern Ireland had been introduced by the previous Labour government in 1978.[50] At the same time, compliance was less than comprehensive because homosexuality remained illegal in a number of other jurisdictions for which the UK was responsible[51] and the remedial legislation expressly excluded any acts involving the participation or presence of more than two people.[52]

Moreover, the relevant legislation contained exemptions that maintained the criminalization of homosexual activities in the three services of the UK armed forces.[53] These were repealed only in 1994, but they continued to remain a ground for discharging members from the armed forces and the UK's merchant ships,[54] with the *Armed Forces' Policy and Guidelines on Homosexuality* subsequently issued by the Ministry of Defense in December 1994 explicitly upholding the policy that "homosexuality, whether male or female, is considered incompatible with service in the armed forces. This is not only because of the close physical conditions in which personnel often have to live and work, but also because homosexual behavior can cause offence, polarize relationships, induce ill-discipline and, as a consequence, damage morale and unit effectiveness. If individuals admit to being homosexual whilst serving and their Commanding Officer judges that this admission is well-founded they will be required to leave the services."[55]

Would the UK remove what essentially constituted a ban on gays in the military if so required by the Court? Four test plaintiffs, all of whom had been dismissed from the Royal Navy or Royal Air Force for reason of their sexual orientation, challenged the UK's policy before the ECtHR, and won, with the Court finding that the continued investigations into the applicants' sexual orientations and their subsequent discharges violated the respect for private life protected under Article 8 ECHR.[56] The UK government again responded swiftly. Without waiting for the next five-year review of armed forces legislation in 2001 and without debate in Parliament, on January 12, 2000, it passed the Armed Forces Code of Social Conduct, after already having stopped all pending investigations into homosexual conduct.[57] The new policy revoked the Ministry of Defense's ban on gays in the military by making assessments of suitability for (continued) service in the armed forces dependent solely on whether "the actions or behavior of an individual [have] adversely impacted or are [. . .] likely to impact on the efficiency or operational effectiveness of the Service," explicitly excluding the permissibility of considerations of "gender, sexual orientation, rank or status."[58]

The Conservatives were highly critical of these changes, while the Liberal Democrats applauded it;[59] in any event, it appears that there was no real alternative to removing the ban on homosexuals in order to comply with the Court's judgments.[60] Still, the speed with which the Labour administration changed the policy, against the wishes of the military leadership who would have preferred a slower approach,[61] may be somewhat surprising, given that the UK's representatives had until the end argued vigorously for the preservation of the ban before the Court[62] and that prominent Labour representatives had backed the exclusionary policy.[63] At the same time, newspapers reported "signs" prior to the Court's judgment (as early as February 1999) that the government was already paving the way for the ban to be lifted,[64] and prior to the 1997 general elections, Labour had committed to a free vote for MPs on the issue of gays in the military.[65] Given Labour's general pro-gay-rights posture, a free vote effectively presaged the end of the ban;[66] in addition, Labour had pre-committed itself to abiding by a judgment of ECtHR requiring the ban's lifting.[67] Given this prevailing attitude in the Labour Party, it does not surprise that the Labour government in 2000 also lowered the age of consent for homosexual activities from 18 to 16 years, that is, the same age of consent as applicable to heterosexual acts,[68] and, complying with the *A.D.T.* judgment,[69] also removed from the criminal law the offense of homosexual acts among several men that had remained intact after *Dudgeon*.[70]

A second, somewhat related issue cluster has concerned the formal nonrecognition of gender reassignments in the case of transsexuals. In earlier judgments, the ECtHR could not discern a sufficiently evolved consensus across European states as to a shared practice.[71] In 2002, however, the Court changed course and, noting domestic passivity despite recurrent calls to keep the need for legal changes under review, found that "the respondent Government can no longer claim that the matter falls within their margin of appreciation, save as regards the appropriate means of achieving recognition of the right protected under the Convention. Since there are no significant factors of public interest to weigh against the interest of this individual applicant in obtaining legal recognition of her gender re-assignment, [the Court] reaches the conclusion that the fair balance that is inherent in the Convention now tilts decisively in favor of the applicant."[72] Hence, the Court declared violations of Article 8 (for nonrecognition of the acquired gender) and Article 12 ECHR (due to the inability to marry a person of the opposite sex, after gender reassignment had occurred), noting that it could no longer be assumed that the words "man" and "woman" used in the latter provision "must refer to a determination of gender by purely biological criteria."[73]

Although an Interdepartmental Working Group on Transsexual People, following the review of practices in other countries as well as a series of expert interviews, had been in favor of full legal recognition of transsexuals in 2000,[74] a call seconded by the UK Court of Appeals in 2001,[75] the government only tabled a draft bill after the ECtHR's judgments in July 2003[76] and after the House of Lords had issued a declaration of incompatibility under the HRA regarding the Matrimonial Causes Act on April 10, 2003.[77] The bill eventually became the Gender Recognition Act 2004. Removing the violations found in *Christine Goodwin* and *I.* (i.e., legal recognition of new gender and right to marry member of one's original sex),[78] the legislation actually went beyond what was required by these judgments as well as the regulations in other countries. In particular, while the Court's judgments concerned specifically postoperative transsexuals, the Gender Recognition Act does not require that an applicant has undergone any specific medical treatment, nor are there other requirements found in the rules and practices of other states, such as that the applicant must be sterile (as is the case Germany).[79] This liberal scope may surprise somewhat, given that "[t]transsexuals are too few in number, too isolated in society, too different in their concerns from the dominant gay movement, to form powerful movements or lobbies,"[80] but may be due, as with the rights of homosexuals, to long-standing support for the rights of transsexuals at least from parts within the Labour Party.[81]

Respect for Home

The case of *Connors* concerned the eviction of the applicant, together with his family, from a local-authority caravan site for Gypsies and Travelers. Under the statutory regime in force at the material time, the Mobile Homes Act 1983, such evictions from public sites—in contrast to private ones—did not require any justification, nor were they subject to judicial review. The ECtHR viewed this as a disproportionate restriction and hence a violation of Article 8 ECHR.[82] Despite calls for speedy implementation through the adoption of a remedial order[83] and a private members bill introduced in the House of Commons in 2006,[84] the government opted to wait for general legislation to be passed. Eventually, this occurred by way of the Housing and Regeneration Act 2008, which extended the safeguards applying to private caravan sites in the Mobile Homes Act 1983 to sites maintained by public authorities;[85] the required secondary legislation to commence the relevant section, however, entered into force in England only in April 2011[86] and in Wales only in July 2013.[87]

So eventually, full compliance with the *Connors* judgment, and with it greater security of tenure for Gypsies and Travelers, had been achieved. But why such a long delay, given that the necessary changes were straightforward, left little wiggle room, and could be realized through the deletion of a few lines of restrictive text in the definition of "protected sites" in the Mobile Homes

Act 1983[88] (a suggestion that Parliament's Joint Committee on Human Rights had already made in 2004[89])? The answer remains elusive. To be sure, the consultations carried out in both England and Wales served the purpose of addressing and clarifying implementation issues and needs, but they were begun in England only in September 2008,[90] that is, after remedial legislation had been adopted in Parliament and in Wales only at the beginning of 2013.[91] Maybe the urgency did not appear that great, given that the Housing Act 2004 had provided partial relief by empowering the courts to suspend repossession orders against residents of caravan sites, whether publicly or privately run.[92] And while public opinion has not been well-disposed toward Gypsies and Travelers and their caravan sites—in the 2007 Living in Wales survey, for example, 78 percent of respondents indicated that they would not want to live near such a site[93]—this does not seem to be a reasonable cause for any avoidance strategy by the authorities in this specific instance because *Connors* did not require additional caravan sites, only the extension of certain legal protections to those already residing on sites run by local authorities.

Two further and related judgments continued the line of argument begun by the Court in *Connors*. Both concerned violations on account of the applicants' inability to raise their personal circumstances as a defense to be taken into account in determining the proportionality of possession/eviction proceedings against them initiated by public housing authorities.[94] As affirmed by House of Lords jurisprudence, however, judicial review in these circumstances was limited to the question of whether the statutory basis of the acts leading to eviction proceedings as such was incompatible with Article 8 ECHR, or alternatively, whether the public authority's decision in question was one "that no reasonable person would consider justifiable."[95] In this approach, the question of whether an appropriate balance had been struck, in light of the tenant's personal circumstances, between the competing interests at stake in the specific case to be decided was outside the scope of the UK courts' power of judicial review. Although the ECtHR had clarified in *McCann* that its earlier jurisprudence in *Connors* on the necessity of appropriate safeguards in eviction proceedings was confined neither to the situation of Gypsies nor to challenges of statutory law as such,[96] in response, the House of Lords, while allowing for more flexibility as part of determining unreasonableness, was not prepared to green-light a general proportionality test.[97]

Compliance[98] was achieved only when the UK Supreme Court revisited the issue in light of the ECtHR's jurisprudence. While reaffirming that under section 2 of the Human Rights Act, it was not bound to follow the ECtHR's jurisprudence, only to "take [it] into account," the Supreme Court also noted that "[w]here there is a clear and constant line of decisions whose effect is not inconsistent with some fundamental substantive or procedural aspect of our law, and whose reasoning does not appear to overlook or misunderstand some argument or point of principle, we consider that it would be wrong for this Court not to follow that line."[99] And so it did, concluding that "where a court is asked to make an order for possession of a person's home at the suit of a local authority, the court must have the power to assess the proportionality of making the order, and, in making that assessment, to resolve any relevant dispute of fact."[100] The decision was unanimous, which is notable because four of the nine judges on the panel that heard the case had, as members of the House of Lords Appellate Committee, argued against the introduction of an individualized proportionality test as part of domestic judicial review.[101] Apparently, some kind of persuasion had been at work over time to change these justices' opinions.

Remedying Discrimination

Among the several discrimination cases involving the UK that have come before the ECtHR, none illustrates the preference-driven logic of complying with adverse judgments as clearly as the remedial response to the 1985 judgment of *Abdulaziz, Cabales and Balkandali*. Under UK immigration law in force at the material time, it was significantly more difficult for women to obtain entry permissions for their foreign-born husbands or fiancés than it was for men to obtain such permissions for their foreign-born wives or fiancées. Whereas the latter generally received indefinite leave to stay irrespective of the nationality of their husbands, in the case of the former the resident wife had to be a citizen of the United Kingdom and Colonies "who or one of whose parents had been born in the United Kingdom," had to provide evidence of adequate financial resources, and could at first only obtain admission of her husband "for twelve months and fiancés or fiancées for three months, with the possibility, subject to certain safeguards, of applying subsequently to the Home Office for indefinite leave."[102] The UK justified the difference in treatment with the "need to protect the labor market at a time of high unemployment," based on the purported statistical fact that "men were more likely to seek work than women, with the result that male immigrants would have a greater impact than female immigrants on the said market."[103] While the Court conceded that economic considerations might justify discriminatory treatment, it found that the evidence in the present case did not support their relevance and hence found a violation of Article 14 in conjunction with Article 8 ECHR due to unjustified discrimination on the basis of sex.[104]

The Thatcher government responded quickly and removed the impugned discrimination from the amended Immigration Rules within three months after the judgment had been rendered, but not in the manner that the applicants had hoped for: instead of removing the additional hurdles applicable to resident wives and fiancées who wanted to bring their spouses to the UK, it removed the privileged position of male residents and extended to them the same provisions and requirements that applied to female residents. Little else might have been expected from a Conservative Party whose 1979 election manifesto had pledged to "end the concession introduced by the Labour government in 1974 to husbands and male fiancés," to "severely restrict the issue of work permits," and to provide "effective control of immigration."[105] Formally, the solution chosen by the UK was fully compliant because discrimination based on sex no longer existed,[106] and this without "undermining the Government's immigration policy nor further alienating its own supporters."[107] For the applicants and the immigrant community, however, "[t]he apparent triumph . . . in the Court turned out in fact to be a defeat, and a worse defeat than if the case had been found in favor of the UK authorities."[108]

The largest set of related judgments involving the UK comprises sixty-six judgments (thirty-four on the merits, thirty-two recognizing friendly settlements) that concerned gender discrimination between widowed men and women with respect to social security benefits and tax allowances. Under legislation in force since 1992, certain benefits—namely, widow's payment, widowed mother's allowance, and widow's pension[109]—were available, as indicated by their names, only to widows, but not to widowers. The same was true of the so-called widow's bereavement allowance,[110] which provided for an income tax reduction over two years following the husband's death. When the Court found most of these two schemes to violate Article 14 ECHR in conjunction with Article 1 of Protocol No. 1 guaranteeing the protection of property,[111] the legislative sources of the Convention violation had already ceased to exist. In light of earlier, similar cases already pending before the Court[112] that were ended by way of friendly settlements,[113] the relevant benefits and payments had been replaced in 1999 with gender-neutral ones available to both men and women,[114] whereas the widow's bereavement allowance had been abolished without replacement.[115] Still, a string of applications

concerning the situation prior to the reforms—which only applied prospec-
tively from the dates of their entry into force and did not entitle to recover
benefits for earlier periods[116]—had already reached the Court. The UK either
settled pending cases[117] or paid just satisfaction as awarded.[118]

One important takeaway from these cases is that discrimination as a result
of a general policy or law can in principle always be remedied in two ways,
with different consequences for at least one part of the affected set of people:
the desired relative benefit or treatment at issue can either be made available to members of the previously excluded or disadvantaged group on equal
terms (leveling upward), or it can be eliminated (leveling downward). In both
versions, because the groups at issue now receive, or are eligible for, the same
benefits or treatment, discrimination as such is eliminated, but while the formal outcome is the same, the concrete consequences for those affected can be
quite different in tangible and meaningful ways, and one may reasonably surmise that governmental preferences for which course of action to pursue will,
inter alia, depend on the size and political power of the affected groups. If
that is the case, then it is not surprising that the comparatively small number
of people to which the regulations at issue in *Abdulaziz, Cabales and Balkandali* applied drew a short straw, whereas the much larger number of current
(or potential future) widows and widowers with their greater electoral power
stacked the deck in favor of extending the benefit at issue, at least in part,
rather than scrapping it altogether.

Freedom of Expression

Freedom of expression is an integral element of democratic systems of governance and a core political right. Like some other rights, and in contrast—at
least formally—to the First Amendment of the United States Constitution,[119]
the exercise of this freedom has been made subject to a limitation clause that
permits restrictions in the service of a set of permissible objectives, such as
the protection of national security or the reputation or rights of others.[120] In
close to a dozen judgments (two are summarized in the Appendix), the UK's
domestic restrictions on the freedom of expression have been found by the
Court to violate the Convention.[121]

Three of these concerned the freedom of the press and related to injunctions imposed to prevent the publishing of articles on thalidomide children,
the settlement of their pending compensation claims,[122] and excerpts from the

book *Spycatcher*,[123] respectively.[124] In the case of the thalidomide children, the injunction was justified by the common-law doctrine of contempt of court on the argument that the integrity of the courts was said to be damaged by the exertion of pressure on the litigants (the pressure principle) and the public prejudgment of the judicial outcome (the prejudgment principle) as a consequence of the report's publication. In response to the judgment, the UK adopted the Contempt of Court Act 1981. Revision of domestic contempt of court law had already been some time in the making,[125] but was stalled during the transition from the Labour to the Conservative government.[126] Eventually, the 1981 Act took a minimalist compliance[127] approach in that it limited the prejudgment principle to instances where a publication "creates a substantial risk that the course of justice in the proceedings in question will be seriously impeded or prejudiced," and only where said proceedings are active.[128]

The pressure principle, by contrast, was left intact, despite suggestions as to its abolition in the domestic Phillimore report, as was the law on intentional contempt, for which it sufficed to act in the knowledge that one's act would in all probability have an effect on ongoing proceedings.[129] As one commentator noted, "The rather flat conclusion must be that the Act has done little to change the law of contempt and to meet the objections made to it. This is not surprising, since it is the fruit of an appraisal which has assumed that the law should be left fundamentally unchanged. The law of contempt is judge-made and judge-centered law. Its reform has been supervised by judges and lawyers, and its passage through Parliament was largely scrutinized by lawyers. The Act may not be a repressive measure, but let no-one be misled [. . .] into believing it to be a 'liberal measure.'"[130] When the restriction on the freedom of the press came to the Court again in the *Spycatcher* affair,[131] the cases were closed on the basis simply of the payment of just satisfaction.[132] It is questionable whether this fully satisfied the requirements of the judgments, though. As Conor Gearty remarks, "Had the public body involved not been a court, it is surely the case that a direction from the government requiring regard for the Convention in future similar situations would have been the very least that would have been expected."[133]

The execution of two judgments finding an unjustified infringement of the freedom of speech due to disproportionate penalties in defamation suits can, by contrast, be considered satisfactory. Prior to the domestic judgment in *Miloslavsky*,[134] where the violation originated in a jury award against the applicant of £1.5 million in libel damages, the Court of Appeal had no power to decrease such awards, short of ordering a new trial. Under legislation adopted in 1990 and a subsequent amendment of its rules, it now possesses such powers[135] and has used them accordingly on subsequent occasions.[136] However, in the *Steel and Morris* ("McLibel") case, the Court of Appeal's award (£36,000 and £40,000), already reduced from the trial court's award, was still found to be disproportionate by the ECtHR in view of the low incomes of the applicants.[137] This aspect of the judgment was considered complied with in light of the understanding that domestic courts would take into account the ECtHR's reasoning in future proceedings.[138] As with other instances where compliance results from the existence of the presumptive guiding function of ECtHR jurisprudence, or the granting of previously lacking discretionary decision-making powers, it is generally difficult to make conclusive assessments as to the scope and depth of compliance beyond noting that the formal existence of the option results in satisfactory compliance, when what matters for appraisals of compliance as "broad" or "minimalist" is how such optional decision-making powers are being used in practice.

Freedom of Association

Three judgments against the UK concerned violations of the rights of trade and labor unions in violation of Article 11 ECHR. The execution of the first of these can be easily understood as a result of a change in legislative majorities.[139] The issue at stake in *Young, James, and Webster* concerned the question whether dismissal from employment for refusal to join a trade union with which the employer had negotiated a closed shop agreement violated the applicants' right of association in its negative form, that is, the freedom to abstain from association and from joining a union.[140] By introducing the closed shop system in 1974,[141] the then-governing Labour Party explicitly repealed the previous prohibition of closed shops and the right of not belonging to a union instituted by its predecessor Conservative government under Prime Minister Edward Heath, which itself had made good on a 1970 election manifesto promise but soon came to labor under its attempt at rearranging industrial relations in Britain.[142] While the 1974 act provided, under certain conditions, for unfair dismissal proceedings, a revision in 1976 retained only "genuine religious" objections as a permissible ground for dismissal to be considered unfair,[143] a ground that did not cover the applicants' objections.

By the time the Court issued its judgment, the political tables had yet turned once more and the Conservative Party had assumed power again on a platform that had explicitly avowed a reform of the closed shop system.[144] This was done by way of the Employment Act 1980 which did not prohibit closed shop agreements as such but made them conditional on the approval of the affected employees and provided for a greater list of permissible objections. Interestingly, the Conservative government did not strive for a friendly settlement once it had come to power but explicitly wanted a decision by the Court on the closed shop system,[145] presumably as backing for additional restrictions on closed shop agreements already envisaged as part of the Employment Act 1982 and additional subsequent legislation.[146]

In a 2002 judgment,[147] the Court took issue with the permissibility under UK law of using financial incentives to make employees renounce certain union rights. One might expect the Labour Party to have been sympathetic to these applications, all of which commenced in 1996 under the last John Major government, but ending supervision of the judgment's execution nonetheless took almost six years.[148] Labour indeed was sympathetic and adopted the Employment Relations Act 2004, which provided for an employee's right not to have offers such as those at issue in the case made. In addition to making judicial proceedings before employment tribunals available in the case of an infringement, the law further strengthened the rights of union members in other areas as well,[149] on the belief "that the principle underlying the decision of the Court extends beyond the facts in *Wilson* [*et al.*] and is applicable to a number of other comparable circumstances."[150] Not strictly required by the judgment, this can thus be seen as an instance of broad compliance that was made possible through the change of government and its general prolabor preferences.

Why then the delay in closing the case? The issue of contention concerned an interpretive disagreement. Whereas the Council of Europe Secretariat took issue with the fact that trade unions had not been given a remedy of their own, that is, independent of their members,[151] the government argued that the unions' interests were sufficiently protected by the remedy available to the latter.[152] After some back-and-forth, the issue was ultimately left unresolved, and the case was closed on the basis that no new clone cases appeared to have been lodged with the Court.[153] Although the rights of individual union members had been broadened, the execution of this judgment nonetheless leaves the impression of restrictive compliance; after all, one formal beneficiary of the judgment, the unions themselves, remained dependent on their members to bring cases to vindicate the rights under the 2004 Act, and when no member was prepared to do so, the union would be left without a remedy of its own.

Execution of the last judgment in this subset, rendered in 2007, occurred faster but likewise stuck close to the facts of the decided complaint. The case involved the inability of trade unions in the UK to expel members who held membership in political parties that espoused views diametrically opposed to their own (as opposed to concrete political activities undertaken as a member of that party, which since 2004 were recognized as a legitimate expulsion ground).[154] Specifically, the applicant union's attempt to expel one of its members who was also actively affiliated with the far-right British National Party had failed because legislation recognized present or former party membership as "protected conduct" that did not constitute a legitimate reason for expulsion.[155] The ECtHR, however, continued its line of jurisprudence begun with the two earlier judgments and highlighted once more the "freedom" aspect of Article 11 ECHR: "As an employee or worker should be free to join, or not join a trade union without being sanctioned or subject to disincentives [. . .], so should the trade union be equally free to choose its members. Article 11 cannot be interpreted as imposing an obligation on associations or organizations to admit whosoever wishes to join. Where associations are formed by people, who, espousing particular values or ideals, intend to pursue common goals, it would run counter to the very effectiveness of the freedom at stake if they had no control over their membership."[156] Given the specific circumstances of the case, including that the affected union member was not expected to suffer any perceivable hardships as a result of expulsion and that the union had not engaged in any "abusive and unreasonable conduct" against him, the Court found the limits on expulsion outside "any acceptable margin of appreciation."[157]

Against the Court's broadly formulated position, the legislative remedy, adopted one year later and specifically in response to the Court's judgment,[158] may appear narrow in that it was tailored very closely to the factual aspects underlying the ECtHR's judgment. Expulsion from a trade union for membership in a political party was enabled by excluding such membership from "protected conduct" where "membership of that political party is contrary to . . . (a) a rule of the trade union, or, (b) an objective of the trade union."[159] To count as such an "objective," it had to be "reasonably practicable for the objective to be ascertained by a person working in the same trade, industry or profession" (in the case of an exclusion), or by a member of the union (in a case of expulsion).[160] Closely mirroring the ECtHR's own language,[161] the act also provided safeguards to (prospective) union members by requiring that permissible exclusions and expulsions had to be fair and in accordance with union rules and without having the effect of depriving affected individuals of their livelihood or imposing other exceptional hardships.[162] As the related debate in the House of Commons makes clear,[163] the primary concern was to limit the exception to the permissible expulsion of members with extremist political party memberships, while preventing those with Labour, Liberal, or Conservative credentials to be removed because the union leadership disliked their otherwise legitimate political opinion. In any event, the UK's response to this judgment shows that ECtHR judgments are carefully studied and that possible exceptions and limitations hinted at by the Court are duly noted and may, as in this case, directly influence remedial legislation.

Few of the issues raised by the judgments discussed in this chapter, while certainly important to the applicants and to others in similar situations, may be said to be of such a politically fundamental nature that reasonable decision-makers would not see room for compromise and accommodation, at least in the mid to long run. As a consequence, if political importance is indeed only marginal, then the outcome of compliance with them may be said to be not all that surprising because it is for the most part not particularly costly. But what if the judgments impose sovereignty costs in an area comprising a core responsibility of the modern state, the protection of law and order? One might then expect greater political contention and a greater reluctance to comply. Chapter 5 examines whether this is the case.

CHAPTER 5

Compliance with General Measures II: Security, Crime, and Justice

Judgments Concerning National Security

When it comes to the politically sensitive issue of national security, governments can be expected to be particularly keen to safeguard their freedom to act in ways that they consider necessary for the protection of their country's safety. Judicial intrusion into this domain has thus frequently been seen by the other two branches of government at best as a nuisance, at worst as a threat to protecting national security. And courts in many countries have correspondingly chosen to stay away from the potential minefield of adjudicating issues impinging on national security by employing various judicial techniques of abstention, such as the political questions doctrine in the United States.[1] In the United Kingdom, the House of Lords, deciding in a 1984 judgment that banning members of trade unions from employment in certain intelligence agencies for alleged national security reasons was not subject to judicial scrutiny, had argued along similar lines: "National security is the responsibility of the executive government; what action is needed to protect its interest is [. . .] a matter upon which those upon whom the responsibility rests, and not the courts of justice, must have the last word. It is par excellence a non-justiciable question. The judicial process is totally inept to deal with the sort of problems which it involves."[2]

The European Court of Human Rights does not define for respondent states the content of their national security objectives or what measures they should adopt in their pursuit. What it does require, though, is that states observe their human rights commitments under the Convention in the domain of national security as in any other policy area, thus circumscribing their freedom of choice in designing laws and policies to fight terrorism and other threats. With respect to the United Kingdom, the ECtHR had issued a total of twenty-three adverse judgments until 2010 that involved measures aimed at protecting national security, triggered particularly by the conflict in Northern Ireland, but more recently also the threat of Islamist terrorism: thirteen judgments involving physical integrity rights under Articles 2 and 3 ECHR, four judgments on detention arrangements in violation of Article 5 ECHR, and six on fairness issues adjudicated under Article 6 ECHR.

Of the judgments regarding the right to physical integrity, two addressed substantive violations while eleven concerned procedural shortcomings of police investigations. In the *Ireland* interstate case (1978), the Court held that the so-called five techniques (including hooding, sleep deprivation, and subjection to noise) employed by UK security forces in aid of interrogations of terrorist suspects in 1971, while staying below the level of torture, qualified as inhuman and degrading treatment in violation of Article 3 ECHR; so did the pattern of physical assaults at the Palace Barracks detention center, which was indicative of an (at least officially tolerated) administrative practice.[3] The *McCann and Others* judgment (1995) concerned the killing in 1988 of three IRA members suspected of planning a bombing mission in Gibraltar. The Grand Chamber of the Court found, by the smallest margin of ten to nine, that the deadly use of force in the case failed to meet the criterion of having been "no more than absolutely necessary [. . .] in defense of any person from unlawful violence," as required by Article 2 (2) lit. a ECHR. The majority found fault, in particular, with the fact that the security force operatives appeared to have been trained and instructed to shoot to kill and had, inter alia, not stopped the suspects from entering Gibraltar in the first place.[4]

The judgments concerning the procedural aspect of Article 2 ECHR arose as a result of deficient inquiries into the deaths of the applicants' next of kin. In *McKerr* (2001) and five related cases, the ECtHR found that the UK had failed to comply with its obligation to conduct effective investigations into the deaths at issue, all of which had occurred in Northern Ireland between 1982 and 1996 at the hand of the police or the security forces, or which suggested collusion between the security forces and the actual killers.[5] (Full compliance with these judgments has still not been achieved, and they are thus discussed below in the section on judgments still being supervised by the Committee of Ministers). And in *Brecknell* (2007) and four other judgments,[6] the complaints concerned the lack of independence of fresh investigations into several shootings that had occurred in Northern Ireland in 1975 and 1976, after new claims alleging collusion between loyalist paramilitaries and the Royal Ulster Constabulary and Ulster Defence Regiment in the commission of these shootings had been made by a former Northern Ireland police officer in 1999. As noted in the section on just satisfaction, because by the time of the judgments the source of the violation already no longer existed, payment was all that was required for compliance.

Given the delicate role of the Northern Ireland conflict in UK politics, it is not unreasonable to expect a reluctant, lukewarm, or even resistant response by the UK to the execution of these judgments, and this is indeed what can generally be observed. By the time the *Ireland* judgment was handed down in 1978, the issue at stake had already effectively become moot because the UK had abandoned the impugned five techniques in response to primarily domestic opinion shortly after the events in question and had compensated the victims of maltreatment; indeed, it had argued that because of that, the case did not need to go forward in the first place.[7] Furthermore, on February 8, 1977, the UK attorney general had proclaimed before the Court the UK's "unqualified undertaking, that the 'five techniques' will not in any circumstances be reintroduced as an aid to interrogation."[8] Although this was considered sufficient by the Committee of Ministers to close its supervision of the case,[9] some authors have expressed "grave doubts as to whether the action taken by the United Kingdom [. . .] was sufficient to ensure broad compliance with the Court's judgment."[10] Not only did the call by the Irish government for prosecution and punishment of those found to have committed the acts in violation of the Convention remain largely unheeded,[11] but despite the abandonment of the five techniques, "interrogations in depth"[12] continued and allegations of maltreatment at the hands of the police in Northern Ireland had actually increased as recently as 1976 and 1977.[13] As Churchill and Young conclude, "[T]he difficulty in evaluating compliance in this case was that a change in the law was not necessary, since the powers conferred on the security forces by law did not require amendment. What required amendment was official tolerance of, or complicity in, behavior which was already unlawful under the law of Northern Ireland and was in breach of existing disciplinary regulations."[14] The limitation of the government's response to the impugned use of the specific five techniques addressed in the judgment—rather than a broader tackling of the use of coercion, ordered, or tolerated—supports the expectation of minimalist compliance, preserving as it does, at least until further challenge, the government's freedom to use, or at least not officially prohibit, other coercive techniques that officials believe might yield useful information.

As in *Ireland*, the *McCann and Others* (1995) judgment, seen at the time as the Court's "most controversial decision [. . .] yet,"[15] gave rise to considerable political irritation in the UK, especially in the quarters of the Conservative Party. Deputy Prime Minister Michael Heseltine called the judgment "incomprehensible" and noted that the government would "do absolutely nothing at all" in response to it because it would not "be swayed or deterred in any way by this ludicrous decision of the court."[16] Some Tories, including Prime Minister John Major, went so far as to question Britain's continuing membership in the Convention system.[17] While not following up, the Major government, in parallel with attacks on the ECJ,[18] launched an attempt to restrict the Court's powers and sent a Foreign Office document to that effect to all member states of the Council of Europe,[19] arguing for "more consistent recognition of the need to respect different circumstances, traditions and laws and the ways in which standards are implemented in different countries" in order "to ensure that judgments are not made against national interests."[20]

Despite this diplomatic saber rattling, the UK did pay the just satisfaction award of almost £34,000 (for costs and expenses) within the three-month time limit set by the Court, and the Committee of Ministers closed the case on that basis.[21] But was payment really sufficient to constitute compliance in light of the judgment? Individual measures did not appear indicated, but Council of Europe documents note that the applicants' representatives had requested unspecified general measures. On the one hand, the "lack of appropriate care in the control and organization of the arrest operation"[22] that the Court adduced in justification of its finding of a violation of Article 2 ECHR could be interpreted as requiring at least a formal review of their planning and execution. On the other hand, one could argue that the violations were so closely connected to the specific facts of the case that these shortcomings could not be generalized. This is the position that the Committee of Ministers eventually took, with officials at the Council of Europe apparently having been swayed not to ask for general measures due to the "considerable political problems" that the case had already generated.[23] While the Committee's stance has been judged unsatisfactory by some observers,[24] both takes on the *McCann* judgment are possible, and it is not surprising that the UK government opted for, and the other government representatives in the Committee of Ministers accepted, the narrower interpretation.

The violation found in *Fox, Campbell and Hartley* had already been addressed shortly after the applicants' complaints had been lodged in 1986. Under new legislation adopted in 1987, the sufficiency of mere suspicion to make an arrest—in place in Northern Ireland since 1922[25]—was replaced with an objective reasonable suspicion test that would be subject to judicial review.[26] This change, although coinciding with the applications in *Fox, Campbell and Hartley*, was primarily an enactment of amendments proposed by a domestic review of previous legislation,[27] and it is the domestic report, not the Convention, that is repeatedly referenced in the bill's parliamentary debates.[28] The amendment brought domestic law into line with the language of Article 5 (1) lit. c ECHR, and in the subsequent judgment of *O'Hara* (2001), in which the application, inter alia, of a reasonable suspicion arrest standard in a related piece of legislation was challenged, the ECtHR essentially accepted the UK's application of the standard in domestic practice as being in conformity with the Convention.[29]

In three of the six judgments relating to fairness issues in proceedings related to national security—*John Murray*; *Averill*; and *Magee*[30]—the Court found that the denial of access to counsel during the first twenty-four to forty-eight hours of detention, combined with provisions in national law according to which it was permissible to draw adverse inferences from a detainee's silence during his detention, violated the applicants' right to a fair trial under Article 6 (1) in conjunction with Article 6 (3) lit. c ECHR. The legislative change required by these judgments was less than forthcoming, giving rise to two interim resolutions—four and six years after the first judgment in this set—in which the Committee of Ministers regretted the delay and "strongly encourage[d]" the UK to adopt all necessary measures to give effect to the judgments.[31] At the time of the first judgment in 1996, the Major government hesitated to change a relevant legislative bill currently before Parliament to bring it in line with the judgment,[32] so that remedial legislation was only adopted in 1999 after Labour had come to power. It still took until April 1, 2003, in the case of England and Wales, and until March 1, 2007, in Northern Ireland, before the relevant sections entered into force.[33]

It is unclear whether these delays were the result of inadvertence or were intentional. For England and Wales, implementation was made conditional on the entry into force of a new code of practice covering the detention, treatment, and questioning of persons by police officers, a code that was to include a provision that requires officers to inform detainees of their right of access to legal advice at any time during detention. For Northern Ireland, additional reviews of criminal evidence legislation and practice codes were said to have caused the delay. In any event, the enacted legislative solutions did comply with the Court's judgments by disallowing adverse inferences from an accused's silence prior to having had access to a lawyer, and they prompted the Committee to end its supervision.[34]

Still, the argument can be made that the UK did no more than it strictly had to, even though broader alternatives presented itself, most notably granting detainees access to a solicitor from the very beginning of their detention, instead of the pattern of frequently delayed access,[35] which would have precluded the problem from arising in the first place. Reading the Court's conclusion in *John Murray* in isolation—"there has therefore been a breach [. . .] of the Convention as regards the applicant's denial of access to a lawyer during the first 48 hours of his police detention"[36]—appears to point in the same direction, but the Court had also accepted the justifiability of restrictions in certain circumstances[37] and refused to affirm an unqualified right of access to a solicitor during the early stages of detention in subsequent judgments.[38] The UK's remedial response did thus have the Court's backing, but the fact remains that the execution of these judgments resulted in a situation that continued to deprive detainees of the fullest protection possible in favor of maintaining certain advantages for the law enforcement authorities (express statements made by detainees during interrogation, for example, continued to be admissible even if made without a solicitor present).[39] It was only in 2010 that the new UK Supreme Court followed the position of a unanimous ECtHR Grand Chamber that held that a fair trial requires that "as a rule, access to a lawyer should be provided as from the first interrogation of a suspect by the police."[40]

Another set of three judgments concerns the relationship of national security and labor regulation. Under Northern Ireland fair employment legislation in force since 1976, persons alleging unjustified discrimination could lodge a complaint with the Fair Employment Agency and, since 1989, the Fair Employment Tribunal, *except* when the refusal of employment or a contract was done for purposes of securing national security or public order, with the certificate by the secretary of state being "conclusive evidence that it was done for that purpose."[41] In its judgments, the ECtHR found that the categorical nature of these certificates unduly deprived the applicants of access to a court or tribunal to hear their case.[42] The UK responded swiftly and provided for an appeals procedure against national security certificates in the Northern Ireland Act 1998.[43] The appeals, however, are not heard by ordinary courts, but instead by a tribunal especially created for this purpose, presumably to safeguard security-sensitive information from being disclosed to the public.[44] What may be most significant in this context, though, is the fact that appointments to serve on the tribunal were entrusted, with little statutory guidance, to the Lord Chancellor of Great Britain,[45] responsible for the administration of the judiciary and a member of the cabinet. This assured that control over the composition, and thereby over what might be called the "attitudinal disposition" of the tribunal, remained in the hands of the government. While appeals to the Court of Appeal (N.I.) were made possible, leave to do so had to be granted first.[46]

The remaining security-related judgments concern violations of the detention regime under Article 5 ECHR. In *Brogan and Others* (1988) and *O'Hara* (2001), the Court found that the detention period of up to a total of seven days without any judicial review permitted under UK law was in breach of a detainee's right under Article 5 (3) ECHR to be brought "promptly" before a judge or to be released instead.[47] In *Fox, Campbell and Hartley* (1990), the Court took issue with the fact that police constables had been authorized to arrest persons without a warrant on the basis of subjective suspicions that they could be terrorists. The ECtHR found this to be a breach of Article 5 (1) lit. c ECHR, which requires reasonable suspicion, a phrase the Court interpreted as demanding an objective, rather than a merely subjective, test.[48] Finally, in the judgment of *A. and Others* (2009), the Court found fault with the United Kingdom's discriminatory detention regime under Part 4 of the Anti-Terrorism Crime and Security Act 2001, which could result in the potentially indefinite detention of individuals certified as "suspected international terrorists" (but not national ones).[49] In addition, several applicants had been unable to effectively challenge their detentions because the charges against them were based on information in "closed" evidence that was not accessible to them or their counsel.

The government's response to the *Brogan* judgment revealed the straightforward intention to evade the implications of the Court's judgment through reliance on the Convention's derogation clause, Article 15 ECHR, which provides that "[i]n time of war or other public emergency threatening the life of the nation any High Contracting Party may take measures derogating from its obligations under this Convention to the extent strictly required by the exigencies of the situation." The United Kingdom submitted its derogation on December 23, 1988, less than a month after the *Brogan* judgment had been issued (November 29, 1988), and justified the human rights restrictions at issue in *Brogan* with the emergency situation in Northern Ireland, with the effect that the applicability of the Article 5 ECHR guarantees was being suspended and the relevant provisions of domestic law left in force.[50] Notably, the Court had not ruled that long precharge detention periods were unlawful as such, but only that the long delay of bringing detainees before a judicial officer for review of the legality of their detention had been at odds with the guarantee of Article 5 (3) ECHR. British officials had also been aware at the time that with such judicial review, other countries were able to detain suspects for much longer periods of time without running afoul of the Convention,[51] yet no such change came about at the time; instead, the derogation was renewed on March 23, 1989, with respect to follow-up legislation that maintained the detention regime intact.[52] The domestic situation was changed only with the adoption of the Terrorism Act 2000, after Labour had come to power, which made an extension of the initial forty-eight-hour precharge detention limit subject to control by a judicial authority. The extension limit of up to an additional five days as such, however, was kept.[53] The derogation with respect to Article 5 (3) ECHR was withdrawn in 2001.[54] In circumstances in which Article 15 ECHR can be legitimately invoked, minimizing state obligations under the ECHR and ECtHR judgments must then be considered formally compliant with the rules of the Convention.

One judgment specifically originating with the more recent threat of Islamist terrorism is *A. and Others* (2009). Shortly after the September 11, 2001, terrorist attacks, the UK government enacted the Anti-Terrorism, Crime and Security Act 2001, whose Part 4 included provisions that allowed the potentially indefinite detention of foreign nationals certified by the secretary of state as suspected international terrorists due to the inability to deport them. While detainees could challenge their designation before the Special Immigration Appeals Commission, they were precluded from accessing certain "closed" materials against them that were kept secret due to the sensitivity of their contents. Expecting that this detention regime would probably be incompatible with Article 5, the UK lodged a formal derogation under Article 15 of the Convention on December 18, 2001. In its judgment, the Court found that while the reason for the derogation, a threat to the life of the nation, could be justified, the concrete measures disproportionately and unjustifiably discriminated between nationals and foreigners and could thus not be said to be "strictly required by the exigencies of the situation," as required by Article 15 (1) ECHR, resulting in a violation of Article 5 (1) ECHR. The inability of several applicants to challenge their detentions due to the inaccessibility of critical, but closed materials furthermore led to violations of Article 5 (4) ECHR, and the inability to claim compensation—because, domestically, they were considered lawfully detained—to a violation of Article 5 (5) ECHR.

This judgment represents one of those instances in which domestic change resulting in compliance preceded the ECtHR's decision. On December 16, 2004, that is, more than a month before the applications in the *A. and Others* case had been lodged with the ECtHR on January 22, 2005, the Appellate Committee of the House of Lords had issued one of its rare declarations of incompatibility under the HRA with respect to the discriminatory detention regime. In response, as of March 2005, the government withdrew the UK's derogation and replaced the impugned detentions with a "control order" regime under the Prevention of Terrorism Act 2005 that could be applied to nationals and nonnationals alike. Through such control orders, the secretary of state could impose various obligations on the person to whom they were addressed, such as restrictions on communication or electronic tagging,[55] but also house arrest or detention, but when measures such as the latter would derogate from Convention rights, they would have to be imposed by a court upon an application by the secretary of state,[56] and a new derogation notice would have to be submitted to the Council of Europe. The control order regime, which applied to a total of fifty-two persons,[57] was later replaced by the system provided for in the Terrorism Prevention and Investigation Measures (TPIM) Act 2011, which enables the secretary of state, subject to judicial scrutiny, to impose a more circumscribed but still substantial set of restrictive measures[58] through the issuing of so-called TPIM notices. Finally, while legal challenges to control orders and notices still face(d) the problem of closed materials, the House of Lords Appellate Committee had decided in June 2009 that domestic courts must take into account the ECtHR's position in *A. and Others* with a view to enabling the accused to obtain sufficient information to mount an effective defense;[59] It is now up to the lower courts to decide requests of access to such materials on a case-by-case basis.

Once again, the UK's response is narrowly compliant with the issues decided in *A. and Others*. On the one hand, the discrimination between nationals and nonnationals was removed, and judicial challenges to the use of closed materials, when necessary for an effective defense, were made possible. On the other hand, the possibility of indefinite detention was not formally ruled out,[60] and even though denial of access to closed materials could be challenged in court, this did neither ipso facto mean that such access would in fact be granted nor that it would be granted on a scale necessary for the most effective defense possible. If "[t]he first duty of government is to safeguard [. . .] national security,"[61] as the 2011 Green Paper on Justice and Security emphasized, then we should expect governments to make only those changes in response to an adverse judgment that are absolutely necessary and to reduce their arsenal of counterterrorism instruments and tactics as little as possible.

The one Convention violation related to the UK's antiterrorism regime that the probably largest number of people has come into touch with concerns the stop-and-search authorizations under section 44 of the Terrorism Act 2000. Under this and the following sections, police constables were authorized to conduct searches of vehicles, their passengers, and of pedestrians "for the purpose of searching for articles of a kind which could be used in connection with terrorism" and, importantly, irrespective of whether "the constable has grounds for suspecting the presence of articles of that kind." (By contrast, under section 43, which authorized police officers to stop and search persons suspected to be terrorists, the decision to conduct a search required reasonable suspicion.) For these search powers to be available in a defined geographical area, a senior police officer first had to issue an authorization, valid for (renewable) periods of up to twenty-eight days and subject to confirmation by the secretary of state, if he or she "consider[ed] it expedient for the prevention of acts of terrorism." Noncompliance with police requests to submit to such searches was made a criminal offense.[62]

Yet what might have been conceived as an exceptional broadening of police search powers ended up being an enduring measure in some parts of the UK. In the Metropolitan Police District (Greater London), for example, authorizations had been successively issued and confirmed under a rolling program, with the section 44 stop-and-search regime continuously in place since entry into force of the Terrorism Act 2000 in February 2001. Country-wide, searches under section 44 increased significantly over the years, from just above 10,000 in 2001–2002, to over 210,000 in the peak year 2008–2009, with a total of over 640,000 people and vehicles having been stopped and searched between 2001 and 2010. Most of the searches occurred in the metropolitan London area (in 2009–2010, for example, the share was 96 percent). Across the full ten years, a mere 0.9 percent of the searches resulted in arrests, mostly, however, not for terrorism, but for other offenses (5,265 out of 5,552 arrests, or 94.8 percent).[63] Not a single terrorism-related conviction originated with a section 44 search in Great Britain.[64] Because of its doubtful necessity, its potential for abuse, and its discriminatory use against ethnic minorities,[65] the section 44 regime had been repeatedly criticized domestically well before the ECtHR declared it incompatible with the respect for private life under Article 8 ECHR. Specifically, the Court found section 44 to be "not in accordance with the law" because the discretionary powers it conferred were "neither sufficiently circumscribed nor subject to adequate legal safeguards against abuse."[66]

A few days after the Court's judgment became final (on June 28, 2010, when the Grand Chamber rejected a rehearing request), the new coalition government of Conservatives and Liberal Democrats that had assumed power after the general elections of May 6, 2010, suspended the broad use of section 44 powers. Following a review of section 44 as part of an examination that also included other antiterrorism measures—in its program for government, the coalition had pledged to "introduce safeguards against the misuse of anti-terrorism legislation"[67]—the government repealed and replaced the section 44 regime with more restricted search powers, first through an urgent remedial order under the HRA (effective March 18, 2011) and then via formal legislation in 2012.[68] Under the new regulations, searches of vehicles and pedestrians could still be conducted irrespective of any reasonable suspicion on the part of the police constable who does the search, but the objective is now limited to searching for evidence that the person is a terrorist or the vehicle is used for a terroristic purpose (i.e., no longer "articles" that could be used for terrorism). More important, these search powers only become available within a specified geographical area and subject to new maximum (but renewable) periods of fourteen days when the senior police officer authorizing them "reasonably suspects that an act of terrorism will take place" and "reasonably considers that [...] the authorization is necessary to prevent such an act."[69] In other words, the standard of expediency has been replaced with reasonable suspicion, which requires some substantiation as to the existence of a threat. The Code of Practice for the Exercise of Stop and Search Powers seeks to provide further safeguards regarding the exercise of the powers under the new regime.

With the new regime demanding reasonable suspicion of the existence of the threat of a terrorist act, it is more circumscribed than the one it replaces and can be considered to comply with the ECtHR's judgment.[70] At the same time, it also intentionally retains the option to authorize "no suspicion" searches when deemed necessary. The government itself had noted that the "[r]epeal [of section 44 *et seq.* of the Terrorism Act 2000] would be the simplest way of implementing the ECtHR judgment"[71] but opted to replace it with another, more restricted regime that was seen as useful and "operationally justified in exceptional circumstances."[72]

In all of the above cases, the UK has taken measures to respond to the violations found in the ECtHR's judgments which has, on the whole, resulted in an improvement of the human rights situation of those in the crosshairs of the state's security apparatus, and this despite the fact that neither terrorists themselves nor the occasional "civil libertarian activists"[73] that may raise human rights concerns from time to time in their stead tend to have much political leverage to bring about change in their favor. At the same time, habitual compliance cannot tell us about the specific choice of measures to remedy a violation. Such choice is not automatic but is based on considerations of conflicting objectives that may be nowhere as starkly put into relief as in national security cases, protecting people while also safeguarding the basic rights of potential or real terrorists. It is one of the core functions of governments to provide for national and human security in its various dimensions, and so it is not surprising that governments will seek to keep the arsenal of instruments considered effective for that purpose as broad, and restrictions as small, as possible. The fact that the design of minimalist remedial measures can be justified by reference to the stipulated needs of the security forces or the exigencies of a situation does not negate that fact that it is still a choice between alternatives.

Reforming the Life Imprisonment Regime

Over the time period relevant for the present study, the UK's life imprisonment regime came to employ several different classifications, each with its own review and release specifics:

- *Mandatory life sentences* are imposed on those convicted for murder.[74]
- *Discretionary life sentences* have been available since at least 1861 for a series of serious crimes when the judge finds that an indeterminate sentence is appropriate in light of the continuing danger of the offender.[75]
- *Detention at Her Majesty's Pleasure* (HMP) is a status reserved for juveniles under the age of eighteen convicted for murder.[76]
- *Custody for life* applies to young people between the ages of eighteen and twenty-one when convicted of any crime for which the law fixes the penalty of life imprisonment.[77]
- *Automatic life sentences* are, since 1997, imposed on all offenders when convicted of a serious violent or sex crime for a second time.[78]
- Finally, the status of *technical lifers* is given to those who had been sentenced to life imprisonment but were subsequently transferred to a mental hospital without a court having made such order on sentencing.[79]

An important role in review and release proceedings used to be assigned to the secretary of state for the Home Department, who under the various schemes had final authority to decide on the release of life prisoners, with the Parole Board having only an advisory function and no binding authority to order release.

The UK's response to the judgments involving the life-imprisonment regime reveals an incrementalist version of minimalism in that each judgment was read narrowly and only followed with regard to the specific facts of the case, ultimately requiring decisions on each separate subregime for it to change throughout. The most obvious strategy of avoidance was revealed in the first relevant case decided by the Court in 1987, in which it found that neither the procedure before the Parole Board nor judicial review afforded the applicant a sufficient review of the legality of his continued detention in conformity with Article 5 (4) ECHR. The Parole Board could not order a detainee's release but only make recommendations to the home secretary, who was free to disregard them, while judicial review of Parole Board proceedings was insufficient as it was limited to charges of illegality, irrationality, and procedural impropriety and could not result in a finding as to the lawfulness of the detention as such.[80] The UK's response to the judgment was limited to pointing out that in light of domestic jurisprudence, it was unlikely that life sentences for such minor offenses such as the applicant's would be imposed again in the future.[81] That, however, was not the issue before the ECtHR. As Churchill and Young note, "The British Government's attempt to limit the implications of *Weeks* by treating it as a special case failed to take account of the reasoning of the Court,"[82] so that "despite the apparently broad implications [. . .] the government failed to bring domestic law into line with the Convention."[83] The limited response is indicative of the intention to avoid the substantive consequences of the ECtHR's judgment and also highlights the failure of the Committee of Ministers' supervision in this case, letting the response pass as satisfactory without pressing for any legal reform.

It took the further judgment in the case of *Thynne, Wilson and Gunnel*,[84] which reaffirmed the *Weeks* reasoning, for the UK to eventually adopt a legislative remedy. New legislation in 1991 made the Parole Board's release decision in the case of discretionary lifers binding on the secretary of state.[85] Again, the UK government, under Prime Minister John Major, opted for restrictive execution. Although in its own pleadings before the Court, the administration had argued that it was impractical to operate two different release regimes for mandatory and discretionary lifers and despite repeated proposals and suggestions in the House of Commons as well as the House of Lords to expand the new review regime to other life imprisonment categories, the administration stuck to its narrow reform design;[86] in other words, for all other lifers, the Parole Board's recommendation remained advisory and the secretary of state continued to be free to depart from them.[87]

The piecemeal approach would be replicated with regard to the review and release procedures in other life-imprisonment categories. Following two 1996 judgments relating to detention of juveniles at Her Majesty's Pleasure,[88] such detainees were also put under the jurisdiction of the Parole Board's Discretionary Lifer Panel.[89] Notably, it remained the prerogative of the home secretary to set the "tariff" for HMP detainees, that is, the minimum time to be served before a prisoner would be eligible for release.[90] This allocation of authority—the home secretary, a member of the executive, here exercised an essentially judicial function—was subsequently found to violate the fairness guarantee of Article 6 (1) ECHR by the Court in 1999,[91] resulting in the transfer of the tariff-setting power to the courts.[92] And in 2002, reversing itself,[93] the Court further held that the practical reality of mandatory life sentences had changed to an extent that "it may now be regarded as established in domestic law that there is no distinction between mandatory life prisoners, discretionary life prisoners and juvenile murderers as regards the nature of tariff-fixing,"[94] so that mandatory lifers also had the right to have their tariffs set by a court and to regular reviews of the legality of their continued detention after their tariffs had expired.[95] As a result, in 2003, the UK provided for the judicial setting of tariffs in these cases and extended the Parole Board's review and release powers to mandatory lifers.[96]

Finally, and apart from three related judgments involving excessive delays in the review of detention after expiry of the tariff,[97] the ECtHR ruled that technical lifers, that is, life prisoners who had been transferred to a psychiatric hospital by the secretary of state without a court order, also had a right to review by a court with the power to order release.[98] Although the UK had abolished the technical lifer status in April 2005, with the release of relevant detainees henceforth to be determined by the Parole Board (while at the same time eliminating some of the benefits of the technical lifer status),[99] those detainees that had been transferred to a mental institution but had not been given technical lifer status yet (transferred lifers) appeared excluded from the review benefits this change had brought. Only in late 2008 did the UK provide evidence that transferred lifers were now also subject to the review jurisdiction of the Parole Board, which could order their release, if appropriate.[100]

The minimalist-incremental approach pursued by successive United Kingdom governments in the extension of the release review scheme for life prisoners is not all that surprising when one considers public opinion in this area, which has generally been in favor of a strict and stringent penal system. The regularly conducted British Crime Survey—since April 2012 known as the Crime Survey for England and Wales—had repeatedly revealed a prevailing opinion by large majorities of respondents (in the vicinity of three-quarters) that sentences handed down by UK criminal courts were considered too lenient[101] (even the death penalty, although abolished in Great Britain for most crimes in 1965 and for all remaining crimes and the entire United Kingdom by 1998, still enjoys widespread, albeit downward-trending, popular support).[102] Against this background, and in the absence of any strong constituency to press for the rights of those sentenced to imprisonment for life, it is politically understandable that neither Tories nor Labour, notwithstanding any contrary normative convictions on the part of individual decision-makers, went out of their way to extend the review scheme initially granted for discretionary life prisoners to other life imprisonment areas on their own initiative.[103]

Legal Aid and Representation

Several cases against the United Kingdom concerned violations of the right to legal aid and representation protected by Article 6 (3) lit. c ECHR. Because the expansion of legal aid increases public spending, we might expect that compliance in this area proceeds narrowly, in order to protect public coffers. While again proceeding incrementally, the record of compliance appears, on the whole, to be satisfactory. Litigation before the ECtHR has resulted in the extension of legal aid and/or representation to various fora in which defendants are liable to be subject to penalties tantamount to criminal punishments,[104] including disciplinary proceedings in prison[105] and certain proceedings before the magistrates' courts.[106] The pledge contained in a friendly settlement to provide for legal aid with respect to certain civic actions in Guernsey was also honored.[107]

But in this area, too, we find clear instances of minimalist and restrictive execution beyond incrementalism. In the context of the deficiencies of the Scottish legal aid scheme for criminal appeals addressed by the Court in the 1990 *Granger* judgment,[108] the government first sought to comply by way of a practice note by the Scottish Lord Justice General advising the appeals courts that they should adjourn proceedings ex officio and make representations to the Legal Aid Board to review its decision denying assistance if they found that the issues at stake were such that legal assistance was in the "interests of justice."[109] Assessments of the latter, however, are naturally subject to judicial discretion and varying opinions, and it was not long before the ECtHR found issue with the manner in which the guidance note had fared in practice.[110]

Compliance with these judgments was ultimately Janus-faced. On the one hand, while remedial legislation provided for legal aid in all criminal appeals proceedings on the sole basis, in most circumstances, of financial eligibility, on the other hand, it at simultaneously abolished the previously automatic right to appeal and made it subject to the requirement of having to seek leave to appeal first.[111] The UK had thus followed up on insinuations to this effect made during pleadings[112] and thereby effectively counteracted the broad granting of legal aid. Once again, this response was formally compliant, given that the Court has not interpreted Article 6 ECHR as requiring a general right of appeal,[113] but the replacement of one barrier with another of a different sort did little to pay tribute to the spirit of the Court's judgment, which arguably aimed at increasing the chances for effective appeals proceedings when these where already provided for. Instead, compliance resulted "paradoxically in the cutting back of appeal rights in order to ensure Scots law meets European human rights standards."[114]

Under Article 6 (3) lit. c ECHR, the right to counsel is explicitly protected only in criminal cases; exceptionally, however, the Court has affirmed the right to legal assistance in civil cases in violation of the guarantees of the umbrella provision of Article 6 (1) ECHR when absence, or denial, of legal aid and assistance would result either in inherently unfair proceedings or thwart the applicant's effective access to a court.[115] This principle was prominently applied in the *Steel and Morris* case. The applicants had been the defendants in a defamation suit brought against them by the McDonald's Corporation, which resulted, with a total of 313 courtroom days, in the longest trial ever, civil or criminal, in English history.[116] The ECtHR held that the denial of legal assistance under UK law in what became known as the "McLibel" suit fundamentally breached the principle of the equality of arms and thus resulted in an unfair trial.[117] In executing the judgment, which was admittedly driven by the unusual circumstances of the case, the UK again chose to prevent future violations through "guided" domestic discretion. While legislation adopted in 1999 (England and Wales), 2003 (Northern Ireland), and 2007 (Scotland) continues to exclude defamation cases from regular legal aid, it allows for discretionary "exceptional funding" in special circumstances; formal guidance documents based on the Court's reasoning delineate what these are and when legal aid should be granted.[118]

Prisoner Correspondence

Another issue area that is characterized by a minimalist-incrementalist approach to compliance concerns the question of the extent to which the correspondence of prisoners should be subject to control and censure. In the case resulting in the very first judgment against the UK in 1975, two letters by the applicant to his member of Parliament and to a chief constable through which he sought to exculpate himself from charges of having been involved in a prison brawl had been stopped by the prison governor. The home secretary, who had discretion with regard to allowing or disallowing prisoner correspondence, subsequently denied leave to contact a solicitor regarding the same matter, presumably to prevent the applicant from initiating proceedings for libel against one of the prison guards, but with the government "advanc[ing] the prevention of disorder or crime and, up to a certain point, the interests of public safety and the protection of the rights and freedoms of others" as justification.[119] The Court found this intervention to be unnecessary in a democratic society and in violation of Article 8 (denial of right to correspondence) and Article 6 (1) ECHR (no access to a court).[120]

To the extent that one accepts the authorities' attempt to prevent litigation as the underlying reason for the denial of leave, the remedial response can be considered rationally minimalist. Whereas prison governors were obliged to provide inmates with necessary facilities to contact a solicitor, if so requested, under revised prison regulations announced soon after the judgment in August 1975,[121] in cases concerning prison matters itself this applied only after they had first ventilated their concerns "through the normal internal channels (e.g. by petition to the home secretary or by application to the Board of Visitors or to a visiting officer of the secretary of state)."[122] This remedy preserved the prison authorities' filter function and, in the view of some observers, continued to impose "conditions impeding or hindering access to the courts, particularly as exhaustion of the prison complaints procedure could take up to a year."[123] In any event, the Home Office explicitly expected that the "prior ventilation rule" would assure that the number of litigations against staff would not increase.[124]

The prior ventilation rule quickly came before the ECtHR as well, and the UK, in reaching a friendly settlement with the applicant, undertook to abolish it and to replace it with a simultaneous ventilation rule,[125] shortly before the Court found it incompatible with both Articles 8 and 6 (1) ECHR in two subsequent cases.[126] Together with several other liberalizations concerning content and addressees of correspondence, these changes were deemed sufficient to close a group of cases relating to pre-reform incidents.[127] When the Committee of Ministers subsequently found that the simultaneous ventilation rule also violated the Convention,[128] it had already been abandoned in response to a High Court judgment,[129] but only with respect to legal communications (i.e., with lawyers, the Convention bodies, or, in the case of foreigners, consulates); it remained in place with regard to all other types of correspondence and was only abolished for good in 1989.

Two further adverse judgments in this issue area followed.[130] The first occurred in 1992 when the Court found that the practice in Scotland of opening all incoming letters from the European Commission of Human Rights as well as letters to and from the applicant's solicitor to check whether they contained any prohibited material was disproportionate.[131] The UK responded by narrowing the applicable rules so that correspondence was to be opened only when there existed "reasonable cause" to suspect an illicit enclosure, only in the prisoner's presence, and without reading the letter (the prison governor, however, retained discretion to decide that correspondence with a legal adviser should be read in exceptional, specifically listed cases).[132] Finally, a 2009 judgment found that monitoring the correspondence of a prisoner suffering from a life-threatening condition with a medical specialist whose credentials were not in doubt was disproportionate.[133] The United Kingdom complied by extending protection of such correspondence across all of its jurisdictions,[134] but it notably tailored that protection very narrowly and nearly verbatim to the circumstances that gave rise to the case decided by the ECtHR, that is, the existence of a life-threatening condition or illness.[135]

The UK responses to these cases reflect the "reluctant and piecemeal approach to reform"[136] in this area, an approach that can be interpreted as seeking to retain on the part of the prison authorities as much control as possible over prisoner correspondence and that required successive instances of litigation to strengthen the right to privacy within the "closed society"[137] of the UK prisons.

Police Immunity for Negligence

An interesting case in which the issue of compliance was "resolved" by a change in the ECtHR's jurisprudence is that of *Osman* (1998). The case arose out of the 1988 killing of Ali and the wounding of Ahmet Osman by one of the latter's former schoolteachers who had formed an attachment to the boy. Osman's relatives subsequently brought tort proceedings against the Metropolitan Police, alleging negligence in exercising their duty of care because they had been aware of his eventual killer's disturbing behavior since 1987 but failed to arrest, interview, or take other measures to prevent wrongdoing on the latter's part. The case, however, was struck out by the Court of Appeal[138] for lack of reasonable cause of action on the basis of a House of Lords precedent that granted, on public policy grounds, immunity to the police in tort proceedings relating to actions in pursuit of the investigation and suppression of crime.[139] The ECtHR, however, found that the apparently automatic granting of immunity to the police by the Court of Appeal violated the applicants' right to access to a court and that "they were entitled to have the police account for their actions and omissions in adversarial proceedings."[140]

Osman turned out to be a highly controversial decision, giving rise to "a whole industry of comment and meta-comment"[141] and a "barrage of academic and judicial criticism"[142] in the UK that targeted Strasbourg's apparent misunderstanding of the UK law on negligence and its interference with "English concepts of 'public interest.'"[143] The ECtHR's judgment seemed to suggest that the claimants in *Osman* deserved a judgment on the merits to determine whether the police's duty of care had been breached, but under UK common law, the issue in the striking-out proceeding was precisely to first determine whether such a duty of care indeed existed (or should be created).[144] The ECtHR thus appeared to distill from an Article 6 ECHR claim regarding access to a court a substantive tort right when no such right existed under domestic law—an apparent usurpation of the role of domestic lawmaker and in contrast to the Court's own previous case-law.[145]

When the UK government promised a more circumspect application of the relevant domestic precedent in the future and appealed, by way of a circular, to police chief officers that they "exercise considerable caution before applying for a strike-out on [grounds of public policy immunity],"[146] this intervention by the executive in the business of the independent judiciary caused a stir among the latter.[147] Still, initially, the UK courts, including the House of Lords, appeared to respond to *Osman* with "a wholesale retreat from public policy immunity,"[148] or at least with a strict consideration of the domestic test used to determine the existence of negligence claims,[149] but the exceptions allowing for tort claims remained few and far between, with "the most recent pronouncements by the House of Lords demonstrate[ing] a return to the broad exclusionary rule enunciated in *Hill* [the precedent]."[150] Indeed, it was the ECtHR that retreated in 2001, when it upheld the duty-of-care test as Convention-compliant in a case involving the alleged negligence of public care authorities.[151] Noting that "its reasoning in *Osman* was based on an understanding of the law of negligence [. . .] which has to be reviewed in the light of the clarifications subsequently made by the domestic courts and notably the House of Lords,"[152] the Court now found that UK negligence law did not provide blanket immunity, but that the relevant test involved the "careful[ ] balancing [of] the policy reasons for and against the imposition of liability" and that the ECtHR could not and should not impose its own view in the matter.[153]

Covert Surveillance

Covert surveillance is a practice widely used by law enforcement agencies to gain an informational advantage on suspected lawbreakers which, by its very nature, interferes with the target's privacy. The United Kingdom has in this respect for a long time stood apart from other Council of Europe member states by refusing to regulate covert surveillance practices through formal legislation,[154] leaving it to the discretion of the secretary of state to determine the necessity of its use as well as the issuing of any administrative guidelines. Demands for legislative reform had been repeatedly voiced in the 1970s and early 1980s,[155] without, however, yielding any results. The Thatcher government began to change its opposition to legislation in this area only under the pressure of two developments.[156] First, the planned privatization of the state-owned telecommunications sector, part of the Conservatives' 1983 election manifesto, would henceforth put the actual implementation of such operations into the hands of a private enterprise, giving the passage of legal regulations a new urgency. Second, notwithstanding strong difficulties in bringing covert surveillance cases before domestic courts,[157] one such case had made its way to the ECtHR, which was expected, in light of earlier jurisprudence in the *Klass* case,[158] to issue a judgment against the United Kingdom. And so it did. In the 1984 *Malone* judgment, the Court found that the absence of statutory rules on the scope and manner of exercise of the secretary of state's discretion in intercepting communications and the metering of phone conversations could not be considered to be "in accordance with the law" as required by the limitation clause of Article 8 (2) ECHR.[159]

The government's response—the Interception of Communications Act 1985¯is an archetypal example of minimalist compliance.[160] The act addressed the absence of a legislative foundation for covert surveillance simply by clothing the previously existing administrative practice in the fabric of formal legislation[161] while disregarding the substantive issues addressed by the Court in the *Klass* judgment.[162] Moreover, the Act covers only phone tapping—the technology involved in *Malone*—and, somewhat less explicitly, phone metering but leaves out the regulation of all other forms of covert surveillance techniques, a notable omission given the rapid development, already in the 1980s, of other aural and video surveillance technologies. Not surprisingly, the act was criticized in parliamentary debates as "setting out to regulate canal traffic in the age of the high speed train and the motorway."[163] Furthermore, although establishing a tribunal to hear complaints about illegitimate phone tapping, there is no requirement to inform targets that they have been subject to such surveillance, making the tribunal's existence less significant.[164] Finally, the permissible objectives for which phone tapping could be legitimately undertaken had remained intentionally broad, comprising national security, "preventing or detecting serious crime," and "safeguarding the economic well-being of the United Kingdom."[165] In the context of national security, the allegedly subversive activity triggering surveillance did not itself have to be illegal.[166] In sum, the administration chose the path of minimalist execution despite the fact that more rights-friendly practices could have been adopted in light of the *Klass* judgment.[167]

And so the incremental process known from other issue areas repeated itself. In 1997, the ECtHR again found the UK in violation of Article 8 ECHR in a case dealing with the interception of calls made on an internal telephone system at Merseyside police headquarters, an area not covered by the Interception of Communications Act 1985.[168] At that time, several other cases involving surveillance techniques and devices other than phone tapping that had also remained unregulated were making their way through the British court system and toward the ECtHR,[169] prompting a still reluctant[170] government to adopt Part 3 of the Police Act 1997, which provided legislative authorization for certain surveillance techniques, such as those involving trespass by the police,[171] and it apparently was passed in the hope of being able to avoid further findings of Convention violations.[172] Once more, however, the effort reflected a largely procedural approach to the issuing of warrants without setting out any new substantial standards to protect a target's privacy. As Nick Taylor has argued, the failure to establish "mandatory judicial supervision of authorization procedures [. . .] at best marginally satisfie[d] the criteria for authorization laid down in Klass [v. Germany]" and "[t]he basis for allowing surveillance [in the Police Act 1997] was unduly broad and appeared to be wider than the administrative guidelines [it] replaced."[173] Taylor concludes: "The Act represented an opportunity missed to provide a comprehensive framework for the regulation of all technical surveillance operations. Again though it could be argued that the impetus for the legislation was the European Convention, the Act appeared to represent an attempt to head off future adverse rulings from Strasbourg rather than being a meaningful attempt to respect the private life of the individual. Though Article 8 [ECHR] reflects a minimum standard to be achieved, the Police Act appeared to be a minimalist attempt to achieve it."[174]

A more comprehensive reform was only begun when Labour came to power after the 1997 general elections. Labour had already promised to reform the Interception of Communications Act 1985 to close a loophole relating to cell phone taps.[175] With the looming entry into force of the Human Rights Act[176] and taking account of a report by the nongovernmental organization JUSTICE that called for a comprehensive reform of UK surveillance regulations,[177] Parliament adopted the Regulation of Investigatory Powers Act 2000 (RIPA). Although the act remedied the lack of legal regulation for the types of issues found to be in violation of the Convention in *Halford* and *Khan* and thus presented a significant step forward in this respect,[178] its protection of privacy in other respects was less than comprehensive. While setting relatively rigorous authorization requirements for intrusive surveillance (e.g., placing bugs in an apartment), lesser standards applied to so-called directed surveillance (e.g., placing the bug "merely" in the hallway of an apartment building). Controversially, RIPA 2000 made it an offense to fail to comply with a notice to disclose encrypted material, leading one commentator to conclude that "[i]t is in such instances where a minimal interpretation of the Convention has led to the statutory rubber stamp for somewhat illiberal state action."[179] And Helen Fenwick discerned an element of evasion in the adoption of RIPA 2000 as a whole: "Under the rhetoric about protecting human rights [. . .] lies an unadmitted concern—to keep scrutiny of [surveillance] matters outside the courts [. . .] whereas had powers of surveillance remained on a non-statutory basis they would have been vulnerable to challenge under Article 8 of the Convention."[180]

Notwithstanding the fact that the application and operation of the regime under RIPA 2000 was later deemed by the Court to be in conformity with the Convention,[181] it is easy to see that both Conservative and Labour governments, while responding to certain deficiencies identified in the ECtHR's jurisprudence, also sought to maintain flexibility in the domestic framework applying to covert surveillance. Nor is there an end to litigation concerning covert surveillance and of debates concerning the tensions between surveillance, security, and the maintenance of freedom. The first applications dealing with the fallout from the Edward Snowden revelations, claiming that generic surveillance by the UK and the sharing of data with US intelligence services have violated certain privacy rights under the ECHR, have been lodged in Strasbourg.[182]

Military Justice

Just as with elements of the UK's justice system in general, so aspects of its military justice system relating to courts-martial, summary trials, and detention review proceedings have been found to be incompatible with the Convention in a number of cases. Although some resistance among the military leadership to changing what might be seen as an integral part of military organizational culture that has been in place nearly unchanged since the mid-1950s might be expected,[183] such opposition surprisingly appears not to have been voiced, at least not publicly or loudly. The first two judgments on the UK military justice system were issued in 1997 and found that the structure of army and air force courts-martial violated the requirements of judicial independence and impartiality under Article 6 (1) ECHR because the central role of the officer convening the court-martial, who simultaneously played a key role in the prosecution of the defendant, was highest in rank among the tribunal members (with the others remaining subject to his overall command) and acted as confirming officer of the court-martial's decision with the power to alter the sentence as he saw fit.[184] This arrangement, the ECtHR found, objectively justified the applicant's misgivings as to the independence and impartiality of the court martial and thus compromised, at a minimum, its appearance in this respect, which was sufficient for a breach of Article 6 (1).[185]

The UK court-martial system had already begun to be modified prior to the Court's judgments with the passage of the Armed Forces Act 1996, whose relevant parts were adopted in anticipation of the Court's rulings.[186] This appears to have occurred willingly and without major objection, with the minister of state for the armed forces at the time noting that the government "recognize[s] . . . that there is a need to remove the impression, however mistaken, that the chain of command can have undue influence over court-martial proceedings."[187] The 1996 Act eliminated, inter alia, the role of the convening officer and allocated his duties to several different bodies; replaced the role of the confirming officer with a three-member reviewing authority with the power to modify findings of guilt and sentencing; and provided for a new right of appeal against court-martial sentences to the civilian Courts-Martial Appeal Court.[188] Based on these changes, the Committee of Ministers ended its supervision of this set of cases.[189]

Although an ECtHR chamber subsequently took issue with certain elements of the new system in 2002,[190] one year later, on the basis of further information and clarifications—prompted, among other things, by a 2002 House of Lords decision that took issue with the ECtHR's reasoning and finding in the *Morris* judgment[191]—the Grand Chamber of the Court decided that concerns especially as to the problematic role of the nonjudicial reviewing authority in Army disciplinary proceedings were outweighed by the fact that, ultimately, it was always the fully independent Court-Martial Appeal Court that made the final decisions in contested cases.[192] Still, additional fairness issues were addressed in further judgments:

- Concerning naval courts-martial, the ECtHR found several violations of Article 6 (1) ECHR concerning both the system in place before[193] and after[194] commencement of the Armed Forces Act 1996; the 1996 act yielded compliance with the first two judgments, whereas additional legislative and practical measures remedied the violations found in the third.[195]
- The fact that a commanding officer (CO) decided on pretrial detention when he was also likely to play an important role in the subsequent trial was seen by the Court to compromise the impartiality required by Article 5 (3) ECHR.[196] Notably, the UK at first kept the commanding officer's role in this respect, but added a right to legal assistance as well as the option to appeal to the CO's immediate superior,[197] and only subsequently required that soldiers in predetention had to be brought before a judicial officer/judge advocate.[198]
- The system of summary trials by a soldier's commanding officer as sole judge without access to legal representation was likewise seen to run afoul of the guarantees of fairness and impartiality under Article 6

ECHR.[199] The United Kingdom, however, opted to maintain the scheme of summary trials essentially intact, adding instead the option to choose trial by court martial instead of summary hearings and, when the CO did end up deciding summarily, an automatic right of appeal to the Summary Appeal Court.[200] And while legal aid and/or representation are available for appeals and court martial proceedings, they continued to be excluded from summary trials, despite the ECtHR's explicit finding in this respect. Supervision was closed nonetheless,[201] ostensibly in light of the availability of legal aid and representation in the optional court-martial or any subsequent summary appeals proceedings, the ECtHR apparently being convinced by the UK that other safeguards assured a reasonably fair summary trial.[202]

The ECtHR's judgments, combined with the coming into force of the HRA in 2000 and the looming prospect of domestic litigation addressing human rights issues in the UK military justice system,[203] thus triggered a number of meaningful reforms. These triggers benefited from the fact that UK armed services legislation is regularly updated, providing a readily available vehicle to address issues as they arose. Since the 1950s, Parliament has passed armed forces acts in five-year intervals, responding to a constitutional requirement that has its origins in the 1688 bill of rights and its prohibition of a standing army unless approved by Parliament.[204] More recent changes, by contrast, had their source exclusively domestically. The motivation for the major overhaul of disciplinary proceedings enacted in the Armed Forces Act 2006, resulting in a harmonized system with single prosecutorial and judicial institutions for all three services, came out of the Strategic Defence Review 1998[205] and went far beyond the issues addressed by the ECtHR. There is no publicly available indication that the reforms of the military justice system were particularly contentious politically or were strongly opposed from within the military, except maybe on the margins. That said, we do observe here as in other areas an apparent wish to keep long-established elements of the system in place, and, rather than replace them, to seek to achieve compliance with the Convention by way of optional or additional procedures.

CHAPTER 6

Judgments Pending Before the Committee
of Ministers

As of June 2017, ten judgments rendered against the United Kingdom until 2010, covering three different (sets of) issues, still remained under Committee supervision.

Faulty Investigations into Wrongful Deaths
in Northern Ireland

A set of six judgments rendered between 2001 and 2003 that is still under supervision concerns violations of the procedural aspect of the right to life under Article 2 due to what the Court perceived as shortcomings in the investigations into the applicants' relatives' deaths.[1] In light of hundreds of similar domestic cases dealing with deaths in Northern Ireland during the period known as the Troubles (late 1960s to 1998), the issue of effective investigations extended reached well beyond the cases decided by the ECtHR,[2] with the latter adding a further stimulus to ongoing reform efforts that had come out of the Criminal Justice Review agreed upon as part of the 1998 Good Friday Agreement. The Court had highlighted various procedural shortcomings, including, inter alia, the lack of independence of the investigating police officers from those involved in the events at issue, the absence of publicly available information on decisions not to prosecute suspects, the fact that the soldiers and police officers who shot the applicants' next of kin could not be required to testify as witnesses in the inquests concerning the deceased, and that inquest proceedings did not allow verdicts or findings that could play an effective role in criminal proceedings (they could, for example, not pronounce on the lawfulness of the force resulting in the victim's death).[3]

A host of general measures has since been adopted by the UK, and the Committee of Ministers has considered many of these as sufficiently remedying a number of shortcomings addressed in the judgments.[4] Some of them, however, have since been shown to be ineffective in practice, resulting in follow-up litigation and further adverse findings against the UK,[5] while the bodies charged with investigating past cases of violent deaths—the Office of the Police Ombudsman for Northern Ireland; the Historical Enquiries Team; and the Police Service of Northern Ireland, Legacy Investigations Branch (continuing the work of the Historical Enquiries Team)—have become subject to various criticisms, including bias in favor of the state and military, and lack of sufficient resources.[6] A number of individual measures in these cases, including inquests, are also subject to some outstanding issues.[7] As envisaged in the 2014 Stormont House Agreement (SHA), which lays down principles of cooperation and policy agreed upon by the major Northern Ireland political parties and the Irish and British governments, the new Historical Investigations Unit (HIU), which is independent from the police and fully compliant with the positive obligations under Article 2 ECHR, is to take over the roughly 1,700 cases currently dealt with by one of the other mechanisms, with the UK government having pledged "full disclosure to the HIU."[8]

Both the creation of the HIU and the ability to make full disclosure require new legislation which more than two and a half years after the conclusion of the SHA has still not come about (neither of these was addressed in the 2015 Fresh Start Agreement).[9] One major point of contention that subsequently arose was the UK government's insistence on a national security exception to the onward disclosure to relatives and the public of information revealed by the state to the HIU. A draft bill leaked in September 2015 would have provided the secretary of state with the power to prevent disclosure to affected families of sensitive information on undefined national security grounds, without the possibility of appeal. Several NGOs have voiced their concern that the government might use such an exception not only to protect genuine national security interests but also to conceal or cover up embarrassing involvements of its own agents in criminal activity.[10] Further developments that have delayed or impeded progress include the withholding of resources;[11] the plan by the secretary of state for Northern Ireland, revealed in September 2016, to first initiate a "more public phase" discussing the design of the legacy bodies before moving forward with their creation; and intervening parliamentary elections in both Northern Ireland in March 2017, after the power-sharing government between Sinn Fein and the Democratic Unionist Party had collapsed, and in the UK in June 2017, which effectively brought Northern Ireland–related government business to a standstill.[12]

The fact that these judgments have still not been fully complied with well over fifteen years after the first of them was rendered is clearly grounds for concern, and the delay in adopting appropriate general measures in these cases had been criticized by Parliament's Joint Committee on Human Rights as early as 2006.[13] What is equally clear is that the Convention-related issues remain intricately entangled with the conflict's legacy and the continuing ethno-national divisions, which make them politically highly sensitive in the two principal communities involved. On the one hand, Unionists and members of Parliament have complained that full transparency is demanded for the 10 percent of conflict-related deaths in Northern Ireland having some possible form of state involvement, but that there is too little focus on the remaining 90 percent caused by non-state terrorist groups,[14] with the Northern Ireland First Minister Arlene Foster perceiving, and rejecting, such imbalance as an attempt to "rewrite the past."[15] Arguing along similar lines, the secretary of state for Northern Ireland, James Brokenshire, recently restated the government's intention to "continue to reject attempts to place the state at the heart of every atrocity or somehow to displace responsibility away from those who carried out terrorist attacks, namely the terrorists themselves" and that that it needed to be assured that "where prosecutions do take place terrorists are not treated more favorably than former soldiers and police officers."[16]

On the other hand, in light of what British Irish Human Rights Watch has called the "entrenched culture of Government secrecy"[17] with respect to military and especially paramilitary activities in Northern Ireland, it is not unrealistic to expect that available restrictions on full disclosure might indeed be used to limit publication of information even when not strictly, or no longer, relevant for national security reasons, but rather to protect former military and police personnel and the reputation of the state itself. In a similar vein, the NGO Relatives for Justice (RFJ) has alleged that what it sees as the UK government's foot-dragging and at best lukewarm support for legacy institutions is motivated by its wish "to hide the illegal and criminal activities of its operatives and the political control and cover guaranteed to those who did its dirty work. It is calculating that the embarrassment of accusations of cover-up is less damaging that the revelations of wrongdoing, human rights violations and war crimes which have underpinned its long fight with republicans."[18]

In light of this perceived lack of a good faith with respect to complying with these judgments, RFJ and applicant representatives have called on the Committee of Ministers to initiate noncompliance proceedings against the UK under Article 46 (4) ECHR.[19]

Needless to say, the political dynamics affecting the manner and modalities of dealing with the conflictual history of Northern Ireland are complex and require greater in-depth research and analysis than can be undertaken in this book. Here, only the barest surface can be scratched, and while the research question motivating this book mandates that the attempts to deal with the conflict's legacy be examined through the analytic lens of compliance with the Court's judgments, these are only one factor among several, and not necessarily the most important one, that have conditioned "Northern Ireland's 'piecemeal' approach to the past."[20] What can certainly be said sixteen years after the *McKerr* judgment was issued in May 2001 is that successive UK governments have not exactly rushed toward committing all necessary resources for the establishment of independent and effective institutions capable of identifying the possible responsibility of UK-directed operatives for, or their collusion in, wrongful deaths in Northern Ireland in Article 2–compliant proceedings. And while the need to do so has been reaffirmed in the SHA, the process appears now to be undermined by the lack of political agreement between the principal stakeholders as to how to balance investigations into state and non-state killings as well as with respect to the acceptability of a national security exception. If nothing else, the proposal to include such an unreviewable veto option strongly puts in relief the government's preference for the retention of ultimate control over which information is made public and which is not, a preference well in line with the expectations of minimalist compliance

Indefinite Retention of Biometric Data

The judgment of *S. and Marper* (2008) concerned a violation of the right to respect for private life due to the fact that the Police and Criminal Evidence Act 1984 permitted the retention of fingerprints and DNA sample material taken as part of criminal investigations without any time limit, even if the accused was subsequently acquitted. While accepting as legitimate the aim pursued by such retention, the Court concluded that "the blanket and indiscriminate nature of the powers of retention of the fingerprints, cellular samples and DNA profiles of persons suspected but not convicted of offences [. . .] fails to strike a fair balance between the competing public and private interests."[21] Importantly, the Court noted with approval the data-retention scheme in place in Scotland, which permits retaining biometric data for three years in the case of people charged, but not convicted, of sexual or violent crimes, with the possibility of a further two-year extension.[22]

While the two applicants' biometric samples were destroyed immediately after the judgment, legislative changes took considerably longer. In England and Wales, remedial legislation, forming part of the Protection of Freedoms Act 2012,[23] received royal assent in May 2012, with the relevant sections fully in force since May 2014. The act provides for a much more detailed and differentiated regime regulating the retention and destruction of biometric data than was previously the case, taking its principal cues from the Scottish example. In general, biometric data taken during investigations that do not result in a conviction will have to be destroyed again. As in Scotland, such data may be retained for three years when the person in question has been charged with a qualifying violent or sexual offence and for two years when the person is subject to a Penalty Notice for Disorder.[24] In addition, data may also be kept for three years for those arrested but not charged with a qualifying offense, subject to the approval of the newly created Biometric Commissioner. In the case of people subject to a National Security Determination, biometric data can likewise be retained absent any formal charges for (renewable) periods of up to two years, with the Biometric Commissioner having the power to order its destruction if he or she considers that retention because of national security concerns is no longer justified. In addition to the legislative changes, the UK reported the destruction or deletion of more than 7.7 million DNA samples, over 1.7 million DNA profiles, and well over 1.6 million fingerprints that did not meet any of the above criteria.[25]

Competence issues (the Northern Ireland Assembly does not have the power to legislate with respect to national security exceptions) and a consequential drafting error in the relevant legislation (the Criminal Justice Act (Northern Ireland) 2013) that required amendment before the legislation could be commenced have so far prevented entry into force of a new Convention-compliant regime in Northern Ireland. And just when commencement was expected for October 2015, "unforeseen circumstances"— including the recognition that some of the data otherwise scheduled to be destroyed might be needed to enable the HIU to conduct effective investigations into unsolved deaths in Northern Ireland, and the interruptions of the

Northern Ireland Assembly's parliamentary business in preparation of UK
and Northern Ireland elections in 2015 and 2017—prevented it from coming
to pass.[26] The most recent information provided by the UK, dating from April
2017, indicates that compliance with this case is now closely connected with
the "resolution to the wider outstanding issues in relation to the legacy of the
Troubles in Northern Ireland."[27]

In this case, then, continued supervision is not the result of willful noncompliance, but rather of the length of domestic legislative processes, mis-
haps along the way, and the fact that the reform in one constituent part of the
UK had become entangled with another issue: the creation of new institutions to investigate Troubles-related deaths. Indeed, the substance of the new
regime in England and Wales, which also functions as the blueprint for the
one in Northern Ireland, has in the meantime already received the Council
of Europe's as well as the Court's blessing.[28] It appears that the UK carefully
adhered to the basic thrust of the ECtHR's decision, with its emphasis on a
differentiated and proportional regime, while also making sure that the new
rules continue to permit the government to use biometric data as part of anti-
terrorism operations, irrespective of formal criminal charges and prosecution. As in many other judgments assessed so far, the general inclination to
comply with a judgment does not prejudice the precise manner in which such
compliance will occur, and while the national security exemptions can be
rationally justified and safeguards are in place through the mandated review
by the biometrics commissioner, they still tip the balance somewhat back in
the government's direction.

What may be qualified as satisfactory substantive outcome should not dis-
tract from the fact, however, that the Labour government, while still in power
prior to the 2010 general election, had first pursued a much more restrictive response to the Court's judgment. Initially, the government intended to
comply with the judgment through secondary legislation, that is, authorizing the secretary of state to make regulations on retention of biometric data
that would need to be approved by both houses of Parliament to become law
but would offer much less opportunity for parliamentary scrutiny and debate
than primary legislation.[29] While this approach was abandoned in favor of
primary legislation with full parliamentary vetting, the proposed substantive
provisions sought, by the government's own admission, to "push the bound-
ary of the judgment in relation to our wish to have protection for the public" (e.g., by providing for a retention period of DNA profiles for six years,
irrespective of the nature of the offence). Parliament's Joint Committee on

Human Rights considered it "unacceptable that the Government appears to have taken a very narrow approach to the judgment by purposely 'pushing the boundaries' of the Court's decision in order to maintain the main thrust of its original policy on the retention of DNA,"[30] "with as few changes as possible to its original policy."[31] The Labour government's solution included in the Crime and Security Act 2010 was not entered into force, however.[32] The new incoming coalition government following the 2010 general elections, composed of David Cameron's Conservative Party and Nick Clegg's Liberal Democrats, had different plans and promised in their government manifesto "to adopt the protections of the Scottish model for the DNA database."[33] This, then, is an instance where a change of government with different policy preferences has had a tangible impact on the design of the remedial measures adopted to comply with an ECtHR judgment.

Prisoner Voting Rights

The remaining two judgments in the data set, *Hirst (no. 2)* (2005) and *Greens and M.T.* (2010), deliver the strongest blow yet to the compliance pull hypothesis with respect to liberal democracies. Just satisfaction for cost and expenses, but not for nonpecuniary damages, has in fact been duly paid in both cases, but the necessary legislative changes to bring UK law into compliance with the Convention, as interpreted by the Court, have not yet been made, and it appears that they also will not be made in the foreseeable future, with these and subsequent cases having raised the more general question of the demarcation of the legitimate decision-making authority between the Court and the member states.

Hirst (no. 2) addressed the question whether the United Kingdom's blanket voting ban imposed on prisoners violated Article 3 of Protocol No. 1.[34] That provision stipulates that the "High Contracting Parties undertake to hold free elections at reasonable intervals by secret ballot, under conditions which will ensure the free expression of the opinion of the people in the choice of the legislature." Although articulated as an obligation for the state, not in terms of a subjective right, the Court had previously interpreted it as including the active right to vote, arguing that the guarantee would otherwise become farcical.[35] In the 2005 *Hirst (no. 2)* judgment, on appeal from a 2004 chamber judgment, the Grand Chamber of the Court held, by twelve votes to five, that while the aim pursued by the ban could be considered legitimate, its indiscriminate scope to (nearly[36]) all prisoners irrespective of the length of their sentence and the gravity of their offence was too blunt an instrument and disproportionate, resulting in a violation of the Convention.[37]

Although other ECtHR judgments had also met with strongly worded criticism from at least some political quarters within the UK, none has engendered such long-lasting opposition as the issue of prisoner voting rights.[38] In response to *Hirst (no. 2)*, the Labour government conducted two rounds of domestic consultations, in 2006–2007 and in 2009, on how to implement the judgment that did not, however, result in the introduction of a parliamentary bill in time for the 2010 general elections. As a result, the elections were held with the impugned blanket ban still in place. In light of the UK's failure to comply with *Hirst (no. 2)* and the inflow of clone cases as a result of it, in 2010 the Court issued a pilot judgment, *Greens and M.T.*, in which it gave the UK six months from the date that the judgment became final to introduce remedial legislation.[39] The judgment became final on April 11, 2011, when the UK's request for a referral to the Grand Chamber was rejected.

Subsequently, however, the UK government asked for, and was granted, an extension of six months until after the anticipated Grand Chamber judgment in the then-pending case of *Scoppola v. Italy (no. 3)* which also concerned prisoner voting rights and in which the UK participated as third-party intervener. The judgment in *Scoppola (no. 3)* was issued in May 2012. It upheld *Hirst (no. 2)* while finding for Italy, because under Italian law the loss of the franchise was proportionately linked to the severity of the crime and could be regained by those who had been deprived of it indefinitely.[40] On November 22, 2012, the last day of the granted extension, the UK coalition government introduced a legislative initiative, the Voting Eligibility (Prisoners) Draft Bill, as required by *Greens and M.T.*[41] The draft bill laid out three alternatives: a voting ban for those sentenced to four or more years in prison; a voting ban for prisoners sentenced to more than six months; and a reaffirmation of the blanket ban currently in place, which was clearly a noncompliant option. A joint select committee composed of members of both houses was set up to conduct prelegislative scrutiny. The committee issued its report on December 18, 2013, and recommended compliance with *Hirst (no. 2)* through enfranchisement of all prisoners with sentences of twelve months or less and of those within six months of the end of their prison term.[42] The coalition government noted the report, but stated, without further explanation, that it would "not be able to legislate for prisoner voting in this Parliament."[43] As a result, the 2014 elections to the European Parliament and the 2015 general elections in the UK were held subject to the blanket ban. In the meantime, the Court had unfrozen the adjourned proceedings, and although many applications were declared inadmissible, three new judgments finding violations with respect to a total of 1,047 applicants were issued in 2014, 2015, and 2016.[44] In none of the cases did the Court award any just satisfaction, not even for costs and expenses, arguing that successful applications required only the filling in of the Court's application form, which did not require any legal assistance.

Why such a delay in implementation? One part of the explanation has to do with the specific policy preferences with respect to prisoner voting rights of all governments in power, as well as of popular majorities, since the *Hirst (no. 2)* judgment was rendered in 2005; another part involves a more general critical stance as to the role of the ECtHR in British law and politics. The immediate response by the then Labour government to the judgment was objection on substance, coupled with defiance as to compliance. As Prime Minister Tony Blair told the House of Commons, "The current position in law is that convicted prisoners are not able to vote, and that will remain the position under this Government."[45] Indeed, although originally enacted under a Conservative government, Labour had deliberately[46] upheld the ban when it extended the franchise to remand prisoners and mental health detainees not convicted of a crime in 2000.[47] As noted, the government nonetheless launched domestic consultations on the issue, which, however, it considered inconclusive. As Jack Straw later frankly observed, these were mainly undertaken with a view to keeping prisoner voting rights from becoming a "nasty pre-election issue"; also, given the dominant preferences in both major parties, "wild horses would not have got a majority into the 'Aye' lobby in favor of a change."[48] The Joint Committee on Human Rights noted in this regard that the obvious foot-dragging raised "serious questions about [the Government's] reluctance to deal with this issue."[49] Still, formally, the government paid lip service to its duty to comply, with a justice minister, Michael Wills, noting in 2009 that while "some degree of voting being extended to some serving prisoners is legally unavoidable," this was to be done "in a proportionate manner" with the aim of keeping prisoners sentenced to four years or more from voting "in any circumstances"[50] and providing a graduated scheme for those sentenced to less than four years.[51]

The 2010–2015 coalition government likewise opposed the implications of the *Hirst (no. 2)* judgment, with Prime Minister David Cameron remarking in the House of Commons that "[i]t makes me physically ill even to contemplate having to give the vote to anyone who is in prison. Frankly, when people commit a crime and go to prison, they should lose their rights, including the right to vote." At the same time, Cameron suggested that a pure avoidance strategy might have to give way to a more pragmatic course, if only to avoid the costs of noncompliance in light of a continuous inflow of clone cases: "But we are in a situation that I am afraid we have to deal with. This is potentially costing us £160 million, so we have to come forward with proposals, because I do not want us to spend that money; it is not right."[52] (It later turned out that the ECtHR, as noted above, refrained from awarding compensation in relevant clone case.) Shortly after these remarks, the minister for political and constitutional reform, Mark Harper, affirmed that the "Government will [. . .] bring forward legislation providing that the blanket ban in the existing law will be replaced," adding that "[g]overnments have an absolute duty to uphold the rule of law. And at this of all times we must avoid risking taxpayers' money in ways that the public would rightly condemn. In the light of this, [. . .] the only responsible course is to implement the judgment, and to do so in a way which ensures the most serious offenders continue to lose the right to vote."[53]

No tangible results followed, however. Just how little support for enfranchising prisoners existed in Parliament had become evident on February 10, 2011, when a motion that advocated keeping the blanket ban intact was carried by 234 votes in favor and only 22 against.[54] Importantly, while the debate also addressed the rationales for the policy decision of keeping prisoners from voting, it very much focused on the jurisdictional question of which institution had the proper authority to decide the issue, the British Parliament or the European Court of Human Rights. The motion itself had declared that "legislative decisions of this nature should be a matter for democratically-elected lawmakers."[55] In debate, Gary Streeter argued that "[t]his matter is not really about whether prisoners in this country have the right to vote, but about whether this House has the right to make its own laws for its own people," adding that "[t]he rights taken on itself by the ECHR is the clearest case of mission creep that we will ever see. It is the ECHR's decision to award itself more power—much more power than the authors of the convention ever intended—that we must challenge today. That decision has led to a steady trickle of judgments and pronouncements over the past 30 years that have frequently left the British public baffled and extremely angry."[56]

Other contributions noted as the principal challenge the "Court's tendency towards micro-management"[57] and that *Hirst (no. 2)* raised the "question of whether we have confidence in the workings of another court system. That is the tension that underlines so much of what we are discussing today—whether we are talking about a credible court, with the extension of its remit as a living instrument, and so on."[58] For those answering in the negative, it was simply "unacceptable that unelected European judges think that they can tell elected Members of this British Parliament how we should treat British criminals who break British laws."[59] Some linked the problem to the permissible limits of treaty interpretation: "The central questions are whether the interpretation of the treaty that we signed has gone beyond what the original treaty contained, and who, thereafter, has the right to make a decision on the matter. Should it be this Parliament or an unelected European institution that makes such decisions? The clear evidence is that it should be this House, and that the interpretation has gone beyond the terms of the original treaty."[60] Not mincing words, Dominic Raab concluded that it was "time that we drew a line in the sand and sent this very clear message back: This House will decide whether prisoners get the vote, and this House makes the laws of the land, because this House is accountable to the British people."[61]

No legislative initiatives are to be expected from a Conservative-led government in the near future. Indeed, in their manifesto for the 2015 general election, the Conservatives had campaigned, inter alia, on the claim that "[w]e have stopped prisoners from having the vote"[62] and announced their intention to "scrap the ECHR"; and in the most recent 2017 election manifesto, prisoner voting is not even mentioned as an issue.[63] Frustrated with the inaction, in late 2015 the Committee of Minsters adopted an interim resolution in which it expressed its "profound concern that the blanket ban [. . .] remains in place" and called for "high-level dialogue" to discuss how the UK will comply with the relevant judgments.[64] The most recent action plan (October 2016) indicates that the ensuing dialogue has revolved in particular around "collating ideas and options to help [the UK] address this judgment *without* amending section 3 of the Representation of the People Act 1983" since "Parliament continues to oppose passing such legislation."[65] How this may be possible is not made clear for fear that "premature disclosure of options which may not be deliverable or meet the expectations of the Committee of Minsters would harm the ability of the United Kingdom to implement the required general measures"; with the impending Brexit negotiations expected to consume much of the Government's time and resources, no "definitive time scale" was announced, the UK only foresaw being able to present the feasible options within the next nine to twelve months.[66] (Incidentally, the UK's exit from the EU also takes away potential future nudging from the CJEU, whose 2015 *Delvigne* decision can be read as implying the incompatibility of blanket bans with the EU's Charter of Fundamental Rights, which, since the Treaty of Lisbon, has the status of binding primary law[67]).

While extending the franchise to prisoners has received some lobbying and support from NGOs such as the AIRE Centre, the Prison Reform Trust, Liberty, and UNLOCK, public opinion has also remained consistently against extending suffrage to prisoners. In representative public opinion polls taken in 2010, 2011, 2012, and most recently in 2015, 50 percent, 69 percent, 63 percent, and 67–69 percent of respondents, respectively, were in favor of maintaining the ban unchanged despite an adverse ruling by an international human rights court.[68] Majorities rejecting prisoner enfranchisement can be observed across all demographic subgroups, political affiliations, and geographic regions. These issue-specific results go hand in hand with a skeptical attitude of the public toward the ECtHR as such. The 2011 survey also asked whether respondents thought that "it is right or wrong that the European Court of Human Rights should be able to make rulings on things the British Parliament or courts have decided." Overall, 63 percent responded that "the British Parliament and Supreme Court should have the final say, rather than a foreign court," with the majority among voters identifying themselves as Conservatives (84 percent) being the largest and those for voters inclined toward Labour (51 percent) and the Liberal Democrats (55 percent) being smaller. Comparable overall majorities also agreed that British membership in the Convention regime had been "abused by lawyers making spurious cases on behalf of criminals" and was, "on balance . . . a bad thing" (57 percent), that it had been an obstacle to fighting terrorism (58 percent), and that Britain should denounce the Convention in favor of a purely domestic bill of rights (55 percent).[69] In light of these public sentiments, it does thus not surprise that lawmakers have been in no hurry to change domestic legislation in line with the guidance offered by the ECtHR.

So *Hirst (no. 2)* and its clone cases are the one set of judgments in which the stipulated compliance pull has so far—well over a decade after the first final judgment—failed to bring about any, if only minimally compliant, remedial response to the Court's decision.[70] The consultations and legislative scrutiny that were undertaken at various points in time and initially seemed to be first steps toward remedial legislation in hindsight appear to have been wasted efforts. Technically, despite the government's claim to the contrary, executing *Hirst (no. 2)* is rather "straightforward, requiring only a one-clause Bill amending s. 3 of the Representation of the People Act 1983."[71] It is the political will in Parliament to enact such a bill that has been demonstrably absent, given the prevailing preferences among both lawmakers and the general public against prisoner enfranchisement. NGO lobbying and peer pressure by the Committee of Ministers[72] did not result in meaningful change to successive governments' position on this issue, and there is no reason to expect that this will change in the near future. With the issue having become entangled with the broader issue of the UK's continued involvement in the Convention scheme, and of a domestic bill of rights that the current government promised to bring forward during the current session of Parliament, compliance with *Hirst (no. 2)* appears ever more unlikely, revealing the UK's reservation costs beyond which it is not prepared to venture. Michael Gove, the lord chancellor and secretary of state for justice, put the key issue succinctly in late 2015 when he noted in the context of addressing the slim chances of a legislative solution to the prisoner voting problem that "you have a clash between two principles: on the one hand, our desire to respect the judgment of the European Court of Human Rights but, on the other hand, our desire to recognize that, ultimately, [. . .] parliamentary sovereignty is the essence of our democracy. In having to choose between the two—it is always difficult and I would rather not—I err on the side of saying that we must respect the democratic principles of parliamentary sovereignty."[73]

CHAPTER 7

Minimalism as the Strategy of Choice for the Reluctant Complier

The analysis of the execution of the judgments rendered by the European Court of Human Rights against the United Kingdom presented in the preceding chapters shows that the United Kingdom has a very satisfactory *formal* compliance record overall. Except for the prisoner voting-rights judgments, which remain unexecuted, successive UK governments—whether led by the Conservative Party, by Labour, or by the coalition between Tories and Liberal Democrats—have taken individual and/or general measures in response to all other judgments issued against the UK, measures that for the most part could, at the time they were taken and on the basis of largely defensible interpretations of the Convention and relevant judgment(s), be considered minimally compliant. Remedial action is also observable with respect to the judgments other than those concerning prisoner voting that are still pending before the Committee of Ministers, although here either not all measures necessary to close the case have been adopted so far or those that have been adopted have later been revealed to fall short of the requirements for full compliance. Just satisfaction, the one measure with regard to which states retain no margin of appreciation as to execution, has always been paid by the UK as awarded, even in cases that were strongly opposed in substance by the government in power, such as *McCann* or *Hirst (no. 2)*. The prisoner voting-right judgments being the only instances where there has been prolonged and deliberate noncompliance on the part of the UK with respect to the adoption of general measures,[1] one can conclude that the descriptive part of H_{NORM} holds surprisingly well for a country that even before the recent turn toward increasingly rancorous criticism often has had an unenthusiastic relationship with the Convention control bodies.

But has this behavior been normatively motivated, with "begrudging compliance" being driven by "long-standing traditions of respecting human rights, the rule of law, and [. . .] [the UK's] international obligations,"[2] or is it the result of recurrently applied pressure to otherwise compliance-disinclined governments? It seems quite clear that the second alternative has little traction in the UK case. Beyond some naming and shaming, there is little evidence of enforcement action in the form of sanctions or electoral pressures. To be sure, human rights interest groups, such as Liberty, JUSTICE, Stonewall, or the AIRE Center, have repeatedly campaigned and lobbied for change and have employed recourse to the ECtHR as part of strategic litigation or have materially supported litigants with whose cause they sympathized. But to the extent that such campaigns and lobbying occurred both before and after an ECtHR judgment, their existence cannot by itself explain the positive response of the government only after a judgment has been issued. There must be something germane to the nature of legally binding judicial pronouncements that effectively changes the political calculus of the relevant decision-makers, and I suggest that this something is inherently normative in character. Even if we qualify naming and shaming as enforcement, it bears pointing out that this technique can be successful only if the actor that is being subjected to it shares certain values and normative commitments with those engaging in it. If that is not the case, then it is not at all clear why the target should feel ashamed in the first place and be motivated to change its behavior.

Popular pressure has likewise not been a relevant source of enforcement in the UK. First, as regards the applicants themselves, in most cases, they hailed from social groups—prisoners, suspected or convicted criminals and terrorists, immigrants, homo- and transsexuals, people deprived of rights in isolated or quite specific circumstances—that did not themselves constitute a politically majoritarian force that could be expected to generate sufficient (ultimately electoral) pressure to compel the government to take implementing decisions that went against its own preferences. Second, if there has been popular pressure, then it appears that it has more often than not been *against* compliance with the Court's judgments, fueled in part by tendentious negative media reporting of human rights benefitting primarily "foreign criminals" and other seemingly "undeserving" segments of the population.[3] It can of course not be excluded that there have been instances of "private" enforcement outside of the public's eye, where stakeholders with leverage have threatened some form of sanction and have received concessions as a result, but if enforcement were the *conditio sine qua non* behind compliance with the Court's judgments, then there should have been either many more documented instances of such enforcement in primary source materials as well as in the academic literature, or instances of noncompliance should have been much more numerous. Since this is not the case, the fact of overwhelming compliance with the Court's judgments despite the absence of meaningful enforcement provides strong support for the normative constraint hypothesis H_{NORM}.

At the same time, as the discussion of the individual and general remedial measures adopted by the United Kingdom has repeatedly shown, formal compliance can in many cases be achieved in different ways. There is no determinism at work in the context of the Court's (mostly declaratory) judgments that would point to one, and only one, precisely defined remedial measure, or set of measures, that alone could remedy the violation declared by the Court. And when some freedom of choice remains, as I argued in the theory section, it will likely be exploited and made use of in light of the implementing actor's own prevailing politico-legal preferences. In most circumstances, this situation will then translate into implementation guided by the desire to minimize change and its legal, political, and/or material ramifications. Evidence of such compliance behavior has been documented aplenty in this chapter, irrespective of the political colors of the government in power at the relevant time, lending credence to hypothesis H_{RC-1}.

What has also become clear, however, is that in a number of cases and constellations it is difficult to make a clear-cut determination as to whether a remedial measure is minimalist or not. This is particularly the case when violations are remedied by making procedural changes, such as enabling the involvement of parents in proceedings relating to access to their children where it was previously lacking.[4] In such a context, the legally mandated involvement of parents formally remedies the previous shortcoming, but whether it results in substantively greater involvement or greater influence is a question the answer to which depends on how the new rules are being used and applied in practice. The best, although by no means perfect, indicator that the achievement of formal compliance through reformed procedures is not just a cover for otherwise continuing impediments to the effective enjoyment of the rights to be protected by procedural guarantees is the absence of subsequent clone cases and follow-up litigation. To determine whether satisfactory compliance at the formal level of law or policy is minimalist or broad in terms of subsequent implementation and practice thus often requires additional research that could not be undertaken for this project. Hence, in many cases, especially those listed in the Appendix, the degree of compliance is simply given as "satisfactory" at the level of formal legislative or policy change, without forcing upon it a classification of either narrow/minimalist or extensive/broad compliance.

In sum, then, the UK case provides strong empirical evidence for the operation of the behavioral logic of rational choice within normative constraints. Even in the absence of meaningful enforcement, the United Kingdom has generally complied with the judgments rendered against it while at the same time having sought to contain, where possible, their domestic impact through minimalist compliance.

PART II

Germany

CHAPTER 8

The Convention and Court Within Constitutionalized Rights Protection

In a 2008 study, the authors noted that "Germany ranks among the lower case-count states, especially when considered on a *per capita* basis."[1] With a total of 184 compliance-relevant ECtHR judgments rendered between 1978 and 2015, that assessment still remains valid. As shown below, many of these judgments involve violations that may be regarded as minor and require "corrections at the margin,"[2] rather than major revisions, of national law, policy, or administrative practices, especially when compared to the systemic deficiencies and recurrent violations of physical integrity rights impugned by the Court in other countries. At the same time, Germany's ECHR history is not free of violations with systemic dimensions or infringements of Articles 3 and 5 which, together with Articles 2 and 4, protect the core set of physical integrity rights. Irrespective of the classification of violations into systemic or isolated, or grave or minor, every violation restricts the affected individuals' ability to live their life as they see fit, and every finding of a violation, with its concomitant obligation to make amends, constrains the relevant public authority's freedom of action. For these individuals and authorities alike, the consequences of the ECtHR's judicature will often be highly important, even if disinterested observers might view the specific instantiations of some rights as marginal or "second-order" rights. Ultimately, the relative importance of enjoying certain rights cannot be established in an abstract, quasi-objective manner but must include the subjective appreciation of such rights by those affected.

Germany is often portrayed, as in Alice Donald and Philip Reach's recent study on the role of parliaments in securing compliance with the ECtHR's judgments, as a country with a "strong culture of compliance . . . with human rights norms and judgments" whose own constitutional bill of rights, according to some, provides "a higher level of protection than the Convention" so that "little is left for correction by the Strasbourg Court."[3] That may well be, but as this part of the book will show, even in a country with a "prevailing human rights culture [that] has ensured the acceptability of the Court,"[4] preference-led behavior resulting in minimalist or restrictive compliance occurs across a range of cases, even those concerning presumably minor issues, because it is the preferences of the concrete actors involved that count, not the relative significance of a case for the polity as a whole. In addition, the German case study also illustrates that what is required to comply with a judgment can change over time as a result of the changing assessment of the nature of the violation at issue, whose systemic character may only reveal itself after the accumulation of similar cases, leading to different requirements as to the remedies necessary for full compliance.

Germany and the Convention

Germany is one of the original signatories of the Convention and was one of the first states to recognize both the right of individual petition as well as the jurisdiction of the Court.[5] Domestically, in line with German constitutional law, the Convention has the legal force of a federal statute with binding effect for the executive and judicial branches of government.[6] Doctrinal arguments for a supraconstitutional, constitutional, or at least supralegislative status of the Convention failed to take hold in judicial practice.[7] The Convention has precedence over all earlier legislation as well as over all legal acts of lower status (e.g., the laws of the German *Länder*).[8] As regards situations in which federal legislation adopted after the ECHR's ratification is in conflict with the Convention, the principle of *lex posterior derogat legi priori* would formally give effect to the law adopted later in time, but judicial practice is based on the assumption, absent explicit evidence to the contrary, that the parliament—the Bundestag—did not intend to violate Germany's treaty obligations, so that the interpretation and application of subsequent federal law should aim, through interpretation, for as much conformity with such commitments as possible (the principle of the so-called public international law friendliness [*Völkerrechtsfreundlichkeit*] of the German legal order).[9]

Importantly, Germany's constitution—the *Grundgesetz* (Basic Law), adopted in 1949—includes its own bill of rights, covering many of the same rights and freedoms that are included in the Convention, and establishes a judicial supervisory mechanism in the form of constitutional complaints that can be lodged with the Bundesverfassungsgericht (Federal Constitutional Court [FCC]).[10] The FCC exercises a strong form of judicial review.[11] Its decisions are legally binding on all "constitutional organs" at the federal and state (*Länder*) level as well as on all courts and administrative authorities, and when they decide upon the constitutionality of legislation or the compatibility of state law with federal law, they "shall have the force of law," that is, they bind everyone.[12] Unlike the US judicial system, in which any court can determine the constitutionality of a piece of legislation, in the German system this authority is reserved for the FCC, and lower courts that harbor doubts as to the constitutionality of legislation have to adjourn the proceedings and submit the relevant question to the constitutional court. Although constitutional complaints cannot be based directly on an alleged violation of the ECHR, due to its lack of constitutional status, the ECHR, and the ECtHR's jurisprudence, can be invoked as interpretive aids in determining the scope of related rights in the Basic Law.[13] At the same time, because of the existence of a detailed domestic-rights catalogue and extensive jurisprudence interpreting it, while references to the ECHR and ECtHR have been increasing over time in the jurisprudence of the high courts, they remain numerically small,[14] and lower courts especially prefer to rely on the national constitution and the FCC's jurisprudence.[15] Even when the influence of the ECHR and ECtHR seems obvious, explicit references to the ECtHR's case law are often lacking.[16]

Because domestic remedies need to be exhausted before the ECtHR can consider a case, and because a constitutional complaint provides an effective remedy in the human rights domain, all German cases before the ECtHR will previously have been submitted to the FCC in order to meet this particular admissibility requirement. The FCC may either have decided not to accept a particular case for decision because it did not view it as establishing a prima facie violation of the constitution, or it may have rendered a judgment on the merits, but in either case an adverse ECtHR judgment against Germany by implication also creates some friction between the two courts' interpretations of the right(s) at issue. The FCC's comparatively strong and influential position, both domestically and internationally,[17] and past evidence concerning its history with the Court of Justice of the European Union that shows that it does not shy away from conflict with international courts in the case of disagreements, make the FCC an important interlocutor when it comes to implementing ECtHR judgments and incorporating its jurisprudence into domestic law.

The primary responsibility for the execution of ECtHR judgments, however, rests with the government, and in particular the Ministry of Justice, which will assist (and prod) other governmental actors when their action is needed to achieve compliance and will also submit draft bills to parliament if legislation needs to be changed. Although the Bundestag also has a Human Rights Committee, such remedial bills have in the past more often been taken care of by the Legal Affairs Committee.[18] Notably, the ECtHR's institutional legitimacy and its right to issue judgments that require adjustments of national law and policy are not as such contentious or fundamentally questioned, and no widespread "hostile attitude" has so far developed against the Court among governmental institutions, political parties, or the public as a result of disliked jurisprudence.[19] This is in marked contrast to the United Kingdom's repeatedly strained relationship with the Court and has been linked in particular to the high repute in which the FCC and its practice of human rights adjudication are held domestically.[20]

The Universe of Judgments Involving Germany

Until the end of 2015, the Court had issued 267 merits, striking-out, or inadmissibility judgments involving Germany (see Table 5). Of these, 178 had found at least one violation of the Convention, while 78 had found none, and 11 had been declared inadmissible or struck out of the Court's list (with 6 of these requiring some form of execution), resulting in a total of 184 compliance-relevant judgments. As of March 10, 2017, 169 (91.8 percent) of these had been complied with, while 15 (8.2 percent) still awaited a final resolution by the Committee of Ministers (the two oldest of these, dating from April 2010, however, were closed soon thereafter, on April 19, 2017).

Table 6 shows the distribution of the 219 distinct violations found in the 178 merits judgments against Germany across articles and principal issue areas. The most frequently infringed provision accounting for more than half of all violations is Article 6 ECHR, especially with respect to its reasonable time requirement for criminal and civil proceedings, followed by Article 5 ECHR, which comprises several arrest- and detention-related rights, with nearly half of the violations involving Germany's preventive detention regime; the latter also gave rise to all nine violations of the principle of *nulla poena sine lege*, which is enshrined in Article 7 ECHR. In third place are violations of the right to an effective domestic remedy under Article 13 ECHR,

Table 5. Judgments Involving Germany and Their Compliance Status as of March 10, 2017

Year	Number of Judgments	At Least One Violation	No Violation	Struck Out/ Inadmissible	Executed	Pending
1968	1	—	1	—	—	—
1978	3	2	1	—	2	—
1981	1	—	1	—	—	—
1982	1	1	—	—	1	—
1983	2	1	1	—	1	—
1984	1	1	—	—	1	—
1985	1	1	—	—	1	—
1986	3	1	2	—	1	—
1987	3	—	3	—	—	—
1988	1	—	1	—	—	—
1989	2	1	1	—	1	—
1991	1	—	1	—	—	—
1992	4	2	2	—	2	—
1993	1	—	1	—	—	—
1994	2	1	1	—	1	—
1995	1	1	—	—	1	—
1996	1	—	1	—	—	—
1997	3	3	—	—	3	—
1999	3	—	2	1	—	—
2000	3	2	1	—	2	—
2001	15	11	3	1	12	—
2002	9	6	2	1	6	—
2003	12	10	1	1	11	—
2004	5	5	—	—	5	—
2005	14	10	3	1	10	—
2006	10	6	2	2	8	—
2007	11	6	4	1	7	—
2008	9	6	2	1	7	—
2009	21	18	3	—	18	—

(*continued*)

Table 5. Judgments Involving Germany and Their Compliance Status as
of March 10, 2017 (*Continued*)

Year	Number of Judgments	At Least One Violation	No Violation	Struck Out/ Inadmissible	Executed	Pending
2010	35	29	6	—	27	2
2011	40	31	8	1	30	1
2012	21	11	9	1	8	3
2013	6	3	3	—	2	1
2014	11	3	8	—	1	2
2015	10	6	4	—	1	5
Total	**267**	**178**	**78**	**11**	**170**	**14**

Source: Extracted from author's own compliance data set.

with all save one of these infringements concerning the lack, in the past, of an
effective remedy to speed up excessively long judicial proceedings. Another
type of violation that has occurred with some frequency concerns the protection of family life, primarily under Article 8 ECHR, as a result of state interference in parent-child relationships, including the discriminatory denial of
access to their children to fathers based on marital status (under Article 14
ECHR) and more recently on the basis of biological versus legal fatherhood.
There have been no violations of Article 2 ECHR (right to life), and violations
of Article 3 ECHR have been rare, with only three findings of degrading or
inhuman treatment (i.e., unacceptable treatment that does not reach a level of
intensity to qualify as torture).

Table 6. Violations Found in 178 Merits Judgments against Germany (through 2015)

Type of Violation	Count	Percent (rounded)
Inhuman or Degrading Treatment (Article 3)	**3**	**1.4**
Right to Liberty and Security of the Person (Article 5)	**27**	**12.3**
thereof: unlawful instances of preventive detention	13	
other unlawful detentions	4	
length of detention on remand	4	
fairness and/or excessive length of habeas corpus proceedings	6	
Right to Fair Proceedings Within Reasonable Time (Article 6)	**116**	**53**
thereof: excessive length of proceedings	97	
unfair proceedings	12	
lack of access to a court	4	
infringement of presumption of innocence	3	
No Punishment Without Law (Article 7)	**9**	**4.1**
Right to Respect for Private and Family Life (Article 8)	**19**	**8.7**
thereof: parental rights issues (including access to children)	10	
respect for private life and privacy	7	
expulsion and exclusion of aliens	2	
Freedom of Expression and of the Press (Article 10)	**8**	**3.7**
Right to an Effective Remedy (Article 13)	**24**	**11**
thereof: absence of effective remedy against excessively long proceedings	23	
Freedom from Discrimination (Article 14)	**9**	**4.1**
thereof: discrimination against unmarried fathers regarding access to children	4	
Other Violations (Right of Assembly, Protection of Property)	**4**	**1.8**
Total	**219**	**100**

Source: Author's own compliance data set; HUDOC.

CHAPTER 9

Compliance with Just Satisfaction Awards and Individual Measures

As in Part I, I will look separately at the different types of measures that may have to be adopted to comply with a judgment, focusing in this chapter on compliance with the obligation to pay just satisfaction as awarded by the Court and to take individual measures in the applicant's case when this is the principal remedial measure required.

Just Satisfaction

With respect to all merits judgments as well as in the six compliance-relevant striking-out judgments in which just satisfaction had been awarded by the Court or pledged by the government,[1] Germany fulfilled its financial obligation and disbursed the relevant funds within the three-month time limit or with small delay.[2] This behavior meets expectations. In most cases (save when awards are linked to politically highly contentious conflicts as in the judgments against Turkey concerning Northern Cyprus), financial compensation is usually a judgment's least costly consequence,[3] especially for comparatively wealthy states such as Germany,[4] and does not, by itself, involve the sovereignty costs of having to make substantive changes to administrative or judicial decisions, or to general law and policy, which often tend to be more contentious politically.

As in the case of the UK, in a number of instances, the Convention violation found was of such a nature, as appraised at the time of the judgment's execution, that the payment of just satisfaction was deemed sufficient to achieve compliance. Such an appraisal can change in light of subsequent information—for example, as provided by a continuing influx of similarly situated clone cases—that indicates that individual violations are part of a larger structural or systemic shortcoming, resulting in the need to adopt general measures as well. This was the case with judgments finding length of proceedings violations against Germany, in which supervision of a first set of judgments was closed solely upon payment of compensation, but the later ones, because similar cases kept coming to the Court, required the adoption of additional general measures, partly due to their consideration not only under Article 6 (1) ECHR, but also in light of Article 13 ECHR. It is worthwhile pointing out that what is seen as constituting a series of isolated incidents and what is seen as qualifying as a systemic defect requiring general measures is itself a matter of judgment, without there being an "objective" standard to provide a strict dividing line between the two.[5] The existence of structural deficiencies may be evident when there are hundreds or thousands of similar applications in close succession, but it is less so when the number is one or two dozen over many years, as in the German context.

And so until the mid-2000s, neither the Court nor the Committee had formally qualified the length of German civil or criminal proceedings as a systemic problem.[6] Regarding the special case of the length of constitutional complaints, the Committee of Ministers was seemingly convinced by German arguments that the problems with excessively long proceedings before the Federal Constitutional Court related to a post-reunification wave of complaints that had begun to abate again by the mid-1990s, and that support staff had been increased in order to speed up proceedings.[7] As a result, all judgments finding length-of-proceedings violations that did not appear to reveal any structural shortcomings at the time (twelve),[8] or with respect to which general measures adopted in response to the earlier judgments concerning the FCC (ten)[9] or between the complaint and the ECtHR's judgment (one)[10] had been considered sufficient, were closed on the basis of the payment of just satisfaction, if awarded,[11] resulting in full compliance.[12] Nine further judgments that concerned isolated past violations without ongoing effects likewise required only just satisfaction to remedy them. Five of these involved the excessive length or unlawfulness of past detentions,[13] two cases concerned violations of respect for the applicants' private lives due to disproportional search and seizure warrants,[14] one judgment addressed unfair detention review proceedings,[15] and the last one concerned the unfairness of civil proceedings for the reimbursement of male-to-female transgender medical treatment.[16]

Individual Measures

When a Convention violation has continuing effects for the applicant, the obligation to provide reparation necessitates remedial measures that eliminate such lingering effects of the violation, to the extent that such measures are available under domestic law. Judgments where compliance requires individual, but not general, measures, include those in which it is not a law, policy, or general practice as such that is not in conformity with the Convention but only its concrete application in the complainant's case. The violation often results from the failure, in the Court's view, to balance appropriately the interests of the individual with those of the broader community in circumstances that would, however, in principle allow for a different balancing. Except for one case, where the nature of the violation did not yield a reasonable spectrum of choices,[17] most judgments in which individual measures were required for compliance provided for a certain, if small, latitude in choosing the means to comply with them.

Expulsion and Indefinite Exclusion

The government's responses to the two judgments in *Yilmaz* (2003) and *Keles* (2005), concerning violations of the right to respect for two foreign nationals' private life (which is protected under Article 8 ECHR) due to their expulsion and the indefinite exclusion orders imposed on them subsequent to their criminal convictions, reveal what may be considered a weakly restrictive approach to compliance. In the ECtHR's view, the permanent exclusions were disproportionate in light of the applicants' personal situations, given that they had family relations in Germany (including children) and had possessed residence permits prior to their expulsion.[18] The broadest response would have been to revoke the relevant orders and allow the applicants to remain in Germany so that they could continue their family lives there. However, since the Court did not impugn the expulsion orders as such, but only the indefinite duration of the exclusion, the competent authorities acted fully in conformity with the judgment's *ratio decidendi* when they transformed the indefinite exclusion orders into time-limited orders of about seven years' length in each case.[19] While the preference of excluding the two applicants from German territory thus continued to guide the decisions after the ECtHR's judgment, it is difficult to say without systematic comparison whether the length of seven years was particularly long or not in light of the relevant offenses. Suffice it to note for present purposes that whatever the precise principles that guided these decisions, the authorities appreciated the remaining range of options below the "indefiniteness" threshold by imposing exclusion orders of significant length.

Parent-Child Relations

The execution of three judgments issued up to 2010 that concern parental guardianship rights and a father's access to his child,[20] which are protected under the right to family life (Article 8 ECHR), reveal both the difficulty of assessing what remedial measures are called for in a given case as well as problems that result from the need to have several interested parties cooperate in remedying the situation. The balancing of interests in these areas is particularly difficult because it is not only the applicants' rights but also the interests of the children that need to be taken into account.

The first judgment in this set, *Kutzner* (2002), can be considered fully complied with. The case concerned the 1997 revocation of the applicants' parental authority over their two daughters, aged four and six at the time, and the latter's subsequent placement in separate and unidentified foster homes without any access to their biological parents for the first six months, which had been justified by the parents' alleged lack of sufficient intellectual capacity for child-rearing.[21] The Court found that the gravity of this decision was disproportionate in relation to the legitimate aim of assuring the children's upbringing in a sufficiently adequate environment, not least in light of contradictory expert reports and the fact that there were no indications whatsoever of any neglect or ill-treatment.[22] In executing the judgment domestically, the local youth office brought together the various stakeholders in the case, and the competent court subsequently undertook a fresh examination of the case with the aid of two new expert psychologists. It eventually revoked its earlier order denying custody and guardianship, so that the children could be reunited with their parents in late 2003.[23]

Executing the judgment thus took almost two years, resulting in a separation of over six years, which is clearly regrettable in such a time-sensitive issue area as parent-child relations. Fully restoring parental authority after it had previously been fully revoked may appear as a broader form of compliance than necessary. After all, the ECtHR had particularly taken issue with the fact that the domestic authorities had turned immediately to "by far the most extreme measure, namely separating the children from their parents," rather than considering less drastic alternatives first.[24] But these less drastic measures that the Court—and indeed German law[25]—envisaged, such as educational support or the partial transfer of guardianship rights, are premised on the children living with their parents. So anything short of returning the two children to their parents would likely have fallen short of minimum compliance.[26] What is notable is that human rights NGOs favoring the applicants' side were also involved in the execution process,[27] but their presence and any potential pressure cannot explain the outcome of the execution process because experts from at least two NGOs—the German Association for the Protection of Children and the Association for the Protection of the Rights of the Child[28]—had already taken the applicants' side in the early stage of the original proceedings but had obviously failed to prevent the withdrawal of parental authority, which then led to the proceedings in Strasbourg.

The second judgment in this group, *Haase* (2004), addressed a violation of the proportionality principle in the context of the withdrawal of parental rights over seven children that had been ordered, without hearing either the parents or the children, on a sole expert's opinion that recommended strict separation of the parents and their children due to suspicions of neglect and maltreatment. In its decision, the Court did not address the justifiability of the separation as such, only the decision-making process and its implementation.[29] The Committee of Ministers, for its part, was satisfied with the fact that the parents' access restrictions to their children had subsequently been progressively lifted, while the issue of the restoration of parental rights and custody (which was eventually revoked for all children except the youngest[30]) was being addressed in separate applications pending before the FCC and the ECtHR, and it thus decided to close its supervision of the case in 2005.[31] Both the FCC (in 2005) and the ECtHR (in 2008) eventually rejected the new applications as manifestly ill-founded, arguing that the approaches of the relevant authorities complied with the requirements of Article 8 ECHR in working toward a possible reunion of the family while paying full attention to the best interests of the children and granting the parents sufficient involvement in the decision-making process.[32]

The *Haase* case shows the difficulty in assessing both the facts of the case as well as the sufficiency of the measures adopted in response to a judgment. While the Court itself accepted the subsequent domestic proceedings as Convention compliant, the issue of state intervention in parent-child matters has remained contentious domestically. On the one hand, there have been a number of prominent cases in the media where child neglect and maltreatment have resulted in the death of young children and in which the public authorities appeared inattentive or negligent.[33] On the other hand, a large number of parents have complained about allegedly capricious youth welfare offices and psychological experts who are said to opt overeagerly for separation of children from their parents,[34] and, inter alia, petitioned the European Parliament regarding this matter.[35] It is no easy task balancing parental rights and the rights of children to special protection, and it is even more difficult to assess from an outsider's perspective the appropriateness of the measures adopted in individual cases.

As regards the *Haase* judgment, it appears reasonable to conclude that in light of the circumstances of the case, the national authorities, by improving procedural safeguards and enabling contact with the children, acted sufficiently in conformity with the Court's judgment. The Court's decision, after all, had criticized the domestic authorities' approach and not their substantive rationale for intervening as such. At the same time, to the extent that one accepts that at least a certain share of the claims by other parents in childcare cases are meritorious, one might conclude instead that reliance on the dissemination of judgments and the direct applicability of the Convention to guarantee widespread compliance with the Convention in this issue area may not be sufficient, complicated as it already is by the decentralized organization of child welfare services and the fact-driven appraisal and decision-making in individual cases. Suffice it to note here that the Court has occasionally had to deal with additional complaints against Germany concerning parent-child relations.[36]

One judgment rendered slightly before the one in *Haase* concerns the *Görgülü* case.[37] The execution of this judgment should have been rather straightforward, but it presented unexpected difficulties that kept it on the Committee's agenda for four and a half years.[38] The applicant, a Turkish citizen residing in Germany, had sought to obtain access rights to, and custody over, his biological son, who was born out of wedlock and whom the mother, who had no interest in caring for the child, had given up for adoption right after birth in 1999 without the father's knowledge or consent, despite earlier assurances to allow custody to be transferred to him.[39] In 2001, a decision by the Naumburg Higher Regional Court denied the applicant's requests and green-lighted the adoption proceedings initiated by the son's foster parents. Before the ECtHR, Mr. Görgülü charged that the decision of putting the foster parents' rights above his own as the biological father violated his right to family life under Article 8 ECHR. The Court, in light of the fact that the father was indisputably willing and able to care for his son, agreed, arguing that the domestic court had exceeded its margin of appreciation in failing to consider seriously all available means for reuniting father and son, even in light of the objective to minimize stress for the son.[40] As to execution, the Court took the unusual step of prescribing that "[i]n the case at hand this means making it possible for the applicant to at least have access to his child."[41]

The subsequent implementation efforts reveal the difficulties of abiding by an adverse judgment when key private and public actors involved in relevant decision-making obstruct such efforts. Although in March 2004 the court of first instance transferred custody to the applicant subsequent to the ECtHR's judgment and granted visitation rights pending a final custody decision, on appeal the Naumburg Higher Regional Court again quashed the decision, arguing that the ECtHR's judgments had no binding effect domestically. Even after a decision by the Federal Constitutional Court in October 2004 affirming that domestic judges had to take into account the judgments of the ECtHR,[42] the same judges at the Naumburg Higher Regional Court again quashed a lower court order providing for access rights in December 2004, prompting the FCC to quash that decision in turn and to reinstate the order of the court of first instance.[43] The apparently intentional disregard of the ECtHR and FCC jurisprudence by the Naumburg appeals judges, who had considered the ECtHR judgment "fraught with ideology,"[44] ultimately resulted in sharply worded criticism by the FCC[45] as well as criminal charges of "perversion of justice" against two judges at the Naumburg court.[46] After the removal of this particular judicial obstacle, in February 2005, for the first time in three years, Mr. Görgülü had contact with his child, but several subsequent visits over the next years again failed, mostly due to repeated obstruction by the foster parents as well as the youth welfare office. Several additional judicial proceedings intervened concerning both the modalities of access and the issue of custody.[47] Only in February 2008 did the father receive custody on a provisional basis, with the son living with him since then. In August 2008, Mr. Görgülü received permanent custody.[48]

While it is true, as then minister of justice Brigitte Zypries noted at the time, that domestic decisions that clearly run counter to the ECtHR's judgment have always eventually been rectified,[49] such long delays regarding time-sensitive family relationships are obviously unfortunate and undesirable. The case also highlights the difficulty that federalist systems can encounter in achieving compliance with an international obligation when state and local authorities that have subject-matter jurisdiction in the relevant area fail to live up to that obligation as a result of different political, legal, or personal views and preferences, even in an essentially (on the surface) apolitical case. While one could surmise that the ethnicity of the father may have played a role, there is no incontrovertible evidence to prove that it did. In any event, the preferences on the part of the state-level Naumburg Court of Appeals were apparently strong enough for it to try to defy even the Federal Constitutional Court, a court in a clearly defined hierarchically superior position. Although the foster parents' repeated boycotts of scheduled visits—hoping for some time to adopt the child, they had an interest of their own to obstruct access between the natural father and the son—cannot be attributed to the state as such, it appears that the state-appointed ex officio guardian did not exert sufficient pressure on the latter to make sure that scheduled meetings between father and son would actually take place.[50] In light of the fact that as early as three months after the child's birth, both Mr. Görgülü's paternity as well as his willingness to take care of his son had been established,[51] the subsequent course of events cannot but dissatisfy disinterested observers: "Nine years, six courts, more than fifty decisions, several (sometimes parallel) proceedings and more than one hundred participants (from the youth office to the ECtHR) are disproportionate to obtain [what the German constitution in Article 6 (2) GG considers] a 'natural right' [of parental care and upbringing] in the case of a single child."[52]

One particular decision—indeed the aspect that has given rise to most commentary and debate in the academic literature[53]—is the Federal Constitutional Court's seminal 2004 judgment in this case, in which it addressed the domestic effect of the Convention and of the Court's judgments. The question of whether the domestic judiciary as one of the three branches of government is bound by the ECtHR's judgments had previously not been answered uniformly by the courts.[54] The FCC decided the issue in favor of what could be called "conditional bindingness" of ECtHR judgments: German public authorities, including the courts, are under an obligation to 'take into account' the relevant decisions of the Strasbourg court in the case at hand and have to abide by it to the extent possible, within the boundaries of 'a methodologically justifiable interpretation of the law.'[55] At the same time, while courts need to have visibly dealt with any relevant ECtHR judgment, they retain some discretion to deviate from strict adherence and execution in light of applicable domestic law:

In taking into account decisions of the ECHR, the state bodies must include the effects on the national legal system in their application of the law. This applies in particular with regard to a partial system of domestic law whose legal consequences are balanced and that is intended to achieve an equilibrium between differing fundamental rights.

[. . .] The decisions of the ECHR may encounter national partial systems of law shaped by a complex system of case-law. In the German legal system, this may happen in particular in family law and the law concerning aliens, and also in the law on the protection of personality [. . .], in which conflicting fundamental rights are balanced by the creation of groups of cases and graduated legal consequences. It is the task of the domestic courts to integrate a decision of the ECHR into the relevant partial legal area of the national legal system, because it cannot be the desired result of the international-law basis nor express the will of the ECHR for the ECHR through its decisions itself to undertake directly any necessary adjustments within a domestic partial legal system.[56]

The FCC decision thus explicitly preserves a degree of discretion on the part of the domestic judiciary. While defensible on normative grounds, not least because of the impact such execution may have on parties not involved in the proceedings before the ECtHR,[57] this position can also be understood as a rational-strategic move, clothed in the language of normative balancing of two bodies of law, that seeks to preserve some institutional decision-making freedom while at the same time affirming a commitment to the Convention. The FCC's decision subsequently gave rise to some back-and-forth between the judges in Karlsruhe and Strasbourg about who should have the final say in human rights disputes.[58]

The *Görgülü* case, then, is significant for two reasons. First, it illustrates that compliance with a judgment by the Court may be delayed and impeded when substate actors—both private and public—whose cooperation is required to achieve execution refuse to abide by the Court's judgment due to their own apparent interests and preferences in the case. Second, while the case, based on its facts, appeared to be limited to the applicant's individual circumstance, the intransigence especially on the part of the local judicial authorities prompted the FCC to render a landmark judgment that spelled out for the first time the precise role of the ECtHR's judgments within domestic law, albeit with the final say reserved for domestic courts and thus, ultimately, the FCC itself. It is in this way that judgments in individual cases may ultimately have consequences not only for the applicant and in other similarly situated cases in the same issue area, but also for many others due to the doctrinal positions that they articulate.

Political Extremists in the Civil Service

The *Vogt* judgment,[59] by contrast, is of greater political salience. The Court was presented with the following question: did the dismissal of a teacher due to her membership in the Communist Party under a domestic policy that viewed membership in parties on the far right and left as incompatible with the constitutional loyalty demanded from civil servants violate the freedom of expression under Article 10 ECHR and/or the freedom of association under Article 11 ECHR? By the narrowest of margins—ten votes against nine—the Court found violations of both provisions, arguing that the government failed to show "convincingly that it was necessary in a democratic society to dismiss [the applicant]. Even allowing for a certain margin of appreciation, the conclusion must be that to dismiss Ms. Vogt by way of disciplinary sanction from her post as secondary-school teacher was disproportionate to the legitimate aim pursued."[60] The finding came somewhat as a surprise, given that the Court had been sympathetic to the very same German policy in two previous judgments where it had found for the government.[61] In *Vogt*, it sought to differentiate the factual situations in these cases as one of access to the civil service (*Glasenapp* and *Kosiek*) versus dismissal from it (*Vogt*), with stricter standards applying to the latter.[62]

The *Vogt* judgment concerned a firmly established, but no less strongly contested, domestic policy. Federal law prescribes that civil servants have to "satisfy the authorities that they will at all times uphold the free democratic constitutional system within the meaning of the Basic Law" and "by their entire conduct bear witness to the free democratic constitutional system within the meaning of the Basic Law and act to uphold it."[63] In 1972, the chancellor and the prime ministers of the *Länder* jointly adopted the "Decree on Employment of Extremists in the Civil Service" (the so-called *Radikalenerlass*), which provided, inter alia, that "civil servants' membership of parties or organizations that oppose the constitutional system—and any support given to such parties or organizations—shall . . . as a general rule lead to a conflict of loyalty."[64] In 1975, the FCC upheld this restriction for civil service membership as constitutional.[65] Such a broad restriction on civil service membership across all areas of activity was a remarkable oddity among Western democracies, even during the Cold War,[66] and in 1986, a Commission of Inquiry of the International Labour Organization found that the *Radikalenerlass* violated ILO standards against employment discrimination and called upon Germany to reexamine both the policy as well as its application to individual cases.[67] Germany, however, refused, pointing, inter alia, to the nonbinding nature of the Commission's findings and recommendations.[68]

What consequences, by contrast, were to be drawn from the Court's legally binding judgment? Formally, by the early 1990s, the *Radikalenerlass* had been repealed in all of the *Länder*,[69] that is, prior to the ECtHR's judgment, but by that time, critics report that more than 13,000 concrete proceedings had been conducted under the policy, at the end of which 1,250 persons had been denied, and 265 removed from, civil service jobs because of membership in mostly left-wing parties, but sometimes also in ostensibly innocuous organizations such as Amnesty International.[70] In its response to the judgment, the German government pursued a friendly settlement with the applicant as to the provision of reparation in her individual case; by the judgment of September 2, 1996, the Court accepted the substance of the friendly settlement as appropriate.[71] Formally, this response in the individual case was sufficient to comply with the judgment and to close its supervision.[72]

At the same time, Germany's response also qualifies as an instance of restrictive implementation that took advantage of the fact that ECtHR judgments are formally binding only in the decided case. Despite this, Germany could have taken the *Vogt* judgment as (political) motivation to review the prior practice in its entirety and to provide for a legal basis to have previous professional bans reassessed before domestic courts, but the government refused to accept such implications.[73] This refusal supports the argument that the path taken reflects rational calculation in line with prevailing political preferences. Indeed, on four subsequent occasions (in 1996, 2002, 2007, and 2012), the successive Kohl, Schröder, and Merkel governments rejected demands coming from the left-wing Partei des Demokratischen Sozialismus (PDS) and its successor party, Die Linke, to draw any broader implications from the judgment.[74] In the absence of a clear legal provision in disciplinary codes allowing for the reopening of domestic proceedings following the *Vogt* judgment, the courts rejected all such applications from persons who had suffered removal from the civil service because their cases failed to reveal, as required, any new facts (which the ECtHR judgment—in somebody's else's case, to boot—did not formally constitute) to warrant reopening.[75] Although fewer civil service job denials for reason of presumably radical political convictions occur today, the issue continues to rouse public opinion in the occasional case that does arise.[76]

In any event, the decision to stay narrowly within the obligation assumed under the Convention and to limit the consequences of the *Vogt* judgment to the decided case, rather than interpreting the judgment in a broader spirit and to take it as a stimulus to review and redress past practices in general, was legally sufficient.[77] It was arguably also a rational choice from the viewpoint of governmental decision-makers. This is particularly so given the fact that the major parties—the Social Democrats (SPD) and the Christian Democratic and Social Unions (CDU and CSU), at least one of which has always formed part of government since the creation of the Federal Republic—had authored and supported the *Radikalenerlass*.[78] Executing the judgment broadly might have been taken as implying that the policy pursued through the *Radikalenerlass*—referred to by the newsweekly *Die Zeit* as "disastrous McCarthyism"[79]—had been, at least in part, illegitimate in retrospect, but such execution would also have reduced future discretion in regulating access to the civil service, a weakening of control that cannot be assumed to be in the government's interest. Importantly, the issue is not whether governments should be able to regulate access to civil service posts—they clearly should—but that any restrictions, especially when involving the political dispositions of applicants or officeholders, need to observe a sense of proportion.[80]

Reopening of Domestic Proceedings

In cases where the Convention violation results from a final domestic judgment that might have turned out differently absent the violation, the only way to provide the applicant with *restitutio in integrum* would require quashing the faulty decision and reopening the case. While reopening of proceedings is an individual measure, its availability depends on the existence of appropriate legislation that allows for it. As the Convention's *travaux préparatoires* with respect to Article 41 ECHR (Article 50 ECHR [1950]) make clear, however, the version ultimately adopted explicitly reflected the preference of those states that rejected a direct cassatory effect of the ECtHR's judgments in favor of the value of legal certainty represented by the finality of domestic judicial decisions. Substantive justice in the individual case would thus require separate national regulations on the reopening of proceedings following an adverse ECtHR judgment. While Germany's procedural codes recognized several valid reasons for the reopening of proceedings, until the law was amended in 1998 ECtHR judgments were not among them.

As a consequence, two judgments rendered in the 1980s must be considered formally complied with, given that that the applicants received just satisfaction, but at the expense of substantive individual justice because a reopening of proceedings was legally not possible. In *Pakelli*,[81] the issue that gave rise to a violation of the right to free legal assistance protected under Article 6 (3) lit. c ECHR centered on a decision by the Federal Court of Justice (FCJ) not to appoint a defense counsel in hearings related to revision proceedings in a criminal case. In *Barthold*,[82] the Court found a violation of the applicant's freedom of expression (Article 10 ECHR) due to prohibitory injunctions issued by German courts as part of unfair competition proceedings that prevented Barthold, a veterinary surgeon by profession, from voicing his concerns as to the need of the creation of an emergency veterinary service. In rejecting Pakelli's constitutional complaint in 1985, the Federal Constitutional Court upheld the position that there was no legal requirement under either the Basic Law or the Convention to provide for the reopening of domestic proceedings in response to an adverse ECtHR judgment.[83] The domestic judgments in these two cases thus remained formally in place.

Although there had been broad support for the introduction of such a reopening ground among academic commentators for some time,[84] its actual introduction in 1998 may have come somewhat as a surprise, given that there had been no subsequent cases against Germany before the ECtHR that had touched on this issue.[85] A first effort in 1993 by members of the then-opposition Social Democrats had failed to yield any legislative changes,[86] but an essentially identical proposal tabled in 1996 turned out to be more successful.[87] Initially, the proposal had been broader and also sought to make it easier for victims of Third Reich injustice to have judgments against them quashed.[88] While the category of the "obvious mistake in the application of the law" (*offensichtlicher Rechtsfehler*) introduced for this purpose met with criticism in parliamentary debate, the proposed reopening of criminal proceedings in response to ECtHR judgments was broadly welcomed.[89] The proposal declared such a step to be necessary in order to strengthen the "idea of unalienable human rights," out of "respect for international treaties and international judicial bodies."[90] Parliament's legal committee, with the votes of the governing coalition, eventually scrapped all proposed changes, except the ECtHR reopening provision and altered it from being mandatory to being conditional.[91] Reopening proceedings would be permissible only to the extent that the outcome of the final domestic judgment depended on the aspect found to have violated the Convention.[92] Based on this version, the *Code of Criminal Procedure* was amended accordingly.[93]

Since the addition of the provision, only one judgment has fallen squarely within its ambit. In the case of *P.S.*, the Court found a violation the fairness of proceedings (Article 6 (1) ECHR) in conjunction with a criminal defendant's right to examine, or have examined, witnesses against him (Article 6 (3) lit. d ECHR).[94] Although by now available, the applicant apparently chose not to avail himself of the option to lodge a request for reopening.[95] Indirectly, the provision also affected another case. In *Stambuk*,[96] the Court had found a violation of the applicant's freedom of expression (Article 10 ECHR) due to the imposition of disciplinary punishment under state-level Rules of Professional Conduct of the Medical Practitioners' Council for having featured in a press article on his work, which was in breach of the Council's non-advertisement regulations. Although not a criminal offense, the relevant state law had been amended as of February 2003 to allow for the reopening of disciplinary proceedings, referencing as valid reasons those listed in section 359 of the German *Code of Criminal Procedure*.[97] (Whether the applicant actually requested reopening of his case is not known.)

The addition of a new ground for reopening criminal proceedings came shortly before the Committee of Ministers called upon all Convention parties to consider adopting in their domestic codes of procedure provisions allowing for the reopening of proceedings following an adverse judgment by the Court.[98] While many states followed suit, reopening, at least initially, was often limited to criminal proceedings.[99] In 2006, Germany also provided for the reopening of civil proceedings in light of adverse ECtHR judgments by inserting an identically worded ground into the code of civil procedure.[100] The principal justification for this change was the recognition that in certain circumstances, reopening of civil proceedings would be the only way to provide for full restitution and that Germany would thus join those states which allowed for the fullest effect to be given to ECtHR judgments.[101] The applicants in the two cases that could have benefitted from this new provision—those in *Storck*[102] and *Schüth*,[103] decided in 2005 and 2010, respectively—could not rely on it, however, because it did not apply retroactively to cases that had become res judicata domestically before the provision's entry into force on December 31, 2006.[104] An attempt to construct a general right to reopening in civil matters prior to that date by one of the applicants was eventually rejected by the FCC in 2013,[105] and so just satisfaction constituted the principal remedy in both cases.[106]

The introduction of new reopening grounds into the German codes of criminal and civil procedure is notable for three reasons. First, both occurred without having been directly prompted by an adverse judgment. Second, the reopening in response to an adverse, outcome-relevant decision by the ECtHR in civil proceedings, even when implying statutory law, goes beyond what has been granted to the judgments of the Federal Constitutional Court when it strikes down domestic legislation as incompatible with the Basic Law. In such cases, only criminal proceedings can be reopened, but not civil ones, although the execution of decisions based upon the voided law becomes barred.[107] Third, as its name already indicates, the Committee of Ministers' recommendation did not create a legal obligation for Convention parties, and no material repercussions follow from its nonimplementation. In other words, states remained free to decide against broadening their reopening provisions. If governments nonetheless take the long-resisted step and weaken the finality of domestic judgments by including new reopening grounds in the absence of any material or other meaningful repercussions, then the best explanation appears to be that a new normative preference has come to prevail that views the finality of judgments as less important within the domestic legal system than the achievement of procedural and substantive justice in the individual case. At the same time, precisely because providing for reopening was not a legal requirement, Germany saw it expressly as within its margin of appreciation to impose temporal restrictions on the reopening of civil proceedings with a view to protecting the legitimate expectations of other parties in disputes concluded prior to December 31, 2006.[108]

Threatened Maltreatment

In *Gäfgen*, the applicant, while in police custody because he was suspected of having abducted a child still believed to be alive, was threatened by a police officer upon order of the Frankfurt am Main deputy chief of police, with "considerable pain at the hands of a person specially trained for such purposes if he did not disclose the child's whereabouts."[109] Faced with this threat, Gäfgen caved in and led the police to the boy's location, where, however, he was found dead (it subsequently transpired that Gäfgen had killed the boy shortly after kidnapping him). The Court's Grand Chamber, reversing an earlier decision by a seven-judge chamber,[110] found that the threat of physical pain, while staying below the intensity required for a finding of torture, amounted to inhuman treatment as prohibited by Article 3 ECHR. Importantly, although the two principal police officers involved had subsequently been prosecuted domestically for coercion and incitement to coercion, the ECtHR considered their sentences—(suspended) payment of fines of €60 for 60 days and €90 for 120 days, respectively—"manifestly disproportionate to a breach of one of the core rights of the Convention"[111] and thus incapable of either exerting a deterrent effect or providing sufficient redress to the applicant. As a result, Gäfgen could still claim to be a victim of a violation of Article 3 for the purpose of proceedings before the Court.

Since the causes of the violation were unique to the case, no general measures beyond publication and dissemination of the judgment appeared necessary. In terms of individual measures, closure of the case hinged on the outcome of Gäfgen's domestic compensation action for the harm suffered as a result of the treatment (he had also been awarded just satisfaction for cost and expenses, which had been promptly paid). A court of first instance had awarded Gäfgen €3,000 in August 2011 (instead of the €10,000 claimed by him), and an appeals court upheld the award in October 2012.[112] The state of Hesse then wired the amount to the first instance court, but because Gäfgen was in a state of private insolvency at the time, the question arose whether the payment could be paid out to him personally or would have to go to the insolvency administrator. The question was decided in September 2013 in favor of the first alternative, and payment was made on December 30, 2013,[113] ending supervision of the case.[114] While it had given rise to public debate about the permissibility of physical pressure in "ticking-bomb" scenarios, both the government and parliament sided with the ECtHR by affirming the unacceptability of the use of torture under any circumstance.[115]

Challenging Transfer Proceedings

In two related cases, *Smith* and *Buijen*, which were decided in 2010—and closed only in April 2017, thus making them the last ones to be closed in the data set of judgments against Germany under consideration here[116]—the applicants had confessed to charges of trafficking in narcotic substances and had waived their right to appeal upon the assurance of the public prosecutor in charge of their cases that they would subsequently be transferred to their country of nationality, the Netherlands, under Article 11 of the Convention on the Transfer of Sentenced Persons,[117] a provision that allows for the conversion of a sentence in accordance with the law of the receiving state. The head of public prosecution, however, later refused to endorse the transfer under Article 11, permitting it only under Article 10 of the Transfer Convention, which requires the receiving state to execute the terms of a sentence as specified by the sentencing state (allegedly, the prosecutor who had made the promise had been unaware of the difference between the two articles). Despite Germany's assertions to the contrary, the Court found that it had not been shown that an effective remedy to challenge the decision not to initiate transfer proceedings as promised existed in domestic law, resulting in a violation of Article 6 (1) ECHR due to the lack of access to a court that could review the applicants' specific complaints.[118]

Already back in 2003, one of the applicants had agreed to being transferred to the Netherlands under the Article 10 procedure and had been released in 2007 after having served two-thirds of his sentence;[119] since these developments had occurred prior to the judgment, this extinguished the need for additional individual measures, other than the payment of just satisfaction. The other applicant, by contrast, had absconded. In September 2012, ten years after the domestic judgment in his case, statutory limitations on executing his sentence kicked in and the search for him was ended.[120] The continuing supervision of the case for almost another five years had principally to do with the question of whether Germany also needed to adopt general measures to remedy the alleged absence of an effective remedy. Germany continued to reiterate its position already articulated before the Court that German law does in fact provide for the possibility to challenge decisions of judicial authorities in transfer proceedings,[121] so that legislative action was not necessary. One can only guess that the Committee kept the case pending to wait for evidence that the claimed domestic remedy had in fact been successfully relied upon to challenge relevant decisions under the Transfer Convention. While Germany's final action report lacks such evidence, it provides excerpts from the relevant statute and points out that no similar applications have reached the ECtHR since the present cases.[122] In the end, this absence appears to have been deemed sufficient by the Committee to end supervision of these two judgments.

While there have been a number of problems impeding smooth compliance with several judgments, just satisfaction awards have been paid and eventually satisfactory individual measures have been adopted in all of them, if on minimalist terms and conditioned by narrow formalist reasoning. Chapter 10 shows that carefully attuning remedies to the judicial signal sent by the ECtHR is also observable with respect to the adoption by Germany of general measures.

CHAPTER 10

Compliance with General Measures

Judgments that find a Convention violation resulting from the formally correct application of domestic legislation or reliance on high court jurisprudence, or from other administrative or factual practices, require the adoption of appropriate general measures to remove the source of the violation and prevent its recurrence.

Remedying the Excessive Length of Proceedings—Again

Supervision of a set of fifty-four judgments (plus another seventeen judgments rendered in 2011) concerning the excessive length of judicial proceedings and the lack of an effective domestic remedy was ended in 2013.[1] The fact that these judgments, dating from the mid-2000s onward,[2] were supervised for a much longer time than earlier judgments on the reasonable time requirement under Article 6 (1) ECHR, which had been closed following the payment of just satisfaction, results from the fact that the continuing inflow to the Court of similar complaints made it no longer possible to classify them as isolated occurrences for which compensation was a sufficient remedy. As the ECtHR eventually noted in the 2010 *Rumpf* judgment, the "violations found in the present judgment were neither prompted by an isolated incident nor were they attributable to a particular turn of events in this case, but were the consequence of shortcomings of the respondent State. Accordingly, the situation in the present case must be qualified as resulting from a practice incompatible with the Convention."[3] Applying its pilot judgment procedure for the first time against a Western European country,[4] the Court ordered Germany to "introduce without delay, and at the latest within one year from the date on which this judgment becomes final, a remedy or a combination of remedies in the national legal system in order to bring it into line with the Court's conclusions in the present judgment."[5]

The *Rumpf* pilot judgment was the Court's response to Germany's "almost complete reluctance"[6] to comply with the 2006 *Sürmeli* ruling, in which the ECtHR had continued its jurisprudence begun with *Kudła v. Poland* (2000) on the scope of the obligation under Article 13 ECHR to provide an effective remedy to address Convention violations before appropriate national institutions. In *Sürmeli*, the ECtHR had vetted all domestic remedies available in Germany to address the problem of excessively long proceedings and had found them lacking in light of the requirements of Article 13. According to the Court, domestic "remedies available to a litigant for raising a complaint about the length of proceedings are 'effective' within the meaning of Article 13 of the Convention if they prevent the alleged violation or its continuation, or provide adequate redress for any violation that has already occurred. A remedy is therefore effective if it can be used either to expedite a decision by the courts dealing with the case, or to provide the litigant with adequate redress for delays that have already occurred."[7] While both preventive as well as compensatory remedies were thus considered compliant with Article 13, the judges clearly expressed their preference when noting that "the best solution in absolute terms is indisputably [. . .] prevention" and that "[s]ome States have understood the situation perfectly by choosing to combine two types of remedy, one designed to expedite the proceedings and the other to afford compensation."[8]

The need to provide for an adequate domestic remedy did not come as a total surprise to the government. Indeed, already in May 2002 the Ministry of Justice had contacted a number of lawyer associations and interest groups in Germany to request their opinion as to whether the ECtHR's *Kudła* judgment required any changes in German civil and criminal procedure law, but no concrete legislative initiatives followed.[9] And while parliament, in response to a 2003 FCC judgment,[10] did enact a new law in 2004 providing for redress in certain cases where judicial proceedings themselves infringed the right to be heard by a court,[11] the specific issue of the excessive length of proceedings was not covered by it.[12] A subsequent effort begun in 2005 by the Ministry of Justice to introduce a legal remedy if a court failed to act (*Untätigkeitsklage*), and announced by the government in the *Sürmeli* pleadings,[13] would have empowered appellate courts to order trial courts to speed up proceedings and to set concrete deadlines. Not surprisingly, it met with opposition from members of the judiciary who viewed such orders as intrusions into judicial independence, and in 2007—that is, after the *Sürmeli* judgment—the government abandoned the plan to introduce a bill on the issue.[14]

And so it took a series of additional adverse decisions and the Court's *Rumpf* judgment[15] before Germany eventually adopted legislation to remedy shortcomings that the government had been aware of since the early years of the new millennium. The Act on Legal Redress for Excessive Length of Court Proceedings and of Criminal Investigation Proceedings was formally introduced as a bill in October 2010, received parliamentary approval in November 2011, and entered into force on December 3, 2011,[16] one day after the deadline set by the Court set in the *Rumpf* pilot judgment. The Act provides, inter alia, that anyone suffering from excessively lengthy proceedings, including proceedings before the Federal Constitutional Court,[17] has a right to compensation for pecuniary and nonpecuniary damages resulting from such delays. For nonpecuniary damages, guided by the just satisfaction practices of the ECtHR,[18] the act lays down a standard amount of €1,200 per year of delay, with the possibility of down- and upward adjustments, depending on the nature of the case (including the possibility of merely symbolic satisfaction). One precondition is that the claimant has raised the issue of (threatened) delay first with the court seized of the substantive case to give it an opportunity to take measures to avoid further delay (*Verzögerungsrüge*). While this requirement has been introduced with the expectation that courts so reproved will likely seek to avoid further delays,[19] no element of compulsion is involved. The delay reprimand thus by itself constitutes no effective legal remedy to speed up proceedings, and its receipt need not be formally acknowledged, nor does a court have to justify its past or intended future conduct in light of it.[20]

Although the ECtHR soon afterward gave its (tentative) blessing to the new legislation,[21] Germany's remedial response remains partial and, in the eyes of the German bar association, "evidently only the second-best option."[22] What it does is domesticate compensation proceedings for excessive-length cases, so that claimants instead of having to go to Strasbourg can now apply to a competent domestic court. And while the requirement of the prior delay reprimand, which may simply be voiced orally during hearings,[23] may result in the speeding up of proceedings in some cases, the claimant's position in this regard has not been substantially improved because it would already have been within the discretion and powers of a court to accelerate cases if notice of expected delays had been given informally. In any event, doubts exist as to the effectiveness of this instrument in the absence of any binding obligation to provide redress by accelerating proceedings.[24] Indeed, as the explanatory report points out, a principal reason for its introduction was to avoid abuse on the part of litigants who knowingly accept excessive delays only to then request compensation ("endure and liquidate"),[25] and so it has been characterized as a legal hurdle primarily aimed at avoiding payment in cases in which litigants have failed to raise the objection properly or lack interest in initiating yet another set of court proceedings.[26]

When compared with the double-pronged alternative identified as ideal by the Court, the adoption of this partial, compensatory remedy is in line with the theoretical expectations articulated here. Parliament had for several years been disinclined to adopt a legislative reform that many parliamentarians viewed as unnecessary, with some opposition remaining even after the *Rumpf* judgment.[27] Litigants suffering from long proceedings as the eventual beneficiaries constitute a dispersed group, both geographically and across time, that faces significant collective-action hurdles, even if supported by the bar association's preference for a stronger remedy in the form of action against judicial failure to act (*Untätigkeitsklage*).[28] The judiciary, on the contrary, is a much more concentrated stakeholder group that also forms a branch of government. The judges' principal interest group was quite vocal in its opposition to any stronger measures than the delay reprimand ultimately adopted (which it also disliked due, inter alia, to its implicit assignment of responsibility for delays to the courts) because it would interfere with judicial independence if one court would be allowed to tell another how to run its business. Even the determination of a court's alternative courses of action as part of compensation proceedings was considered to be an illegitimate meddling with the reviewed court's autonomy.[29] This quasi-absolutist understanding of judicial independence of course overlooks the fact that lower courts are routinely instructed by higher courts to reconsider cases in light of different legal interpretations, and it disregards the fact that such directive remedies with a view to accelerating proceedings are available in other Council of Europe member states,[30] without the courts in these states being substantially deprived of their independence as a result.

It is this preference for autonomy of a governmental actor involved in this problem area that is reflected in the remedial solution adopted, a remedy that eschews effective ex ante prevention in favor of ex post compensation. Since Germany was already subject to compensatory claims before the ECtHR, the reform in essence only changed the forum, whereas the introduction of a strong preventive remedy with binding force for its curial addressees—an option on the table from 2005 to 2007—would have meant a more far-reaching structural change. While such a change may have seemed unwarranted in light of the overall satisfactory record concerning the length of judicial proceedings in Germany, it would have empowered litigants to a greater extent than the option eventually chosen. In light of the preferences involved and the overall strategic context, the decision in favor of the latter corresponds with the expectation of rational choice within normative constraints.

Parent-Child Relations

With respect to four of the eight judgments in which compliance required general measures to remedy infringements of the right to protection of family life, either in light of Article 8 only or in conjunction with the nondiscrimination provision of Article 14, the reform that brought domestic legislation into compliance with the Convention actually preceded the ECtHR's judgments, and in two others, it had already been initiated in response to jurisprudence by the FCC; in other words, the ECtHR identified past violations on the basis of rules that were no longer in force or were scheduled to be amended soon. The first set of four judgments implicated a legal provision in force at the material time that treated noncustodial divorced fathers and noncustodial fathers of out-of-wedlock children differently with respect to the issue of access to their children. While divorced fathers automatically had a legal right of access that could be curtailed only if the interests of the children so required, unmarried fathers did not have such a right *unless* the mother or a guardianship court determined that such access was in the children's best interest; in other words, granting a right of access was seen as an exception to the rule, as reflected in much judicial practice.[31] In addition, for children born out of wedlock, the law established that custody was exercised solely by the mother. In the first judgment on the issue, the Court found violations of Article 8 ECHR (right to family life) and Article 6 (1) ECHR (fairness of proceedings) on the basis of "an insufficient involvement of the applicant in the decision-making process [related to granting access],"[32] before it concluded in the later cases that the access decisions based on the legal regime in force at the time constituted a violation of Article 14 ECHR (prohibition of arbitrary discrimination) in conjunction with Article 8 ECHR.[33] The Court noted that "very weighty reasons" were required to justify "a difference of treatment on the ground of birth out of or within wedlock [. . .]. The same is true for a difference in the treatment of the father of a child born of a relationship where the parties were living together out of wedlock as compared with the father of a child born of a marriage-based relationship. The Court discerns no such reason in the instant case."[34]

When the judgments were issued, the relevant provisions were no longer valid law, having been amended in December 1997, with effect of July 1, 1998.[35] Parental authority was henceforth to be shared between parents, irrespective of marital status (section 1626 (1) German Civil Code); joint custody was now in principle possible for unmarried parents but remained subject to the mother's veto (section 1626a Civil Code); and children henceforth had a right of contact with both parents, and both parents the right, as well as obligation, to have contact with their children (section 1684 Civil Code). The Committee of Ministers considered these reforms sufficient to remedy the violations identified by the Court and ended its supervision of these cases.[36] Although the four applications had been lodged between June 1993 (*Sahin*) and July 1996 (*Hoffmann*), and thus before the reform passed parliament, there is no indication in the preparatory documents that the pending cases played any role in motivating the reform.[37] Instead, reference is made to judgments of the Federal Constitutional Court and to academic and political debates, going back at least to 1991, on the necessity of a reform in light of changed social realities.[38] While the reform removed discrimination between married and unmarried fathers with respect to access rights, it remained more restrictive with regard to custody which in the case of unmarried fathers—but not divorced ones—required the approval of the mother (who received custody by default).

This aspect was eventually addressed by the Court in the 2009 *Zaunegger* judgment, in which the Court found, against a leading 2003 FCC judgment,[39] that the legally mandated discriminatory treatment, and hence the German courts' refusal to award joint custody in the absence of an affirmative declaration by the mother as part of a joint declaration, could not be objectively justified because "there was not a reasonable relationship of proportionality between the general exclusion of judicial review of the initial attribution of sole custody to the mother and the aim pursued, namely the protection of the best interests of a child born out of wedlock."[40] Remedial legislation entered into force in May 2013. It provides that unmarried fathers can petition a court to award joint custody that shall be granted by way of a simplified procedure if no reasons concerning the child's well-being argue against it.[41] The legislative response was facilitated by the fact that the FCC had echoed the ECtHR's position in 2010 when it reversed itself, declared the relevant Civil Code provision unconstitutional,[42] and decreed provisionally that family courts should award joint, or partial joint custody, when appropriate (both the ECtHR's and the FCC's decisions are mentioned as reasons for introducing remedial legislation).[43] Although aware of a potentially more beneficial response for unmarried fathers—the conferral, by law, of joint custody, as practiced in a number of other COE countries[44]—the government favored a facultative opt-in procedure, as a middle-of-the-road approach between automatic conferral and requiring an application without a presumption in favor of the applicant father.[45] The Committee considered the new law sufficiently compliant.[46]

A second set of two cases decided in 2005 concerned the discrimination in the allocation of child benefits on the basis of the nature of foreign applicants' residence status, also resulting in violations of Article 14 in conjunction with Article 8 ECHR.[47] Under section 1, para. 3 of the 1994 Child Benefits Act, aliens could receive child benefits only if they had a residence permit (*Aufenthaltsberechtigung*) or a provisional residence permit (*Aufenthaltserlaubnis*); as a consequence, aliens with a more limited residence title for exceptional purposes (*Aufenthaltsbefugnis*) were denied such assistance. The applicants in the present cases, all Polish nationals, had entered Germany in 1985 and 1987. Although not qualifying for asylum-seeker status, they had received residence permits for exceptional purposes, which had been regularly renewed. Because of this residence status, however, child benefits either had not been granted (in *Niedzwiecki*) or had been ended after the change in the law in 1994 (in *Okpisz*).

The ECtHR's judgments in these cases had no ascertainable effect of their own since the Federal Constitutional Court had already ruled in 2004 that the relevant provision also violated the Basic Law's nondiscrimination clause (Article 3 GG), and it had ordered the law to be changed by January 1, 2006.[48] The FCC acknowledged as legitimate the objective of granting child benefits only to those whose stay in Germany was likely to be permanent, but it also found the type of residence title to be an insufficient indicator for these purposes. Remedial legislation was adopted in December 2006 and entered into force with retroactive effect as of January 1, 2006.[49] The amendment removed the impugned discrimination by making child benefits in principle available to all foreigners with a valid residence title, provided that that title also included a work permit. The reform took "gainful employment [and] integration into the German labor market as an indicator for permanent stay in Germany"[50] but continued to exclude from eligibility for child benefits those whose stay—despite a work permit—was intended to be temporary, as in the case of students, au pairs, or seasonal workers.[51] Notably, no mention at all is made in the government's legislative proposal of ECtHR's judgments; only the FCC is cited as a reason for the reform.[52] In terms of substance, this omission was inconsequential, as the ECtHR in its judgments had simply pointed to the FCC's decisions as support for its own finding of a Convention violation, without adding any original arguments of its own.[53]

As in the *Zaunegger* case discussed above, the *Brauer* judgment (2009) triggered change that likely would not have come about in its absence. The ECtHR here took issue with a law dating from 1969 that, while recognizing for the first time the inheritance rights of children born out of wedlock vis-à-vis their fathers (previously, such children and their fathers were not even considered legally related), denied such rights to those that were born prior to the cut-off date of July 1, 1949—that is, those that had already come of age at the time of the adoption of the law (in the instant case, this meant that in the absence of other direct heirs the applicant's potential inheritance would fall to the state). In 1976 and 1996, the FCC had twice upheld the constitutionality of that provision, on the grounds of both the difficulties of establishing paternity in earlier times and the protection of the legitimate expectations of the legally recognized heirs. Parliament, nodding to the FCC judgments, maintained the exception as well when passing the Children's Rights Improvement Act in 2002.[54] The European Court, by contrast, decided that it could not "find any ground on which such discrimination based on birth outside marriage can be justified today" and declared a violation of Article 14 in conjunction with Article 8. Notably, it stipulated that "the aspect of protecting the 'legitimate expectation' of the deceased and their families must be subordinate to the imperative of equal treatment between children born outside and within marriage."[55]

Two years later, remedial legislation passed parliament. It pursued the only substantive option available by granting to children born outside of marriage a statutory right of inheritance in respect of their fathers and paternal relatives, irrespective of their date of birth.[56] And still, there was a restrictive element: the law had retroactive effect only with respect to relevant inheritance cases that occurred *after* the date of the ECtHR's judgment (i.e., May 28, 2009); all cases that had arisen earlier thus remained subject to discriminatory treatment. The government justified this new cut-off point by arguing that it was only from the date of the ECtHR's judgment that the (at that time, sole) legal heirs could no longer expect the discriminatory regime to continue, whereas in all earlier inheritance cases the legitimate expectations of the legal heirs did deserve continuing protection.[57] This, of course, is not an altogether unreasonable argument; still, the chosen option remains more restrictive than the alternative of giving full retroactive effect to the new nondiscriminatory regulation. That this broader type of compliance would have created significant practical as well as normative problems of its own is a point well taken, but as speakers from the opposition parties pointed out in parliamentary debate, they would not have been insurmountable because the reopening of concluded inheritance cases was not unheard of and the number of relevant cases seemed manageable, given that at the time of the law's adoption, the potential claimants were already older than sixty-two years.[58] Moreover, the adopted solution chose to disregard the Court's above-cited explicit argument that the elimination of discrimination trumped the protection of legitimate expectations in this field.[59] So in the end, the governing coalition simply preferred one type of injustice over another, a preference that resulted in more restrictive implementation of the judgment than would have been the case without the limitation regarding retroactivity.

Finally, in the 2010 *Anayo* judgment,[60] the Convention violation resulted from the German courts' refusal, based on their interpretation of relevant provisions on parental access in the civil code in force at the time, to grant the applicant access to his twin children who had resulted from a two-year liaison with a married woman that had ended in 2005; by the time of the twins' birth in December of that year, the woman had returned to her husband, who under German law was considered their legal father. Regarding the rights of biological fathers of children who are not their legal fathers, it took almost two years before remedial legislation was first proposed, with the delay being due, according to one source, to some unspecified "political problem that could not be resolved."[61] When it was, things moved along relatively swiftly and the act entered into force in July 2013.[62] It now provides for access rights for biological fathers if they have shown serious interest in their child and if access is not contrary to the child's best interest and well-being; the law also provides for incidental paternity tests if biological fatherhood is in doubt.[63] The first draft bill identifies the ECtHR's judgments as the sole motivation,[64] with the regulations responding narrowly to the points addressed by the ECtHR, rejecting along the way remedial designs that went beyond what was minimally required to comply, such as extending a general right to probable biological fathers to have their paternity clarified even in the absence of an intention to participate in the child's life, allowing direct challenges for biological fathers to the mother's husband's status of legal fatherhood,[65] or regulating related constellations (e.g., involving homosexual parents) not addressed in the ECtHR's judgment.[66]

The reason why supervision of the case was closed only in early 2017[67] has to do with the taking of satisfactory individual measures in the case because the legal parents, who had so far not informed the twins about their true biological descent, appealed a 2013 first-instance decision in favor of granting supervised access to the applicant. This decision was then quashed by the Karlsruhe Higher Regional Court in 2015, which based its ruling, however, solely on the legal parent's apparent inability to cope with such access, as described in an expert's report. In a decision issued in October 2016, the Federal Court of Justice in turn quashed the higher regional court's decision and remanded the case for a fresh review.[68] Expressly invoking the ECtHR's jurisprudence,[69] the FCJ noted that the interests of the legal parents and their refusal to grant access cannot be determinative of a decision against such access. Since the courts become involved only if access is not voluntarily granted, biological fathers who are not legal fathers must not be typified as "troublemakers" ex ante, as this would make the legally afforded possibility of access illusory by creating a presumption against its desirability. Instead, a "comprehensive assessment" of the children's best interests has to be conducted in which the situation and interests of the legal parents are an important, but not exhaustive, aspect.[70] Notably, the FCJ instructed the lower court to hear the children themselves and, if the legal parents refused to do so, to provide them (they were already ten years old at the time of FCJ decision) with information about their biological descent in a suitable manner prior to subsequent access proceedings.[71] Since the violation identified by the ECtHR resulted not from the earlier denial of access as such, but the manner in which domestic proceedings had been conducted—namely, domestic courts' failure to fairly consider and balance the competing interests at stake[72]—affirming requisite procedural safeguards in the highest civil court's jurisprudence was sufficient to close the case.

Unfairness of Criminal Proceedings

Two sets of ECtHR judgments addressed aspects of unfairness in criminal proceedings based on provisions in federal law. The first set comprises two judgments that addressed the ostensibly trivial question of interpreter costs. Article 6 (3) lit. e ECHR provides that, to assure a fair criminal trial, every defendant has the right "to have the free assistance of an interpreter if he cannot understand or speak the language used in court." Under German domestic law, however, the applicants in the first case, *Luedicke, Belkacem and Koç*,[73] upon having been convicted of various criminal offenses, were themselves charged with the interpreter costs.[74] Before the ECtHR, the German government argued that Article 6 (3) lit. e ECHR was to assure a fair trial during proceedings but did no longer apply once a defendant had been found guilty.[75] Notably, in 1975, during the preparation of the relevant piece of domestic legislation, the issue of whether foreigners lacking a sufficient command of the German language should be relieved of interpreter costs was raised and discussed, but ultimately rejected, in line with the dominant opinion in judicial decisions and the academic literature at the time.[76] The Court did not follow the government's argument and instead found that the word "free" meant "neither a conditional remission, nor a temporary exemption, nor a suspension, but a once and for all exemption or exoneration."[77]

Since the violation was based directly on the correct application of domestic law, full compliance in response to the Convention violation required changing the relevant legal provision. Because the violation revolved around a very specific issue that did not suggest any great occasion for politicization, one might have expected a relatively swift execution along the lines suggested by the Court's reasoning. This is what happened, although with some minor delay. In August 1980, motivated explicitly by the ECtHR's decision,[78] the Court Costs Act was amended to exclude interpreter costs from those for which a defendant convicted in a criminal trial could be held liable.[79] At the same time, Germany insisted before the Committee of Ministers that the adoption of legislative measures was essentially a voluntary measure that was not as such required by the Convention and was thus exempt from supervision by the Committee.[80] The Committee, however, rejected that line of reasoning.[81] While the legislative outcome was appropriate in light of the ECtHR's judgment, note that it was also specifically restricted to criminal proceedings; Germany could have extended the judgment's logic to other legal proceedings below the threshold of criminal law in which defendants, if convicted, face state-imposed adverse consequences, but it chose not to.

It was precisely this omission that gave rise to the *Öztürk* judgment.[82] In this case, the applicant had been fined for causing a road accident, a misdemeanor, and had also been charged with interpreter costs incurred during subsequent judicial proceedings. He objected to these based on the Court's judgment in *Luedicke, Belkacem and Koç*. Before the ECtHR, the government argued that Article 6 (3) lit. e, by its very terms, applied only to people "charged with a criminal offence" and did thus not cover misdemeanor proceedings. The Court, sitting in plenary session, took a different position. Arguing that the term "criminal offence" in the Convention had to be given an autonomous interpretation to prevent states from circumventing its provisions simply by reclassifying certain acts as noncriminal,[83] the Court found that the term "criminal offence" covered all those regulations "that make their perpetrator liable to penalties intended, *inter alia*, to be deterrent and usually consisting of fines and of measures depriving the person of his liberty,"[84] a characterization that applied to the fine imposed on Mr. Öztürk. As a consequence, a less than unanimous Court found Germany in breach of the ECHR.[85]

The execution of the Öztürk judgment went less smoothly than that in *Luedicke, Belkacem and Koç* and took a full five years, a long time given that the issue was of the same low complexity as in the earlier case, requiring only an extension of the amendment then made to the law of misdemeanors. The overwhelming response to the judgment in academic journals and judicial opinions was, however, one of reserved skepticism. The distinction between crimes and misdemeanors was seen as so fundamental and justified that their lumping together for purposes of Article 6 ECHR was broadly criticized and rejected. The German government shared this assessment and engaged in domestic foot-dragging. Another case (*Lutz*) was pending at the time in which the Court had to decide whether the presumption of innocence addressed in Article 6 (2) ECHR also applied to misdemeanor proceedings, with the German government arguing, and hoping, for a reversal of the Court's earlier interpretation. While the Court did not find a violation, it stuck by its earlier position on the autonomous interpretation of the term criminal offence as including misdemeanors.[86] Because the domestic legal provision on interpreter costs in misdemeanor proceedings had not yet been changed, further applications based on the same fact patterns reached Strasbourg. In 1988, the European Commission of Human Rights reaffirmed the Court's position in *Öztürk* and *Lutz* in two reports,[87] quelling the German government's hopes for a change in the position of the Strasbourg control bodies. The pending proceedings were concluded by way of friendly settlements,[88] and in June 1989 Germany finally amended the law to exempt defendants in misdemeanor proceedings from having to pay interpreter costs,[89] not without adding, however, that such costs could still exceptionally be imposed if the defendant had caused these through fault of his or her own[90] and that they would in any event be covered only to the extent that they were "truly" necessary for mounting an effective defense.

Still, these attempts at minimal restrictions notwithstanding, in executing the *Öztürk* judgment, Germany had no meaningful range of options. The only alternative to exempting misdemeanor defendants from interpreter costs was outright noncompliance. Under these circumstances, and given the widespread preference for the status quo, the only remaining strategy was to delay execution and to use the next case before the Court to reargue the case for the distinction of criminal and misdemeanor proceedings, as Germany did. Once this strategy did not pay off with the desired result, however, the preference for the status quo could no longer be sustained both for normative and cost/benefit reasons. Normatively, sustained noncompliance was not a palatable option, but rationally, it made sense to "nationalize" the payment of translator costs once the Court's jurisprudence appeared settled, rather than continue to suffer adverse judgments and to bear not only the costs of additional just satisfaction awards but also the costs of defending further cases that did not offer any prospect of success.

The second set in this group of cases comprises four judgments that revolved around the violation of the equality of arms required for adversarial trials under Article 5 (4) ECHR. Three of these were decided together in 2001 and concerned the fact that counsel for the applicants, who were being held in detention on remand, were denied access to the latter's criminal files on the basis of a provision in the German *Code of Criminal Procedure* (section 147 (2)) that in the version in force at the material time allowed the public prosecutor to deny access if he or she considered that such access might compromise ongoing investigations, without possibility of judicial review.[91] By the time the ECtHR issued its judgments, that provision had already been amended.[92] While not guaranteeing access to the prosecutor's files, the amended provision now at least enabled judicial review of the prosecutor's decision to deny access;[93] this proved sufficient enough a response for the Committee to close its supervision of these cases.[94] It is unclear to what extent the domestic legal change was prompted by Strasbourg's jurisprudence, though. All three cases had been pending since 1994 and were jointly referred to the Court by the Commission on December 9, 1998,[95] so that Germany was on notice that the relevant domestic norm was being challenged. Also, the Court had made clear in earlier judgments that it considered a defendant's access to the investigative case file an important element of fair adversarial proceedings in detention-related review cases under Article 5 (4) ECHR.[96] The report accompanying the German draft legislation, however, contains no reference to the cases pending before the Court. Instead the legislative change is justified with the increasing criticism of the old regulation in the academic literature and the fact that the prosecutorial denial of access to case files had also been made subject to judicial control in other contexts.[97] It will be fair to say that the addition of a judicial control element is the minimum response required to afford fairer proceedings to defendants in detention on remand, with its effectiveness depending largely on judicial practice in applying the provision, a practice that soon gave rise to disagreements as to its scope.[98]

This change was not the end of the story, however. In the subsequent *Mooren* (2009) judgment, concerning criminal proceedings regarding charges of tax evasion, the Grand Chamber of the Court again found a violation of the fairness requirement in Article 5 (4) ECHR—conceded by Germany—because the prosecutor-denied access to documents had not been sufficiently remedied in the course of challenges to the applicant's detention on remand. It was, in any case, not sufficient for the prosecution to offer the applicant's counsel an oral account of the evidence on which the charges were based.[99] Germany responded with a further amendment of the relevant provision of section 147 (2) of the *Code of Criminal Procedure* to emphasize that in cases where the accused is in detention on remand (or where placement in detention has been requested) and access to documents has been denied, the relevant pieces of information necessary for the defendants to challenge the legality of their detention have to be made available to them or their counsel "in appropriate form,"[100] which, "as a general rule," means access to the relevant files (thus retaining some discretion as to the modalities of access). Germany also took the opportunity with the amendment, as the explanatory notes make clear, to phrase it in such a way as to permit the denial of direct access because it might jeopardize the investigation not only in the defendant's case but also in those against other parties.[101] Thus, once again, while "habitual compliance" did occur, it did not result in the broadest possible improvement in the applicant's human rights situation— academic commentators had already proposed more far-reaching, unconditional access rights[102]—but instead combined taking measures that met the minimum requirements for compliance with adding a restrictive element that may be in the interest of the law enforcement authorities but not those subject to investigation.

The Right to Privacy

At the time, no other decision against Germany had received as much publicity, not only in academic circles but also in the general media, as the Court's
judgment concerning a complaint by Princess Caroline von Hannover.[103]
The reason seems clear: the press had a special motivation to report on the
case because its subject matter fell squarely within its own backyard—the
freedom of the press, or rather its limits, when weighed against celebrities'
right to privacy. Further legal and political salience was added to the case
by the fact that the Strasbourg judges took on directly the jurisprudence
of the Federal Constitutional Court. Princess Caroline, the eldest daughter of Prince Rainier III of Monaco, had litigated in German courts against
the publication of a series of photos in the tabloid press that showed her in
various unofficial circumstances and private settings. The princess argued
that these publications violated her right to privacy.[104] In ruling on her constitutional complaint, the FCC had decided in a landmark 1999 judgment
that pictures showing Caroline with her children deserved special protection and could not be published, but that other pictures of her alone or with
other adults could be published without her consent on the ground that she
was a "contemporary public figure *par excellence*" (*absolute Person der Zeit-
geschichte*) who, as a result of that status, and in distinction to merely relatively public figures, had to endure the general public's interest in her life,
even if only for entertainment purposes, and to tolerate pictures taken of her
in environments that could be characterized as "public."[105] The ECtHR, by
contrast, argued that his approach "afford[ed] the person very limited protection of their private life or the right to control the use of their image" and
was thus inappropriate for people who did "not exercise any official functions."[106] Instead,

> the decisive factor in balancing the protection of private life against
> freedom of expression should lie in the contribution that the pub-
> lished photos and articles make to a debate of general interest. It is
> clear in the instant case that they made no such contribution, since
> the applicant exercises no official function and the photos and arti-
> cles related exclusively to details of her private life. Furthermore, the
> Court considers that the public does not have a legitimate interest
> in knowing where the applicant is and how she behaves generally in
> her private life even if she appears in places that cannot always be

described as secluded and despite the fact that she is well known to the public. Even if such a public interest exists, as does a commercial interest of the magazines in publishing these photos and these articles, in the instant case those interests must, in the Court's view, yield to the applicant's right to the effective protection of her private life.[107]

The ECtHR hence concluded that Germany, through its courts, had breached Article 8 ECHR by failing to provide sufficient protection of the applicant's right to privacy.

The judgment elicited a wave of mostly negative reactions in the media—including from reputable outlets,[108] which cried censure and feared the end of investigative journalism[109]—as well as somewhat more balanced but still largely critical commentary in academic journals.[110] A coalition of major media associations, broadcasters, and nearly seventy editors-in-chief called on the Schröder government to request a rehearing before the Grand Chamber of the Court.[111] The government declined to do so,[112] however, with some support from the FCC.[113] The FCC justices presumably feared that a referral might have led, as one justice put it, to a "petrification"[114] of Strasbourg's jurisprudence as a result of the greater authority of Grand Chamber judgments, and FCC considered it apparently more advantageous to give domestic courts a chance first to address and actively shape the consequences of the ECtHR's chamber judgment.[115] The government adduced the same reasons and preferred to choose a wait-and-see position with respect to jurisprudential developments in Germany as well as at the ECtHR.[116] While the issue of just satisfaction was settled by way of a friendly settlement involving the payment of €115,000,[117] the crucial question was how German courts would react in future privacy cases, caught between the jurisprudence of the ECtHR and their own constitutional court.

All in all, it appears that Strasbourg's position came to trump the FCC's earlier doctrine. While some state courts occasionally continued to rely on the FCC's jurisprudence, the Federal Court of Justice, the highest domestic court in civil and criminal matters, effectively jettisoned the legal construct of the "contemporary public figure *par excellence*," which it had previously used as the principal criterion to assess the permissibility of the publication of pictures of celebrities, and began to balance the freedom of the press and the right to privacy on the basis of the information value that the reporting at issue had within the given context at the material time; in this assessment, celebrity status was just one factor among several.[118] Yet, while acknowledging that the mere satisfaction of curiosity did not suffice to establish information value and that the depicted people and events, taken together with the accompanying text, had to have some contemporary historical significance, the FCJ also emphasized that the latter must not be interpreted too narrowly: "[E]specially with a view to the public's information needs, [the term contemporary history] does not only comprise events of historico-political significance, but contemporary history in general, that is, all issues of general societal interest, and is therefore in turn determined by the public's interests. Contributions aimed at entertainment can also generate public opinion; such contributions may in certain circumstances even stimulate and influence the formation of public opinion in more enduring a manner than factual information."[119] The FCC subsequently greenlighted the FCJ's new approach as constitutionally unproblematic.[120] In particular, it noted that the notions of absolute and relative public figures, developed as auxiliary concepts in the context of statutory interpretation, were not constitutionally required and could be replaced with another balancing approach.[121] As long as the FCJ engaged in a reasonably substantive appraisal of the information value of a given photo in the context of its accompanying text, such approach was legally acceptable. The FCC also agreed with the FCJ that the information value of contributions of a predominantly entertaining nature, including reporting about the private lives of celebrities,[122] could provide "occasion for socio-critical considerations" and thus "for a matter-of-fact debate of general interest."[123]

It is difficult to assess these observable changes in doctrine in terms of narrow and broad compliance. On the one hand, the FCJ and FCC adopted the ECtHR's balancing approach even though they did not necessarily have to abandon their own existing conceptual instruments, which seems to imply broad compliance; after all, although taking issue with the application in practice, the ECtHR had not required the replacement of the legal concept of the "contemporary public figure *par excellence*," only that it be interpreted more narrowly and applied with greater foreseeability than had been the case in the dispute before it.[124] On the other hand, the scope of compliance in this context specifically depends, arguably, less on the doctrinal framework used to balance competing rights and interests, and more on the application of such balancing framework in practice. Did German courts henceforth protect celebrities' right to privacy better by prohibiting more frequently the publication of photos in circumstances that they would have allowed under the old test? Because under both the old and the new tests, domestic courts retain(ed) a margin of appreciation in assessing the circumstances of the cases before them, the counterfactual evidence is difficult to establish with certitude. The extent to which these jurisprudential developments had tangible effects on the freedom of the press is unclear. One early study concluded that the actual effects on the nature and quality of coverage of celebrities in the yellow press appear to have been negligible,[125] whereas media representatives claimed that the judgment's aftermath "had [...] severely curtailed the freedom of information and of the press."[126] Hyperbolic fears that investigative journalism as such had been put in existential jeopardy,[127] however, have clearly not materialized.

While not necessarily qualifying as an instance of restrictive compliance as here understood, the emphasis of both the FCJ and the FCC on the information value of publications aimed solely at entertainment and their contribution to societal discourses of social or political relevance makes sure that the new test, like the old one, continues to provide protection for this type of content, against the privacy interests of those depicted. One could well see this as an attempt to use the interpretive opportunities left open by the *von Hannover* judgment—in particular, the question of what may constitute a contribution to debates of general interest—to assert a position close to the FCJ's and FCC's original preferences within the lexical confines of the ECtHR's decision. In any event, in several subsequent judgments involving Germany,[128] the ECtHR further clarified the criteria for balancing freedom of expression and respect for private life[129] and signaled approval of the new domestic approach and its application in practice:

> [I]n accordance with their case-law, the national courts carefully balanced the right of the publishing companies to freedom of expression against the right of the applicants to respect for their private life. In doing so, they attached fundamental importance to the question whether the photos, considered in the light of the accompanying articles, had contributed to a debate of general interest. [...]
>
> The Court also observes that the national courts explicitly took account of the Court's relevant case-law. Whilst the Federal Court of Justice had changed its approach following the *von Hannover* judgment, the Federal Constitutional Court, for its part, had not only confirmed that approach, but also undertaken a detailed analysis of the Court's case-law in response to the applicants' complaints that the Federal Court of Justice had disregarded the Convention and the Court's case-law.

In those circumstances, and having regard to the margin of appreciation enjoyed by the national courts when balancing competing interests, the Court concludes that the latter have not failed to comply with their positive obligations under Article 8 of the Convention. Accordingly, there has not been a violation of that provision.[130]

All of the five judgments came out in favor of the freedom of expression and of the press.[131] One way to interpret this string of judgments is in terms of mutual accommodation. The domestic courts adopted the ECtHR's framework, while the latter affirmed the margin of appreciation of the former, as long as its own jurisprudence was properly acknowledged and the eventual balance struck was reasonably justifiable, an arrangement that still left sufficient freedom for domestic courts to come out either one way or the other.

Reforming the Preventive Detention Regime

ECtHR judgments concerning national law and policy in the areas of security and crime tend to figure more prominently, and controversially, in the public sphere than judgments in other issue areas. The judgment of *M.* is no exception in this respect.[132] At issue in this case was the possibility, laid down in section 66 (1) of the *Strafgesetzbuch* (*German Criminal Code*), to keep a person convicted of violent crimes in so-called preventive detention after the expiry of the criminal sentence if he or she was believed to be a continuing danger to society, subject to certain conditions. At the time of the applicant's original sentencing, the law limited preventive detention subsequent to a prison sentence to up to ten years, after which the detainee had to be set free. In 1998, the law was changed, however, to enable continuing preventive detention beyond ten years unless a court decided that a detainee no longer posed a threat to society and could be set free.[133] The applicant in *M.*, after having been convicted of various violent crimes in the past, was ordered by a court to be kept in preventive detention following his last prison sentence, which ended in 1991. In 2001, however, shortly before the expiry of the previous ten-year limit, a court ordered that M. be kept in detention, relying on the 1998 amendment and assessments provided, inter alia, by a forensic psychiatrist that M. still posed a danger to the public. M.'s constitutional complaint, in which he argued that the extent of his preventive detention contravened the constitutionally protected right to liberty (Article 2 (2) GG) and that the extension based on the 1998 amendment violated the prohibition of ex post facto criminal laws (Article 103 (2) GG), was rejected by the Federal Constitutional Court in 2004. As to the former claim, the FCC found that the requirements for extending preventive detention (including an external expert's opinion) met the heightened proportionality demands for the continued deprivation of liberty beyond the original period of confinement; as to the latter contention, the justices argued that the prohibition applied only to "measures which expressed sovereign censure of illegal and culpable conduct and involved the imposition of a penalty to compensate for guilt"[134] but not to measures aimed at correction and prevention.

A unanimous chamber of the European Court of Human Rights disagreed and instead found violations of Article 5 (1) and 7 (1) ECHR, respectively. In the ECtHR's view, "there was not a sufficient causal connection between the applicant's conviction by the sentencing court in 1986" and the extension of preventive detention in 2001, as required by Article 5 (1) lit. a ECHR, nor was there any "sufficiently concrete and specific" threat of offenses similar to past ones that could justify detention (under Article 5 (1) lit. c ECHR), nor reliance on a substantiated assessment that the applicant was of "unsound mind" (Article 5 (1) lit. e ECHR).[135] In addition, proceeding on the basis of an autonomous interpretation of the Convention, the Court qualified preventive detention as a penalty for purposes of Article 7 (1) ECHR. Because the 1998 amendment on which the extension of M.'s preventive detention was based changed preventive detention from the previously determinate maximum length of ten years into one of potentially unlimited duration, the extension ran afoul of the principle of *nulla poena sine lege* enshrined in that article.[136] Germany sought a rehearing before the Grand Chamber, but the request was rejected on May 10, 2010.[137]

Germany's response to the *M.* judgment followed quickly on its heels, in part because the new coalition government that came to power after the 2009 general elections had already agreed on an overhaul of the preventive detention regime as part of its legislative agenda.[138] Parts of the reform were motivated by this domestic stimulus, but other parts were a direct response to the ECtHR's judgment and the awareness of other related cases still pending before it. And while Germany did not ignore the Court's reasoning, the approach pursued illustrates the logic of watering down the amendments required to comply with the ECtHR's judgments with elements intended to maintain preventive detention as broadly available as possible. Germany did this by, on the one hand, amending the provisions on preventive detention in the criminal code and, on the other, by adopting new legislation on the detention of mentally disturbed criminals.[139] The main changes introduced into the criminal code were the following:

- The offenses that a defendant has to have committed to qualify for primary or unconditional preventive detention—that is, preventive detention ordered at the time of sentencing—were essentially limited to intentionally committed violent crimes, in particular offenses against life, physical integrity, personal freedom, and sexual self-determination,[140] for which a prison sentence of at least two years has been imposed. A further condition that required two previous convictions of at least one year each was specified to require convictions for violent crimes, eliminating the possibility that an offender repeatedly sentenced for thievery might end up in preventive detention after a first conviction for a violent crime.[141] In contrast, for sexually motivated crimes, the statute of limitation for convictions to be included was extended from five to fifteen years. Restricting preventive detention to violent crimes had long been demanded domestically and had been part of the government's announced program,[142] so that this change cannot be directly attributed to the ECtHR's judgments.
- The overall reduction in the scope of primary preventive detention was coupled with a broadening of the possibility for a sentencing court to reserve a decision on preventive detention for a later time (reserved preventive detention).[143] While this option had been available since 2002 in circumstances in which the continuing threat of a defendant, while not certain, was nonetheless probable, it was now broadened to be available also in cases of first-time convictions for violent crimes with a sentence of five years or more. Under the old regime, a decision on whether to activate reserved preventive detention had to be taken at the latest six months before a detainee became eligible for parole, but under the amended version it can be taken up to the last day of the completion of the full sentence. The decision is to be based on the convict's personality, the crime(s), and, as a supplement, his or her development in prison up to the time of the decision.
- Last but not least, the option of ordering preventive detention subsequently, that is, after and separate from conviction and sentencing (retrospective preventive detention),[144] was significantly curtailed for future cases. Instead of being available generally, its applicability was

henceforth limited to persons who had to be released from a psychiatric hospital because the incapacity that resulted in their committal no longer existed, but for whom further confinement was advisable because "a full appraisal of the person, his deeds and, complementarily, of his development up to the point of decision suggests that he will commit, with a high probability, felonies that will result in physical or mental damage to the victims."[145] The government justified the change by noting that the earlier rule, due to its strict requirements such as the emergence of new relevant facts after conviction, had been of limited relevance in practice.[146]

Importantly, the reform did not remove the possibility of unlimited preventive detention, because the temporal aspect as such had not been criticized by the ECtHR in the *M.* judgment, only its retroactive imposition. The curtailment of retrospective preventive detention while expanding reserved preventive detention also sought to better address the causal nexus requirement because the latter was linked more directly to the initial conviction and sentence. The government did not stress this point but only noted that the issue of the compatibility of retrospective preventive detention with the ECHR, which it continued to affirm, had been raised in academic writings and might be addressed by the ECtHR in currently pending proceedings.[147] What the government did expressly note was that the broadening of (aspects of) primary and reserved preventive detention was specifically intended to compensate for the putative loss in protection incurred as a result of the elimination of most of retroactive preventive detention.[148]

The government's strategic response becomes most obvious when considering the new regulations of the second element in the remedial legislation, the Therapy Detention Act (with the German name, *Therapieunterbringungsgesetz*, abbreviated as ThUG). This act was designed at the time specifically with a view to enabling the (continued) detention of persons who otherwise might have had to be released as a result of the legal implications of the *M.* judgment.[149] It does so by enabling their committal, for renewable periods of up to eighteen months (section 12 ThUG), to a closed therapeutic institution if their propensity to commit crimes is causally linked to the existence of a mental disorder (section 1 ThUG). This term receives no further definition in the act. The legislative materials make clear, however, that it is intended to cover phenomena beyond mental illness in its clinical sense: "Social deviations or social conflicts alone, without personal impairments of the person concerned, are not classified as a mental disorder. By contrast, specific disorders of personality, behavior, sexual preference, of impulse or drive control can signal a psychic disorder. This applies in particular to anti-social personality disorder and various disorders of sexual preferences, such as pedophilia or sadomasochism. Ultimately, the term 'mental disorder' covers a broad spectrum of phenomena, of which only some are qualified as a mental illness in the practice of psychiatric-forensic assessments."[150]

Furthermore, to avoid the characterization of such committal decisions as criminal sanctions, resulting in potentially new violations of the *nulla poena sine lege* principle, the law provides that the committal decision has to be taken by a civil, not a criminal court, and that suitable institutions with a "medical-therapeutic orientation" have to be "spatially and organizationally distinct from institutions of the penal system" (section 2 ThUG). Whether the detainee receives the best treatment appropriate for his supposed disorder and whether it can be improved at all, are irrelevant factors, as long as the institution offers treatment that does not rule out a positive effect on the detainee's disorder.[151] It seems reasonably clear that the detention part is the politically desired driving motor of the new act, not its therapy-focused elements,[152] with its approach to "forensic psychiatry without diagnosis"[153] drawing strongly worded criticism from the principal association of psychiatrists in Germany.[154] In any event, the German high courts subsequently saw no legal problem in defining mental disorder broadly and without requiring any impairment of criminal responsibility.[155]

These amendments, however, were not the last word in the recurrent reform efforts surrounding the preventive detention regime. Further changes became necessary when the Federal Constitutional Court, in a leading judgment issued on May 4, 2011, reversed its 2004 decision and declared the entire preventive detention regime, in both its current and previous manifestations, to be unconstitutional due to the failure to observe the so-called distance requirement (*Abstandsgebot*): The FCC argued that preventive detention as legislated and implemented in practice was not sufficiently distinct from detention in prison as a penal sanction and hence constituted a disproportionate interference with the right to liberty under the Basic Law.[156]

An examination of the legislative response[157] to this domestic judicial stimulus is beyond the scope of this chapter. What bears mentioning, however, with a view to Germany's response to the *M.* judgment, is the way that the FCC dealt with the ECtHR's reasoning in its own decision. The FCC reaffirmed the position expressed in the *Görgülü* judgment that the ECHR, and the ECtHR's interpretations of it, remain hierarchically below the Basic Law and may on occasion not be fully complied with by the courts if the ECtHR's judgments conflict with domestic law. At the same time, the FCC accepted the ECtHR's position that both retrospective extensions as well as subsequent separate orders of preventive detention—irrespective of its quality as a criminal penalty or not—could not be justified under Article 5 (1) lit. a ECHR for lack of a sufficient causal connection between the original sentencing and the later aggravation of the deprivation of liberty, and that the only ground remaining that could cover preventive detention was provided by Article 5 (1) lit. e ECHR, which authorizes the detention, inter alia, of people of unsound mind.[158]

Accordingly, the FCC held that preventive detention would be permissible only in the case of individuals who met the mental disorder criterion laid down in the ThUG—also emphasizing its flexible scope, which can cover nonclinical dissocial/antisocial personality disorders, with all the attendant discretion that this implies—and that the institutions for its execution had to provide meaningful therapeutic offerings. Concerning the qualification of preventive detention as a punishment for purposes of the prohibition of ex post facto laws under Article 7 (1) ECHR, however, the FCC did not follow the ECtHR and reaffirmed the doctrinal distinction between detention as punishment and detention as a preventive measure under national law. In the end, the FCC also concluded that retroactive extensions of preventive detention were unconstitutional, but it relied on a different justification: the protection of legitimate expectations in a rule-of-law society, which entailed that no harsher measures would be imposed on detainees than those in force at the time of their offense. While the substantive outcome was thus equivalent, the FCC's decision also made clear again that there would be no blind obedience to the ECtHR's interpretations.[159]

The follow-up to the *M.* judgment, whose supervision by the Committee of Ministers was closed in 2014 together with that of twelve related judgments,[160] is not unexpected. While remedial legislation had been passed within a year of the Court's judgment, this response sought to maintain the availability of the instrument of preventive detention as broadly as possible, narrowing primary and retroactively ordered preventive detention while expanding the range of cases in which it could be reserved at the time of sentencing.[161] In the case of retrospective preventive detention, the new legislation took advantage of the fact that the notion of unsound mind in Article 5 (1) lit. e ECHR has not received a definite definition in the ECtHR's jurisprudence, and so it created a new and similarly indeterminate category of mental disorder that would permit preventive detention of individuals whose dangerousness resulted from a condition below the threshold of mental illness or insanity. Indeed, the ECtHR itself noted on several occasions that "it appears that the notion of 'persons of unsound mind' [. . .] in Article 5 § 1 (e) of the Convention might be more restrictive than the notion of 'mental disorder' ('*psychische Störung*') referred to in section 1 § 1 of the Therapy Detention Act" and harbored doubts "whether [a] dissocial personality alone could be considered as a sufficiently serious mental disorder so as to be classified as a 'true' mental disorder."[162] So far, however, the Court has either chosen to base the violation of the Convention on other grounds[163] or has found that in the concrete cases before it, the attested disorder was sufficiently severe to constitute a true mental disorder that reached the threshold of being of unsound mind.[164]

The FCC, for its part, followed the ECtHR's arguments to some extent but stopped short of accepting them wholesale. No discernible pressure beyond the threat of additional litigation had been exerted against Germany inter- or transnationally to bring about compliance; if anything, domestic public opinion, fueled by the often well-publicized instances of recidivist violent criminals (despite comparatively low numbers overall) tended to be strongly against a relaxation of the regime,[165] and while parts of the reform had already been planned by the incoming coalition government (e.g., restriction of preventive detention to violent crimes), others had not (e.g., retroactive preventive detention only in cases of mental disorder). Those affected or threatened by preventive detention, owing to their numbers, the nature of their crimes, and their living situation (usually in detention), were, in any event, not in a position to exert meaningful political pressure for broader changes in their favor. Still, even if remedial measures could have been even more favorable (and thus broader), the ECtHR's judgments, the ensuing "dialogue"[166] and "mutual give and take"[167] between the ECtHR and the FCC, and the remedial legislation adopted did improve the overall legal and living situation of preventive detainees while also accommodating the vested interests of the public at large and "allow[ing] the German legal system and its inner logics to remain 'intact.'"[168]

Miscellaneous Judgments

The execution of the only judgment that concerned a Convention violation based on state legislation went smoothly. The applicant had complained about unjustified discrimination on the basis of sex in that under the

Baden-Württemberg state law, only men were required to serve in the fire service or to pay a fire service levy instead. The ECtHR agreed and found a violation of Article 14 ECHR in conjunction with the rarely invoked Article 4 (3) lit. d ECHR (excluding work that is part of normal civic obligations from the prohibition of "forced or compulsory labor").[169] Subsequent to the Court's judgment, Baden-Württemberg and two other *Länder* with similar laws stopped collecting fire service levies and refrained from imposing new ones.[170] The FCC, reversing itself on the issue,[171] and explicitly acknowledging the ECtHR's decision, also declared the impugned provisions null and void due to their incompatibility with the Basic Law's own nondiscrimination provision (Article 3 (3) GG).[172] While it is unclear whether the decisive behavioral impact can be attributed to the ECtHR's or the FCC's decision, the result in either case fully removed the source of the violation and thus the possibility of its recurrence.[173]

In the 2003 *Herz* judgment,[174] the Court found a violation of the applicant's right under Article 5 (4) ECHR to have the legality of his temporary detention in a psychiatric hospital in 1996 reviewed even after the six-week detention order against him had ended and he had in fact escaped from the hospital. Domestic courts had rejected his subsequent requests for review on the argument that he no longer suffered adverse consequences as a result of the order's expiry. In 1998, shortly after the events in question, and reported in the ECtHR's judgment, the FCC had ruled that the right to have the legality of certain public acts reviewed persisted even after their effects had lapsed,[175] and lower courts appear to have followed this new jurisprudential line when examining relevant requests.[176]

The 2006 *Jalloh* judgment was the first one in which the Grand Chamber of the Court found an infringement by Germany of Article 3 ECHR, due to the forcible administration of emetics to a person suspected of having swallowed a small drug package (which indeed he had) as well as of the fair-trial guarantee of under Article 6 (1) ECHR because the evidence thus procured was subsequently used in the criminal trial against the applicant despite it having been obtained in violation of the Convention.[177] While German law does not address the use of emetics specifically, a provision in the *Code of Criminal Procedure* (section 81a) that authorizes "bodily intrusions effected by a doctor [. . .] for the purpose of examination without the accused's consent"[178] has been interpreted by many, though not all, German courts pronouncing on the issue as permitting the forcible administration of emetics. In Germany, the *Länder* are primarily responsible for domestic law enforcement, and several of them had resorted to the practice on a regular basis (resulting, incidentally, in at least two fatalities in 2001 and 2005). The ECtHR's judgment did not leave any discretion to the authorities and, upon instruction by the Federal Ministry of Justice, the forcible administration of emetics was first suspended and then abandoned shortly afterward in the relevant *Länder*[179] (taking emetics voluntarily remains permissible, however).[180]

CHAPTER 11

Exploiting Choice Within a Domestic Human Rights Culture

The empirical findings in this part closely parallel those of the United Kingdom case study. All judgments rendered against Germany during the time period under consideration had been sufficiently complied with as of April 2017—if sometimes with substantial delay—and their supervision by the Committee had consequently been ended. And yet, although Germany's compliance record with ECtHR judgments may thus be viewed as very satisfactory,[1] and there has so far not been any animosity toward the Court akin to that observable in the United Kingdom, this does not imply an unqualified rights-favoring position beyond minimum requirements. Instead, "patterns of restrictive or evasive implementation" are discernible in Germany as well,[2] as illustrated by Germany's responses to the judgments addressing presumptive political radicals in the civil service, the preventive detention regime, and the discovery process in criminal proceedings. At a general jurisprudential level, the FCC has reiterated in several leading judgments that from the vantage point of the domestic legal order and of the courts, there can be no blind obedience to Strasbourg's judgments, but that the latter's domestic execution may have to be adjusted to be made to fit that order,[3] which will usually imply some sort of restrictive reading. The FCC tendency to guard jealously its independence as the ultimate arbiter of German constitutional affairs against external encroachments is emblematic of a general inclination to retain final, if sometimes only marginal, decision-making power on the part of domestic authorities, rather than to concede infringed rights to the fullest extent possible.[4] That such restrictions and the retention of final review and decision-making authority can be justified on the merits, and are not mere whim, is a point well taken—after all, the possibility of limiting the enjoyment of individual rights in view of the protection of the interests of others and of the political community as a whole is part and parcel of virtually all human rights documents, whether national or international—but the important insights are, first, that such considerations almost always come into play, and second, that different alternatives as to how restrictions are to be substantively and procedurally institutionalized usually exist.

Again, as in the UK case, the analysis of German remedial responses has yielded no significant evidence for the relevance of political or material enforcement as a major factor in explaining compliance with the Court's judgments, neither at the national nor at the international level. One might argue that (the threat of) repeat litigation in the absence of a remedial response may affect the cost-benefit calculations of governments—as it apparently did in the context of the *Öztürk* judgment—which could then be qualified as a type of enforcement. Yet while repeat litigation indeed has material consequences—through the expenditure of resources to defend cases in Strasbourg and as a result of additional just satisfaction awards—such consequences are predicated on the assumption that the respondent state will continue to live up at least to its procedural and financial obligations under the Convention, both of which are, however, as little subject to hard enforcement as is the execution of the original leading judgment. Follow-up costs thus materialize and may act as enforcement only when one assumes that the state will actually abide by the financial obligations imposed on it by subsequent clone cases, that is, once we accept the existence of some sort of compliance pull effect with respect to them.

One instance that can be said to have involved enforcement was the *Görgülü* case. Here, successful execution required repeat interventions by the Federal Constitutional Court against the decisions of the regional Naumburg Court of Appeal, which had failed to take due account of Strasbourg's findings and reasoning. To the extent that the Naumburg Court and its judges suffered (the threat of) adverse consequences from its initial recalcitrance, the FCC's interventions can be classified as instances of vertical judicial enforcement of the ECtHR's *Görgülü* judgment by a federal court higher up in the domestic legal-institutional hierarchy, something that does occur with some frequency in hierarchically organized institutional contexts. The FCC, however, was itself not forced by any other actor to comply with the *Görgülü* judgment, and, as was shown above, while articulating a ECtHR-friendly position at the same time used the occasion to reassert the domestic judiciary's final authority with respect to the implementation of ECtHR judgments.

Last but not least, comparable to the adoption of the HRA in the UK, the inclusion of ECtHR judgments as possible grounds for reopening criminal and civil proceedings resulted in legal change in Germany that constituted broader compliance with the spirit of the Convention than was legally required as a remedial consequence triggered by judgments of the Court. The reopening reform appears to be best explained as being part of a general diffusion of ideas among Council of Europe member states that had come around to viewing the reopening of proceedings as the normatively most appropriate remedy to findings of certain Convention violations.[5] It is, in any event, unclear what material or political benefits Germany could have expected to derive from these reforms that would make them more amenable to a rational-instrumentalist explanation, not least given the fact that so few cases in the past had raised, or were expected to raise in the future, the issue of the reopening of domestic proceedings.[6] Regardless, such reforms show that changes to law and policy that enhance the depth of compliance with the ECtHR's judgments can at times be motivated by normative considerations and shifting political views even without being legally required or being motivated by obvious instrumentalist cost-benefit calculations.

It is somewhat otiose to ponder what the compliance record might have looked like had the Court decided some of the cases with higher-stake political and/or material consequences against Germany, such as the complaints lodged in 1975 by members of the terrorist Red Army Faction against their detention conditions and their alleged status as political prisoners,[7] the applications by former German Democratic Republic (GDR) officials against the legality of their punishment for the harsh (and sometimes lethal) GDR border-policing regime,[8] or the complaints taking issue with certain elements of Germany post-reunification land reform[9] and arguing for Germany's responsibility, as successor to the GDR, to indemnify those having been expropriated under the latter's socialist regime.[10] The point made most recently by Shai Dothan that the ECtHR and other courts will often act strategically and manipulate the judicial signal they send so as to maximize the probability of compliance with their judgments is a point well taken.[11] For positivist, observational assessments, however, we are left with the judgments actually rendered, and here Germany's record, like that of other liberal democracies, shows respectable levels or even near-perfect formal compliance, if repeatedly minimalist or restrictive in substance, without any instance in the German case (so far at least) of sustained, intentional noncompliance. As Donald and Leach have recently noted in their case study on

Germany, "The prevailing attitudes, including among parliamentarians and the public, are generally very conducive to compliance. The higher rate of adverse ECtHR judgments against Germany increased the political salience of Strasbourg decisions, but even as regards the most contentious issues politically, debates have still concerned *how* to comply with ECtHR judgments, not *whether* to do so."[12]

Human Rights Compliance as Normatively Constrained Rational Choice

In the recent past, research in international relations on the causes of state and governmental behavior has been dominated by two paradigmatic approaches: rationalism, on the one hand, and constructivism, on the other.[1] Whereas rationalist approaches highlight the centrality of interests, preferences, and of cost-benefit analyses in explaining specific outcomes within particular strategic contexts, constructivist approaches foreground the constitutive role of norms with respect to actor interests and identities as well as their regulatory function by stipulating the appropriate behavior expected of actors with a given identity. As noted in Chapter 1, it has become increasingly accepted that each approach by itself sheds only partial light on the determinants of politically relevant behavior and that, as a result, they often yield not so much alternative but, rather, complementary explanations of social and political phenomena.[2] This book has sought to contribute to this joint research agenda by proposing a hybrid theory of compliance specifically by liberal democracies with the judgments of the European Court of Human Rights, arguing that the best explanation of the observable patterns of behavior analytically separates the *why* from the *how* of compliance, illuminating the why part by reference to a hypothesized normative constraint effect exerted by the Court's judgments on liberal democracies, and explaining the how of compliance on the basis of rational choice theory.

Evaluation of Hypotheses

The empirical evidence presented in the two country case studies generally supports the plausibility of the theory of rational choice within normative constraints articulated in this book. Hypothesis H_{NORM} had predicted that liberal democracies will strive to comply with the Court's judgments and will do so for normative reasons. With the exception of the *Hirst (no. 2)* judgment and its clone cases, this has generally been shown to be the case: governments, whether on the left or on the right of the political spectrum, have always paid just satisfaction as awarded; have taken individual measures in the applicant's case if necessary to provide reparation; and have, where required to achieve compliance, adopted general measures to remedy violations that originated in legislation or general policy or practices. Subject to the caveat that absence of evidence is not evidence of absence, such measures have been adopted with little empirically identifiable pressure that could be qualified as enforcement by political or material means. The recurrent deferral of adopting legislative measures to remedy the violation identified in the UK prisoner voting cases also shows, however, that such voluntary compliance may reach its limits even in the case of liberal democracies when the intervention of the Court into domestic law and policy is seen as being excessively activist and "illegitimate" to the extent that it appears to usurp powers of self-government that are believed to be more properly located and exercised at the national level; UK resistance to the banning of smacking as a permissible practice of parental discipline appeared similarly motivated.

When the perceived sovereignty costs generated by the legal obligation of compliance with an adverse judgment do not exceed a country's reservation cost, the usual strategy of respondent governments is to seek to minimize the consequences for domestic law and policy by exploiting the available spectrum of choices in designing and adopting a remedial response, as predicted by hypothesis H_{RC-1}. Although assessments as to whether a concrete remedial measure is minimalist or not in response to a particular violation of the Convention cannot always be made clearly and determinatively (if only because changes and reforms that appear satisfactory at the formal level of legislation, procedure, or policy guidelines may be implemented restrictively in practice), the case studies reveal that in many, if not most, cases remedial responses can be characterized as more restrictive or minimalist than available alternatives. The fact that a chosen minimalist measure can be justified by reference to the exigencies of the situation or the objectives pursued and is thus not arbitrary or capricious does not detract from the fact that it is still minimalist; after all, broader measures could also have been justified by reference to different objectives or to a different interpretation of the perceived exigencies of a given situation. Instances of broad compliance (if not with a specific judgment, then with the spirit of the Convention) also exist, as evidenced by the adoption of the HRA in the UK or by the introduction of the judgments of the ECtHR as reopening grounds in the German codes of criminal and civil procedure; but as expected by hypothesis H_{RC-2}, these can be linked to changes in general preferences among political majorities. Here again, there is no evidence that governments were compelled, through enforcement, to adopt these measures.

Although the specific requirements for compliance in some cases and circumstances may remain contentious, the overall observable patterns of compliance with the Court's judgments by the UK and Germany are in line with the hybrid constructivist-rationalist theory articulated here, and there is little compelling evidence that would suggest that a rationalist model linking successful compliance to the presence of enforcement would have more explanatory leverage. This does not exclude per se the possibility that political pressure has played a role in bringing about compliance in some cases, or that instrumentalist cost-benefit calculations have motivated remedial action in others; but on the whole, the theory of rational choice within normative constraints is able to explain most observations of compliance with adverse judgments by the ECtHR by the two liberal democracies here studied, certainly more so than the rationalism-only alternative. Neither is it the case that we observe any pervasive "à la carte compliance" according to which "states rarely comply with *all* of the obligations within a ruling."[3] Germany and the UK (again, with the exception, so far, of the prisoner voting-rights judgments) have generally adopted all three types of measures—just satisfaction, individual, and general measures—if necessary to comply with particular judgments. They might have occasionally tried to argue that certain individual or general measures were not necessary, but when the Committee of Ministers insisted on them, they have exercised choice not with respect to the types of measure to be taken, but with respect to their substantive content and design.

The record of compliance elucidated so far thus reveals the ECHR context as one that fits Karen Alter's definition of the judicialization of politics "where citizens, organizations, and firms see law as conferring upon them rights, and where politicians conceive of their policy and legislative options as bounded by what is legally allowed."[4] In terms of the distinction between the dynamic and the constrained views of courts so prominent in analyses of the CJEU,[5] the ECtHR provides evidence for aspects of both. The Court quite clearly has acquired political power of its own that it has used to push for remedies and reforms in a wide variety of issue areas, triggering changes that have often gone against the policies and outcomes preferred by the relevant decision-makers at the time. It is, in any event, demonstrably not the case that the ECtHR simply gives voice to preferences already held domestically by polit-ical majorities in government, the public, or both. At the same time, being dependent on other actors to implement its decisions, its political power is, like that of any other international court,[6] necessarily subject to constraints. In the countries and judgments examined in this book, the ensuing politics of implementation—stylized by some even as a "political battle"[7]—have over-whelmingly revolved around determining (and usually containing) the scope and depth of the Court's domestic impact, not whether there should be any impact at all. As the UK's position on the issue of prisoner voting rights has shown, however, it is not a foregone conclusion that this will always be the case. This variable reach of the Court's judgments is in part a consequence of what Nico Krisch has termed the "open architecture of European human rights law," that is, an order "in which the relationships of the constituent parts are governed not by legal rules but primarily by politics."[8] To be sure, there is a legal obligation to abide by the Court's judgments, but the specific content of that obligation is nowhere expressly defined in the Convention and has instead emerged as a result of, and continues to be shaped by, subsequent practices that are in essence political.

Importantly, if the behavioral logic outlined here is correct, then it strongly suggests that mere appeals to governments to comply more speedily with adverse judgments and do so more broadly in order to prevent clone and follow-up cases may be of little avail, at least in the short run, simply because there are usually few sufficiently powerful political incentives for govern-ments to do so and bear the related costs when these may as well be deferred into the future and then possibly become another government's problem.

Strategies of Minimizing Impact

The case studies have revealed a number of strategies that governments have pursued with a view to limiting the impact of the ECtHR's judgments domes-tically. Some of these strategies have relied upon elements in the ECHR's institutional design, whereas others have exploited interpretive possibilities afforded by the indeterminacy of legal language and the declaratory character of the ECtHR's judgments. Among these strategies are the following:

- **LIMITING COMPLIANCE TO THE APPLICANT'S CASE**

  Remedial measures are limited to the applicant's case, even though broader implications with respect to other persons in similar contexts could be drawn.

- **THE "EXCEPTIONAL CASE" ARGUMENT**

  The need to adopt general measures is argued away by emphasizing the exceptional occurrence of the violation at issue, which is unlikely to be repeated.

- **INCREMENTALISM**

  General measures are limited to the issue or subregime at issue in the decided case, despite its implications for other areas of domestic law or policy; while in accordance with the formal legal obligation under Art. 46 (1) ECHR, this approach elects to disregard a judgment's potentially broader "spirit" and chooses not to address related issues preemptively.

- **RETENTION OF DISCRETION**

  Instead of making a particular benefit whose lack has been found to violate the Convention generally available, that benefit will be made available only subject to an assessment and decision by a specified authority. This way, at least some decision-making authority and discretion is being retained.

- **EXPLOITING AMBIGUITY AND VAGUENESS**

  The fact that a provision or term in the ECHR has not (yet) been given a definitive interpretation by the Court, or that a passage in the judgment itself is open to different understandings, is exploited by imposing one's own interpretation as to what is required and permissible and what is not.

- **LEVELING DOWNWARD**

  In discrimination cases, instead of making the desired benefit available to the disadvantaged group, it will be taken away from the previously advantaged one.

- **COUNTERREFORMS**

  One restriction is removed, as required by the judgment, while another unprohibited measure is imposed elsewhere to counteract the effect of the removal.

- **FINANCIAL COMPENSATION INSTEAD OF SUBSTANTIVE CHANGE**

  Rather than provide for full *restitutio in integrum*, governments sometimes prefer to provide reparation through financial compensation (just satisfaction) instead or are prepared to accept the risk of subsequent clone cases with additional awards of just satisfaction rather than make substantive changes to law and policy in a timely manner.

- **DEROGATION**
  Where the conditions for the invocation of Article 15 ECHR are met—the existence of a "time of war or other public emergency threatening the life of the nation"—states can relieve themselves from strict observance of most, though not all, substantive obligations under the ECHR. While a valid derogation does not suspend the duty to comply with a previously rendered judgment, it will prevent further clone cases from coming to the Court and will dispense with the need to enact legislative changes.

Many examples for these strategies as employed in practice have been adduced in the United Kingdom and the Germany case studies, and there is no a priori reason to expect that the governments of other liberal (as well as not-so-liberal) democracies that feel inconvenienced by a judgment of the Court would not employ them as well. Some evidence that other Council of Europe member states also engage in such minimization and avoidance strategies already exists,[9] and additional research is needed to reveal the extent to which these and additional strategies are used across different types of states, governmental actors, issue areas, and remedial measures.

Sequence and Causality

One argument against the use of compliance as an analytical concept to assess state behavior is that the existence of compliance may be wrongly taken to imply causality.[10] I argued above that while this note of caution is well taken and that compliance is indeed a descriptive concept, in the case of adverse judgments compliance and causal effectiveness will often go together. Often is not always, though. As revealed by the empirical cases, there are four principal scenarios with different implications as to the likelihood of the Court's judgments having played a causal role in affecting state behavior. First, in a number of instances the individual or general measure later found to comply with the Court's judgment had actually been adopted prior even to the lodging of the complaint with the Strasbourg control bodies, so that one cannot credit the Court's later judgment with triggering domestic change. In such cases litigation usually serves the purpose of an ex post confirmation of the incompatibility of the pre-reform's law or policy with the Convention, possibly in the hope of financial compensation for material or immaterial damages. What is conceivable is that the domestic measures had been triggered by the Court's judgment against another state on a comparable law or policy,[11] which would then need to be shown separately. In either case, for any subsequent payment of just satisfaction, when awarded, the Court's judgment would still be the trigger cause since there would otherwise be no reason for a state to pay in the absence of the award (this holds in principle for all just satisfaction awards).

Second, in other cases, applications had already been lodged in Strasbourg, and the Commission had sometimes already issued its report in the pre-1998 system, putting the government on notice that an adverse judgment might be on its way. Governments may then choose not to wait for the final judgment but engage in what may be termed proleptic compliance instead. When this is the case, the expectation of an adverse judgment may contribute to bringing about change, though not necessarily exclusively, although the precise content of the measures adopted would not yet have been affected by the Court's specific *ratio decidendi* as laid out in the judgment.

Third, there are instances where remedial measures followed once the judgment had been issued and responded to the critiques of the given law or policy contained therein, but other domestic forces driving reform efforts were also at play (e.g., an incoming government may have already announced reform plans of its own). Here the judgment may not have been the sole or even primary reason for pursuing reforms but contributed to shaping the specific terms of the reform. Last but not least, there are many cases in which it is quite clear that the government would not have adopted any individual or general measures in the absence of the Court's judgment; in these cases, the claim that the judgment caused change, interacting with a state's disposition toward complying with adverse judgments, is strongest.

In short, then, the argument that compliance and causality usually go together in the case of the satisfactory domestic execution of adverse judgments by the ECtHR—an argument that can in principle be extended to compliance with judgments of international courts more generally—needs to be qualified somewhat. In most cases, the Court's decisions will play an at least contributory causal role in the absence of which there would have been either no change, or different change, of domestic laws, policies, and practices. On occasion, however, judgments will be merely ex post legal assessments that have no role in motivating domestic reforms.

Normative Implications

The empirical evidence on compliance by liberal democracies with the judgments of the European Court of Human Rights presented in this book is, despite occasional "hiccups" resulting in delayed implementation and the as yet uncertain outcome of the prisoner voting rights saga, generally encouraging with respect to the role that judicial institutions may play in inter- and transnational relations. "Compliance without enforcement" is possible,[12] after all, even against the substantive legal and policy preferences of the governments involved. What this requires, however, is a normative commitment on the part of domestic decision-makers to human rights and their institutionalized protection beyond the state. Where such commitment is lacking, or has been incompletely acquired, voluntary compliance is less likely. As Bas de Guy Fortman has written in a related context, "[A] judiciary committed to the human rights venture and convinced of its basic ideas is not to be regarded as a substitute for a human rights culture at all levels of decision-making."[13] Such normative commitment is also of critical importance for the effectiveness of the one enforcement mechanism that is regularly employed against noncomplying respondent states—social pressuring through naming and shaming at the Council of Europe and elsewhere—because the efficacy of naming and shaming is predicated on the idea that the target actually shares certain values with the actors engaging in the practice and thus has something to feel ashamed about. In other words, social enforcement, while implicating a rationalist logic of action, has a normative core.

It may be disappointing to some that the solid formal compliance record of liberal democracies is being purchased at the price of often minimalist compliance. As unsatisfactory as such minimalism may be, especially for those directly affected as well as from the vantage point of efficiency due to its tendency to produce avoidable follow-up litigation, one might also argue that it is the (even normatively) acceptable result of balancing the authority of two types of institutions—the ECtHR, which is specifically intended to safeguard human rights at the regional European level, on the one hand, and the governments of the states subject to its jurisdiction, which serve their domestic constituencies, on the other—each of which has its own defensible claim to democratic legitimacy. In many of the cases discussed in this book, the Court's positions, however principled they may have been, are not the only "correct" or defensible ones that a reasonable interpreter of the Convention would necessarily have to arrive at. Allowing states some margin of appreciation within which to give such decisions effect domestically and to "form" that response in light of the preferences of domestic majorities can itself be seen, within certain limits, as a normatively appropriate balancing of the decision-making of two legitimate sites of politico-legal authority. Inefficiencies resulting from minimalist compliance are then simply costs that have to be accepted as part of operating a governance system in which such actors negotiate, over time and through repeated interaction, the appropriate relationship and balance between majority preferences and the human rights interests of individuals and political minorities. Viewed this way, the logic of rational choice within normative constraints can thus be seen not only as a positive theory of observable state behavior in response to adverse ECtHR judgments, but also as a normative one that vindicates minimalist compliance as democratically legitimate.

Further Judgments Against
the United Kingdom

This appendix lists the judgments against the UK rendered through 2010 that for reasons of space could not be discussed in the main body of the UK case study. Each entry briefly presents the main issue(s) and the Convention article(s) violated and summarizes the remedial measures adopted. The assessment of the depth of compliance in this Appendix is based on the scheme shown in the following table.

Table A1. Categories for Assessing the Depth of Compliance with ECtHR Judgments

Assessment of Compliance	Description
Broad	Remedial response results in enhanced rights protection beyond narrow reading of the judgment, for example, by applying the same remedy to related areas of law and policy not at issue in the case.
Full	Violation is remedied in full, without any meaningful broader or narrower alternatives readily apparent.
Satisfactory	Remedial response addresses source of violation at formal level of legislation, procedure, or practice in a way that, in principle, allows for the prevention of a recurrence of the violation.
Minimalist/Restrictive	Remedial measure responds narrowly to the violation found by the Court, eschews broader alternatives, and/or seeks to retain discretionary decision-making on the part of state authorities.

Table A2. Right to Life

Judgment:	*Paul and Audrey Edwards* (March 14, 2002)
Final Resolution:	CM/ResDH(2009)145 (December 3, 2009)
Issue:	Death of a mentally ill prisoner at the hands of his cell mate, who was considered dangerous; UK authorities had, inter alia, failed to meet their positive obligation under Article 2 to protect the lives of persons in its custody and had carried out an ineffective investigation into the applicants' next-of-kin's death.
Violations:	Article 2, Article 13
Remedial Response:	Remedial measures included, inter alia, the requirement to conduct a cell-sharing risk assessment for every new prisoner and improved transmission of relevant information on detainees to prison operators. The procedural shortcomings are addressed especially by the coming into force of the Human Rights Act. Disagreement persisted between the applicants and the government as to the sufficiency of the individual measures—a further investigation into the circumstances of the applicants' son's death—an issue on which the Committee of Ministers sided with the government.
Assessment:	Satisfactory compliance

Table A3. Freedom from Torture, Inhuman, Or Degrading Treatment/Punishment

Judgment:	*McGlinchey and Others* (April 29, 2003)
Final Resolution:	CM/ResDH(2007)133 (October 31, 2007)
Issue:	Lack of appropriate medical services for heroin addict while in prison, resulting in her death
Violations:	Article 3, Article 13
Remedial Response:	Transfer of health services for prisoners from Prison Services to Primary Care Trusts with a view to improving quality and appropriateness of medical services for drug abusers; additional resources to fund clinical drug-addiction treatment in prison and drug rehabilitation programs
Assessment:	Satisfactory compliance
Judgments:	*Z. and Others* (May 10, 2001); *E. and Others* (November 26, 2002)
Final Resolution:	CM/ResDH(2011)290 (December 2, 2011)
Issue:	Failure to protect children from inhuman/degrading treatment in the form of sexual or physical abuse and neglect by family members
Violations:	Article 3, Article 13
Remedial Response:	New legislation in England, Wales, and Scotland adopted well before judgments were issued imposed stronger obligations on local authorities to make enquiries and take action in cases of suspected maltreatment and neglect of children (England and Wales: Children Act 1989; Scotland: Children [Scotland] Act 1995), plus various other measures. A third related case was settled; see *Z. W.* (Friendly Settlement) (July 29, 2003).
Assessment:	Satisfactory compliance
Judgment:	*Keenan* (April 3, 2001)
Final Resolution:	CM/ResDH(2011)290 (December, 2, 2011)
Issue:	Insufficient psychiatric assessment and treatment of psychotic inmate known to be a suicide risk and belated imposition of serious disciplinary punishments, including seven days of segregation, all of which may have contributed to his eventual suicide
Violations:	Article 3, Article 13
Remedial Response:	Improved monitoring procedures and medical treatment of mentally ill detainees
Assessment:	Satisfactory compliance

(*continued*)

Judgment:	*Price* (July 10, 2001)
Final Resolution:	CM/ResDH(2011)286 (December 2, 2011)
Issue:	Detention in 1995 of four-limb-deficient thalidomide victim in standard facilities that were inadequate in view of her special needs
Violation:	Article 3
Remedial Response:	The Disability Discrimination Act 1995, sec. 21, imposes on public service providers, including prisons, the obligation to cater effectively to people with disabilities; the police, however, were exempt under the 1995 act, which was later remedied by the Disability Discrimination Act 2005, sec. 2. These obligations are now superseded by the Equality Act 2010, sec. 20.
Assessment:	Satisfactory compliance (initially restrictive due to exclusion of police)

Table A4. Right to Liberty and Security of the Person

Judgment:	*Allen* (March 30, 2010)
Final Resolution:	CM/ResDH(2012)64 (March 8, 2012)
Issue:	Refusal to allow the applicant to participate in appeal hearings initiated by the prosecutor concerning an earlier decision granting her bail
Violation:	Article 5 (4)
Remedial Response:	Legislation providing for the right to participate in appeal hearings concerning bail in the relevant jurisdictions was adopted shortly after the judgment: Criminal Procedure (Amendment) Rules 2010, S.I. 2010 No. 1921 (L.12), sec. 8 (amending Criminal Procedure Rules 2010, rule 19.17 [4]) (for England and Wales); Act of Adjournal (Criminal Procedure Rules Amendment No. 4) (Miscellaneous) 2010, Scottish S.I. 2010 No. 418, sec. 3 (inserting new rule 4.2 into Criminal Procedure Rules 1996) (for Scotland). In Northern Ireland, judicial practice reportedly already provided for participation rights.
Assessment:	Full compliance
Judgment:	*Saadi* (January 29, 2008)
Final Resolution:	CM/ResDH(2010)67 (June 3, 2010)
Issue:	An asylum-seeker, detained while his application was being processed under a recently instituted fast-track procedure, had only been informed of the reason for his detention, through his attorney, seventy-six hours after it had commenced. The form that detainees were given and which purported to indicate the reason for detention did not include detention for reason of the fast-track procedure. (The judgment is important for the violation it did not find: the Court considering the applicant's detention for seven days not to be excessive under Article 5 (1) lit. f ECHR).
Violation:	Article 5 (2)
Remedial Response:	The relevant form had been revised in 2002 to also include the fast-track procedure as reason for detention.
Assessment:	Full compliance

(*continued*)

Judgments:	*Kolanis* (June 21, 2005); *Johnson* (October 24, 1997)
Final Resolution:	CM/ResDH(2010)1 (September 15, 2010)
Issue:	Unlawful detention for over three-and-a-half years of patient no longer mentally ill due to authorities' inability to procure accommodation in rehabilitation hostel (*Johnson*); delay of over a year of judicial review of continuing lawfulness of detention in hospital after the Mental Health Review Tribunal (MHRT) had recommended conditional discharge (*Kolanis*)
Violations:	Article 5 (1) (*Johnson*), Articles 5 (4) and (5) (*Kolanis*)
Remedial Response:	Change made in domestic case law in 2002 that enabled MHRTs to reconsider and modify their previous decisions to direct conditional discharge when discharge under the originally specified conditions could not be immediately implemented (previously, such decisions were considered final and not subject to change).
Assessment:	Satisfactory compliance
Judgment:	*H.L.* (October 5, 2004)
Final Resolution:	CM/ResDH(2014)133 (September 10, 2014)
Issue:	Detention of an autistic patient without legal capacity to consent as an "informal patient" under the common law doctrine of necessity—permitting detention of persons who might be a danger to themselves or to others—without sufficient procedural safeguards resulting in health-care professionals effectively assuming full control over applicant's liberty, plus lack of adequate procedure to challenge applicant's detention
Violations:	Article 5 (1), Article 5 (4)
Remedial Response:	England and Wales: Deprivation of Liberty Safeguards laid down in sec. 50 and schedules 7 through 9 of Mental Health Act 2007 provide for a new set of administrative safeguards, including the possibility of review of the lawfulness of detention. Northern Ireland: 2010 Guidance by the Department of Health, Social Services and Public Safety advises mental health practitioners about the need to adhere to principles stated by ECtHR in *H.L.*; with formal legislation (Mental Capacity Bill) before the Northern Ireland Assembly in 2015, there reportedly has been widespread adherence to the Guidance.
Assessment:	Satisfactory compliance (with substantial delay)

Judgment:	*Hutchison Reid* (February 20, 2003)
Final Resolution:	CM/ResDH(2010)214 (December 2, 2010)
Issue:	Unfair burden of proof was imposed on the applicant in proceedings for release, who had to show that his mental illness was not treatable, and excessive delays in those review proceedings, which lasted four years and seven months.
Violation:	Article 5 (4)
Remedial Response:	Mental Health (Public Safety and Appeals) Scotland Act 1999, sec. 64 B1 puts the burden of proof on the authorities; plus increase in number of judges at the relevant Court of Session.
Assessment:	Full compliance
Judgments:	*S.B.C.* (June 16, 2001); *Caballero* (February 8, 2000)
Final Resolutions:	ResDH(2002)41 (April 30, 2002) (*Caballero*); CM/ResDH(2010)214 (December 2, 2010) (*S.B.C.*)
Issue:	Automatic denial of pretrial bail under Criminal Justice and Public Order Act 1994, sec. 25, for detainees previously convicted for certain criminal offences
Violations:	Article 5 (3), Article 5 (5)
Remedial Response:	Already prior to the judgments, the provision had been amended by the Crime and Disorder Act 1998, sec. 56, which, phrased as an exception, allows for bail "if the court or, as the case may be, the constable considering the grant of bail is satisfied that there are exceptional circumstances which justify it" (*S.B.C.*, para. 15). Although in principle enabling bail for repeat offenders, by making the decision to do so dependent on a judicial or police officer's assessment of the existence of exceptional circumstances, the change in the law retained as much decision-making competence in such matters for the competent state authorities as possible.
Assessment:	Minimalist compliance: The UK could also have chosen the broader approach of making the grant of bail the standard approach and subjecting that standard to the exceptional option of refusing bail if relevant reasons argued against it, but instead it chose the narrowly compliant solution described above.

(*continued*)

Judgment:	*X. (Merits)* (November 5, 1981); *X. (Just Satisfaction)* (October 18, 1982)
Final Resolution:	DH(83)2 (March 23, 1983)
Issue:	Inability of detainee committed to Broadmoor Hospital (for the criminally insane) to effectively challenge his recall to the institution by the home secretary after he had been conditionally discharged (so-called restricted release)
Violation:	Article 5 (4)
Remedial Response:	The Mental Health (Amendment) Act 1982, sec. 28 (4) and sched. 1 empowered the MHRTs to order—not only recommend—the release of restricted patients.
Assessment:	Minimalist compliance:[1] Narrowly targeted to violation; broader alternative would have been to change scope of habeas corpus proceedings generally.

[1]Similarly: Hoggett 1983, 185; Peay 1982, 798–808 (questioning independence of the MHRTs and the effectiveness of the new safeguards); but see also Churchill and Young 1992, 299 (noting that compliance was achieved) and Gostin 1982, 785 (arguing that UK went beyond requirements of ECtHR's judgment in *X.*).

Table A5. Right to a Fair Trial

Judgment:	*Tsfayo* (November 14, 2006)
Final Resolution:	CM/ResDH(2010)75 (June 3, 2010)
Issue:	The Housing Benefit Review Board (HBRB) that had heard the applicant's application regarding a dispute over housing and tax benefits had not been independent of one of the parties to the dispute since several of its members were councilors from the local authority, which would have been liable to pay part of the benefits, if awarded.
Violation:	Article 6 (1)
Remedial Response:	Since July 2001, well before the judgment and in response to repeated domestic calls for their abolition by the UK Council on Tribunals for reasons similar to those voiced in *Tsfayo*, the HBRBs had been abolished and replaced by independent appeals tribunals set up under social security legislation adopted in 2000 (see Child Support, Pensions and Social Security Act 2000, sec. 68 and sched. 7, para. 6).
Assessment:	Full compliance
Judgments:	*Shannon* (October 4, 2005); *Kansal* (April 27, 2004); *I.J.L., G.M.R. and A.K.P.* (Merits) (September 19, 2000); *Saunders* (December 17, 1996)
Final Resolutions:	ResDH(2004)88 (December 21, 2004) (*Saunders* and *I.J.L., G.M.R. and A.K.P.*); CM/ResDH(2010)146 (September 15, 2010) (*Kansal*); CM/ResDH(2009)141 (December 3, 2009) (*Shannon*)
Issue:	Use of evidence obtained by way of compulsory powers during certain investigations into business wrongdoing in subsequent criminal trials in violation of applicants' right not to incriminate themselves
Violation:	Article 6 (1)
Remedial Response:	As an interim measure, an attorney general guidance note informed prosecutors of the inadmissibility of evidence procured under the use of compulsory powers in subsequent criminal trials, with a few exceptions. This guidance applied broadly to all such evidence, regardless of the specific regime under which it was obtained. These regulations were formalized by legislation in 1999 that removed the admissibility of such evidence from the relevant statutes (Youth Justice and Criminal Evidence Act 1999, sec. 59 and sched. 3; see also Explanatory Notes to Youth Justice and Criminal Evidence Act 199, paras. 199, 200).

(*continued*)

Assessment:	Broad compliance: While difficult to see benefits or specific interests, in the abstract and ex ante, in maintaining the admissibility of such evidence under one regime but not another, this response represents an instance of broad compliance beyond the requirements suggested by the specific aspects of the case decided by the Court.

Judgment:	*S.C.* (June 15, 2004)

Final Resolution:	CM/ResDH(2011)171 (September 14, 2011)
Issue:	Criminal proceedings against an eleven-year old child with low intellectual abilities that were conducted in a manner that did not enable him to participate effectively in his trial for attempted robbery
Violation:	Article 6 (1)
Remedial Response:	Two practice directions issued by the lord chief justice, Trial of Children and Young Persons in the Crown Court (2000) and another on vulnerable defendants (2007), emphasized the necessity as well as various means to accommodate the needs of vulnerable defendants, including children, in the courtroom. In addition, a 2006 amendment of the Youth Justice and Criminal Evidence Act 1999 provided for the possibility for vulnerable defendants to give evidence through a live link from outside the courtroom.
Assessment:	Satisfactory compliance

Judgments:	*Edwards and Lewis* (October 27, 2004); *Dowsett* (June 24, 2003); *Atlan* (June 19, 2001); *Rowe and Davis* (February 16, 2000)

Final Resolutions:	CM/ResDH(2010)214 (December 2, 2010) (*Dowsett, Rowe and Davis* and *Atlan*); CM/ResDH(2011)289 (December 2, 2011) (*Edwards and Lewis*)
Issue:	Failure of the prosecution to disclose to the defense evidence that would have strengthened the latter's case
Violation:	Article 6 (1)

Remedial Response:	Remedied prior to the ECtHR's judgments but after the applications in some of these cases had been lodged; first stipulated in the Criminal Procedure and Investigations Act 1996 and subsequently amended as part of the Criminal Justice Act 2003, the amended law imposes an obligation on the prosecution to disclose all material "that has not previously been disclosed and which might reasonably be considered capable of undermining the case for the prosecution against the accused, or of assisting the case for the accused" (Explanatory Notes to Criminal Justice Act 2003, para. 23), an obligation subject to review by the trial court (see Criminal Procedure and Investigations Act 1996, secs. 3, 4, 7, 9, and Criminal Justice Act 2003, pt. 5).
Assessment:	Full compliance

Judgment:	*Kingsley* (May 28, 2002)
Final Resolution:	CM/ResDH(2010)214 (December 2, 2010)
Issue:	Lack of appearance of impartiality of the Gaming Board for Great Britain, which in 1994 revoked the applicant's certificates regarding his employment as a director in the gaming industry, after some Gaming Board members had previously made remarks as to the applicant's unfitness to direct a casino company
Violation:	Article 6 (1)
Remedial Response:	Reorganization of the Gaming Board and subsequent replacement with the Gambling Commission, with appeal lying to the Gambling Appeals Tribunal, and then to the High Court; in the interim, Gaming Board membership was increased from five to eight to allow greater flexibility of excluding potentially biased members from decision-making panels; formal legislation followed in the form of the Gambling Act 2005 and Gambling Act (Commencement No. 2 and Transitional Provisions) Order 2005, S.I. 2005 No. 2455.
Assessment:	Satisfactory compliance

Judgment:	*P., C. and S.* (July 16, 2002)
Final Resolution:	CM/ResDH(2010)214 (December 2, 2010)
Issue:	Parental lack of effective access to a court and unfair proceedings due to absence of legal representation in care and adoption proceedings brought by local authority; removal of baby from mother at birth and lack of involvement in decisions concerning family matters
Violations:	Article 6 (1), Article 8

(*continued*)

Remedial Response: Since legislation at such was not at issue, only individual deci-
                        sions by a judge and the local authority, the Department of
                        Health pledged that it would keep the Court's ruling in mind
                        in the implementation of the new Adoption and Children Act
                        2002, including with respect future guidance to local authori-
                        ties and adoption agencies.

Assessment: Satisfactory compliance

Judgments: *Beckles* (October 8, 2002); *Condron* (May 2, 2000)

Final Resolutions: CM/ResDH(2010)214 (December 2, 2010)

Issue: Juries had been instructed that they could draw adverse infer-
                        ences from a defendant's silence during police questioning,
                        without having to take into consideration that the defendant
                        may have been specifically advised to remain silent by his or
                        her counsel.

Violation: Article 6 (1)

Remedial Response: In 2001, the Judicial Studies Board, responsible for the
                        training of judges, issued a revised specimen direction to be
                        used for instructing juries that included a more differentiated
                        approach to the evaluation of silence during interrogation,
                        providing, inter alia, that where juries believed a defendant
                        "had or may have had an answer to give, but reasonably relied
                        on the legal advice to remain silent, [they] should not draw
                        any conclusion against him" (quoted in *Beckles*, para. 39).

Assessment: Minimalist compliance: New specimen directions are nar-
                        rowly tailored exactly to details of case—counsel's advice to
                        remain silent has to be taken into account—but still leave it
                        to jurors to evaluate whether they believe that reliance on
                        counsel's advice was in good faith or represented "convenient
                        shield" beyond which to hide (cf. *Beckles*, para. 39).

Judgment: *McGonnell* (February 8, 2000)

Final Resolution: ResDH(2001)120 (October 15, 2001)

Issue: Perceived lack of impartiality by the Royal Court of Guernsey
                        due to the overseeing by the bailiff—Guernsey's chief civil
                        officer—of passage of regulations that he was later called
                        upon to adjudicate as president of Royal Court

Violation: Article 6 (1)

Remedial Response:	Abolition of the bailiff's membership in principal legislative and administrative committees and the right during legal proceedings to object to the presiding judge, who is under an obligation to reveal his prior involvement in any of the issues to be decided by the court
Assessment:	Full compliance

Judgment:	*Scarth* (July 22, 1999)
Final Resolution:	DH(2000)48 (April 10, 2000)
Issue:	Lack of public hearings in recovery of debt proceedings
Violation:	Article 6 (1)
Remedial Response:	Under Civil Procedure Rules 1998, S.I. 1998 No. 3132 (L. 17), sec. 39.2 (1), all hearings are to be held in public, including those on small claims at issue in this case, except where a court finds that a limited list of considerations (such as national security or the interests of children) require a private hearings.
Assessment:	Full compliance

Judgment:	*McMichael* (February 24, 1995)
Final Resolution:	DH(97)508 (October 29, 1997)
Issue:	Lack of fair adversarial proceedings due to withholding of confidential reports and other documents from parents in custody hearings
Violations:	Article 6 (1), Article 8
Remedial Response:	The Children's Hearings (Scotland) Rules 1996, S.I. 1996 No. 3261 (S. 251), rule 5 (3), provide that any document or information furnished to the members of a children's hearing shall also be made available to all other relevant persons in relation to the child whose case is being considered.
Assessment:	Full compliance

Judgments:	*O., W., B., R., and H.* (all Merits) (July 8, 1987)
Final Resolutions:	DH(90)3 (*O.*), DH(90)4 (*B.*), DH(90)5 (*W.*), and DH(90)6 (*R.*) (March 12, 1990); DH(88)22 (December 9, 1988) (*H.*)
Issue:	Lack of involvement of parents in decisions concerning access to their children committed to public care and absence of effective judicial remedies to determine the merits of the related public care orders
Violations:	Article 6 (1), Article 8 (except for *O.*)

(*continued*)

Remedial Response:	The revised Children Act 1989 mandated the involvement of parents and guardians in the decision-making process and also empowered the courts to review the merits of such cases and to make consequential access orders, where deemed appropriate.
Assessment:	Satisfactory/full compliance (at level of procedure)

Judgment:	*Campbell and Fell* (June 28, 1984)

Final Resolution:	DH(86)7 (June 27, 1986)
Issue:	Nonpublic decisions of the Board of Visitors, a disciplinary body adjudicating prisoner matters, lack of legal representation at board hearing and of adequate facilities to prepare defense; lack of access of a court due to delay in granting access to legal advice concerning potential claims for compensation; interference with regard to right to respect for correspondence (discussed above)
Violations:	Article 6 (1), Article 6.3.b and c, Article 8, Article 13
Remedial Response:	Decisions of the Board of Visitors are henceforth to be made sufficiently public, with right to publicly funded legal representation (implementation by way of policy circular to chairmen of Boards of Visitors and prison governors).
Assessment	Satisfactory compliance

Table A6. Right to Respect for Private and Family Life

Judgment:	*M.A.K. and R.K.* (March 23, 2010)
Final Resolution:	CM/ResDH(2012)65 (March 8, 2012)
Issue:	Hospital staff, suspecting sexual abuse of a nine-year-old girl, had conducted tests in the absence of parental consent and without a court order, and also had restricted the father's access to the child over four days before finally consulting a dermatologist, who diagnosed the visible bruising as a rare skin disease. The ECtHR considered this approach to be in breach of domestic law and disproportionate.
Violations:	Article 8, Article 13
Remedial Response:	Revised statutory guidance had been issued in 2006, 2008, and 2010, pointing out that the correct way in cases of suspicion of abuse is to request a judicial Emergency Protection Order to restrict access, rather than maintain informal arrangements, with various documents also stressing the critical role of parental consent when conducting medical tests or treatment.
Assessment:	Satisfactory compliance
Judgment:	*A.D. and O.D.* (March 16, 2010)
Final Resolution:	CM/ResDH(2012)66 (March 8, 2012)
Issue:	Deficient manner in which social service authorities had conducted a (faulty) family risk assessment that resulted in the placement of the second applicant in foster care and his belated return to his family; the risk assessment had been triggered by the diagnosis of several bone fractures and the suspicion of parental abuse; the fractures, however, eventually turned out to be the result of a rare medical condition (brittle bone disease).
Violations:	Article 8, Article 13 in conjunction with Article 8
Remedial Response:	The UK has sought to prevent a recurrence of similar violations by way of issuing revised statutory guidance in 2006 and 2010, which, among other things, highlights the procedures to be followed, including medical examinations, when a child is considered to be at risk.
Assessment:	Satisfactory compliance

(*continued*)

Judgment:	*Dickson* (December 4, 2007)

Final Resolution:	CM/ResDH(2011)176 (September 14, 2011).
Issue:	In the absence of provision for conjugal visits, the applicants (a prisoner sentenced to life imprisonment and his wife) requested but were denied artificial insemination facilities by the secretary of state in accordance with a general policy to honor such requests only in exceptional circumstances. The Court found that the policy was too rigid and did not allow for a proper balancing of the different interests at stake.
Violation:	Article 8
Remedial Response:	The relevant policy has subsequently been amended, with the restriction of "very exceptional circumstances" having been eliminated and replaced by a proportionality test to be conducted by the secretary of state, whose decision can be challenged by way of judicial review. In the case of the applicants, individual measures became unnecessary because Mr. Dickson had become eligible for unescorted home leave in 2007.
Assessment:	Satisfactory compliance

Judgment:	*Wainwright* (September 26, 2006)

Final Resolution:	CM/ResDH(2011)290 (December 2, 2011)
Issue:	Disproportionate manner in which strip searches were conducted on the applicants in deviation from standard procedures when visiting their son/brother in prison, justified by the possibility that they might be smuggling drugs. Except for battery, no means of obtaining redress existed at the material time.
Violations:	Article 8, Article 13
Remedial Response:	Various policy instruments, drawing attention to *Wainwright*, have since emphasized the need to conduct strip searches in strict conformity with applicable rules, breach of which will make strip searches unlawful.
Assessment:	Satisfactory compliance

Judgment:	*Keegan* (July 18, 2006)

Final Resolution:	CM/ResDH(2009)144 (December 3, 2009)
Issue:	Forcible entry by the police into the home of the applicants, mistakenly believing it to be the home of an armed robber after having failed to exercise due diligence in ascertaining the identity of the current residents

Violations:	Article 8, Article 13
Remedial Response:	Shortly before the judgment, on January 1, 2006, a new police practice code issued under authority of the Police and Criminal Evidence Act 1984, sec. 66, relating, inter alia, to searches had entered into effect and highlighted the necessity of first making appropriate investigations as to the accuracy of any information before requesting a warrant. The requirement has been reenacted in the Revised Code of Practice for Searches of Premises by Police Officers and the Seizure of Property Found by Police Officers on Persons or Premises (effective October 27, 2013), para. 3.1 (before making an application for a search warrant, an "officer must take reasonable steps to check the information is accurate, recent and not provided maliciously or irresponsibly").
Assessment:	Satisfactory compliance

Judgment:	*Roche* (October 19, 2005)

Final Resolution:	CM/ResDH(2009)20 (January 9, 2009)
Issue:	Inadequate access to information about mustard- and nerve-gas tests performed on applicant at Chemical and Biological Defense Establishment at Porton Down in 1963 (overall, 3,000 service personnel had been subject to nerve gas tests and 6,000 to mustard gas tests in 1962 and 1963.)
Violation:	Article 8
Remedial Response:	Compliance in terms of general measures was provided by the Data Protection Act 1998, with a number of additional initiatives having been taken to facilitate access to information by those who had participated in the tests. The delay in execution appears to have been due to the adoption of individual measures in the case because certain documents that the applicant needed to prove a causal link between the tests and his medical condition—chronic obstructive pulmonary disorder—could not be located. In July 2007, the Pension Appeal Tribunal found the link substantiated, and from January 2008, the applicant received an increased pension due to the disability he sustained as a result of participating in the tests.
Assessment:	Full compliance

(*continued*)

Judgments:	*M.G.* (September 24, 2002); *Gaskin* (July 7, 1989)
Final Resolutions:	ResDH(2000)106 (July 24, 2000) (*Gaskin*); CM/ResDH(2010)137 (September 15, 2010) (*M.G.*)
Issue:	Lack of access to social service records relating to the applicants' time spent in public care
Violation:	Article 8
Remedial Response:	While the Access to Personal Files (Social Services) Regulations, S.I. 1989 No. 206, was adopted just prior to the *Gaskin* judgment, imposing a duty on social service agencies to provide access to information held on an individual, it had no retroactive effect. Full compliance occurred only in 1998, when a general right of access to information, whether held by public or private bodies, was established by the Data Protection Act 1998, secs. 7 and 68.
Assessment:	Initially restrictive, later full (albeit incidental) compliance: Although the Data Protection Act of July 16, 1998, remedied the violation found in these cases, it did so as a by-product because it was primarily a (just-in-time) response to the UK's duty to transpose EU directive 95/46/EC on the protection of individuals with regard to the processing of personal data scheduled to enter into force October 25, 1998 (see Directive 95/46/EC of the European Parliament and of the Council of 24 October 1995 on the Protection of Individuals with Regard to the Processing of Personal Data and on the Free Movement of such Data, 1995 *O.J.* [L 281] 31–50 [November 23, 1995]).
Judgment:	*T.P. and K.M.* (May 10, 2001)
Final Resolution:	CM/ResDH(2008)84 (October 8, 2008)
Issue:	Lack of adequate involvement of mother in authority's decision to take child into public care on allegations of sexual abuse due to withholding of crucial evidence
Violations:	Article 8, Article 13 (lack of remedy)
Remedial Response:	Legal shortcomings had been addressed by new instruments adopted in 1991 that require the disclosure of all materials to be used in care proceedings to the other parties; see Family Proceedings Rules 1991, S.I. 1991 No. 1247 (L.20), Rule 4.23 (1), and Family Proceedings Court (Children Act 1989) Rules 1991, S.I. 1991 No. 1395 (L.17), Rule 17.
Assessment:	Satisfactory compliance

Judgment:	J.T. (March 30, 2000)
Final Resolution:	CM/ResDH(2014)131 (September 10, 2014)
Issue:	Inability to change "nearest relative" appointed to fulfil certain guardianship functions during involuntary detention in mental health institution; settlement included UK's pledge to amend the legislation so as to enable such a change.
Violation:	Friendly Settlement (Article 8)
Remedial Response:	England and Wales: Mental Health Act 2007, secs. 23–26, in force since November 2008, provide psychiatric detainees with right to challenge appointment of "nearest relative" in court and to propose a more agreeable replacement. Northern Ireland: reform of the relevant legislation has been stalled again and again for many years, but in April 2014, the High Court (Queen's Bench Division) interpreted the relevant Articles 32 and 36 of the Mental Health (Northern Ireland) Order 1986 in a way that now permits challenges by patients in line with those available under English and Welsh law.
Assessment:	Satisfactory compliance (with substantial delay)

Table A7. Freedom of Expression

Judgment:	*Hashman and Harrup* (Judgment of November 25, 1999)
Final Resolution:	CM/ResDH(2011)180 (September 14, 2011)
Issue:	So-called binding over orders had been imposed on the applicants that required them to "keep the peace and be of good behavior" after they had, as "hunt saboteurs," sought to disrupt a hunt by blowing a hunting horn and shouting at the dogs, but despite the fact that this behavior had not been found to constitute a breach of the peace. Due to the lack of specificity of the terms used in the order, the ECtHR found that the restrictions on the applicants' freedom of expression could not be considered "prescribed by law" (Article 10 (2) ECHR), because it was impossible to foresee what kind of behavior would breach the order.
Violations:	Article 10
Remedial Response:	Although guidance was sent to prosecutors in 2000 not to ask for binding over orders unless there was past conduct that, if repeated, would constitute a breach of the peace, practice directions to the relevant courts remained outstanding, resulting in a 2005 interim resolution (CM Res. DH(2005)59 of July 5, 2005). In 2007 such a practice direction was finally adopted. It specified that "[r]ather than binding an individual over to 'keep the peace' in general terms, the court should identify the specific conduct or activity from which the individual must refrain" (Consolidated Criminal Practice Direction, pt. III, para. 31.3, http://webarchive.nationalarchives.gov.uk/20080814090439/justice.gov.uk/criminal/procrules_fin/contents/practice_direction/pd_consolidated.htm).
Assessment:	Satisfactory compliance (with substantial delay of eight years)

Judgment:	*Bowman* (Judgment of February 19, 1998)
Final Resolution:	CM/ResDH(2007)14 (February 28, 2007)
Issue:	Conviction for distributing antiabortion leaflets prior to the 1992 general election in breach of the legally mandated preelection expenditure limit of £5 for unauthorized third parties with respect to promoting or prejudicing the election of specific candidates (At 50p, the original cost-limit in the Representation of the People Act 1983, sec. 75 [1] lit. b [ii] had been even lower, but it was increased to £5 in 1985 by the Representation of the People Act 1985, sec. 14 (3)).
Violations:	Article 10

Remedial Response: In 2000, this limit was raised to £500 with respect to influenc-
ing the election of candidates in general elections and to £50
with respect to candidates in local elections though amending
the Representation of the People Act 1983 by way of the Political Parties, Elections and Referendums Act 2000, sec. 131.

Assessment: Minimalist compliance: Despite the increase, the limits
remain quite low, continuing to preclude many supportive
activities by third parties in favor of a particular candidate. A
broader option would have been to abolish the statutory limit,
but this went against prevailing preferences, inter alia, among
the major parties in the UK (see Fifth Report of the Committee on Standards in Public Life [Neill Committee], The
Funding of Political Parties in the United Kingdom [October
1998], Cm 4057–I, 111, 126–131).

Table A8. Right to Marry

Judgment:	*B. and L.* (September 19, 2005)
Final Resolution:	CM/ResDH(2010)187 (December 2, 2010)
Issue:	Prohibition of marriage between a father-in-law and his daughter-in-law, unless both of their former spouses had died
Violation:	Article 12
Remedial Response:	Prohibition removed in all British jurisdictions shortly after the ECtHR's judgment: in England and Wales by Marriage Act 1949 (Remedial) Order 2007, S.I. 2007 No. 438; in Scotland by Family Law (Scotland) Act 2006, sec. 1; and in Northern Ireland by Law Reform (Miscellaneous Provisions) (Northern Ireland) Order 2006, S.I. 2006 No. 1945 (N.I.14)
Assessment:	Full compliance

Table A9. Prohibition of Unjustified Discrimination

Judgment:	*J.M.* (Judgment of September 28, 2010)
Final Resolution:	CM/ResDH(2012)231 (December 6, 2012)
Issue:	The Child Support Act 1991 provided for reduced child maintenance when an absent parent was in a new relationship, whether married or unmarried, but did not apply to same-sex relationships.
Violation:	Article 14 in conjunction with Article 1 of Protocol No. 1
Remedial Response:	Since 2004, well before the application in *J.M.* (September 6, 2006), the Civil Partnership Act 2004, and further legislation adopted under it, provided that same-sex partnerships are recognized in the same way for purposes of child maintenance as are heterosexual relationships.
Assessment:	Full compliance
Judgment:	*Clift* (Judgment of July 13, 2010)
Final Resolution:	CM/ResDH(2011)288 (December 2, 2011)
Issue:	Under the Criminal Justice Act 1991, prisoners sentenced to fixed-terms sentences of more than fifteen years, when applying for early release, required the approval of the secretary of state in addition to a positive recommendation from the Parole Board, whereas for those with fixed sentences of less than fifteen years and life sentences, the latter sufficed.
Violation:	Article 14 in conjunction with Article 5
Remedial Response:	As of August 2, 2010, new legislation (Coroners and Justice Act 2009, sec. 145) initiated before the Court's judgment, but after the introduction of the application (January 29, 2007), made the Parole Board's early release decisions binding on the secretary of state, thus removing the latter's discretion.
Assessment:	Full compliance
Judgment:	*O'Donoghue and Others* (Judgment of December 14, 2010)
Final Resolution:	CM/ResDH(2011)288 (December 2, 2011).
Issue:	Regulations introduced in 2005 required a Certificate of Approval from immigrants, subject to a fee of £295, if they wanted to marry in a church other than the Church of England.
Violations:	Article 14 in conjunction with Article 12 and Article 9; Article 12

(*continued*)

Remedial Response:	By the time of the ECtHR's judgment in 2010, payment of the fee had already been suspended as of April 9, 2009, and remedial legislation—the Asylum and Immigration (Treatment of Claimants, etc.) Act 2004 (Remedial) Order 2011, S.I. 2011 No. 1158—had been introduced in response to a similar finding by the Appellate Committee of the House of Lords in 2008. With its coming into effect in May 2011, the certificate of approval scheme was abolished. The order's Explanatory Notes only refer to domestic decisions as reason for the change; the House of Lords case is R. (Baiai and Others) v. Secretary of State for the Home Department, 2008 UKHL 53.
Assessment:	Full compliance

Judgment:	*P.M.* (Judgment of July 19, 2005)
Final Resolution:	CM/ResDH(2009)143 (December 3, 2009)
Issue:	According to the Income and Corporation Taxes Act 1988, as amended by Finance Act 1988, sec. 36, married or divorced fathers could deduct maintenance payments made in respect of their children for tax purposes, but unmarried fathers could not.
Violation:	Article 14 in conjunction with Article 1 of Protocol No. 1
Remedial Response:	In 2000, the tax deductibility of such payments had been abolished by Finance Act 1999, sec. 36, except when one party to a marriage was born before April 6, 1935. Because this change, already noted in the judgment (para. 19), occurred well before the case had even been lodged with Strasbourg (on February 14, 2003), it is clear that the ECtHR's decision did not have any causal effect on its abolition. The continuing discrimination of parents sixty-five years and older at the time between those that were or had been married and those that had not was eliminated in 2005 as part of an overhaul of tax regulations in order to accommodate civil partnerships (Tax and Civil Partnership Regulations 2005, S.I. 2005 No. 3229, sec. 67). No reason for this change is given; see Explanatory Memorandum to the Tax and Civil Partnership Regulation 2005, para. 7.10. The regulation has been superseded by Income Tax Act 2007, sec. 454.
Assessment:	Full compliance

Table A10. Protection of Property

Judgment:	*Stretch* (June 24, 2003)
Final Resolution:	ResDH(2005)101 (October 26, 2005)
Issue:	Interference in the peaceful enjoyment of property due to a public authority's denial of the optional extension of a lease apparently lawful at the time of its conclusion, but later said to have been ultra vires
Violation:	Article 1 of Protocol No. 1
Remedial Response:	Remedied prior to judgment by Local Government (Contracts) Act 1997, sec. 2, which provides that contracts beyond a local authority's statutory powers will have effects as if the local authority had had power to enter into them and had properly exercised that power
Assessment:	Full compliance

Table A11. Right to Free Elections

Judgment:	Matthews (February 18, 1999)
Final Resolution:	ResDH(2006)57 (November 2, 2006)
Issue:	Residents of Gibraltar, a Crown dependency not formally part of the United Kingdom, could not vote for the European Parliament, despite the fact that the UK had extended large parts of the European Economic Community (EC) Treaty to Gibraltar upon accession to the EC in 1972. In 1976, however, the Labour government had requested that Gibraltar be excluded from the first direct elections to the European Parliament (EP). Several subsequent proposals for inclusion of Gibraltar failed, in part due to the argument that this would require an amendment of the 1976 EC act that would likely be vetoed by Spain. For background, see The European Parliament (Representation) Bill, House of Commons Research Paper 07/78 (December 4, 2002).
Violation:	Article 3 of Protocol No. 1
Remedial Response:	After the Matthews judgment, the UK proposed such an amendment, which Spain indeed rejected. After a 2001 interim resolution lamented the delay in the judgment's execution, the UK took unilateral action and included Gibraltar in one of its existing electoral regions in time for the 2004 EP elections.
Assessment:	Full compliance. It is not entirely clear, however, why the UK waited until 2003 with the implementation of an option that had been suggested since the mid-1980s. Prior to the ECtHR judgment, extension of the EP franchise to Gibraltar was apparently not a priority, despite favorable domestic opinion. The Court's decision may have provided the UK with welcome justification to justify a unilateral approach, given Spanish opposition to an EU-level solution.

NOTES

Introduction

1. See for example Lovat and Shany 2014, 253n2; Bates 2010, 2; Open Society Justice Initiative 2010, 52; Goldhaber 2007, 2, 189–190; Greer 2006, 1; Helfer and Slaughter 1997.

2. See generally Lambert Abdelgawad 2016.

3. See ECtHR Annual Report 2011, 149, http://www.echr.coe.int/Documents/Annual_report_2011_ENG.pdf.

4. See ECtHR Annual Report 2015, 197, http://www.echr.coe.int/Documents/Annual_Report_2015_ENG.pdf

5. Madsen 2016, 174.

6. See for example Lamprecht 2015, 259–267.

7. "Neither the ECHR, nor the legal positions of the ECtHR based on it, can cancel the priority of the Constitution. Their practical implementation in the Russian legal system is only possible through recognition of the supremacy of the Constitution's legal force." Quoted in Smirnova 2015; for discussion, see Pustorino 2016.

8. See, e.g., Madsen 2016, 174; Oomen 2016; Dzehtsiarou and Greene 2011; and the contributions to Arnardóttir and Buyse 2016; Popelier, Lambrecht, and Lemmens 2016; Flogaitis, Zwart, and Fraser 2013.

9. Madsen 2016, 175. Throughout this book, ellipses not included in the source text will be identified through the use of square brackets.

10. High Level Conference on the Future of the European Court of Human Rights, Brighton Declaration, April 20, 2012, http://www.echr.coe.int/Documents/2012_Brighton_FinalDeclaration_ENG.pdf; High-Level Conference on the 'Implementation of the European Convention on Human Rights, Our Shared Responsibility,' Brussels Declaration, March 27, 2015, https://www.coe.int/t/dghl/standardsetting/cddh/reformechr/Declaration-Brussels_EN.pdf.

11. Protocol No. 15 Amending the Convention on the Protection of Human Rights and Fundamental Freedoms, June 24, 2013, Council of Europe Treaty Series—No. 213, http://www.echr.coe.int/Documents/Protocol_15_ENG.pdf. As of October 17, 2017, thirty-six states had ratified Protocol No. 15, see Chart of Signatures and Ratifications of Treaty 213, https://www.coe.int/en/web/conventions/full-list/-/conventions/treaty/213/signatures?p_auth=j8tQv0bQ.

12. Protocol No. 16 to the Convention on the Protection of Human Rights and Fundamental Freedoms, October 2, 2013, Council of Europe Treaty Series—No. 214, http://www.echr.coe.int/Documents/Protocol_16_ENG.pdf. For analysis, see Gionnopoulos 2015; Voland and Schiebel 2017. As of October 17, 2017, eight states had ratified Protocol No. 16, see Chart of Signatures and Ratifications of Treaty 214, https://www.coe.int/en/web/conventions/full-list/-/conventions/treaty/214/signatures?p_auth=j8tQv0bQ.

13. Brussels Declaration, 2, https://www.coe.int/t/dghl/standardsetting/cddh/reformechr/Declaration-Brussels_EN.pdf.

14. Steering Committee for Human Rights 2015, 59–60.

15. Since 2000, PACE has issued eight reports examining problems in the execution of ECtHR judgments, the most recent report being from September 2015; see Parliamentary Assembly of the Council of Europe 2015.

16. The Effectiveness of the European Convention on Human Rights: The Brighton Declaration and Beyond, PACE Resolution 2055 (2015) (April 24), para. 4, http://assembly.coe.int/nw/xml/XRef/Xref-XML2HTML-en.asp?fileid=21754&lang=en.

17. Committee of Ministers 2017a, 47.

18. Ibid., 59.

19. Helfer 2014b, 41.

20. Ryssdal 1996, 67

21. Warbrick 1991, 140; for similar assessments, see Leuprecht 1993, 791, 800; Harmsen 2001, 34.

22. Carter and Trimble 1995, 309.

23. See, e.g., Gerards and Fleuren 2014; Keller and Stone Sweet 2008; Barkhuysen and van Emmerik 2005; Blackburn and Polakiewicz 2001; Churchill and Young 1992.

24. See Krisch 2008, 197, and 2010, 127n95 (noting the absence of "systematic studies" on compliance rates with ECtHR judgments); Janis, Kay, and Bradley 2008, 104 ("It is just this sort of general study that is most lacking"); Posner and Yoo 2005, 65, 66 (absence of "good data to corroborate . . . whether compliance with EC[t]HR judgments has been high or low").

25. See only Donald and Leach 2016, 303 (noting "an unprecedented focus on national implementation of Convention standards and [ECtHR] judgments").

26. Social scientists had for a long time bypassed the ECtHR in favor of the CJEU/ECJ; see only Christoffersen and Madsen 2011, 3–4. Beginning with Moravcsik 1995, this picture has been slowly changing. Since then they have examined such issues as the political origins of the Convention (Moravcsik 2000); its role as an element in democratic governance in Europe (Cichowski 2006); principal-agent relationships between the Court and respondent states (Hawkins and Jacoby 2006 and 2008); the politics of judicial appointments and the significance of judicial biases (Voeten 2007, 2008, 2011); the legal cultures and judicial identities represented on the Court (Arold 2007; Bruinsma 2006); citation patterns among the Court's precedents (Lupu and Voeten 2012); changes in the ECtHR's jurisprudential trajectory across time, as conditioned by historical contexts (Madsen 2007 and 2011); the relationship between the Court and nongovernmental organizations (NGOs) (Hodson 2011; Cichowski 2011); and spillover effects of ECtHR policy-making to countries not party to the case decided by the Court (Helfer and Voeten 2014).

27. Fisher 1981.

28. Early unpublished conference papers include Zorn and van Winkle 2000 and 2001; von Staden 2007.

29. Greer 2006, chaps. 2 and 6.

30. Keller and Stone Sweet 2008.

31. Stone Sweet and Keller 2008, 4.

32. Ibid., 19, 19n43.

33. Motoc and Ziemele 2016.

34. Hawkins and Jacoby 2010, 74.

35. Anagnostou 2013, 11.

36. Anagnostou and Mungiu-Pippidi 2014, 225; for critical commentary, see Voeten 2014.

37. Hillebrecht 2014, 25–33.

38. Ibid., 49–50, 58.

39. Grewal and Voeten 2015.

40. von Staden 2016a.

41. Moravcsik 2000.

42. See, e.g., Hillebrecht 2014; Anagnostou 2013; Simmons 2009; Dai 2007.

43. The difference in the cut-off years for the judgments covered—2015 for the quantitative assessment, 2010 for the qualitative case studies—is an artifact of the genesis of this work. While updating the data set by adding a further five years of judgments and their state of compliance was feasible within the time available for final revisions of the manuscript, examining the domestic legal and political processes surrounding the implementation of another five years of judgments for the two countries would have exceeded it. For the main argument I am making here, this divergence is fortunately not significant. An earlier unpublished version of this research also contained additional case studies on Italy, the Netherlands, Denmark, and Norway; see von Staden 2009.

44. Out of the copious literature, see, e.g., Hafner-Burton 2013, 2009, 2005; Cao, Greenhill, and Prakash 2012; Risse, Ropp, and Sikkink 2013 and 1999; Simmons 2009; Carey 2009; Landman 2005; Carey and Poe 2004; Hathaway 2002; Poe, Tate, and Keith 1999; Keith 1999; Poe and Tate 1994.

45. See, e.g., Hafner-Burton 2013, chaps. 2 and 3 (addressing the "calculus of abuse").

46. Mahoney 2002, 104.

47. This phrase is borrowed from the title of a report on the implementation of international human rights decisions prepared by the Open Society Justice Initiative (2013).

48. See especially Alter 2001 and 2009; Stone Sweet 2004; and more recently, Stone Sweet and Brunell 2012; Carruba, Gabel, and Hankla 2008 and 2012.

49. For an overview of the international judiciary, see Mackenzie, Romano, and Shany 2010.

50. Shapiro 1981.

51. Romano 2011, 261–263, 1999, 713–715; see also generally Merrills 2011.

52. As Robert Harmsen has put it, "The Convention community may now be seen to encompass three broad types of national human rights situations: those of established democracies, (post-)transition States, and States in which the basic norms of democratic governance and the rule of law have significantly failed to take hold" (Harmsen 2011, 141).

53. On the origins and history of the Convention and Court, see Robertson 1950; Marston 1993; Simpson 2001; Bates 2010; and most recently, Duranti 2017. On procedure, see, e.g., Mowbray 2012, chap. 2.

54. See, e.g., Bates 2011, 29–33.

55. Text available at https://www.cvce.eu/content/publication/1997/10/13/b14649e7-c8b1-46a9-a9a1-cdad800bccc8/publishable_en.pdf. The Congress of Europe had been organized by the International Committee of Movements for European Unity.

56. References to ECHR (1950) are to the original Convention text as adopted in 1950.

57. These are rare. As of October 2017, twenty-eight interstate applications, several relating to the same situation, had been lodged with the Convention organs over a time span of sixty-some years, only four of which have resulted in a judgment; see ECtHR, "Inter-States Applications," http://www.echr.coe.int/Documents/InterStates_applications_ENG.pdf.

58. In such cases, the Committee merely noted the result and concluded the process by stating that no further measures were required; for an example, see Drzemczewski 1978.

59. The HUDOC database, available at http://hudoc.echr.coe.int, contains over 3,100 entries of decisions taken by the Committee of Ministers under Article 32 ECHR [1950]. While this number also includes follow-up resolutions reporting implementing measures in response to the committee's own merits decisions (about a third), the larger share are decisions on the merits that found at least 2,612 violations of the Convention (based on the sum of all individual violations identified in HUDOC, but excluding the number listed for "generic" violations of Article 6 to avoid double counting because most of the latter are already counted under one of the more specific provisions of that article (e.g., Article 6 (3) lit. c ECHR).

60. Nor did individuals have formal standing before the Court, although the Court had accepted their appearance as part of the Commission's delegation from the beginning; see Lawless v. Ireland (no. 2) (Questions of Procedure) (April 7, 1961). Protocol No. 9, in force since October 1, 1994, removed these restrictions for ratifying states (it was repealed again when Protocol No. 11 entered into force).

61. For dates of acceptance, see Convention for the Protection of Human Rights and Fundamental Freedoms: Declarations Made Pursuant to Former Articles 25 and 46, https://rm.coe .int/168048d4e8.

62. For a rehearing request to be accepted, a case must "raise[ ] a serious question affecting the interpretation or application of the Convention or the Protocols thereto, or a serious issue of general importance" (Article 43 (2) ECHR). Chambers may also exceptionally relinquish jurisdiction to the Grand Chamber prior to issuing a judgment (Article 30 ECHR). Referral requests are rarely accepted. According to a 2011 statistic, only about 5 percent of the requests (110 out of a total of 2,129) were successful (European Court of Human Rights 2011, 4).

63. For the argument that the ECtHR has partly compensated the absence of formal, "direct" embeddedness within the domestic legal systems of state parties through forms of "diffuse" embeddedness, see Helfer 2008.

64. Council of Europe 1975, vol. 1, 300–302, (Article 13 [b]); Bates 2010, 57–58.

65. Council of Europe 1977, vol. 4, 44 ("the Court will not have the power to declare null and void or amend Acts emanating from the public bodies of the signatory States").

66. For a detailed analysis of the Court's practice of awarding just satisfaction, see Ichim 2015.

67. Exceptions are Article 16 ECHR (reserving a state's right to restrict the political activity of aliens), and Article 4 of Protocol No. 4 and Article 1 of Protocol No. 7 (relating to issues of the expulsion of aliens).

68. See Banković et al. v. Belgium and 16 Others (dec.) (December 12, 2001).

69. See Al-Jedda v. United Kingdom (July 7, 2011), paras. 85–86; Al-Skeini and Others v. United Kingdom (July 7, 2011), paras. 149–150; see generally Mowbray 2012, 64–82.

70. For guidance on how the admissibility criteria are being applied, see European Court of Human Rights 2014a.

71. Compare this with the approach in Article 44 of the American Convention on Human Rights which permits such suits; see Burgorgue-Larsen and Úbeda de Torres 2011, 111.

72. During the first two years after the introduction of the new admissibility criterion— when it could be applied only by chambers, not by single-judge formations—it had been invoked in forty-two cases, resulting in the inadmissibility of twenty-six of them; see European Court

of Human Rights 2012a, 10; for further examples, see European Court of Human Rights 2014a, 88–96; for a critical review, see Vogiatzis 2016.

73. Protocol No. 15 will reduce from six months to four the time period within which an application has to be lodged following the final domestic decision. It will also eliminate one of the safeguards that attached to the "significant disadvantage" requirement added by Protocol No. 14, namely, that even a minor case would have to be considered by the ECtHR if "has not been duly considered by a domestic tribunal." As a remaining safeguard, allegations of minor breaches will have to be considered if "respect for human rights as defined in the Convention and the Protocols thereto requires an examination of the application on the merits" (Article 35 (3) lit. b ECHR).

74. ECHR, "Overview 1959–2015" (2016), 5, http://www.echr.coe.int/Documents /Overview_19592015_ENG.pdf.

75. See ECHR, "Analysis of Statistics 2015" (2016), 4, http://www.echr.coe.int/Documents /Stats_analysis_2015_ENG.pdf. In 2014, that percentage was even higher (97.4 percent): see ECHR, "Analysis of Statistics 2014" (2015), 4, http://www.echr.coe.int/Documents/Stats _analysis_2014_ENG.pdf.

76. "Explanatory Report to Protocol No. 14," reproduced in Council of Europe 2004, 28.

77. Leach 2013, 161.

78. On the pilot judgment procedure, see, e.g., Leach et al. 2010; for a critique of its use in the context conflict and post-conflict cases, see Kurban 2016.

79. Committee of Ministers 2017b, Rule 11 (2).

80. European Human Rights Advocacy Centre 2012.

81. See Greer 2006, chap. 2 and 155–165.

82. See Hawkins and Jacoby 2010, 66–76; Hillebrecht 2014, 46–47.

83. See Grewal and Voeten 2015, 502.

84. See Anagnostou and Mungiu-Pippidi 2014, 215.

85. The term "execution" is close to the descriptive concept of "implementation," but it has a clear directional element in that the execution of a judgment has to aim at compliance with that judgment, so that supervision of a judgment's execution implies supervision of compliance with it. While the Convention contains no express guidance as to the scope and extent of the Committee's supervisory powers, the term "supervision" implies at least some degree of "scrutiny or inspection" (Leuprecht 1988, 106).

86. Ryssdal 1996, 63.

87. Lambert Abdelgawad 2008, 36.

88. See, e.g., the Committee's final resolution concerning the first judgment it supervised under Article 54 ECHR (1950), concerning the Case "Relating to Certain Aspects of the Laws on the Use of Languages in Education in Belgium" v. Belgium (Merits) (July 23, 1968), in which it merely stated that "the Committee, in virtue of its obligations under Article 54 of the European Convention on Human Rights, took note of the measures taken by Belgium [. . .] in the context of its constitutional reform" without expressing an opinion as to whether these measures sufficiently complied with the judgment. The resolution is included in the Communication from the Committee of Ministers to the Assembly (statutory report), COE Doc. 3170 (October 3, 1972), reproduced in Council of Europe 1984, 105.

89. "Rules Adopted by the Committee of Ministers Concerning the Application of Article 54 of the European Convention on Human Rights of February 1976," reproduced in Council of

Europe 1984, 149 (appendix 2). See esp. Rule 3: "The Committee of Ministers shall not regard its functions under Article 54 of the Convention as having been exercised until it has taken note of the information supplied in accordance with Rule 2 and, when just satisfaction has been afforded, until it has satisfied itself that the State concerned has awarded this just satisfaction to the injured party." No substantive standards as to individual and general measures are being set; see Flauss 1988, 410, 419; Ress 1995, 865.

90. Tomkins 1995, 59; see also Klerk 1998, 77.

91. See Sundberg 2004, 1532. In one instance, the Committee, without awaiting the outcome of the domestic legislative process, ended its supervision after the Netherlands informed it that a bill remedying the relevant situation had been introduced to parliament; see Committee of Ministers (CM) Res. DH(82)2 (June 24, 1982) (Winterwerp v. Netherlands). As it turned out, it took eleven and a half years before the bill became law, with additional cases concerning similar situations having come to the Commission and Court in the meantime; see Klerk 1998, 75.

92. See Bartsch 1988; Sundberg 2004, 1516–1517; Lambert Abdelgawad 2008, 37.

93. Cf. Flauss 1988, 421.

94. Lambert Abdelgawad 2008, 38.

95. See generally ibid., 35–38.

96. See Ress 1995, 867; Drzemczewski and Tavernier 1998, 220 (noting "l'attitude plus exigeante du Comité des Ministres dans son rôle de surveillance depuis quelques années").

97. See Brighton Declaration, paras. 26, 27, http://www.echr.coe.int/Documents/2012 _Brighton_FinalDeclaration_ENG.pdf; Brussels Declaration, 2, 7–8, https://www.coe.int/t/dghl /standardsetting/cddh/reformechr/Declaration-Brussels_EN.pdf.

98. Committee of Ministers 2017b, Rule 6 (2). A separate provision (Rule 12) covers the supervision of the execution of the terms of friendly settlements. The 2001 rules are reproduced in Lambert Abdelgawad 2002, 50–52, and the pre-amendment 2006 version can be found in Lambert Abdelgawad 2008, 71–80. The Committee has also adopted working methods to formalize its procedures; they are available, together with the rules, at http://www.coe.int/en/web /execution/rules-and-working-methods.

99. Çalı and Koch 2014, 302.

100. For the Department's mandate, see http://www.coe.int/en/web/execution/presentation -of-the-department; see also Drzemczewski 1990, 100.

101. Information provided by a high-ranking official within the Department for the Execution of Judgments of the European Court of Human Rights, Council of Europe, Strasbourg, October 1, 2007.

102. Cf. Leuprecht 1988, 106.

103. Çalı and Koch 2014, 313–314.

104. Cf. Jönsson and Tallberg (1998, 372), who speak of "post-agreement compliance bargaining."

105. Lambert Abdelgawad 2008, 36.

106. Macdonald 1999, 430; Sundberg 2001, 583; somewhat more critical is Greer 2006, 158.

107. This is true, if only in hindsight, even of the earlier practice of closing supervision on the promise of adopting certain measures since it appears that these promises have eventually indeed always been kept, if at times with significant delay.

108. The chronological list that was used for the list of all judgments issued up to the year 2010 is dated November 3, 2011 (on file with author). The Court has since discontinued the chronological list, and I used HUDOC to generate judgment lists for the years 2011–2015.

109. I did the same in the few instances where judgments were issued separately with respect to different applicants whose cases had previously been joined under a single case name.

110. In the case of chamber judgments that have been successfully referred to the GC for a rehearing, the date of the final judgment relevant for execution purposes is the date of the GC judgment (see Article 44 (1) ECHR). For revision judgments, by contrast, the date of the original merits judgment has been retained because that judgment had usually already become final and thus triggered the respondent state's obligation to execute it, although the content of that obligation might then later have changed as a result of the revision judgment.

111. Note that the Court has developed the practice of recognizing friendly settlements in "decisions," not judgments, especially since the entry into force of Protocol No. 14 in 2010, which added a new Convention provision to that effect (Article 39 (3) ECHR). While such decisions are also submitted to the Committee for supervision (Article 39 (4) ECHR), they are not included in this data set. The incidence of friendly settlements is thus underreported when only looking at judgments (indeed, the HUDOC execution database, available at http://hudoc.exec .coe.int, identifies a total of 3,013 friendly settlements as having been concluded over the same time period, 1960–2015). Compliance with unilateral declarations, also primarily recognized in decisions, is, by contrast, not supervised by the Committee of Ministers, but applicants have the option of requesting their application to be reinstated should a state fail to abide by the terms of the declaration.

112. That information has been collected primarily from HUDOC, and the lists of final resolutions adopted by the Committee of Ministers are available at http://www.coe.int/en/web /execution/closed-cases. After the HUDOC Exec execution database became available in January 2017 (at http://hudoc.exec.coe.int), the status of all pending judgments has been rechecked.

113. A formal compliance status has been unavailable in HUDOC and HUDOC Exec for two remaining observations, the striking-out judgments Shevanova v. Latvia and Kaftaïlova v. Latvia (both December 7, 2007). Since they do not appear in the lists of outstanding just satisfaction awards (http://www.coe.int/en/web/execution/payment-information) either, however, they have likely been complied with.

114. A total of 343 judgments had been issued up to the end of 1995.

115. See only Interim Resolution CM/ResDH(2008)69 (September 18, 2008), in Collection of Interim Resolutions 1988–2008, COE Doc. H/Exec(2008)1, 174, https://rm.coe.int /168059ddae, covering 244 cases.

116. See only Interim Resolution CM/ResDH(2015)45 (March 12, 2015), in Collection of Interim Resolutions 2009–2015, COE Doc. H/Exec(2015)9, 90, https://rm.coe.int/168059ddb0, covering 221 cases.

117. See only Interim Resolution CM/ResDH(2010)224 (December 2, 2010), in ibid., 29, covering 2,183 cases concerning the excessive length of judicial proceedings in Italy (including many applications decided by the Committee of Ministers under former Article 32 ECHR [1950]).

118. See only Interim Resolution CM/ResDH(2012)234 (December 6, 2012), in ibid., 117, covering 390 cases.

119. Grewal and Voeten (2015, 502–503) try to navigate this issue by including in their data set only so-called lead cases as ostensibly independent observations. In terms of assessing compliance, this research strategy creates issues of its own: first, lead cases are by definition cases that require new *general* measures; the assessment of compliance with judgments that are limited to individual remedial measures is thus marginalized. Eliminating merits judgments

with Importance Level 3 has the same effect—these may not raise novel legal issues but will often require the adoption of new individual measures—and in addition excludes from examination most friendly settlements as a distinct compliance-relevant type of judgment. Second, not all clone cases raise exactly the same issues or have the same violation profile in terms of the specific provisions violated as the lead case with which they are being jointly supervised, so for a more accurate appreciation of the link between specific violations and compliance, they would need to be considered together with the lead case(s).

120. It bears noting that the number of judgments against a country involving a particular violation does not by itself provide an accurate reflection of the magnitude of the problem in terms of the number of people affected. First, while most judgments address complaints by individual applicants, some application numbers cover several hundred persons (see, e.g., Alesiani and 510 Others v. Italy [February 27, 2001]), while other judgments may dispose of over a thousand individual applications at the same time (see, e.g., McHugh and Others v. United Kingdom [February 10, 2015]). Second, the introduction of the pilot judgment procedure in 2004 has led to a situation in which hundreds or even thousands of applications involving the same alleged violation may be adjourned pending the outcome of the pilot case and its execution. This procedure was not yet in place when the first waves of clone cases reached the Court in the 1990s. Last but not least, the number of complaints submitted depends on people actually knowing about the ECtHR and then being willing and able to submit an application, aspects that can be expected to vary by country, issue area, and socioeconomic background; see, e.g., Boyle and Thompson 2001.

121. See only European Court of Human Rights 2007, para. 25.

122. The data files for the Polity IV Project, Political Regime Characteristics and Transitions, 1800–2016, are at http://www.systemicpeace.org/inscrdata.html.

123. See Marshall, Gurr, and Jaggers 2017, 14–17. Both the democracy and autocracy variables are constructed on the basis of scores for the "competitiveness of political participation [. . .], the openness and competitiveness of executive recruitment [. . .] , and constraints on the chief executive," with the autocracy variable additionally reflecting the "regulation of participation" (ibid., 14, 16).

124. These are Andorra (four judgments, compliance rate of 100 percent); Bosnia and Herzegovina (thirty-seven, 57 percent), Iceland (sixteen, 94 percent), Liechtenstein (seven, 86 percent), Monaco (two, 100 percent), San Marino (eleven, 82 percent), and Malta (forty-five, 80 percent).

125. Andorra (four judgments) and Monaco (two) also have compliance rates of 100 percent.

Chapter 1

1. See, e.g., Simmons 2002; Hafner-Burton 2005 and 2009; Hafner-Burton and Tsutsui 2005; Dai 2007; Morrow 2007; Mitchell and Hensel 2007.

2. Guzman 2008, 211; on problems with making reputation bear the burden of explaining compliance, see Brewster 2009a and 2009b; Geisinger and Stein 2008.

3. Simmons 2009, 112 (emphasis added).

4. Ibid., 125.

5. Ibid., 127–148.

6. See Checkel 2001; Risse 2000; Goodman and Jinks 2004.

7. Checkel 2005, 804 (references omitted); for other constructivist-leaning work, see Koh 1998 and 1999; Chayes and Chayes 1995; Goodman and Jinks 2013.

8. Risse and Sikkink 1999, 22–25, 34.

9. Katzenstein, Keohane, and Krasner 1998, 682; Finnemore and Sikkink 1998, 910; March and Olsen 1998, 952; Keohane 2000, 130; Fearon and Wendt 2002, 67–68.

10. Finnemore and Sikkink 1998, 911; see, similarly, Checkel 1997, 488–489; Ruggie 1998, 885; Goodman and Jinks 2004, 700–702; March and Olsen 2008, 702.

11. James March and Johan Olsen have suggested four such relationships: the clearer logic dominates the less clear one; one logic determines the principal decision constraints, whereas the other refines the decision within those constraints; the logics follow a development path in which the impact of one logic subsides as that of the other grows stronger; or one logic is simply conceived as a special case of the other; see March and Olsen 1998, 952–953, and 2008, 701–705.

12. Jepperson, Wendt, and Katzenstein 1996, 68.

13. See, e.g., Carruba and Gabel 2015, 192–193; Dothan 2015, e.g., 23, 71.

14. Beach 2005.

15. Conant 2002. Conant uses a rationalist framework to address the variable reach of compliance, but the prior decision of whether to comply with an ECJ judgment in the first place is not theorized as such and touched upon only in passing; see ibid., 217.

16. Hillebrecht 2014, 32.

17. See also Young 1979, 4, 104; Fisher 1981, 20; Mitchell 1994, 30; Raustiala and Slaughter 2002, 539.

18. Neyer and Wolf 2005, 42; see Martin 2013, 606–607, on "the dangers of inferring causal effect from observed compliance."

19. Viljoen and Louw 2007, 6; Hawkins and Jacoby 2010.

20. Compare this with the outcome values used in Zürn and Joerges 2005 of "initial noncompliance," in which behavior subsequently changes in appropriate directions, and of a "compliance crisis," in which no such subsequent change takes place; Zürn 2005, 9; Neyer and Wolf 2005, 47.

21. Cf. Kapiszewski and Taylor 2013, 811; Dai 2013, 87 and 2005, 367; Hathaway 2002, 1964–1965; Kingsbury 1998, 348; Volcansek 1986, 8–9.

22. Cf. Martin 2013; Howse and Teitel 2010; Simmons 2009, 19; Janis 2000.

23. Paulson 2004, 436; Zürn 2005, 8–9.

24. Note that the *assessment* of compliance and noncompliance needs to be kept separate from the *consequences* that attach to them. To that extent, the speed-limit example given by Chayes and Chayes (1995, 17) is misleading. If you go, say, 54 mph in a 50-mph zone, you are formally noncompliant; it is just that the authorities will generally not bother to enforce the speed limit in the case of such minor infractions. In other words, the question here is not the range of acceptable compliance, but the range of noncompliant behavior that will not trigger enforcement action.

25. See, e.g., Pressman and Wildavsky 1984; Pülzl and Treib 2007; Hill and Hupe 2002.

26. Raustiala and Slaughter 2002, 539; Victor, Raustiala, and Skolnikoff 1998, 4–6; Jacobson and Brown Weiss 1998, 4. Agreements that are self-executing can generally dispense with domestic implementation, but these are rare in international regulatory regimes; see Jacobson and Brown Weiss 1998, 4.

27. Raustiala and Slaughter 2002, 539.

28. Raustiala 2000, 392.

29. See, e.g., Council of Europe 2016, 7–8; Motoc and Ziemele 2016; Kapiszewski and Taylor 2013, 807; Volcansek 1986.

30. Raustiala 2000, 394.

31. Ibid., 398.

32. Young and Levy 1999, 6.

33. Downs, Rocke, and Barsoom 1996; Martin 2013, 592.

34. See only Keller and Marti 2016, 832. These secondary obligations mirror those applicable under the law of state responsibility (see generally Crawford 2013, part 5) which, however, at least as codified by the International Law Commission (ILC), formally apply only to breaches of primary obligations that are owed to states. See ibid., 460, and Article 33 (1), ILC Articles on the Responsibility of States for Internationally Wrongful Acts (2001), reproduced in ibid., 717–718.

35. Martin 2013, 605.

36. Huneeus 2014, 441; Hawkins and Jacoby 2010, 30–40.

37. Where the measures that eventually result in compliance are initiated or adopted only after the case is already pending—that is, after the government has been informed about it—then such compliance may instead be an instance of what may be called "anticipatory" or "preemptive," compliance, with the respondent state expecting to lose the case (e.g., on the basis of relevant other ECtHR case law involving third parties or due to the signals sent by the Court during the proceedings) and already beginning to adopt remedial measures prior to the issuing of a binding judgment. In such a case, the Court's anticipated decision would still exert some causal influence.

38. The Court awards just satisfaction only if requested by the applicant; in addition, in some instances it has argued that the finding of a Convention violation in itself provides sufficient just satisfaction; see Laffranque 2014, 87–88, 92–94; Ichim 2015, 135–141.

39. Shany 2014, 14.

40. Ibid., chap. 2; von Bogdandy and Venzke 2013, 55–57.

41. See von Staden 2016b, 458; Shany 2013, 1313.

42. For the ECtHR, compare Lovat and Shany 2014, 256–258.

43. Helfer 2014a, 466–470; for a definition of judicial effectiveness that places compliance at its center, see Helfer and Slaughter 1997, 290.

44. See, e.g., Helfer's additional categories of *erga omnes* effectiveness, embeddedness effectiveness, and effectiveness in developing international law (Helfer 2014a, 470–480). For empirical evidence of the ECtHR's *erga omnes* effectiveness with respect to lesbian, gay, bisexual, and transgender (LGBT) rights litigation in Europe, see Helfer and Voeten 2014.

45. Sunstein 1994, 20.

46. See Kutz 1994. Kutz points out that, strictly speaking, the legal terms at issue here are not so much indeterminate, which would suggest that they give no indication whatsoever as to their meaning, as underdetermined, in that they allow for several possible interpretations.

47. See generally Hart 1994, 124–136 (discussing the "open texture" of law).

48. See Barak 2005, 7.

49. Ibid., 9.

50. See only Venzke 2012, 46 ("[s]table meaning is [. . .] the result of the absence of dispute"); Hart 1994, 126.

51. Venzke 2012, 58.

52. Dworkin 1978, 134ff.

53. If they did, then we should see hardly any cases before courts that hinge on disagreements as to the meaning of the legal rules at issue since rational actors with the same information

should come to the same conclusion as to the meaning of the applicable law. Indeed, as Hart has poignantly noted, the "canons" of interpretation "make use of general terms which themselves require interpretation" (Hart 1994, 126).

54. Barak 2006, 273.

55. While the interpretive decisions of judges are thus guided at least in part by their juridical Weltanschauung, their choice set is the same constrained by past interpretive practices and inherited standards of legal argumentation; see Venzke 2012, 48–49.

56. As Hans Kelsen noted, "Authentic interpretation, whether general or individual, is a law-creating act. [. . .] The decision of a judicial or administrative authority applying a general norm—which has several meanings—to a concrete case can correspond to only one of these meanings and must thus exclude others. It is by the decision that one of several meanings of the applied norm becomes binding in the concrete case; and it is mainly, although not only with respect to its interpretive function that a judicial or administrative decision has a law-creating character" (Kelsen 1950, xv). See similarly Dworkin 1998, 6; von Bogdandy and Venzke 2013, 55–57.

57. See Helfer and Slaughter 2005, 918.

58. See Sundberg 2004, 1516 ("La question de savoir si un arrêt dénonce un problème structurel nécessitant des mesure générales, ou s'il ne fait que signaler une défaillance ponctuelle dépend directement du libellé des arrêts, lu à la lumière et dans le contexte des autres informations disponibles sur le cas d'espèce. En effet, la simple lecture du dispositif de l'arrêt n'est normalement pas suffisante pour comprendre la violation"); Barkhuysen and van Emmerik 2005, 19 ("[I]t is not always clear from a judgment which abstract measures should be taken to prevent future violations"); Keller and Marti 2016, 840 ("The first step for implementation is always to identify what a judgment actually demands [, with] declaratory relief remain[ing] vague and ambiguous in this respect").

59. Galanter 1983, 136 (emphasis added).

60. Chayes and Chayes 1995, 17; Raustiala 2000, 397.

61. On the latter, see Keller and Marti, 2016, 845–850.

62. Exceptions are "pilot" and so-called Article 46 judgments in which the Court provides explicit guidance as to how the respondent state must address certain systemic problems; see generally Leach et al. 2010; Sicilianos 2014.

63. Wildhaber 2000; European Court of Human Rights 2007, para. 23 ("Only in extremely rare cases can the Court consider a consequential order aimed at putting an end or remedying the violation in question. The Court may, however, decide at its discretion to offer guidance for the execution of its judgment").

64. Occasionally, as part of states' positive obligations, the Court also stipulates obligations of means; see, e.g., Kelly and Others v. United Kingdom (May 4, 2001), para. 96 (noting that a state's obligation to undertake effective investigations into cases of unlawful killings "is not an obligation of result, but of means").

65. E.g., Lambert Abdelgawad 2008, 7.

66. See Leach 2013; Cremer 2014.

67. See Lambert Abdelgawad 2014, 117.

68. Compare this to the practice of the Inter-American Court of Human Rights (see generally Pasqualucci 2013, chap. 6), which, however, is also explicitly authorized by Article 63 (1) of the American Convention on Human Rights to order reparations. No such authorization exists in the European Convention.

69. The Convention also includes a denunciation clause (Article 58 (1) ECHR) whose invocation, however, does not remove the obligation to comply with judgments issued before the denunciation became effective (cf. Article 58 (2) ECHR).

70. Leeb 2001, 18, 13–14; Ichim 2015, 12.

71. See only Polakiewicz 1993, 112–113; Leeb 2001, 17–18. In the absence of a recognized legal obligation, the Committee of Ministers, in Recommendation No. R(2000)2 (January 19, 2000), had called on ECHR parties to provide for reopening in response to adverse judgments voluntarily. Many states have in the meantime done so; see Leach 2011, 94.

72. Cf. Polakiewicz 1993, 199–204.

73. On measuring compliance with human rights judgments, see also Kapiszewski and Taylor 2013, 808–812; Hillebrecht 2009.

74. See, similarly, Neyer and Wolf 2005, 43.

75. Katzenstein 1996, 5.

76. In the following, I drop the qualifier "European" and only refer to "liberal democracies." It goes without saying, though, that the arguments in this work apply only to the regional European context. Liberal democracies elsewhere, although they also engage in rights protection, may do so in quite different ways; cf. only Ignatieff 2005.

77. See generally Held 2006, chap. 3.

78. Erman 2005, 2.

79. Linz 1992, 183.

80. Dahl 1992, 235 (emphasis omitted).

81. Hafner-Burton 2013, 71–72; cf. also Erman 2005, 2 ("human rights and democracy are mutually constitutive").

82. Statute of the Council of Europe, preamble, para. 3.

83. Ibid., Article 3.

84. Ibid., Article 1.

85. On the concept and measurement of identity, see generally Abdelal et al. 2009b.

86. Cf. Abdelal et al. 2009a, 3. It is in this way that norms can be both *regulative* of state behavior and *constitutive* of their identity, because it is through compliance with human rights norms that states (re)produce their identity as liberal democracies.

87. See, e.g., Hafner-Burton 2013, 71; Davenport and Armstrong 2004; Davenport 1999; Henderson 1993 and 1991; Helfer and Slaughter 1997, 331–335.

88. Bueno de Mesquita et al. 2005; see also Landman 2005, 117ff, comparing the human rights performance of "old," "third-wave," and "fourth-wave" democracies.

89. Neumayer 2005, 950; see also Hathaway 2002, 2019.

90. Landman 2005, 121.

91. See, e.g., Hafner-Burton 2013, 71; Bueno de Mesquita et al. 2005, 456.

92. See, e.g., Dahl 2015, chap. 8; Howard and Carey 2004; Reenock, Staton, and Radean 2014.

93. Cf. Howard and Carey 2004, 284.

94. A strict conceptual distinction is not necessary here, nor is a resolution of the question of whether the rule of law comprises democracy or democracy comprises the rule of law since in practice they usually appear together. As Brian Tamanaha has noted, these terms, plus "individual rights" and "formal legality" "cluster together in liberal democracies as a unified complementary package" (Tamanaha 2004, 110).

95. Weiler 1991, 2421.

96. For similar arguments with respect to the CJEU, see Conant 2002, 217; Schmidt 2014, 781.

97. MacMullen 2004, 422.

98. Risse and Sikkink 1999, 33.

99. Goodman and Jinks 2013, 26.

100. Ibid., 137.

101. Mitchell 2007, 907.

102. Henkin 1990, e.g., 69, 71, 72, 251.

103. Karen Alter, Laurence Helfer, and Mikael Madsen have recently used the same criteria—states' recognition of the obligation to comply, plus the taking of meaningful steps toward compliance—to define the "de facto authority" of international courts; see Alter, Helfer, and Madsen 2016, 7. To the extent that the normative constraint expectation holds, it is, then, from that perspective, the same as saying that the ECtHR has de facto authority vis-à-vis respondent states. Note that Alter, Helfer, and Madsen remain agnostic, however, as to the reasons underlying the recognition of a court's authority (see ibid., 6), whereas I here stipulate a normative logic of action.

104. Hillebrecht 2014, 31–32.

105. Chayes and Chayes 1995, 3

106. For a similar methodological approach, see Deitelhoff 2009, 46.

107. Risse-Kappen 1995, 504.

108. In microeconomics, a reservation price is the highest price a buyer is willing to pay for a good or service and, conversely, the lowest price at which a seller is willing to sell it.

109. Chayes and Chayes 1995, 8 (emphasis added).

110. For discussion of the interaction of heterogeneous motivations and the articulation of a "goal-framing" theory of compliance, see Etienne 2011.

111. Simmons 2009, 123.

112. See von Staden 2016a, 251–252.

113. As Louis Henkin once noted, "[C]ompliance with international human rights law [. . .] is wholly internal" (Henkin 1990, 250).

114. See, e.g., Hafner-Burton 2005 and 2009 on human rights conditionalities in preferential trade agreements mostly between developed and developing countries.

115. While the Committee has recently been empowered to refer cases of noncompliance back to the Court for a judicial determination where it "considers that a High Contracting Party refuses to abide by a final judgment" (Article 46 (4) ECHR), no new sanctions are provided for in the case of a positive verdict.

116. E.g., Council of the European Union 2008, 7. The other current candidate countries are Albania, the former Yugoslav Republic of Macedonia, Montenegro, and Serbia; potential candidates are Bosnia and Herzegovina and Kosovo; see EU enlargement information at http://ec.europa.eu/enlargement/countries/check-current-status/index_en.htm. Except for Kosovo, all other candidates are COE members and parties to the ECHR.

117. See, similarly, Simmons 2009, 122.

118. See ECtHR, "Inter-States Applications," http://www.echr.coe.int/Documents/Inter States_applications_ENG.pdf.

119. See, e.g., Guzman 2008; Tomz 2007, chap. 2; Mercer 1996; Keohane 1984, 105–106.

120. Downs and Jones 2002, S96.

121. Cf. Simmons 2009, 124–125.

122. See Dothan 2015, 16–20.
123. Brewster 2009b, 261.
124. Dothan 2011, 122.
125. Brewster 2009a, 332–333.
126. Dothan 2015, 23 (emphasis added).
127. Cf. Brewster 2009a and 2009b.
128. Downs and Jones 2002, S113.
129. Ibid., S111.
130. Ibid., S112.
131. Geisinger and Stein 2007 and 2008, 1137–1142.
132. Geisinger and Stein 2008, 1139. Also see Downs and Jones 2002, S112n39, who note that while noncompliance with environmental and human rights agreements may have few reputational repercussions in other issue areas, "[t]he reputational damage with respect to a state's *social standing* in the international community might of course be as great or greater" (emphasis added).
133. On intangible sanctions, see Brennan et al. 2013, 224–229.
134. Huneeus 2014, 451.
135. See Hillebrecht 2014, 31–32.
136. See Moravcsik 2000.
137. See Raz 1975.
138. Churchill and Young 1992, 285.
139. Constructivist scholars have argued that plausible instances of persuasion beyond the state can be found, e.g., in the context of the treaty negotiations resulting in the Rome statute of the International Criminal Court (Deitelhoff 2006 and 2009) and national citizenship reforms based on COE initiatives (Checkel 2001, 1999, 1997). The successful operation of persuasion, however, is commonly predicated on an ideal discursive speech situation—involving the existence of shared life worlds, the absence of "relationships of power, force, and coercion" (Risse 2000, 11), and characterized by inclusiveness and sincerity (Ulbert and Risse 2005; Deitelhoff and Müller 2005)—that is recognized as rarely obtaining, or even being sufficiently approximated, in political practice (see Deitelhoff 2009, 43, who thus, at ibid., 45, speaks of isolated "islands of persuasion"). The absence of an ideal speech situation also characterizes the "most institutionalized form of contention" (Tilly and Tarrow 2007, 18), adjudication, which is inherently adversarial in character. While the goal is to persuade the judge(s), litigation is generally ill structured to serve the objective of persuading either of the two disputants of the superiority of the other side's argument.
140. Unilateral declarations are not mentioned in the Convention but have been introduced as part of judicial practice and since April 2012 have been governed by Rule 62A of the ECtHR's Rules of Court; the most recent version of the rules, of November 14, 2016, is available at http://www.echr.coe.int/Documents/Rules_Court_ENG.pdf.
141. Most friendly settlements provide for ex gratia payments without formally recognizing a Convention violation; see Keller, Forowicz, and Engi 2010, 39. Through such settlements states may thus avoid a precedent-setting judgment on the merits. Similarly, while unilateral declarations have commonly been accompanied by an explicit recognition of a breach of the Convention, this has not always been a *conditio sine qua non* (ibid., 146) and became mandatory only with the introduction of Rule 62A (1) lit. b of the 2012 Rules of Court. Even so, the execution of cases settled by way of a unilateral declaration and recognized in a decision (not a judgment)

of the Court is, unlike friendly settlements, not supervised by the Committee of Ministers. In the case of noncompliance with the undertakings pledged as part of a unilateral declaration, however, the applicant can ask the Court for a reinstatement of the application; see European Court of Human Rights 2012b, 2.

142. Beginning with Volcansek, 1986 (see, e.g., 9, 12).

143. Conant 2002, 3 (emphasis in the original).

144. Ibid., 3–4.

145. Martinsen 2015a, 226–227, 236.

146. Martinsen 2015b, 1623.

147. See Çalı and Koch 2011.

148. E.g., Assanidze v. Georgia (April 8, 2004), paras. 202, 203.

149. See generally Lambert Abdelgawad 2008.

150. Committee of Ministers 2008, para. 5.

151. E.g., by way of the Court's "pilot judgments," which address systemic problems and outline the general measures that respondent states need to take; see Leach et al. 2010.

152. For an illustrative case in the context of the CJEU, see Schmidt 2014.

153. See Vaughne Miller, Protocol 11 and the New European Court of Human Rights, House of Commons Library Research Paper 98/109 (December 4, 1998), 8.

154. In 2012, the Council of Europe's Steering Committee on Human Rights noted that "large numbers of applications spend many years pending before the Court without a substantive response," and "the average length of time taken for *prima facie* admissible cases to be communicated [to respondent states] is currently 37 months" (Steering Committee of Human Rights 2012, 52). While setting the goal of dealing with cases "within three years after they are brought," the Court at the same time notes the "impossibility to indicate the length of proceedings before the Court" (European Court of Human Rights 2014b, 9).

155. This goes beyond mere agenda-setting attributed to the conclusion of human rights treaties (Simmons 2009, 127–129) and human rights judgments (Hillebrecht 2014, 29–31; Helfer and Voeten 2014, 82–84), which are said to provide executives that are otherwise institutionally constrained to initiate legislative reforms with the ability to compel the legislature to engage with their own preferred changes and reforms. While the agenda-setting function of ECtHR judgments is a point well taken, it does not yet say anything about the depth of eventual compliance, which may still turn out to be minimalist if a parliamentary majority is unsympathetic to the required changes.

156. See generally Putnam 1988. Note an important difference, though: in the judicialized version of the two-level game, the game is not about identifying, negotiating, and securing the win set of all possible outcomes at the international level that would find majority acceptance at the domestic level (Putnam 1988, 437), but rather to use the normativity of judicial judgments to overcome majority or veto-power opposition.

157. Putnam discusses a similar use of international actions under the label of *synergistic linkage* (Putnam 1988, 446–448; see also Moravcsik 1993, 26–27). Synergistic linkage of issues makes available policy options that were previously beyond domestic reach and allow to trade off drawbacks and benefits of an international agreement in order to secure ratification. In the case of the judicial two-level game; however, no new options as such arise; rather, a previously available option—although not preferred by at least one of the stakeholders involved—is now endowed with normative force so that the metaphor of "tying hands" is more appropriate.

158. See Allee and Huth 2006; Simmons 2002.

159. Hillebrecht 2014, 29.

160. In their study of the *erga omnes* effects of the ECtHR's jurisprudence on LGBT rights, Helfer and Voeten find, inter alia, that such judgments have their strongest effect with respect to increasing the probability of rights-enhancing reforms in states not party to the case decided by the Court where public acceptance of LGBT rights is low but political elites are in principle open to such change; see Helfer and Voeten 2014, 100–105.

161. The conditional withholding of benefits is sometimes distinguished from enforcement, when defined strictly in terms of cost-imposing sanctioning, and characterized as a separate (because positively incentivizing) instrument for exercising influence, but since conditionally withheld (or promised) benefits can be viewed as opportunity costs, I include them under enforcement.

162. This is a variation of the well-known argument that the depth of cooperation as reflected in international law will correlate with the availability of enforcement devices to prevent free riding or to punish it in order to prevent its recurrence (see Downs, Rocke, and Barsoom 1996).

163. Conant 2002, 16–17.

164. Ibid., 24–27.

165. Ibid., 26.

166. Ibid., 18–23.

167. Dai 2007, 71.

168. Ibid., 72–73.

169. Simmons 2009, 136.

170. Ibid., 150–151.

171. Cardenas 2007, 8.

172. A social movement here is understood as "a sustained challenge to power holders in the name of a population living under the jurisdiction of those power holders by means of repeated public displays of that population's worthiness, unity, numbers, and commitment" (Tilly 1999, 257, emphasis omitted).

173. The use of law and adjudication in social movement campaigns is a standard strategy in contentious politics; see, e.g., McCann 1998 and 2006.

174. As Susanne Lohmann (1993, 319) has noted, "[I]t is puzzling that rational political leaders with majoritarian incentives would ever respond to political action" by minority groups or movements. But see Dai 2007, 71.

175. For an overview, see Keller, Forowicz, and Engi 2010, chap. 3.

176. Ibid., 30–31, 52–54, 58.

177. See Committee of Ministers 2017b, Rules 12 and 13.

178. Keller, Forowicz, and Engi 2010, 21–24, 41–49.

179. See ibid., 39, 68, 76–77, 92–93, 140.

180. Ibid., 65, 78.

181. Ibid., 92.

182. See ibid., 67–68, for a comparison of friendly settlements and unilateral declarations.

183. The benefits of friendly settlements for the respondent state might explain the increase in their incidence over time, with the average annual growth rate across all settlements, including unilateral declarations, between 1998 (7 settlements) and 2008 (748 settlements) being 59.5 percent (for absolute figures, see ibid., 203). If settlements indeed have cost-minimizing effects, one might wonder why they are not concluded more often. Suffice it to say that the willingness

to settle is not evenly distributed across the Convention parties, with Poland, Turkey, and Italy in the lead, and Russia rarely settling, despite a burgeoning number of applications; see ibid., 75, 108, 204–207. For the present purpose of studying compliance with the Court's judgments, it is sufficient to take those settlements that have been concluded as the relevant observations without inquiring into the causes of nonsettlement elsewhere.

184. The same applies to remedies voluntarily pledged by respondent states as part of unilateral declarations (usually payment of a specified amount of compensation).

185. The sixteen countries are, in alphabetical order, Austria (ratification of ECHR 1958/ subject to ECtHR's jurisdiction since 1959), Cyprus (1962/1980), Denmark (1953/1959), Finland (1990/1990), Germany (1952/1959), Hungary (1992/1992), Ireland (1953/1959); Italy (1955/1973), Lithuania (1995/1995), Luxembourg (1953/1959); the Netherlands (1954/1959), Norway (1952/1964); Slovenia (1994/1994), Sweden (1952/1966), Switzerland (1974/1974), and the United Kingdom of Great Britain and Northern Ireland (1951/1966).

186. See von Staden 2009 for qualitative analyses of select judgments from four more countries (Denmark, Italy, the Netherlands, and Norway).

187. Cf. King, Keohane, and Verba 1994, 55ff.

188. Cf. Eckstein 1975, 108ff.

Chapter 2

1. Bates 2015, 42.

2. Moravcsik 2000, 239–243.

3. Bates 2010, 317.

4. Donald and Leach 2016, 224.

5. Ibid., 228.

6. Hillebrecht 2014, 102.

7. A note on referencing in this Part and in Part II: all ECtHR judgments and decisions in which the United Kingdom (and in Part II, Germany) is the respondent state will be referenced only by the name of the applicant(s), followed by the date of the judgment in parentheses.

8. For all judgments rendered up to 2005 this has been done in von Staden 2009.

9. See only Duranti 2017; Simpson 2001; Wicks 2000; Marston 1993.

10. Hoffman and Rowe 2013, 33; Kinley 1993, 1.

11. For the text of the declarations, see *Yearbook of the European Convention of Human Rights* 9 (1966): 8–11, 14–15. For background on the first declaration, see Lord Lester of Herne Hill 1998.

12. Dicey 1915.

13. Besson 2008, 36.

14. The Colonial Office had opposed the extension of the Convention to the UK's dependent territories in part for fearing that human rights entitlements might further fuel rising independence movements; see Simpson 2001, 288–291, 476–477; Marston 1993. As a result, the final Convention text made such extension optional (Article 63 ECHR [1950], retained as Article 56 ECHR). Notwithstanding these concerns, the UK extended the Convention to forty-two British dependencies as early as 1953 (Simpson 2001, 6).

15. Simpson 2001, 288–297.

16. Besson 2008, 39. It could, however, be relied upon indirectly as guidance in statutory construction, to resolve conflicts or lacunae in the common law, to "inform the exercise of

judicial [. . .] discretion," and to inform domestic decisions on EU law (on the basis that EU law included the protection of fundamental rights as a general principle of law). Wadham et al. 2007, 4–5; see also Besson 2008, 48–49.

17. The various calls and proposals for incorporation that had been voiced since the late 1960s had accordingly come to naught; see, e.g., Kinley 1993, chap. 1; Feldman 2002, 77–80.

18. See, e.g., Fenwick 2007, 158–160; Ewing and Gearty 1990.

19. Foster 2006, 13.

20. "Bringing Rights Home" is the title of a Labour consultation paper published December 18, 1996; reprinted in *European Human Rights Law Review* (1997): 71–80.

21. Strictly speaking, the HRA incorporates the ECHR only indirectly through reference to the rights included in the Convention and does not give domestic force of law to the Convention as such, as did, by comparison, the 1972 European Communities Act with respect to the Community Treaties; see Fatima 2005, 231; Dwyer 2005, 362–363; Besson 2008, 42.

22. The HRA is thus subject to simple legislative amendment; see Feldman 2002, 80.

23. The text of the HRA can be found in *International Legal Materials* 38 (1999): 464–483, and at http://www.opsi.gov.uk/acts/acts1998/ukpga_19980042_en_1.

24. See Vick 2002, 358–361, for supporting as well as some dissenting positions.

25. Except for the House of Lords when acting in its judicial capacity; see HRA sec. 6 (4).

26. Until March 2015, a total of twenty-nine declarations of incompatibility had been made by UK courts; see Joint Committee on Human Rights, *Human Rights Judgments*, 7th Rep. Sess. 2014–15, HL Paper 130/HC 1088, March 11, 2015, 17.

27. On the history and application in practice of HRA sec. 2.1, see Wicks 2005.

28. Feldman 2002, 83.

29. Churchill and Young 1992, 285.

30. Feldman 2002, 89–90. Section 29 (2) lit. d of the Scotland Act 1998 specifically notes that provisions enacted by the Scottish Parliament under its devolved legislative competence are not to be considered law if they are "incompatible with any of the Convention rights or with Community law." See the Government of Wales Act 1998, sec. 107 (1), and the Northern Ireland Act 1998, sec. 6 (2) lit. c, for similar provisions.

31. Hope 2009, 169, 155–177.

32. Arnold 2010; di Mambro 2010.

33. See Lucinda Maer and Alexander Horne, *Background to Proposals for a British Bill of Rights and Duties*, House of Commons Library Standard Note SN/PC/04559 (February 3, 2009), http://researchbriefings.files.parliament.uk/documents/SN04559/SN04559.pdf; Alexander Horne, Joanna Dawson, Vaughne Miller, and Jack Simson Caird, *A British Bill of Rights?*, House of Commons Library Briefing Paper No. 7193 (May 19, 2015), http://researchbriefings .files.parliament.uk/documents/CBP-7193/CBP-7193.pdf.

34. See "In Full: Brown Speech on Liberty," delivered at University of Westminster, October 25, 2007, http://news.bbc.co.uk/2/hi/uk_news/politics/7062237.stm.

35. *The Coalition: Our Programme for Government* (2010), 11, https://www.gov.uk /government/uploads/system/uploads/attachment_data/file/78977/coalition_programme_for _government.pdf.

36. Commission on a Bill of Rights, *A UK Bill of Rights? The Choice Before Us* (December 2012), vol. 1, 176, para. 12.7, http://webarchive.nationalarchives.gov.uk/20130128112038/http: /www.justice.gov.uk/downloads/about/cbr/uk-bill-rights-vol-1.pdf.

37. See *Protecting Human Rights in the UK: The Conservatives' Proposals for Changing Britain's Human Rights Laws* (2014), https://www.conservatives.com/~/media/files/downloadable%20Files/human_rights.pdf.

38. See *Strong Leadership, A Clear Economic Plan, A Brighter, More Secure Future*, the Conservative Party Manifesto 2015, https://issuu.com/conservativeparty/docs/ge_manifesto_low_res_bdecb3a47a0faf/75. For an analysis of the implications of replacing the HRA and withdrawal from the ECHR, see Dzehtsiarou et al. 2015.

39. See *Forward Together: Our Plan for a Stronger Britain and a Prosperous Future: The Conservative and Unionist Party Manifesto 2017*, 37, https://www.conservatives.com/manifesto; *For the Many, Not the Few: The Labour Party Manifesto 2017*, 80, http://www.labour.org.uk/page/-/Images/manifesto-2017/labour-manifesto-2017.pdf.

40. Donald and Leach 2016, 229.

41. See only Ziegler, Wicks, and Hodson 2015.

42. Davis 2013, 69.

43. Laws 2014, 192.

44. Donald and Leach 2016, 229 (quoting Lord Neuberger).

45. Omitted from this count are twenty-one separate just satisfaction judgments, one revision judgment, and thirteen chamber judgments that were later successfully referred to and decided by the Grand Chamber.

46. Out of the 295 merits judgments against the UK, 226 are single-violation judgments (76.6 percent), whereas 69 judgments found two or more violations of the Convention (23.4 percent).

47. In *Lamguindaz* (Friendly Settlement) (June 28, 1993); *Ian Faulkner* (Friendly Settlement) (November 30, 1999); *J.T.* (Friendly Settlement) (March 30, 2000).

Chapter 3

1. Civil proceedings: *H.* (Merits) (July 8, 1983); *Darnell* (Oct. 23, 1993); *Robins* (September 23, 1997); *Davies* (July 16, 2002); *Foley* (October 22, 2002); *Mitchell and Holloway* (December 17, 2002); *Somjee* (October 15, 2002); *Price and Lowe* (July 29, 2003); *Obasa* (January 16, 2003); *Eastaway* (July 20, 2004); *Blake* (September 26, 2006); *Bhandari* (October 2, 2007); *Richard Anderson* (February 9, 2010). Criminal proceedings: *Howarth* (September 21, 2000); *Mellors* (July 17, 2003); *Henworth* (November 2, 2004); *Massey* (November 16, 2004); *King* (December 16, 2004); *Crowther* (February 1, 2005, no just satisfaction awarded); *Yetkinsekerci* (October 20, 2005); *Bullen and Soneji* (January 8, 2009). Military proceedings: *Jordan (no. 2)* (December 10, 2002); *Crompton* (October 27, 2009).

2. König v. Germany (Just Satisfaction) (March 10, 1980), para. 15.

3. Edel 2007, 93.

4. See CM Res. DH(88)22 (December 9, 1988) (*H.*); DH(94)33 (May 4, 1994) (*Darnell*); DH(98)90 (April 22, 1998) (*Robins*); ResDH(2001)76 (June 26, 2001) (*Howarth*); CM/ResDH(2010)81 (June 3, 2010) (*Henworth*; *Massey*); CM/ResDH(2009)142 (December 3, 2009) (*Yetkinsekerci*); CM/ResDH(2010)214 (December 2, 2010) (*Eastaway*; *Mellors*; *Crowther*; *Blake*; *Bhandari*; *Jordan (no. 2)*)); ResDH(2006)28 (June 21, 2006) (*Davies*; *Foley*; *Mitchell and Holloway*; *Price and Lowe*); ResDH(2006)29 (June 21, 2006) (*Somjee*; *Obasa*); CM/ResDH(2010)80 (June 3, 2010) (*King*); CM/ResDH(2011)288 (December 2, 2011) (*Richard Anderson*); CM/ResDH(2011)182 (*Bullen and Soneji*; *Crompton*) (September 14, 2011).

5. See *Gillow* (Merits) (November 24, 1986) and *Gillow* (Just Satisfaction) (September 14, 1987), closed by CM Res. DH(88)2 (March 4, 1988).

6. *McLeod* (September 23, 1998), closed by CM Res. ResDH(2000)123 (October 2, 2000).

7. *Brecknell, McCartney, McGrath, O'Dowd and Reavey* (November 27, 2007), closed by CM Res. CM/ResDH(2009)19 (January 9, 2009).

8. See further *Goodwin* (March 27, 1996) (journalist held in contempt of court due to refusal to name source of confidential company information), closed by CM Res. DH(97)507 (October 29, 1997); *Steel and Others* (September 23, 1998) (disproportionate police intervention in peaceful protest activities not prescribed by law and without reasonable grounds to expect that applicants' peaceful protest would cause breach of the peace, plus subsequent unlawful detention in police custody), closed by CM Res. ResDH(2003)161 (October 20, 2003); *P., C. and S.* (July 16, 2002) (denial of legal assistance in care and adoption case resulting in unfair proceedings), closed by CM/ResDH(2010)214 (December 2, 2010); *Glass* (March 9, 2004) (medical treatment of mentally and physically disabled child [administration of morphine] against his mother's objections and without court order), closed by CM/ResDH(2011)174 (September 14, 2011); *Gault* (November 20, 2007) (insufficient reasons for denial of bail pending retrial at the end of which the applicant had been acquitted), closed by CM Res. CM/ResDH(2010)66 (June 3, 2010); *Yassar Hussein* (March 7, 2006) (refusal by domestic court to grant cost order despite acquittal based on assumed guilt of applicant), closed by CM Res. CM/ResDH(2010)65 (June 3, 2010); *Financial Times Ltd and Others* (December 15, 2009) (disproportionate judicial disclosure order against journalists that had remained unenforced and later became time-barred), closed by CM Res. CM/ResDH(2012)67 (March 8, 2012).

9. See *William Faulkner* (June 4, 2002) and CM Res. CM/ResDH(2011)36 (March 10, 2011).

10. See *Brennan* (October 16, 2001), closed by CM Res. CM/ResDH(2011)285 (December 2, 2011).

11. *Lloyd and Others* and *Beet and Others* (March 1, 2005), closed by CM Res. CM/ResDH(2010)140 (September 15, 2010).

12. The COE's lists of judgments for which no or incomplete information related to payment has yet been received (available at http://www.coe.int/en/web/execution/payment-information) includes several hundred entries past the payment deadline, with some judgments having been rendered as far back as 2006.

13. See CM Interim Res. DH (96) 251 (May 15, 1996) (nonpayment of just satisfaction awarded in Stran Greek Refineries and Stratis Andreadis v. Greece [December 9, 1994]).

14. See interim resolutions on nonpayment in the Cyprus-related *Loizidou* case: DH(99)680 (October 6, 1999); DH(2000)105 (July 24, 2000); ResDH(2001)80 (June 26, 2001); ResDH(2003)174 (November 12, 2003); payment was eventually made, see CM Res. ResDH(2003)190 (December 2, 2003).

15. See *Omojudi* (November 24, 2009) (deportation to Nigeria because of conviction for sexual assault) and *A.W. Khan* (January 12, 2010) (deportation to Pakistan after conviction for narcotics-related crime), both closed by CM Res. CM/ResDH(2011)82 (June 8, 2011); *Hilal* (March 6, 2001) (threatened deportation of political opposition member to Zanzibar/Tanzania), closed by CM Res. CM/ResDH(2010)138 (September 15, 2010); *D.* (May 2, 1997) (threatened deportation of terminally ill AIDS patient to St. Kitts), closed by CM Res. DH(98)10 (February 18, 1998); *Chahal* (November 15, 1996) (threatened deportation of orthodox Sikh to Punjab/India), closed by CM Res. DH(2001)119 (October 15, 2001); *Lamguindaz* (Friendly Settlement)

(June 23, 1993) (deportation of Moroccan native to country of nationality because of criminal record), closed by CM Res. DH(93)55 (November 9, 1993).

16. *NA.* (July 17, 2008) (threatened removal of ethnic Tamil to Sri Lanka), closed by CM Res. CM/ResDH(2011)84 (June 8, 2011); *S.H.* (June 15, 2010) (threatened removal of ethnic Nepalese to Bhutan), closed by CM Res. CM/ResDH(2011)182 (September 14, 2011).

17. *NA.*, para. 147 (emphasis added).

18. *S.H.*, para. 71.

19. *Soering* (July 7, 1989), para. 111; for discussion, see Lillich 1991.

20. *Soering*, para. 97; see also Farran 1996, 60.

21. CM Res. DH(90)8 (March 12, 1990) (emphasis added).

22. Article IV of the 1972 UK-US extradition treaty provided that "[i]f the offense for which extradition is requested is punishable by death under the relevant law of the requesting Party, but the relevant law of the requested Party does not provide for the death penalty in a similar case, extradition may be refused unless the requesting Party gives assurances satisfactory to the requested Party that the death penalty will not be carried out."

23. *Soering*, paras. 28, 17.

24. For the Court, the existence of this alternative did enter into the assessment of the proportionality in light of Article 3 ECHR of extraditing Mr. Soering to the United States instead, without any resulting prescriptions, however. Ibid., para. 110. See similarly *Jens Soering* (Comm. rep.) (January 19, 1989), diss. ops. Frowein and Trechsel.

25. See *Harkins and Edwards* (January 17, 2012), paras. 85, 86, 91.

26. Warbrick 1990, 1087.

27. CM Res. CM/ResDH(2012)68 (March 8, 2012).

28. Letter from D. Walton, Agent of the Government of the United Kingdom to T. L. Early, Section Registrar, European Court of Human Rights (December 31, 2008), quoted in letter from the Chair of the Joint Committee on Human Rights to John Hutton MP, secretary of state for defense (January 13, 2009), http://www.publications.parliament.uk/pa/jt200910/jtselect/jtrights/85/85we02.htm.

29. *Al-Saadoon and Mufdhi* (March 2, 2010), para. 155.

30. Quoted in ibid., para. 56; see also ibid., para. 66.

31. Ibid., para. 171.

32. CM Res. CM/ResDH(2012)68 (March 8, 2012); see, further, letter from Liam Fox MP, secretary of state for defense, to the chair of the Joint Committee on Human Rights (November 25, 2010), and the annex thereto, both available at http://www.parliament.uk/business/committees/committees-a-z/joint-select/human-rights-committee/human-rights-judgments/al-saadoon-and-mufdhi-v-uk/.

33. *Welch* (Merits) (February 9, 1995).

34. CM Res. DH(97)222 (May 15, 1997), reproduced in *Human Rights Case Digest* 8 (1997): 538–540.

35. *Sander* (May 9, 2000); closed by CM Res. ResDH(2002)36 (April 30, 2002).

Chapter 4

1. Moravcsik 2000, 227.

2. In *Chahal* (November 15, 1996), one issue concerned the fact that the applicant, a Sikh separatist detained for over six years pending his deportation to India, had been unable to

appeal his deportation and detention orders due to domestic law that excluded cases from judicial review in which the reason to deport and detain was based on national security or other political considerations. The HRA empowered domestic courts to review such decisions with respect to their conformity with the Convention; see CM Res. DH(2001)119 (October 15, 2001). The case of *Cuscani* (September 24, 2002) concerned the lack of an interpreter during a sentencing hearing, with the HRA enabling courts to rely directly on Article 6 (3) lit. e to provide such service; see CM Res. ResDH(2006)56 (November 2, 2006).

3. Violations of Article 13 ECHR, either by itself or in conjunction with other Convention articles, had been found in *Silver and Others* (Merits) (March 25, 1983); *Campbell and Fell* (June 28, 1984); *Abdulaziz, Cabales and Balkandali* (May 28, 1985); *Chahal* (November 15, 1996); *Halford* (June 25, 1997); *Smith and Grady* (Merits) (September 27, 1999); *Khan* (May 12, 2000); *Keenan* (April 3, 2001); *Z. and Others* (May 10, 2001); *T.P. and K.M.* (May 10, 2001); *P.G. and J.H.* (September 25, 2001); *Paul and Audrey Edwards* (March 14, 2002); *Armstrong* (July 17, 2002); *D.P. and J.C.* (October 10, 2002); *Taylor-Sabori* (October 22, 2002); *Beck, Copp and Bazeley* (October 22, 2002); *Allan* (November 5, 2002); *E. and Others* (November 26, 2002); *Hatton and Others* (August 7, 2003); *Peck* (January 28, 2003); *McGlinchey and Others* (April 29, 2003); *Chalkley* (June 12, 2003); *Lewis* (November 25, 2003); *Wood* (November 16, 2004); *Bubbins* (March 17, 2005); *Keegan* (July 18, 2006); *Wainwright* (September 26, 2006); *R.K. and A.K.* (September 30, 2008); *A.D. and O.D.* (March 16, 2010); *M.A.K. and R.K.* (March 23, 2010). Two judgments raised issues under Article 13 not remedied by the HRA: *Al-Saadoon and Mufdhi* (March 2, 2010) (judicial office of House of Lords closed over holidays; when it reopened, the applicants had already been handed over to Iraqi authority, nullifying any available judicial remedy) and *MacKay and BBC Scotland* (December 7, 2010) (no formal procedure in Scotland to challenge court-ordered reporting restrictions in criminal trial); see CM Res. CM/ResDH(2012)68 (March 8, 2012) (greater availability of new UK Supreme Court, with Registrar, who may stay any orders, if necessary, reachable by phone when office is closed) and CM/ResDH(2012)108 (June 6, 2012) (Act of Adjournal [Criminal Procedure Rules Amendment No. 3] [Miscellaneous] 2011, sec. 6, provides for statutory basis of challenge proceedings), respectively.

4. Violations of Article 5 (5) ECHR were found in *Brogan and Others* (Merits) (November 29, 1988); *Fox, Campbell and Hartley* (Merits) (August 30, 1990); *Thynne, Wilson and Gunnell* (October 25, 1990); *Hood* (February 18, 1999); *Caballero* (February 8, 2000); *Stephen Jordan (no. 1)* (March 14, 2000); *Curley* (March 28, 2000); *S.B.C.* (June 19, 2001); *O'Hara* (October 16, 2001); *Waite* (December 12, 2002); *Wynne (no. 2)* (October 16, 2003); *Hill* (April 27, 2004); *Thompson* (June 15, 2004); *Lloyd and Others* (March 1, 2005); *Beet and Others* (March 1, 2005); *Blackstock* (June 21, 2005); *Kolanis* (June 21, 2005); *A. and Others* (February 19, 2009) (a post-HRA case, the violation concerned the fact that domestic courts had not found a violation of Article 5 ECHR and therefore did not grant an enforceable claim to compensation).

5. *Brogan and Others* (Merits) (November 29, 1988), paras. 66, 67; CM Res. DH(90)23 (September 24, 1990) (*Brogan and Others*); DH(92)24 (June 15, 1992) (*Thynne, Wilson and Gunnel*).

6. Rights Brought Home: The Human Rights Bill (1997), Cm. 3782 (October 1997), para. 1.18, https://www.gov.uk/government/uploads/system/uploads/attachment_data/file/263526/rights.pdf.

7. Klug 2000, 162–163.

8. *Tyrer* (April 25, 1978), para. 35; for analysis, see Bonner 1979.

9. See "Folly to Drop Birch, Isle of Man Says," *Globe and Mail* (Canada), January 18, 1978; "Isle of Man Fights to Retain Birching," *Globe and Mail*, June 21, 1979; Jeffrey Simpson,

"Corporal Punishment Favored: Manx Speak Loudly, Carry Big Stick," *Globe and Mail*, November 20, 1981. While judicially imposed corporal punishment had been abolished in Wales, Scotland, and England in 1948 and in Northern Ireland in 1968, the Isle of Man parliament (the Court of Tynwald) had considered its abolition in 1963, 1965, and 1977 but explicitly chose to retain it; see Farran 1996, 63.

10. While retaining some authority to legislate over the Isle of Man, Westminster has rarely exercised these reserve powers, especially not against the express wishes of the Manx government, since granting the island increasing autonomy through parliamentary acts in 1866, 1872, and 1878; see generally Kermode 2001.

11. See Ghandhi 1983; Tony Farragher, "Isle of Man Declares an End to 'Brutal' Birching," *Independent* (March 6, 1993), 2.

12. See CM Res. (78) 39 (October 13, 1978).

13. As permitted under Article 63 (4) ECHR (1950) (now Article 56 (4) ECHR). An attempt to renew the declaration by two Labour frontbenchers failed in 1986; see Michael Morris, "Labour Puts Case for Manx Rights: Attempt to Restore Rights of Isle of Man Citizens to Use European Court of Human Rights," *Guardian* (May 1, 1986).

14. Churchill and Young 1992, 287.

15. *Campbell and Cosans* (Merits) (February 25, 1982), para. 38.

16. Churchill and Young 1992, 289; Andrew Moncur, "Parents Get Right to Forbid Caning: New Legislation to be Announced in Queen's Speech," *Guardian* (October 22, 1984).

17. Churchill and Young 1992, 289; David Hearst and Colin Brown, "Caning Bill Upset by Lords' Rebuff," *Guardian* (July 5, 1985).

18. Indeed, in 1993 the Court ruled with the thinnest majority—five votes to four—that at least in the instant case (an eight-year-old boy having "being slippered three times on his buttocks through his shorts with a rubber-soled gym shoe" in an independent school), the punishment did not rise to the level of "degrading" treatment, nor did it find violations of Articles 8 or 13 ECHR; see *Costello-Roberts* (March 25, 1993), para. 32; for critical discussion, see Phillips 1994.

19. See Churchill and Young 1992, 290–291, and CM Res. DH(87)9 (June 25, 1987) (*Campbell and Cosans*). In a number of other cases alleging violations of Article 3 and/or Article 2 of Protocol No. 1 due to corporal punishment in public schools, the UK concluded friendly settlements: see *X.* (Comm. rep.) (December 17, 1981); *Durairaj et al.* (Comm. rep.) (July 16, 1987); *Townend and Townend* (Comm. rep.) (January 23, 1987); *B. and D.* (Comm. rep.) (July 16, 1987); *Three Members of the A. Family* (Comm. rep.) (July 16, 1987). In 1988 it was reported that the UK had paid £51,000 in compensation to sixteen families that had lodged applications with the Commission claiming violations of Article 3 ECHR for corporal punishments received in public schools mostly between 1982 and 1987, that is, during the delay in implementation; see Ngaio Crequer, "Families Receive 51,000 Pounds for School Punishments," *Independent* (September 28, 1988), 4; "Beaten Children Share 51,000 Pounds Compensation: Corporal Punishment in Schools," *Times* (September 28, 1988). Although the Commission had concluded that there had been violations of both Article 3 ECHR and Article 2 of Protocol No. 1, alone and in conjunction with Article 13 ECHR (see *Warwick* [Comm. rep.] [July 18, 1986]), the Committee of Ministers was able to muster the required two-thirds majority for a finding of violation under Article 32 ECHR only with respect to Article 2 of Protocol No. 1, but not with respect to Article 3 ECHR; see CM Res. DH(89)5 (March 2, 1989). In a later case, the Commission again found a violation of Article 3 and referred the case to the Court, where a friendly settlement was reached; see *Y.* (Friendly Settlement) (October 29, 1992).

20. See School Standards and Framework Act 1998, sec. 131.

21. See "Corporal Punishment Outlawed," BBC News, June 16, 1998, http://news.bbc.co.uk /1/hi/education/114325.stm.

22. *A.* (September 23, 1998).

23. Ibid., para. 24. The reasonable chastisement defense had been recognized in UK courts since at least 1860, when it featured in the case of R. v. Hopley, 2 F. and F. 202, 206 (1860).

24. Williams 2007, 271. Right after the judgment had been delivered, the health minister, Paul Boateng, stated that "[t]his Labour government believes in parental discipline. Smacking has a place in that. Our law will do nothing to outlaw smacking" (quoted in Clare Dyer, "Parents to Keep Right to Smack Despite Euro Ruling," *Guardian* [September 24, 1998], 1).

25. The judgment of the UK Court of Appeal's criminal division in Regina v. H. (Reasonable Chastisement)—[2001] EWCA (Crim.) 1024 (Eng.); [2001] 2 FLR 431; [2002] 1 Cr. App. Rep. 39 (April 25, 2001)—noted the ECtHR's judgment and developed a list of five factors to be taken into account in determining whether chastisement could be considered "reasonable": "(i) the nature and context of the defendant's behavior; (ii) the duration of that behavior; (iii) the physical and mental consequences in respect of the child; (iv) the age and personal characteristics of the child; (v) the reasons given by the defendant for administering the punishment" (*Times Law Reports* [May 17, 2001], 329).

26. See CM Interim Res. ResDH(2004)39 (June 2, 2004), and A. against the United Kingdom, Secretariat Memorandum, COE Doc. CM/Inf(2004)6 rev. (April 5, 2004), esp. paras. 45–49.

27. See Williams 2007, 271; Alexandra Frean, "Children's Groups Scent Victory in Campaign for Smacking Ban," *Times* (March 15, 2004), 30; John Carvel, "Human Rights Committee Condemns Smacking," *Guardian* (September 22, 2004) (noting that the Children Are Unbeatable! Alliance, formed in 1998 in response to ECtHR's ruling in A., comprises 350 "anti-smacking" organizations).

28. Keating 2006, 405–406.

29. See Children Act 2004, sec. 58; Children Act 2004: Explanatory Notes, paras. 236–240; Keating 2006.

30. See A. against the United Kingdom, Secretariat Memorandum, COE Doc. CM/Inf/ DH(2005)8 (February 3, 2005), paras. 59–60.

31. See summary of opinions reported in Annotated Agenda, 1013th CM Meeting (December 3–5, 2007), COE Doc. CM/Del/OJ/DH(2007)1013 sec. 4.3 (*s.n. A.*) and in A. against the United Kingdom, Secretariat Memorandum, COE Doc. CM/Inf/DH(2006)29 (June 2, 2006), paras. 49–56.

32. See A. against the United Kingdom, Secretariat Memorandum, COE Doc. CM/Inf/ DH(2008)34 (August 28, 2008), para. 64. On February 20, 2009, the appeal by the Northern Ireland Children's Commissioner was rejected on standing grounds; see "Commissioner Loses Appeal Against Law That Allows Parents to Smack Children," *Irish Times* (February 21, 2009), 7; her attempt to get smacking banned ended for financial reasons, see Gerry Moriarty, "Bid Abandoned to Ban Smacking," *Irish Times* (April 22, 2009), 8.

33. The final resolution was adopted shortly afterward: CM Res. CM/ResDH(2009)75 (September 16, 2009).

34. See A. against the United Kingdom, Secretariat Memorandum, COE Doc. CM/Inf/ DH(2008)34 (Aug. 28, 2008), para. 77.

35. In October 2007, the minister for children, Kevin Brennan, rejected changes to the current law—see Sam Coates, "Total Smacking Ban Is Ruled Out," *Times* (October 26, 2007),

32—and in February 2008, the Sentencing Guidelines Council released new guidelines on dealing with assaults on children, advising that when physical harm as a result of smacking was either not intended or not foreseen, courts should be lenient; see Sentencing Guidelines Council, "Overarching Principles: Assaults on Children and Cruelty to a Child" (February 2008), paras. 12–14, https://www.sentencingcouncil.org.uk/wp-content/uploads/web_Overarching _principles_assaults_on_children_and_cruelty_to_a_child.pdf. The guidelines quickly drew criticism as undermining the effectiveness of the current legal framework; see Christopher Hope, "Smacking Laws 'Unworkable,'" *Daily Telegraph* (February 20, 2008), 1.

36. See David Langton, "Ministers to Review Ban on Smacking," *Independent*, June 16, 2007 (noting that a recent poll revealed that more than two-thirds of parents used smacking as a punishment and that "between 80 and 90 per cent of parents and adults without families were against a complete ban"); Alexandra Frean, "Children's Champions Demand a Total Ban on Smacking," *Times* (January 21, 2006), 4 ("Historically, polls asking parents if they want to ban smacking have come up with a majority response of 'no'").Two recent opinion polls in Wales and Scotland corroborate these assessments; see YouGov—Children 1st Survey (January 30–February 1, 2015), https://d25d2506sfb94s.cloudfront.net/cumulus_uploads/document /8syhbq168m/YG-Archive-150201-Children1st.pdf (67 percent of all Scottish respondents in favor of keeping law unchanged); YouGov—Western Mail Survey (April 9–11, 2014), https:// d25d2506sfb94s.cloudfront.net/cumulus_uploads/document/23dqxm93za/YouGov-Survey -Western-Mail-Welsh-Sample-Smacking-140411.pdf (69 percent of Welsh respondents in favor of not banning the right to smack children).

37. A 2003 representative survey found that over 50 percent of surveyed parents had smacked or slapped their children within the last twelve months, with 9 percent having used more severe physical punishment; see Deborah Ghate, Neal Hazel, Susan Creighton, Steven Finch, and Julia Field, "The National Study of Parents, Children and Discipline in Britain: Key Findings," (2003), http://www.prb.org.uk/publications/Parents%20Children%20and %20Discipline%20Summary%20final.pdf. These findings correspond with those of other studies and surveys; see, e.g., Nobes and Smith 1997; Rosemary Bennett, "Majority of Parents Admit to Smacking Children," *Times Online* (September 20, 2006), https://www.thetimes .co.uk/article/majority-of-parents-admit-to-smacking-children-5zrr08b8z3x (reporting poll results according to which seven out of ten parents smack their children and 80 percent believe in the benefits of smacking).

38. In February 2008, fifty Labour MPs sought to revive support for a new and free vote on the issue; see Patrick Wintour, "Senior Labour MPs Lead Campaign to Ban Smacking: 50 Backbenchers Ask Colleagues for Support—Chief Whip Urged to Hold Free Vote on 'Moral Issue,'" *Guardian* (February 15, 2008), 10. The attempt eventually failed in the House of Commons without a vote.

39. In early 2017, after France had passed anti-smacking legislation—against widespread public opposition—it was reported that the UK was one of only four countries in Europe that still permitted the practice (the others being Switzerland, Italy, and the Czech Republic); Henry Samuel, "France Bans Smacking, Raising Pressure on UK to Follow Suit," *Telegraph*, January 3, 2017, http://www.telegraph.co.uk/news/2017/01/03/france-bans-smacking-raising-pressure-uk -follow-suit/. The French law, however, was soon after struck down again due, reportedly, to technical issues; see "France's Top Court Strikes Down Anti-smacking Law," *France24*, January 27, 2017, http://www.france24.com/en/20170127-france-children-top-court-constitutional -council-strikes-down-anti-smacking-law-rights.

40. See COE webpage on the elimination of corporal punishment at http://www.coe.int/en /web/children/corporal-punishment.

41. See European Committee for Social Rights, Association for the Protection of All Children (APPROACH) v. France, Complaint No. 92/2013 (September 12, 2014) (the quotation can be found in para. 36); APPROACH v. Slovenia, Complaint No. 95/2013 (December 5, 2014); APPROACH v. Czech Republic, Complaint No. 96/2013 (January 20, 2015); APPROACH v. Belgium, Complaint No. 98/2013 (January 20, 2015); APPROACH v. Ireland, Complaint No. 93/2013 (December 2, 2014). The Irish case is particularly relevant since the complaint concerned the defense of "reasonable chastisement" as available under Irish common law. Article 17 (1) of the Revised European Social Charter of 1996 obliges states, inter alia, "to take all appropriate and necessary measures designed: [. . .] to protect children and young persons against negligence, violence or exploitation."

42. Human Rights Committee, "Concluding Observations on the Seventh Periodic Report of the United Kingdom of Great Britain and Northern Ireland" (August 17, 2015), UN Doc. CCPR/C/GBR/CO/7, para. 20.

43. Charlotte England, "Welsh Parents Could Be Banned from Smacking Their Children," *Independent*, January 5, 2017, http://www.independent.co.uk/news/uk/home-news/wales-ban -parents-smacking-children-corporal-punishment-welsh-assembly-bill-amendment-slapping -a7510546.html.

44. For an overview and an oral history of this and many of the following cases, see Johnson 2016.

45. See *Dudgeon* (Merits) (October, 22, 1981), para. 61.

46. Churchill and Young 1992, 320.

47. See Homosexual Offences (Northern Ireland) Order 1982, S.I. 1982 No. 1536 (N.I. 19), Article 3 (1), and CM Res. DH(83)13 (October 27, 1983).

48. See Sexual Offences Act 1967, sec. 1; Goldhaber 2007, 34.

49. See Criminal Justice (Scotland) Act 1980, sec. 80.

50. Churchill and Young 1992, 320.

51. Namely, on the Isle of Man and in Jersey; see Churchill and Young 1992, 321.

52. Homosexual Offences (Northern Ireland) Order 1982, S.I. 1982 No. 1536 (N.I. 19), Article 3 (2) lit. a.

53. See Sexual Offences Act 1967, sec. 1 (5); Criminal Justice (Scotland) Act 1980, sec. 80 (5).

54. See Criminal Justice and Public Order Act 1994, sec. 146.

55. Quoted in *Lustig-Prean and Beckett* (Merits) (September 27, 1999), para. 42. See also statement by Minister of State for the Armed Forces Jeremy Hanley, 241 Parl. Deb., HC (6th ser.) (April 12, 1994), col. 171, and Written Answers, "Armed Forces: Homosexuality Policy Assessment," 570 Parl. Deb. HL (5th ser.) (March 5, 1996), col. 14WA.

56. See *Smith and Grady* (Merits) and *Lustig-Prean and Beckett* (Merits) (September 27, 1999). Two later judgments concerned the same violation: see *Perkins and R.* (October 22, 2002); *Beck, Copp and Bazeley* (October 22, 2002).

57. See statement by Secretary of State for Defense Geoffrey Hoon, 342 Parl. Deb. HC (6th ser.) (January 12, 2000), cols. 287–288.

58. Armed Forces Code of Social Conduct (January 12, 2000), paras. 5, 1, reproduced in Mark Oakes, The Armed Forces Bill, House of Commons Research Paper 01/03 (January 8, 2001), appendix 2, http://researchbriefings.files.parliament.uk/documents/RP01-03/RP01 -03.pdf. On the basis of the adoption of the code, the Committee closed the supervision of

these cases; see CM Res. DH(2002)34 (April 30, 2002) (*Lustig-Prean and Beckett*); DH(2002)35 (April 30, 2002) (*Smith and Grady*); DH(2003)128 (July 22, 2003) (*Beck, Copp and Bazeley*); DH(2003)129 (July 22, 2003) (*Perkins and R.*). The removal of the ban resulted in numerous claims for compensation by soldiers who had been dismissed because of their homosexuality; see Jenny Percival, "End to Ban on Gays May Bring Flood of Claims," *Scotsman*, January 13, 2000, 9 (noting that "[o]ver the past ten years, 654 members of the armed forces have been forced to leave for this reason"). By 2008, the UK had paid out £4 million to 65 individuals, see Martin Hodgson, "£4m MoD Payout to Gay Personnel," *Guardian* (November 8, 2008), 17.

59. For the Tories see, e.g., statement by Iain Duncan Smith: "Surely one of the greatest concerns arising from the judgment is the way in which the convention is being applied to the military. There is a danger that issues such as the role of women in the front line and even our training policy could be decided by the European Court of Human Rights and not by our own Government and armed forces" (342 Parl. Deb. HC [6th ser.] [January 12, 2000], col. 290); statement by Nicholas Soames, noting that the "announcement will be greeted with dismay through all three services, which surely, by their faithful and gallant service over generations, have earned the right to be exempted from these lunatic politically correct nostrums" (342 Parl. Deb. HC [6th ser.] [January 12, 2000], col. 294). For the Liberal Democrats, see statement by Paul Keetch, 342 Parl. Deb. HC (6th ser.) (January 12, 2000), col. 292.

60. See statement by Gerald Kaufman, 342 Parl. Deb. HC (6th ser.) (January 12, 2000), col. 292 ("As Conservative Governments accepted the authority of the European Court of Human Rights throughout their periods in office, it is difficult to see what other decision they could have come to"). The suggestion that the UK should seek an exemption of its military service from the coverage of the Convention similar to that of France had to fail because France's exemption was based on a reservation that could be lodged only at the time of the ECHR's ratification; see statements by Julian Brazier and Geoffrey Hoon, 342 Parl. Deb. HC (6th ser.) (January 12, 2000), col. 295. Also see Jamie Walker, "Gays Sacking Out," *Australian*, September 29, 1999, 12 (noting that at the time that "it was unclear whether the decision spelled the end of the ban on homosexuals, with Ministry of Defence officials pointing out that the Strasbourg judges had confined themselves to the sacking issue, not the legality of the policy itself").

61. See Paul Eastham, "Blair May Give MPs Free Vote on Forces Gays: Tory Fury at Labour's Move over Ban on Homosexuals," *Daily Mail* (September 3, 1999), 41.

62. See Robert Verkaik, "Labour Apology for MOD Gay Ban," *Independent*, May 19, 1999, 14 (noting that the "Government said it would fight to uphold its policy on not allowing gay men and women in the armed forces"); statement by Gerald Howarth, 337 Parl. Deb. HC (6th ser.) (November 8, 1999), col. 685.

63. In 1995, Labour's then shadow spokesman on defense had emphasized "that we in the Labour party have never given the green light to homosexual activity, conduct or relationships in the armed forces [. . .] We fully accept the particular conditions of the armed forces and that homosexual [. . .] relationships [. . .] can undermine and be prejudicial to good order and morale"; quoted in statement by Richard Ottaway, 337 Parl. Deb. HC (6th ser.) (November 8, 1999), col. 685. See also Stephen Grosz, "Gays Have Won a Battle," *Guardian* (September 24, 1999), 24 (noting that "although the last Tory defence secretary supported the ban, the legal defence of it has been maintained by his Labour successor George Robertson").

64. See Michael Seamark and Paul Eastham, "Euro Court 'Clears Way' for Sacked Four to Launch a Challenge: Forces Gay Ban Could Soon be Overturned," *Daily Mail* (February 27, 1999), 38.

65. See Eastham, "Blair May Give MPs Free Vote on Forces Gays," *Daily Mail* (September 3, 1999), 41; see also John Rentoul, "About-Turn Complete as Blair Backs Ban," *Independent*, May 10, 1996, 9 (noting that Labour's defense spokesman had committed the party to lifting the ban in 1995 and that most of the Labour shadow cabinet voted to lift it in 1996). In addition, Labour's 1997 election manifesto declared that "we will seek to end unjustifiable discrimination wherever it exists"; see Labour Party Manifesto 1997, *New Labour: Because Britain Deserves Better*, http://www.politicsresources.net/area/uk/man/lab97.htm.

66. Voting in the House of Commons on a legislative amendment that would have ended the ban in May 1996, only eight Labour MPs sided with the Conservative majority to reject the amendment; see Rayside 1998, 96.

67. See Belkin and Evans 2000, 23n31.

68. See Sexual Offences (Amendment) Act 2000, sec. 1. The Labour majority in the House of Commons had previously passed legislation to this effect in 1998 and 1999, which was blocked, however, both times in the House of Lords; see Explanatory Notes to Sexual Offences (Amendment) Act 2000, paras. 4–5. Then prime minister Tony Blair had already argued in favor of the sixteen-year threshold in 1994 when the Conservative Major government had lowered the age of consent for homosexual acts from 21 to 18 years; see *Sutherland* (Comm. rep.) (July 1, 1997), para. 28. After the remedial legislation had entered into force, the case was settled in *Sutherland* (March 27, 2001). One instance of prosecution begun under the older discriminatory regime (and then discontinued after the change in domestic law) still resulted in a judgment; see *B.B.* (February 10, 2005), closed by CM Res. ResDH(2005)99 (October 26, 2005).

69. *A.D.T.* (July 31, 2000). The *A.D.T.* lawsuit had benefited from support by the LGBT lobby group Stonewall, which saw it as strengthening its case for demanding change of discriminatory domestic gross indecency laws; see Hodson 2011, 134–139.

70. See Sexual Offences Act 2003, sched. 6, paras. 11, 15, repealing the relevant provisions in the Sexual Offences Act 1956 and the Sexual Offences Act 1967; see also CM/ResDH(2010)118 (September 15, 2010).

71. See *Rees* (October 17, 1986), para. 37; *Cossey* (September 27, 1990), para. 40; *X., Y. and Z.* (April 22, 1997); *Sheffield and Horsham* (July 30, 1998). See also B. v. France (March 25, 1992), para. 63 (finding that the different situation in France with respect to the treatment of transsexuals did result in a violation of Article 8 ECHR).

72. *Christine Goodwin* and *I.* (July 11, 2002), paras. 93, 73, respectively. For summaries, see Rudolf 2003. A further clone case is *Grant* (Judgment May 23, of 2006) (failure to recognize acquired gender for purposes of determining legal retirement age [different for men and women]).

73. *Christine Goodwin*, para. 100. The Court's about-face had more to do with a change in interpretation than a change in contextual factors; see Erdman 2003 (linking the change to the Court's abandonment of the "consensus doctrine" in establishing a shared European standard). Note also that the dissents in the previous cases had become more numerous; cf. with respect to a violation of Article 8 ECHR: *Rees* (twelve to three), *Cossey* (ten to eight), *X., Y. and Z.* (fourteen to six), and *Sheffield and Horsham* (eleven to nine). The decisions in *Christine Goodwin* and *I.* were unanimous.

74. *Report of the Interdepartmental Working Group on Transsexual People* (London: Home Office, Communication Directorate, 2000), 20, para. 4.3, http://www.oocities.org/transforum2000/Resources/wgtrans.pdf.

75. See Bellinger v. Bellinger, [2001] EWCA Civ: 1140, [2002] 1 All E.R. 311 (C.A., 2001), paras. 96, 109.

76. See Rains 2005, 393.

77. See Bellinger v. Bellinger, [2003] UKHL 21, [2003] 2 All E.R. 593 (H.L.).

78. CM Res. CM/ResDH(2011)175 (*C. Goodwin* and *I.*) and CM/ResDH(2011)173 (*Grant*) (September 14, 2011).

79. See Gender Recognition Act 2004, sec. 2 (1) (requiring that the applicant "(a) has or has had gender dysphoria, (b) has lived in the acquired gender throughout the period of two years ending with the date on which the application is made, (c) intends to continue to live in the acquired gender until death, and (d) complies with the requirements imposed by and under section 3"); Rains 2005, 396–397; the German legal requirements are set out in ibid., 373–374.

80. Heinze 2001, 290.

81. Forty-eight of the fifty-five House of Commons supporters of Early Day Motion 302, "Civil Rights for Transsexuals," tabled January 17, 1996, hailed from the Labour Party; see http:// www.parliament.uk/business/publications/business-papers/commons/early-day-motions/edm -detail1/?edmnumber=302&session=1995-96.

82. *Connors* (May 27, 2004), paras. 94–95. Previously, the Grand Chamber had affirmed the authorities' right to regulate the use of land, even if privately owned, as gypsy sites, provided that the different interests at stake had been taken into account and properly balanced; see the judgments in *Chapman*; *Beard*; *Coster*; *Lee*; and *Jane Smith* (January 18, 2001).

83. Joint Committee on Human Rights, Monitoring the Government's Response to Court Judgments Finding Breaches of Human Rights, 16th Rep. Sess. 2006–07, HL Paper 128/HC 728, June 28, 2007, 37.

84. See Caravan Sites (Security of Tenure), Bill 206 (July 4, 2006), http://www.publications .parliament.uk/pa/cm200506/cmbills/206/2006206.pdf.

85. See Housing and Regeneration Act 2008, sec. 318.

86. CM Res. CM/ResDH(2013)174 (September 11, 2013).

87. The situation in Wales had been addressed in *Buckland* (August 18, 2012), closed by CM Res. CM/ResDH(2013)237 (November 20, 2103).

88. In Mobile Homes Act 1983, sec. 5 (1).

89. See Joint Committee on Human Rights, Monitoring the Government's Response to Human Rights Judgments: Annual Report 2008, 31st Rep. Sess. 2007–08, HL Paper 173/HC 1078, October 31, 2008, 29.

90. See *Implementing the Mobile Homes Act 1983 on Local Authority Gypsy and Traveller Sites: Consultation* (London: Communities and Local Government Publications, September 2008), https://www.gov.uk/government/uploads/system/uploads/attachment_data/file/11861 /implementingmobilehomesact.pdf. The outcome report was issued two years later: *Consultation on Implementing the Mobile Homes Act 1983 on Local Authority Gypsy and Traveller Sites: Summary of Responses* (London: Communities and Local Government Publications, October 2010), https://www.gov.uk/government/uploads/system/uploads/attachment_data/file/11863 /1736663.pdf.

91. Explanatory Memorandum to The Housing and Regeneration Act 2008 (Consequential Amendments to the Mobile Homes Act 1983) (Wales) Order 2013 (June 12, 2013), 6, http:// www.assemblywales.org/sub-ld9356-em-e.pdf.

92. Housing Act 2004, sec. 211 (amending Caravan Sites Act 1968, sec. 4 [6]).

93. *"Travelling to a Better Future": Gypsy and Traveller Framework for Action and Delivery Plan* (Cardiff: Welsh Government Publications, September 2011), 20, http://gov.wales/docs /dsjlg/publications/equality/110928gypsytravelleren.pdf.

94. *McCann* (May 13, 2008) and *Kay and Others* (September 21, 2010).

95. Kay and Others and Another v. London Borough of Lambeth and Others, Leeds City Council v. Price and Others and Others, [2006] UKHL 10 (March 8, 2006), para. 110.

96. *McCann*, para. 50.

97. Doherty and Others v. Birmingham City Council, [2008] UKHL 57 (July 30, 2008), addendum.

98. See CM Res. CM/ResDH(2012)145 (*McCann*) and CM/ResDH(2012)144 (*Kay and Others*) (September 26, 2012).

99. Manchester City Council v. Pinnock, [2010] UKSC 45 (November 3, 2010), para. 48.

100. Ibid., para. 49.

101. See Lords Hope and Brown as well as Baroness Hale in *Kay and Others* (2006), paras. 110, 207–208, 189–190, and Lords Hope and Rodger in *Doherty* (2008), paras. 56, 123, respectively.

102. *Abdulaziz, Cabales and Balkandali* (May 28, 1985), para. 23.

103. Ibid., para. 75.

104. Ibid., para. 79 ("[T]he Court is not convinced that the difference that may nevertheless exist between the respective impact of men and of women on the domestic labor market is sufficiently important to justify the difference of treatment, complained of by the applicants, as to the possibility for a person settled in the United Kingdom to be joined by, as the case may be, his wife or her husband").

105. See *Conservative General Election Manifesto 1979*, sec. 4: "The Rule of Law, Immigration and Race Relations," http://www.margaretthatcher.org/archive/displaydocument.asp?docid=110858.

106. Supervision closed by CM Res. DH(86)2 (April 11, 1986).

107. Churchill and Young 1992, 330.

108. Gearty 1997, 94.

109. See Social Security and Benefits Act 1992, secs. 36–38.

110. See Income and Corporation Taxes Act 1988, sec. 262.

111. *Willis* (June 11, 2002); *Hobbs, Richard, Walsh and Geen* (November 14, 2006). In contrast to the other benefits, the Court found the widow's pension scheme to be in conformity with the Convention; see Willis, para. 50; *Runkee and White* (May 10, 2007), paras. 40–42.

112. See Welfare Reform and Pensions Act 1999: Explanatory Notes, "3: Bereavement Benefits" ("The UK has been under challenge in the European Court of Human Rights over the present scheme").

113. See *Cornwell* (Friendly Settlement) and *Leary* (Friendly Settlement) (April 25, 2000) (relating to widowed mother's allowance and widow's payment), closed by CM Res. ResDH(2002)95 (*Cornwell*) and ResDH(2002)96 (*Leary*) (both July 22, 2002); *Crossland* (Friendly Settlement) (November 9, 1999) (relating to widow's bereavement allowance), closed by CM Res. DH(2000)81 (May 29, 2000).

114. See Welfare Reform and Pensions Act 1999, secs. 54, 55, replacing "widowed mother's allowance" with "widowed parent's allowance," "widow's pension" with "bereavement allowance," and "widow's payment" with "bereavement payment," all of which are available to men and women alike if they otherwise qualify for them. The *Willis* case was closed by CM Res. ResDH(2003)130 (July 22, 2003).

115. See Finance Act 1999, sec. 34.

116. April 6, 2000 (Finance Act 1999) and April 9, 2001 (Welfare Reform and Pensions Act 1999).

117. See only the Committee of Ministers' final resolutions: ResDH(2002)97 (July 22, 2002) (*Fielding*); ResDH(2002)144 (*Downie*) and ResDH(2002)145 (*Loffelman*) (October 21, 2002); ResDH(2002)161 (December 17, 2002) (*Sawden*); ResDH(2003)148 (July 22, 2003) (*Rice*); ResDH(2004)12 (February 24, 2004) (*Atkinson*); CM/ResDH(2009)41 (January 9, 2009) (seventeen friendly settlements); CM/ResDH(2009)157 (December 3, 2009) (seven friendly settlements). Additional friendly settlements were recognized as decisions; for an example see only *Hughes* (Decision of September 2, 2009). The UK House of Lords had also found that the discriminatory schemes for widowed mother's allowance and widow's payment had no objective justification, but because the HRA did not provide for compensation in these circumstances, the settlements had to occur at the European level; see ibid.

118. In addition to the 2002 *Willis* judgment, see those mentioned in CM Res. CM/ResDH(2009)152 (March 12, 2009) (fourteen judgments, including *Hobbs, Richard, Walsh and Geen*); CM/ResDH(2010)135 (September 15, 2010) (eleven judgments); and CM/ResDH(2010)24 (April 3, 2010) (eight judgments).

119. The first amendment to the United States Constitution reads in its relevant part: "Congress shall make *no* law [. . .] abridging the freedom of speech or of the press [. . .]" (emphasis added).

120. See Article 10 (2) ECHR.

121. One of these did not require any substantive modifications: the violation regarding the freedom of expression in *Steel and Others* related to a police intervention in peaceful protests that was not prescribed by domestic law and thus constituted an unwarranted and disproportionate interference; see ibid., para. 110. Due to the special circumstances of the case, execution entailed only the payment of just satisfaction and the dissemination and publication of the judgment; see CM Res. ResDH(2003)161 (October 20, 2003).

122. *The Sunday Times (no. 1)* (Merits) (April 26, 1979), closed by CM Res. DH(81)2 (April 2, 1981) (announcement of pending Contempt of Court bill deemed sufficient to close case).

123. *Observer and Guardian* and *The Sunday Times (no. 2)* (November 26, 1991).

124. A fourth, related case concerned a journalist's refusal to reveal his source in civil proceedings and the fine that was subsequently imposed on him for contempt of court, the execution of which was achieved by way of Convention-conform interpretation of domestic legislation; see *Goodwin* (March 27, 1996), closed by CM Res. DH(97)505 (October 29, 1997).

125. In 1969, the Interdepartmental Committee on the Law of Contempt had published a report on the law's effect on tribunals of inquiry (The Law of Contempt as it Affects Tribunals of Inquiry, Cmnd. 4078), and in 1974, the Report of the Committee on Contempt of Court (Phillimore Committee Report), Cmnd. 5794, had laid out the cornerstones of a legislative contempt of court reform; see Farran 1996, 269; Sauvain 1975.

126. Churchill and Young 1992, 334.

127. Ibid., 335; see also ibid., 336 ("a less than whole-hearted acceptance of the European Court's judgment").

128. Contempt of Court Act 1981, sec. 2 (2) and 2 (3).

129. Churchill and Young 1992, 336.

130. Young 1981, 253; see also ibid., 249 (noting that the bill's debates proceeded on the apparent assumption that "flexibility is all, certainty is not important, and the value of freedom of expression was scarcely mentioned"). For a similarly critical view of the reform when the act was still at the draft stage, see Tettenborn 1981, 124 ("It is particularly worrying that the bill apparently fails in its principle [objective] of revising the rule in the Times Newspapers case").

131. The issue concerned the maintenance of injunctions on the publications of excerpts from *Spycatcher* after it had already been published in the United States and involved common charges of breach of confidence (*Observer and Guardian*) and contempt of court (*The Sunday Times (no. 2)*).

132. CM Res. DH(92)17 (*Observer and Guardian*), DH(92)18 (*The Sunday Times (no. 2)*) (May 15, 1992).

133. Gearty 1997, 96.

134. *Tolstoy Miloslavsky* (July 13, 1995), closed by CM Res. DH(97)20 (February 9, 1996).

135. Revised Order 59, Rule 11 (4), adopted in light of sec. 8 (2), Courts and Legal Services Act 1990, specifies that "[i]n any case where the Court of Appeal has power to order a new trial on the ground that damages awarded by a jury are excessive or inadequate, the court may, instead of ordering a new trial, substitute for the sum awarded by the jury such sum as appears to the court to be proper, but except as aforesaid the Court of Appeal shall not have power to reduce or increase the damages awarded by a jury" (quoted in *Tolstoy Miloslavsky*, para. 27).

136. See Rantzen v. Mirror Group Newspapers Ltd. (1986) [1994] QB 670 (C.A.), [1993] 4 All E.R. 975 (libel damages reduced from £250,000 to £110,000); Elton John v. MGN Ltd., [1997] QB 586 (C.A), [1996] 2 All E.R. 35 (libel damages reduced from £350,000 to £75,000).

137. See *Steel and Morris* (February 2, 2005), para. 96.

138. See CM Res. CM/ResDH(2011)284 (December 2, 2011).

139. See Churchill and Young 1992, 340–341.

140. *Young, James and Webster* (Merits) (August 13, 1981), closed by CM Res. DH(83)3 (March 23, 1983).

141. As part of the Trade Union and Labour Relations Act 1974.

142. The four years of Heath's government, especially after passing the Industrial Relations Act 1971, which curtailed the power of the unions, saw an unprecedented wave of strikes that prompted no fewer than five declarations of states of emergency; see Callaghan 2005, 723.

143. See Trade Union and Labour Relations (Amendment) Act 1976, cited in *Young, James and Webster* (Merits), para. 23; reenacted by the Employment Protection (Consolidation) Act, sec. 58 (3); see also Farran 1996, 286.

144. See *Conservative General Election Manifesto 1979*, item 2.2 ("The Closed Shop"), http://www.margaretthatcher.org/archive/displaydocument.asp?docid=110858.

145. See Churchill and Young 1992, 338.

146. See Employment Act 1982, secs. 1–14; Employment Act 1988, pt. 1; Employment Act 1990, secs. 1, 2.

147. *Wilson, National Union of Journalists and Others* (July 2, 2002). The applicants had rejected new contracts that linked a wage increase to the renunciation of the right to be represented by their trade union, receiving, as a consequence, lower salaries than colleagues who had signed the contracts.

148. See Annotated Agenda, 1020th CM Mtg. (March 4–6, 2008), COE Doc. CM/Del/OJ/DH(2008)1020 sec. 6.1 (*s.n. Wilson, National Union of Journalists and Others*); the final resolution was adopted three years later: CM Res. CM/ResDH(2011)183 (September 14, 2011).

149. See Employment Relations Act 2004, secs. 29–32.

150. Explanatory Notes to Employment Relations Act 2004, 35, para. 193.

151. In *Wilson, National Union of Journalists and Others*, paras. 46–48, the Court refers to the rights both of the unions and of their members. The Secretariat's position was shared by the Joint Committee on Human Rights, Scrutiny of Bills: 6th Progress Report, 13th Rep. Sess.

2003–04, HL Paper 102/HC 640, June 4, 2004, para. 2.19 ("We consider that failing to provide unions with an avenue for redressing a violation of their right under Article 11 could result in a violation of both the Article 11 right and the right to an effective remedy for that violation").

152. See Annotated Agenda, 928th CM Mtg. (June 6–7, 2005), COE Doc. CM/Del/OJ/DH(2005)928 Vol. I (*s.n. Wilson, National Union of Journalists and Others*).

153. See Annotated Agenda, 1020th CM Mtg. (March 4–6, 2008), COE Doc. CM/Del/OJ/DH(2008)1020 sec. 6.1 (*s.n. Wilson, National Union of Journalists and Others*).

154. Introduced by Employment Relations Act 2004, sec. 33 (3).

155. Trade Union and Labour Relations (Consolidation) Act 1992, sec. 174.

156. *Associated Society of Locomotive Engineers and Firemen (ASLEF)* (February 27, 2007), para. 39.

157. Ibid., para. 52.

158. Explanatory Notes to Employment Act 2008, paras. 100–101.

159. Employment Act 2008, sec. 19, para. 2, amending Trade Union and Labour Relations (Consolidation) Act 1992, sec. 174.

160. Ibid.

161. "For the individual right to join a union to be effective, the State must nonetheless protect the individual against any abuse of a dominant position by trade unions [. . .]. Such abuse might occur, for example, where exclusion or expulsion from a trade union was not in accordance with union rules or where the rules were wholly unreasonable or arbitrary or where the consequences of exclusion or expulsion resulted in exceptional hardship [. . .]"; *Associated Society of Locomotive Engineers and Firemen*, para. 43. See also Joint Committee on Human Rights, Monitoring the Government's Response to Human Rights Judgments: Annual Report 2008, Thirty-first Rep. Sess. 2007-08, HL Paper 173/HC 1078, October 31, 2008, 22 (para. 45) (calling for such individual safeguards with reference to the Court's judgment); 482 Parl. Deb., HC (6th ser.) (November 4, 2008), col. 204 (Mr. Dismore) ("The additional safeguards in clause 19 are the kind of safeguards that the Joint Committee on Human Rights report talked about, and that the ASLEF judgment hinted at").

162. Employment Act 2008, sec. 19, para. 2.

163. 482 Parl. Deb., HC (6th ser.) (November, 4, 2008), cols. 187–214.

Chapter 5

1. See, e.g., Franck 1992; Cole 2014.

2. Quoted in Hanks 1988, 115.

3. *Ireland* (January 18, 1978), paras. 167, 173ff; see also Dickson 2010, 61–68.

4. *McCann and Others* (September 27, 1995), para. 213.

5. *McKerr; Hugh Jordan; Kelly and Others; Shanaghan* (May 4, 2001); *McShane* (May 28, 2002); *Finucane* (July 1, 2003). In *McShane*, the Court also found a violation of Article 34 due to threatening the applicant's solicitor with disciplinary proceedings for disclosing certain documents received in confidentiality in the course of domestic inquest proceedings; see *McShane*, paras. 147–152.

6. *Brecknell; McCartney; McGrath; O'Dowd; Reavey* (all November 27, 2007).

7. Dickson 2010, 150. This does not necessarily mean that the proceedings in Strasbourg had no effect on the UK's decision. The application by Ireland had been lodged shortly after the events in question on December 16, 1971, and had been declared admissible by the Commission

on October 1, 1972; its five-hundred-page report, however, was only issued a good three years later; see *Ireland* (Comm. rep.) (January 25, 1976).

8. See *Ireland*, paras. 99–102. In 1972, Prime Minister Edward Heath had still been less categorical when he remarked that "if any Government did come to the decision, after the most careful thought, that it was necessary to use some or all of these techniques, it would be necessary to come to the House first before doing so," suggesting the possibility of reintroducing the five techniques if they were authorized by legislation; quoted in Dickson 2010, 148n50.

9. See CM Res. (78) 35 (June 27, 1978).

10. Churchill and Young 1992, 295; see also Tomkins 1995, 59 (noting that the "undertaking by the United Kingdom government here took the form merely of a political promise[ ]—there was no formal legal guarantee that the five techniques could not be re-employed").

11. Churchill and Young 1992, 293–294.

12. Prime Minister Edward Heath's words, quoted in Dickson 2010, 148.

13. Churchill and Young 1992, 294; Walsh 1982, 38.

14. Churchill and Young 1992, 295–296.

15. "McCann and Others," Case Note, *Journal of Civil Liberties* 1 (1996): 68.

16. Quoted in Frank Millar and Paddy Smyth, "Britain Plans to Ignore Gibraltar Killings Ruling," *Irish Times* (September 28, 1995), 1.

17. Ibid. By contrast, Shadow Home Secretary Straw called on the government to "observe both the letter and the spirit of this decision" (ibid.); see also Jackson 1997, 57; Dickson 2010, 257.

18. John Rentoul, "Euro-skeptics Back Call to Curb Court's Powers," *Independent*, February 8, 1996, 10.

19. Michael White, "Ministers Seek Curb on Rights: Europe-Wide Offensive After Embarrassing Rulings," *Guardian* (April 2, 1996), 1; Frances Gibb, "Mackay Seeks Curb on European Court," *Times* (April 9, 1996), Home News.

20. Statement by Sir Nicholas Bonsor, Minister of State, Foreign and Commonwealth Office, 273 Parl. Deb., HC (6th ser.) (March 6, 1996), cols. 315 and 314, respectively.

21. See CM Res. DH(96)102 (March 22, 1996). See also statement by Sir Nicholas Bonsor, 273 Parl. Deb., HC (6th ser.) (March 6, 1996), col. 314 ("The Government were left with the duty to pay costs, which we did in accordance with our practice of obeying international law").

22. *McCann and Others* (September 27, 1995), para. 212.

23. According to a Council of Europe briefing note on the case.

24. Dickson 2010, 257–258.

25. Noted by MP Seamus Mallon, 107 Parl. Deb. HC (6th ser.) (December 16, 1986), col. 1100.

26. See CM Res. DH(91)39 (December 13, 1991) and *Fox, Campbell and Hartley*, para. 22 (change introduced by Northern Ireland (Emergency Provisions) Act 1987, sec. 6).

27. See Sir George Baker, Review of the Operation of the Northern Ireland (Emergency Provisions) Act 1978, Cmnd. 9222 (1984) (Baker Report).

28. See debates of the bill in House of Commons and House of Lords between December 16, 1986, and May 13, 1987, http://hansard.millbanksystems.com/bills/northern-ireland -emergency-provisions-bill.

29. See *O'Hara* (October 16, 2001), para. 44.

30. *John Murray* (February 8, 1996); *Averill* and *Magee* (both June 6, 2000).

31. See CM Interim Res. DH(2000)26 (February 14, 2000) and ResDH(2002)85 (June 11, 2002).

32. Dickson 2010, 176–177.

33. See CM Res. CM/ResDH(2010)120 (September 15, 2010); Youth Justice and Criminal Evidence Act 1999, sec. 58. The provision for Northern Ireland—the Criminal Evidence (Northern Ireland) Order 1999, S.I. 1999 No. 2789 (N.I. 8), sec. 36—is essentially the same.

34. See CM Res. CM/ResDH(2010)120 (September 15, 2010). As regards individual measures, it is to be noted that the conviction and sentence of twenty years imprisonment in the Magee case, which was based largely on incriminating statements made prior to access to legal advice, was quashed by the UK Court of Appeal in April 2001 with reference to the ECtHR's judgment; see ibid.

35. Dickson 2010, 174.

36. *John Murray*, para. 70

37. Ibid., para. 63.

38. See *O'Kane* (Decision of July 6, 1999); *Brennan*, paras. 54–55.

39. See generally Dickson 2010, 174–182.

40. Salduz v. Turkey (November 27, 2008), para. 55; the relevant UK Supreme Court decision is Cadder v. H.M. Advocate, [2010] UKSC 43 (26 October 2010).

41. See Fair Employment (N.I.) Act 1976, sec. 42 (2). The act was amended by the Fair Employment (N.I.) Act 1989 which, inter alia, created the Fair Employment Tribunal but left the national security certificate exclusion untouched.

42. *Tinnelly and Sons Ltd.* and *McEldruff and Others* (July 10, 1998) (refusal of public works contracts or security clearance to obtain them); *Devlin* (October 30, 2001) (refusal of employment as administrative assistant with Northern Ireland Civil Service); *Devenney* (March 19, 2002) (dismissal from job as waiter at private hotel).

43. See Northern Ireland Act 1998, secs. 90–92, and Northern Ireland Act Tribunal (Procedure) Rules 1999, S.I. 1999 No. 2131, esp. Rules 7 and 3 (1). The cases were subsequently closed: CM Res. DH(2000)49 (April 10, 2000) (*Tinnelly and Sons Ltd.*; *McEldruff and Others*); ResDH(2003)9 (Feb. 24, 2003) (*Devlin*); ResDH(2004)9 (February 24, 2004) (*Devenney*).

44. See Northern Ireland Act 1998, sec. 91, para. 6, lit. b.

45. See ibid., sched. 11, sec. 1, para. 1.

46. See ibid., sec. 92, para. 2.

47. *Brogan and Others* (Merits) (November 29, 1988), para. 62; *O'Hara* (October 16, 2001), para. 46. The initial detention period of forty-eight hours permissible under sec. 12 (4) of the Prevention of Terrorism (Temporary Provisions) Act 1984 could be extended by the secretary of state for up to an additional five days (sec. 12 [5] of the 1984 act); see *Brogan and Others*, para. 30.

48. *Fox, Campbell and Hartley* (Merits) (August 30, 1990), para. 35. Section 11 (1) of the Northern Ireland (Emergency Provisions) Act 1978 authorized "any constable [to] arrest without warrant any person whom he suspects of being a terrorist" (ibid., para. 16). For a case summary and comment, see Finnie 1991.

49. *A. and Others* (February 18, 2009).

50. See CM Res. DH(90)23 (September 24, 1990). The Court subsequently upheld the derogation in *Brannigan and McBride* (May 26, 1993). As Jackson notes, however, in doing so, it "has been fairly deferential to British claims of exigency" (Jackson 1997, 60); see also O'Boyle 1977, 183. *Brannigan and McBride* spearheaded a series of fourteen additional applications that challenged the UK derogation's legality; see Marks 1995, 71n18. Notably, the UK had repealed a long-standing derogation which had shielded it against the detention-related complaints in the Ireland case in August 1984, shortly before the events in the Brogan case; see *Brogan*, para. 48.

51. See Jackson 1997, 51–52.

52. See *Yearbook of the European Convention of Human Rights* 32 (1989): 8.

53. See Terrorism Act 2000, sec. 41 and sched. 8, pt. 3 ("Extension of Detention under Section 41"). On the basis of this change, the Committee of Ministers also closed supervision of the 2001 O'Hara judgment; see Annotated Agenda, 906th CM Mtg. (December 8–9, 2004), COE Doc. CM/Del/OJ/DH(2004)906 Vol. 1 (*s.n. O'Hara*) and CM Res. CM/ResDH(2010)214 (December 2, 2010).

54. See *Yearbook of the European Convention of Human Rights* 44 (2001): 19–20.

55. Fenwick 2007, 1441.

56. See generally ibid., 1440–1460.

57. Gearty 2013, 92.

58. As listed in Terrorism Prevention and Investigation Measures Act 2011, sched. 1.

59. CM/ResDH(2013)114 (June 6, 2013).

60. Fenwick 2007, 1440, 1443.

61. Justice and Security Green Paper, Cm. 8194 (October 2011), xi, para. 1.

62. Terrorism Act 2000, secs. 43, 44–47. These sections make similar provision to the following sections of the PTA: sec. 13A (inserted by the Criminal Justice and Public Order Act 1994 [c. 33]) and sec. 13B (inserted by the Prevention of Terrorism (Additional Powers) Act 1996 [c. 7]).

63. See David Povey, ed., *Police Powers and Procedures England and Wales 2009/10* (2nd ed.), Home Office Statistical Bulletin 07/11 (London: Home Office, April 14, 2011), 40–41.

64. Review of Counter-Terrorism and Security Powers: Review Findings and Recommendations, Cm. 8004 (January 2011), 16.

65. Ibid., 15–16 (para. 4); Choudhury and Fenwick 2012, 62; Bowling and Phillips 2007.

66. *Gillan and Quinton* (January 12, 2010), para. 87.

67. *The Coalition: Our Programme for Government* (London: Cabinet Office, 2010), 11, https://www.gov.uk/government/uploads/system/uploads/attachment_data/file/78977/coalition_programme_for_government.pdf.

68. See Terrorism Act 2000 (Remedial) Order 2011, S.I. 2011 No. 631; Protection of Freedoms Act 2012, secs. 59–62.

69. Protection of Freedoms Act 2012, sec. 61 (1).

70. See CM Res. CM/ResDH(2013)52 (March 7, 2013).

71. Review of Counter-Terrorism and Security Powers: Review Findings and Recommendations, Cm. 8004 (January 2011), 17, para. 9.

72. Ibid., 18, para. 15.

73. Gearty 2013, 89.

74. Introduced by Murder (Abolition of Death Penalty) Act 1965, section 1 (1); see also Padfield 2002, 5–8.

75. Padfield 2002, 3–5. The relevant crimes include "attempted murder, manslaughter, rape, robbery, arson, criminal damage with intent to endanger life, aggravated burglary, kidnapping, incest, infanticide and sexual intercourse with a girl under the age of 13" (ibid., n. 6).

76. See Padfield 2002, 8–10. This form of detention has been available since 1800 and applied originally to felons acquitted on grounds of insanity; since 1933, it was extended to juvenile offenders under the age of eighteen; see Farran 1996, 139.

77. See Padfield 2002, 10–11.

78. Ibid., 11–14.

79. Described in *Benjamin and Wilson* (September 26, 2002), paras. 19–23.

80. See *Weeks* (Merits) (March 2, 1987), paras. 63–69.

81. See CM Res. DH(89)18 (June 15, 1989). The offense for which Weeks had been convicted involved the robbery of a pet shop with a starting pistol loaded with blank cartridges at age seventeen, resulting in the theft of 35p.

82. Churchill and Young 1992, 315; see also Padfield 2002, 37–38.

83. Palmer 1994, 484.

84. See *Thynne, Wilson and Gunnell* (October 25, 1990).

85. See Criminal Justice Act 1991, sec. 34; see also CM Res. DH(92)24 (June 15, 1992).

86. See the detailed discussion of the progress of the reform proposal through the different legislative stages in Padfield 2002, chap. 4.

87. See Farran 1996, 134–135.

88. See *Singh* and *Hussain* (February 21, 1996). The ECtHR found that the nature and rationale of detention at Her Majesty's Pleasure, although being a mandatory sentence for offenders under eighteen found guilty of the crime of murder, were closer to that of discretionary life sentences. As a consequence, the review procedure, at the time the same as for adult mandatory lifers, failed to meet the requirements of Article 5 (4). The same issue arose in *Curley* (March 28, 2000).

89. See CM Res. DH(98)149 (*Hussain*) and DH(98)150 (*Singh*) (June 11, 1998); CM/ResDH(2011)37 (*Curley*) (March 10, 2011); Crime (Sentences) Act 1997, secs. 28–32. The Parole Board Rules 1997, revised at the same time, remedied the violation later found in *Waite* (December 10, 2002), which concerned the unfairness of proceedings relating to the revocation of the applicant's release on license due to the absence of oral hearings, by providing for such hearings in the context of fully adversarial proceedings; see Annotated Agenda, 906th Mtg. (December 8–9, 2004), COE Doc. CM/Del/OJ/DH(2004)906, vol. 1 (*s.n. Waite*) and CM Res. CM/ResDH(2010)214 (December 2, 2010).

90. Padfield 2002, 79.

91. The two judgments in *T.* and *V.* (December 16, 1999), relating to the much-publicized 1993 killing of a two-year-old boy by two ten-year-olds, also included violations of, inter alia, Article 5 (4) ECHR of HMP detainees but did not require general measures due to the specifics of the cases; see CM Res. CM/ResDH(2007)134 (October 31, 2007).

92. See Criminal Justice and Courts Services Act 2000, sec. 60.

93. See *Wynne (no. 1)* (July 18, 1994), paras. 35–36 (noting, inter alia, that "as regards mandatory life sentences, the guarantee of Article 5 (4) was satisfied by the original trial and appeal proceedings and confers no additional right to challenge the lawfulness of continuing detention or re-detention following revocation of the life license").

94. *Stafford* (May 28, 2002), para. 79. The Stafford case also concerned the unlawful detention of the applicant on account of the extension of his detention by the home secretary for reasons unrelated to his original conviction for life; see ibid., paras. 81–83.

95. See ibid., paras. 87–90. The Court affirmed its position in *Easterbrook*, para. 28, *von Bülow* (October 7, 2003); *Wynne (no. 2)* (October 16, 2003); and *Hill* (April 27, 2004).

96. See CM Res. CM/ResDH(2011)179 (September 14, 2011) (*Stafford; von Bülow; Wynne (no. 2); Hill*); CM Res. CM/ResDH(2010)214 (December 2, 2010) (*Easterbrook*) and Annotated Agenda, 885th CM Mtg. (June 1–2, 2004), COE Doc. CM/Del/OJ(2004)885, vol. 1 (*s.n. Easterbrook*); Criminal Justice Act 2003, pt. 12, chap. 7 ("Effect of Life Sentence") and schedules 21 and 22.

97. See *Oldham* (September 26, 2000) (interval of two years); *Hirst (no. 1)* (July 24, 2001) (intervals of twenty-one months and two years); *Blackstock* (June 21, 2005) (interval of twenty-two months). These cases were closed on the basis of the Crime (Sentences) Act 1997, sec. 28 (7) lit. b, which provides for review at least every two years as well as evidence provided by the UK that discretionary lifer cases are normally reviewed at intervals of eight to eighteen months; see CM Res. DH(2001)160 (December 17, 2001) (*Oldham*); CM/ResDH(2010)119 (September 15, 2010) (*Hirst (no. 1)*; *Blackstock*).

98. See *Benjamin and Wilson* (September. 26, 2002). Reviews of the necessity of the continued detention of technical lifers had not been conducted by the parole board, but by the Mental Health Review Tribunal which had, however, no power to order the release of a patient and whose recommendations were subject to the secretary of state's veto.

99. As noted in the assessment of the case by the Council of Europe Secretariat, "[t]he effect of the abolition [. . .] of the possibility of applying for technical lifer status appears in particular to have been to attach greater restrictions on prisoners who might previously have benefited from such a status (they appear now to have lost the possibility to benefit from unconditional release and to be entitled only to release on life license)"; Annotated Agenda, 1035th CM Mtg. (September 17–18, 2008), COE Doc. CM/Del/OJ/DH(2008)1035 sec. 4.2 (*s.n. Benjamin and Wilson*).

100. See Annotated Agenda, 1043rd CM Mtg. (December 2–4, 2008), CM/Del/OJ/DH(2008)1043 sec. 6.1 (*s.n. Benjamin and Wilson*). After the First-Tier Tribunal (Mental Health), the successor to the Mental Health Review Tribunal, has recommended either detainees' discharge from hospital, or their continuing detention, their case is subject to review, after the expiry of the tariff, by the parole board, which has the power to order release on life license; see CM Res. CM/ResDH(2010)186 (December 2, 2010) (*Benjamin and Wilson*).

101. See Chapman, Mirrlees-Black, and Brawn 2002, 2n2 (reporting that in 1996, 79 percent of respondents found sentencing much (51 percent) or a little too lenient (28 percent); in 1998 the figures were 49 percent and 30 percent, respectively). These figures have remained relatively stable both before and after the 1990s; see, e.g., Roberts et al. 2003, 29 (71 percent majority finding sentences too lenient in 1987) and Allen 2006, 12 and table 1.06 (reporting that 76 percent of respondents perceive sentencing as too lenient).

102. See Moore 2006 (2005 survey results showing support for death penalty in Great Britain at 49 percent, versus 45 percent who are opposed to it).

103. Labour campaigned explicitly on a law-and-order platform in the 1997 general elections, which entailed, inter alia, the pledge to be "tough on crime and tough on the causes of crime" and to institute "stricter punishment for serious repeat offenders." See Labour General Election Manifesto 1997, *New Labour Because Britain Deserves Better*, http://www.politicsresources.net/area/uk/man/lab97.htm.

104. Under the Court's autonomous concepts doctrine, whether a domestic penalty is covered by the Convention's guarantees for criminal proceedings is determined not by its domestic label, but on the basis of the nature of the charge and the nature and severity of the penalty; see Engel and Others v. Netherlands (Merits) (June 8, 1976), para. 82.

105. See *Campbell and Fell* (June 26, 1984) and CM Res. DH(86)7 (June 27, 1986) (publicly funded legal representation in disciplinary proceedings before Board of Visitors); *Ezeh and Connors* (October 9, 2003), *Whitfield and Others* (April 4, 2005), *Black* and *Young* (January 16, 2007), all closed by CM Res. CM/ResDH(2011)178 (September 14, 2011). The Prison (Amendment) Rules 2002, S.I. 2002 No. 2116, provide for legal representation in disciplinary proceedings that

may result in a penalty of additional days of detention. The 2002 rules also rectified the second violation, of Article 6 (1) ECHR, in *Whitfield and Others, Black,* and *Young* concerning the lack of independence and impartiality of the prison authorities responsible for conducting disciplinary proceedings by introducing a separate, independent adjudicator to decide any charges that could result in additional days of detention.

106. See *Benham* (June 6, 1996) and CM Res. DH(97)506 (October 29, 1997); *Perks and Others* (October 12, 1999) and CM Res. DH(2000)93 (July 24, 2000); *Beet and Others* and *Lloyd and Others* (March 1, 2005), and CM Res. CM/ResDH(2010)140 (September 15, 2010), all closed on the basis of the entry into force of the Legal Advice and Assistance (Scope) (Amendment) Regulations 1997, S.I. 1997 No. 997, Regulation 3 (2), which provides for legal representation in all proceedings on nonpayment of a fine or nonobservance of a court order when an adverse decision carries the risk of imprisonment; see further *Hooper* (November 16, 2004), paras. 20–23, CM Res. CM/ResDH(2010)214 (December 2, 2010), and Annotated Agenda, 1007th CM Mtg. (October 15–17, 2007), COE Doc. CM/Del/OJ/DH(2007)1007 sec. 6.1 (*s.n. Hooper*). (Amendment No. 15 to Consolidated Criminal Practice Direction of March 2007 provides for representation in the context of "binding over" orders and the fixing of their terms). One other case related to legal aid and representation is *Brennan* (October 16, 2001) in which the violation of the right to effective legal representation resulted from the proximity, within hearing, of a police officer during the applicant's first consultation with his solicitor; the UK subsequently sent a guidance note to police authorities drawing attention to the case; see CM Res. CM/ResDH(2011)285 (December 2, 2011).

107. See *Faulkner* (Friendly Settlement) (November 30, 1999), CM Res. CM/ResDH(2010)214 (December 2, 2010), and Annotated Agenda, 992nd CM Mtg. (DH), April 3–4, 2007, COE Doc. CM/Del/OJ/DH(2007)992 sec. 6.1 (*s.n. Faulkner*).

108. *Granger* (March 28, 1990). Under the rules in force at the time, the Scottish Legal Aid Board would grant aid only if it found that there were substantial grounds for making the appeal.

109. CM Res. DH(91)29 (November 18, 1991). In the case of such a recommendation, the Manual of Procedure of the Scottish Legal Aid Board, para. 6.12, provided for the automatic granting of legal aid. For a critical view on the sufficiency of this measure, see Gearty 1997, 88.

110. See *Boner* and *Maxwell* (October 28, 1994).

111. See Farran 1996, 171, and Criminal Justice (Scotland) Act 1995, secs. 42, 65; see, further, CM Res. DH(96)155 (*Boner*) and CM Res. DH(96)156 (*Maxwell*) (May 15, 1996). Although legal aid is also granted to request leave to appeal, this stage does not involve any (usually costly) hearings.

112. See *Boner*, para. 42, and *Maxwell*, para. 39.

113. See Grabenwarter 2008, 339; Mole and Harby 2006, 8. In criminal cases, the right to an appeal is provided for by Article 2 of Protocol No. 7 to the Convention (November 22, 1984).

114. Murdoch 1997, 127.

115. See *P., C. and S.* (July 6, 2002), paras. 88–91; Airey v. Ireland (Merits) (October 9, 1979), paras. 26–28.

116. Mark Oliver, "McLibel," *Guardian* (February 15, 2005), http://www.theguardian.com /news/2005/feb/15/food.foodanddrink.

117. See *Steel and Morris* (February 15, 2005); for discussion, see Lillard 2005.

118. See CM Res. CM/ResDH(2011)284 (December 2, 2011).

119. *Golder* (February 21, 1975), para. 45.

120. Ibid., esp. para. 40.

121. Circular Instruction 45/75 (August 6, 1975), reproduced in Cohen and Taylor 1978, 42–43.

122. CM Res. (76) 35 (June 22, 1976), appendix.

123. Churchill and Young 1992, 303; see also Birkinshaw 1981, 139 (noting Home Office's "failure to implement any real change"); Jackson 1997, 71 (implementation of *Golder* had "been eviscerated by bureaucratic artifice").

124. Circular Instruction 45/75 (August 6, 1975), para. 14. Notably, in 1981 the English Court of Appeal ruled that an application to the European Commission of Human Rights could not be classified as the initiation of legal proceedings that would benefit from the prior ventilation rule; see Guilfoyle v. Home Office, [1981] 2 W.L.R. 223; see Birkinshaw 1981, 140.

125. See *Reed* (Friendly Settlement) (Comm. rep.) (December 12, 1981).

126. See *Silver and Others* (Merits) (March 25, 1983) (as in *Golder*, the denial of leave to seek legal advice also resulted in violation of right to access to a court [Article 6 (1) ECHR]; see paras. 80–82); *Campbell and Fell* (June 28, 1984).

127. In addition to *Silver and Others*; *Campbell and Fell*; *Boyle and Rice* (April 27, 1988); *McCallum* (August 30, 1990). The changes in the relevant regulations are set out in *Silver and Others* (Merits), paras. 37, 40, 48–49, and have been viewed as adequate by academic commentators; see, e.g., Churchill and Young 1992, 307, and Birkinshaw 1983, 271. For final resolutions, see CM Res. DH(85)15 (June 28, 1985) (*Silver and Others*); CM Res. DH(86)7 (June 27, 1986) (*Campbell and Fell*); CM Res. DH(88)17 (October 26, 1988) (*Boyle and Rice*); CM Res. DH(90)38 (December 13, 1990) (*McCallum*).

128. See *Byrne, McFadden, McCluskey and Mc Larnon* (Comm. rep.) (December 3, 1985) and CM Res. DH(87)7 (March 20, 1987).

129. R. v. Secretary of State for the Home Department ex parte Anderson [1984] QB 788, 1 ALL E.R. 920.

130. One later case also concerned interference with prisoner correspondence, but because the interference had occurred in contravention of existing UK prison rules, it only required payment of just satisfaction; see *William Faulkner* (June 4, 2002) and CM Res. CM/ResDH(2011)36 (March 10, 2011).

131. *Campbell* (March 25, 1992).

132. See CM Res. DH(93)52 (January 26, 1993).

133. *Szuluk* (June 2, 2009).

134. CM Res. CM/ResDH(2013)88 (May 7, 2013).

135. For England and Wales, Prison and Young Offender Institution (Amendment) Rules 2009, S.I. 2009 No. 3082, sched. 1, section 2, amends the Prison Rules 1999 to provide that "[a] prisoner may correspond [. . .]with a registered medical practitioner who has treated the prisoner for a life threatening condition, and such correspondence may not be opened, read or stopped unless the governor has reasonable cause to believe its contents do not relate to the treatment of that condition." The Scottish amendment is likewise limited to circumstances of life-threatening illnesses; see Prisons and Young Offenders Institutions (Scotland) Rules 2011, Scottish S.I. 2011 No. 331, sec. 50. In Northern Ireland, according to a binding 2012 prison service standing order, communication with outside medical practitioners is only treated as privileged if such correspondence had already been commenced prior to the prisoner's committal; see CM Res. CM/ResDH(2013)88 (May 7, 2013).

136. Churchill and Young 1992, 308.

137. Birkinshaw 1981.

138. Osman v. Ferguson, [1993] 4 All E.R. 344.

139. Hill v. Chief Constable of South Yorkshire, [1989] A.C. 53 (finding absence of duty of care owed by police to victim of serial killer).

140. *Osman* (October 28, 1998), para. 153.

141. English 2001a, 305; see also, e.g., Gearty 2001; Lunney 1999; Monti 1999; Weir 1999.

142. Harlow 2004, 444; for critical views from the high bench, see Hoffmann 1999, 162–164; Hoyano 1999, 923–924.

143. Giliker 2000, 372.

144. See, e.g., Lunney 1999, 240–241.

145. In the ECtHR's own interpretation, Article 6 ECHR guaranteed fair proceedings only in cases where domestic law provided for civil rights and obligations but not a specific configuration of substantive rights as such; see *James and Others* (February 21, 1986), para. 81 ("Article 6 para. 1 [. . .] extends only to 'contestations' (disputes) over (civil) 'rights and obligations' which can be said, at least on arguable grounds, to be recognised under domestic law; it does not in itself guarantee any particular content for (civil) 'rights and obligations' in the substantive law of the Contracting States"); *Lithgow and Others* (July 8, 1986), para. 192.

146. CM Res. DH(99)720 (December 3, 1999).

147. See Rosalind English, "The Law Lords Are Already Fighting Strasbourg over the Human Rights Act," *Times* (June 29, 2000), Features Section.

148. English 2001a, 306.

149. Shircore 2006, 44.

150. Ibid., 46.

151. See Harlow 2004, 444; Gearty 2002; English 2001b; Kingscote 2001.

152. *Z. and Others* (May 10, 2001), para. 100.

153. Ibid., paras. 99, 101.

154. See Cameron 1986, 126–127; Robertson 1973, 55–75.

155. Most notably in the Report of the Committee on Privacy, Cmnd. 5012 (1972) (the Younger Report)—for a brief overview, see Dworkin 1973—and the 1981 Report of the Royal Commission on Criminal Procedure, Cmnd. 8092 (1981); see also Cameron 1986, 129, 132.

156. In its white paper The Interception of Communications in Great Britain, Cmnd. 7873 (1980), the Conservatives had still defended the undesirability of legislation; see also Lloyd 1986, 87.

157. Cameron 1986, 128 (noting that the reason for the lack of domestic opportunities to bring telephone tapping cases before the courts was "that national security interceptions were not carried out for the purpose of prosecution, and it was prosecution practice not to lead evidence from police and customs interceptions directly in court").

158. Klass and Others v. Germany (September 6, 1978). Although finding for Germany, the Court had defined a number of requirements for Convention-conforming phone tapping.

159. *Malone* (Merits) (August 2, 1984).

160. This evaluation is shared by virtually all commentators; see Cameron 1986, 149 ("minimalist interpretation"); Lloyd 1986, 95 ("major question whether [the Act] will achieve its stated objective of ensuring compliance with the requirements of the Convention"); Taylor and Walker 1996, 111 ("Act went no further than the Malone judgment demanded"); Churchill and Young 1992, 324 ("If the Act hardly appears to fulfill the letter of the Court's judgment, even less does

it comply with" its spirit); Fenwick 2007, 1033 ("incomplete reform"). For the Committee of Ministers, the passage of formal legislation sufficed to close supervision; see CM Res. DH(86)1 (April 11, 1986).

161. Baxter 1986, 19; Cameron 1986, 145, 149.

162. Lloyd 1986, 93.

163. 75 Parl. Deb., HC (6th ser.) (March 12, 1985) col. 241, quoted in Taylor and Walker 1996, 111.

164. Taylor and Walker 1996, 113.

165. Interception of Communications Act 1985, sec. 2.

166. Cameron 1986, 136–137.

167. See *Klass and Others*, paras. 51–60 (discussing safeguards and oversight mechanisms available under German covert surveillance legislation).

168. *Halford* (June 25, 1997) (the Interception of Communications Act 1985 did not apply to telephone systems operated by public authorities outside of the public network).

169. See *Khan* (May 12, 2000); *P.G. and J.H.* (September 25, 2001); *Armstrong* (July 16, 2002); *Hewitson* (May 27, 2003); *Chalkley* (June 12, 2003); *Lewis* (November 25, 2003); *Taylor-Sabori* (October 22, 2002); *Allan* (November 5, 2002) (also involving a violation of the fair trial guarantee of Article 6 (1) ECHR, remedied by subsequent quashing of conviction by the Court of Appeal, see [2004] EWCA Crim. 2236, [2004] All ER (D) 114 (August); *Wood* (November 16, 2004); *Elahi* (June 20, 2006); *Copland* (April 3, 2007); *Liberty and Others* (July 1, 2008).

170. The reluctance of the Conservative government with respect to legislating in the field of covert surveillance and privacy rights was visible even with regard to intrusions by private actors, see Privacy and Media Intrusion: The Government's Response, Cm. 2918 (1995), 20; see also Taylor and Walker 1996, 122.

171. Police Act 1997, pt. 3 (entitled Authorization of Action in Respect of Property).

172. Taylor 2002, 71; Fenwick 2007, 1056.

173. Taylor 2002, 71.

174. Ibid.

175. See Andy McSmith and Peter Beaumont, "Labour Vows to Close Loophole on Phone Taps," *Observer*, March 23, 1997, 15.

176. Three additional judgments involved breaches of privacy due to surveillance and were closed in part on the basis that similar occurrences would be subject to the HRA 1998 or were in contravention of domestic codes of practice; see *Foxley* (June 20, 2000) (interception, opening, reading, and copying to file of the applicant's correspondence with his legal advisers on behalf of Trustee in Bankruptcy partly not in accordance with law, partly disproportional), Annotated Agenda, 764th CM Mtg. (October 3, 2001), COE Doc. CM/Del/OJ/OT(2001)764 (*s.n. Foxley*) (Insolvency Act 1986, which authorized trustee in bankruptcy to open applicant's mail, now applies subject to HRA 1998), and CM Res. CM/ResDH(2010)214 (December 2, 2010); *Peck* (January 28, 2003) (release and broadcasting of CCTV footage showing applicant's suicide attempt, without consent or attempt at masking identity), CM Res. CM/ResDH(2011)177 (September 14, 2011) (CCTV Code of Practice 2008, at 7, highlights requirements for CCTV use under Article 8 ECHR); *Perry* (July 17, 2003) (covert videotaping in custody area of police station in violation of applicable code of practice); CM Res. ResDH(2005)100 (October 26, 2005) (circular draws attention to domestic rules and Court's judgment).

177. See Colvin 1998; Home Office, Interception of Communications in the United Kingdom: A Consultation Paper, Cm. 4368 (June 1999), 2.

178. The Committee of Ministers considered the enactment of RIPA 2000 and the adoption of the subsequent code of practice on covert surveillance as well as other secondary legislation sufficient to close the *Halford*, *Khan*, and later clone cases; see CM Res. CM/ResDH(2007)15 (February 28, 2007) (*Halford*); CM Res. ResDH(2005)68 (July 18, 2005) (*Khan*; *P.G. and J.H.*; *Armstrong*; *Hewitson*; *Chalkley*); CM/ResDH(2010)136 (September 15, 2010) (*Elahi*; *Lewis*); CM/ResDH(2011)38 (March 10, 2011) (*Taylor-Sabori*; *Allan*; *Wood*); CM/ResDH(2011)83 (June 8, 2011) (*Liberty and Others*); CM/ResDH(2010)79 (June 3, 2010) (*Copland*).

179. Taylor 2002, 72; for further critiques, see Fenwick 2001, 534–536; Fenwick 2007, 1074–1075.

180. Fenwick 2000, 345; see also Taylor 2002, 72–73 ("an Act that is not so much directed at the protection of privacy, as a measure designed to ensure that the HRA has little impact upon the area").

181. See *Kennedy* (May 18, 2010).

182. See *Big Brother Watch and Others* (appl. no. 58170/13), lodged September 4, 2013, communicated January 9, 2014; *Bureau of Investigative Journalism and Alice Ross* (appl. no. 62322/14), lodged September 11, 2014, communicated January 5, 2015.

183. The post–World War II military justice system for the air force and army was established by the Air Force and Army Acts of 1955, respectively, while that for the navy came into being on the basis of the Naval Discipline Act 1957; see Rowlinson 2002, 18.

184. See *Findlay* (February 25, 1997) (army); *Coyne* (September 24, 1997) (air force). Several clone cases followed: *Moore and Gordon* (air force), *Smith and Ford* (army) (September 29, 1999); *Hood* (army), *Cable and Others* (air force and army) (February 18, 1999); *Mills* (June 5, 2001); *Wilkinson and Allen* (February 6, 2001); *Miller and Others* (October 26, 2004) (all army); *Martin* (October 24, 2006) (army court-martial of civilian family member).

185. See *Findlay*, paras. 73, 76, 80.

186. See statements by Minister of State for the Armed Forces Nicholas Soames and by John Reid, 268 Parl. Deb., HC (6th ser.) (December 13, 1995), cols. 1028, 1032, respectively. Calls for change had been voiced prior to that; see, e.g., statement by John Reid, 193 Parl. Deb., HC (6th ser.) (June 17, 1991), col. 93. The *Findlay* case had been introduced in May 1993 and had been declared admissible in early 1995, with the Commission rendering its report in September 1995, that is, early enough for arguments before, and the findings of, the Commission (roughly comparable to those of the Court) to be considered in the design of the new legislation; see *Findlay* (Comm. dec.) (February 23, 1995) and *Findlay* (Comm. rep.) (September 5, 1995). The impact of the pending application is also hinted at by McCoubrey 1997, 86, and Rowlinson 2002, 20, 32.

187. Quoted in McCoubrey 1997, 87.

188. See Hansen 2013, 241–242.

189. See CM Res. DH(98)11 (February 18, 1998) (*Findlay*); DH(98)12 (February 18, 1998) (*Coyne*); DH(99)719 (December 3, 1999) (*Cable and Others*); ResDH(2000)46 (*Moore and Gordon*) and ResDH(2000)47 (*Smith and Ford*) (April 10, 2000); DH(2000)82 (May 29, 2000) (*Hood*); ResDH(2001)162 (December 17, 2001) (*Wilkinson and Allen*); ResDH(2003)10 (February. 24, 2003) (*Mills*); CM/ResDH(2010)214 (December 2, 2010) (*Miller and Others*); CM/ResDH(2011)172 (September 14, 2011) (*Martin*).

190. See *Morris* (February 26, 2002) (finding violations of Article 6 (1) due to lack of sufficient safeguards to exclude outside pressure on ad hoc lay tribunal members who remained subject to army discipline, and the power of the nonjudicial reviewing authority to substitute findings of guilt and sentences for those reached in the court-martial proceedings).

191. See R. v. Boyd, Hastie and Spear et al. (July 18, 2002), [2002] UKHL 31; see also Rowe 2003, 212.

192. See *Cooper* (December 16, 2003), paras. 131–132. Cooper concerned an air force court-martial, but the Court subsequently extended its reasoning to the essentially similar army court-martials; see *Vaughan and Others* (December) (May 25, 2004).

193. *G.W.* and *Le Petit* (June 15, 2004) (problematic role of convening authority due to superiority of rank vis-à-vis court-martial members; absence of legal basis to challenge composition of court-martial; absence of appeal to judicial authority where guilty pleas had been entered).

194. See *Grieves* (December 16, 2003) (independence and impartiality of navy court-martial compromised, inter alia, because the judge advocate in a naval court-martial [i.e., its legally trained member] is a serving naval officer, not a civilian).

195. See Annotated Agenda, 1028th CM Mtg. (June 3–5, 2008), COE Doc. CM/Del/OJ/DH(2008)1028 sec. 6.1 (*s.nn. Grieves, G.W.,* and *Le Petit*). For final resolutions, see CM/ResDH(2010)214 (December 2, 2010) (*G.W.*) and CM/ResDH(2011)290 (December 2, 2011) (*Le Petit* and *Grieves*).

196. *Hood* (February 18, 1999); *Stephen Jordan* (March 14, 2000); *Thompson* (June 15, 2004); *Boyle* (January 8, 2008).

197. See CM Res. DH(2000)82 (May 29, 2000) (*Hood*), ResDH(2001)73 (June 26, 2001) (*Stephen Jordan*), closed in light of Investigation and Summary Dealing (Army) Regulations 1997, regulations 20–24.

198. CM/ResDH(2011)287 (December 2, 2011) (*Boyle; Thompson; Bell*), closed on the basis of the adoption of the Armed Forces Discipline Act 2000, sec. 11 (1), later replaced by Armed Forces Act 2006, chap. 2, pt. 4; see also Armed Forces Discipline Act 2000: Explanatory Notes, paras. 17–18 (noting that the *Thompson* remedy came out of a further review of pretrial detention arrangements following *Hood*).

199. *Thompson* (June 15, 2004); *Bell* (January 16, 2007).

200. The creation of the Summary Appeal Court was an element that met with some criticism because it was thought to undermine the authority of the CO in exercising military discipline; see, e.g., statements by Lords Inge, Carver, and Chalfont, and Earl Attlee, 607 Parl. Deb. HL (5th ser.) (November 29, 1999), cols. 684–690, 691–695. For the government's position, see the statement by Baroness Symons of Vernham Dean, at col. 699: "Our legal advice is that it is now considered that a right of appeal is also necessary to make the procedures associated with summary dealings compatible with the convention. So I am afraid that, for those who have raised the question of whether the summary appeal court is necessary, the answer is: yes, in terms of the evolving thinking on the matter since 1996, that is indeed the advice." The active chiefs of staff reportedly approved of the proposed changes; see ibid., col. 700.

201. CM Res. CM/ResDH(2011)287 (December 2, 2011) (*Boyle; Thompson; Bell*).

202. See Annotated Agenda, 1035th CM Mtg. (September 17–18, 2008), COE Doc. CM/Del/OJ/DH(2008)1028 sec. 6.1 (*s.n. Thompson*)..

203. Rowe 2002, 204; Rowlinson 2002, 20.

204. Armed Forces Act 2006: Explanatory Notes, para. 14.

205. Ibid., paras. 15–16, 19.

Chapter 6

1. *McKerr; Hugh Jordan; Kelly and Others; Shanaghan* (all May 4, 2001); *McShane* (May 28, 2002); *Finucane* (July 1, 2003). In *McShane*, the Court also found that the UK had breached its

obligation under Article 34 ECHR to enable applicants to communicate freely with the Convention organs by threatening the applicant's solicitor with disciplinary proceedings for disclosing certain documents received in confidentiality.

2. Memorandum from British Irish Rights Watch (March 15, 2007), para. 21, reproduced in Joint Committee on Human Rights, Monitoring the Government's Response to Court Judgments Finding Breaches of Human Rights, 16th Rep. of Sess. 2006–07, HL Paper 128/HC 728 (June 18, 2007), appendix 21. During the conflict, more than 3,700 individuals have reportedly been killed and 40,000 injured; see Dwyer and McAlinden 2015, 15.

3. For the various execution-relevant issues, see Cases Concerning the Action of the Security Forces in Northern Ireland: Summary of the Individual and General Measures Taken and Identification of Outstanding Questions, Memorandum, COE Doc. CM/Inf/DH(2014)16 rev (May 27, 2014).

4. See CM Interim Resolutions ResDH(2005)20 (February 23, 2005); CM/ResDH(2007)73 (June 6, 2007); CM/ResDH(2009)44 (March 19, 2009).

5. See *McCaughey and Others* and *Hemsworth* (both July 16, 2013) (excessive investigative delays concerning deaths at hand of security forces in Northern Ireland).

6. See, e.g., Inspection of the Police Service of Northern Ireland Historical Enquiries Team (2013), http://cain.ulst.ac.uk/issues/police/hmic/2013-07-03_HMIC_HET-report.pdf; The Relationship Between the Police Service of Northern Ireland and the Office of the Police Ombudsman for Northern Ireland (December 2013), http://www.cjini.org/CJNI/files/b9/b97d8f4a-295f-42d5-8e63-ecc2199307c8.pdf.

7. McKerr Group of Cases: Consolidated Action Plan, COE Doc. DH-DD(2016)970 (September 9, 2016). With regard to inquests, the UK Supreme Court had affirmed in 2011 that these must comply with the positive obligations under Article 2 ECHR; see In the matter of an application by Brigid McCaughey and another for Judicial Review (Northern Ireland) (2011) UKSC 20 (May 18, 2011).

8. See Stormont House Agreement, December 2014, paras. 31, 32, 37, https://www.gov.uk/government/uploads/system/uploads/attachment_data/file/390672/Stormont_House_Agreement.pdf.

9. Northern Ireland Executive, "A Fresh Start: The Stormont Agreement and Implementation Plan," November 17, 2015, https://www.northernireland.gov.uk/sites/default/files/publications/nigov/a-fresh-start-stormont-agreement_0.pdf.

10. See the submissions by Pat Finucane Center, COE Doc. DH-DD(2016)1213 (November 10, 2016), 7; Relatives for Justice, COE Doc. DH-DD(2016)1191 (November 2, 2016), 8; the Committee on the Administration of Justice (CAJ), COE Doc. DH-DD(2016)1203 (November 7, 2016), 3–6.

11. Cate McCurry, "DUP Leader Arlene Foster: Why I Blocked Plans to Speed up Troubles Probes," *Belfast Telegraph*, May 4, 2016, http://www.belfasttelegraph.co.uk/news/northern-ireland-assembly-election/dup-leader-arlene-foster-why-i-blocked-plans-to-speed-up-troubles-probes-34683461.html.

12. Consolidated Action Plan: McKerr Group of Cases v. the United Kingdom, COE Doc. DH-DD(2017)530 (May 11, 2017), 3.

13. Joint Committee on Human Rights, Implementation of Strasbourg Judgments: First Progress Report, 13th Rep. Sess. 2005–06, HL Paper 133/HC 954, March 8, 2006, paras. 10, 18.

14. See, e.g., Sarah Priddy, *Implementation of the Stormont House Agreement*, House of Commons Debate Pack No. CDP-2017-0008 (January 5, 2017), 10, 11, 20.

15. Quoted in McCurry, "DUP Leader Arlene Foster," *Belfast Telegraph*, May 4, 2016.

16. Ben Farmer, "Troubles Inquiry into British Soldiers Is 'Unfair', Minister Says As He Calls for 'Inappropriate' System to be Overhauled," *Telegraph*, February 23, 2017, http://www .telegraph.co.uk/news/2017/02/23/troubles-inquiry-british-soldiers-unfair-minister-says -calls/. For the government's position, see also Robert Mendick, "Theresa May: Troubles Inquiries Should Focus on IRA," *Telegraph*, January 20, 2017, http://www.telegraph.co.uk/news/2017 /01/26/theresa-may-troubles-inquiries-should-focus-ira/.

17. Cited in Joint Committee on Human Rights, Monitoring the Government's Response to Court Judgments: Annual Report 2008, 31st Rep. Sess. 2007–08, HL Paper 173/HC 1078, October 31, 2008, 28.

18. Communication from NGO Relatives for Justice to the Committee of Ministers, COE Doc. DH-DD(2017)566 (May 23, 2017), 4.

19. Ibid., 9; Communication from the Applicant's Representative in the Case of Kelly and Others to the Committee of Ministers, COD Doc. DH-DD(2017)13 (January 9, 2017), para. 18.

20. Lawther 2015, 28. On the reforms of various aspects of Northern Ireland's criminal justice system and the legal and political forces affecting them, see McAlinden and Dwyer 2015.

21. *S. and Marper* (December 4, 2008), para. 125.

22. Ibid., paras. 109–110.

23. Available at http://www.legislation.gov.uk/ukpga/2012/9/pdfs/ukpga_20120009_en.pdf.

24. Introduced by the Criminal Justice and Police Act 2001, secs. 1–11, PNDs are intended to enable the police to respond efficiently to "low-level, anti-social and nuisance offending" (Ministry of Justice, Guidance on Penalty Notices for Disorder [June 24, 2014], 4], can be issued on the spot, and involve penalties of £60 or £90.

25. National DNA Database Strategy Board Annual Report 2012–13, 3, 23–24, https://www .gov.uk/government/uploads/system/uploads/attachment_data/file/252885/NDNAD_Annual _Report_2012-13.pdf.

26. See Communications from the UK Concerning the Case of S. and Marper v. the United Kingdom, COE Docs. DH-DD(2015)836 (August 17, 2015), DH-DD(2016)489 (April 20, 2016), and DH-DD(2016)1000 (September 13, 2016).

27. Communication from the UK Concerning the Case of S. and Marper v. the United Kingdom, COE Doc. DH-DD(2017)431 (April 11, 2017).

28. See *Goggins and Others* (July 19, 2011), para. 73; COE Doc. CM/Inf/DH(2011)22rev (May 26, 2011).

29. See Joint Committee on Human Rights, Legislative Scrutiny: Policing and Crime Bill, 10th Rep. Sess. 2008–09, HL Paper 68/HC 395, April 16, 2009, 39–41.

30. Joint Committee on Human Rights, Legislative Scrutiny: Crime and Security Bill; Personal Care at Home Bill; Children, Schools and Families Bill, 12th Rep. Sess. 2009–10, HL Paper 67/HC 402, March 2, 2010, 9–12.

31. Joint Committee on Human Rights, Enhancing Parliament's Role in Relation to Human Rights Judgments, 15th Rep. Sess. 2009–10, HL Paper 85/HC 455, March 26, 2010, 20.

32. See Crime and Security Act 2010, secs. 14–23.

33. The Coalition: Our Programme for Government, 11, https://www.gov.uk/government/uploads/system/uploads/attachment_data/file/78977/coalition_programme_for _government.pdf.

34. See Representation of the People Act 1983, sec. 3 (1): "A convicted person during the time that he is detained in a penal institution in pursuance of his sentence is legally incapable of voting at any parliamentary or local government election."

35. See Mathieu-Mohin and Clerfayt v. Belgium (March 2, 1987), para. 48ff.

36. Exceptions apply currently to prisoners on remand and those committed to prison for contempt of court or for default in paying fines.

37. *Hirst (no. 2)* (Grand Chamber Judgment of October 5, 2005), para. 82.

38. For useful summaries of domestic developments since 2005, see Alexander Horne and Isobel White, Prisoners' Voting Rights (2005 to May 2015), House of Commons Library Standard Note SN/PC/01764 (February 11, 2015), and Jack Simson Caird, Prisoners' Voting Rights: Developments Since May 2015, House of Commons Library Briefing Paper No. CBP 7461 (February 15, 2016).

39. *Greens and M.T.* (November 23, 2010), para. 115 and op. para. 6.

40. See Scoppola (no. 3) v. Italy (May 22, 2012), paras. 96, 108–109.

41. See Voting Eligibility (Prisoners) Draft Bill, Cm. 8499 (November 2012). In light of the bill's introduction, on March 26, 2013, the Court adjourned consideration of over twenty-three hundred clone cases related to the voting ban; see "Court Adjourns 2,354 Prisoners' Voting Rights Cases," Press Release ECHR 091 (March 26, 2013).

42. Joint Committee on the Draft Voting Eligibility (Prisoners) Bill, Draft Voting Eligibility (Prisoners) Bill, Rep. Sess. 2013–14, HL Paper 103/HC 924, December 18, 2013, para. 227.

43. Ministry of Justice, Responding to Human Rights Judgments: Report to the Joint Committee on Human Rights on the Government Response to Human Rights Judgments 2013–14 (December 2014), 29.

44. See *Firth and Others* (August 12, 2014); *McHugh and Others* (February 10, 2015); *Millbank and Others* (June 30, 2016).

45. Human Rights Futures Project, "Prisoner Voting and Human Rights in the UK, LSE Human Rights Futures Project," London School of Economics (June 2013), 10, http://www.lse .ac.uk/humanRights/documents/2013/PrisonerVotes.pdf.

46. See government statements as reproduced in *Hirst (no. 2)*, paras. 16, 24.

47. See Representation of the People Act 2000, secs. 4, 5, and Explanatory Notes to Representation of the People Act 2000, paras. 40–45.

48. Joint Committee on the Draft Voting Eligibility (Prisoners) Bill, Witness Evidence by Jack Straw and David Davis, July 17, 2013, http://www.parliamentlive.tv/Main/Player.aspx?meetingId =13649, at 9:58:38. For an earlier similar assessment, see Joint Committee on Human Rights, Legislative Scrutiny: Political Parties and Elections Bill, 4th Rep. Sess. 2008–09, HL Paper 23/ HC 204, February 1, 2009, para. 1.15. See also *Liberty's Response to the Ministry of Justice's Second Stage Consultation on the Voting Rights of Convicted Prisoners Detained within the United Kingdom* (September 2009), 6, https://www.liberty-human-rights.org.uk/sites/default/files/liberty-s -response-to-the-prisoner-voting-consultation-2.pdf ("The Government's failure to implement the ECtHR's decision reflects a lack of political will which has been manifested in a series of delaying tactics, including the flawed and protracted consultation exercise").

49. Joint Committee on Human Rights, Monitoring the Government's Response to Human Rights Judgments: Annual Report 2008, 31st Rep. Sess. 2007–08, HL Paper 173/HC 1078, October 31, 2008, 26 (para. 62). For further criticism, see Human Rights Committee, Consideration of Reports Submitted by States Parties under Article 40 of the [International] Covenant [on Civil and Political Rights]: Concluding Observations of the Human Rights Committee—United Kingdom of Great Britain and Northern Ireland, UN Doc. CCPR/C/GBR/CO/6 (July 30, 2008), para. 28, http://www.refworld.org/docid/48a9411a2.html.

50. See "Prisoner Voting: Second Stage Consultation" (April 8, 2009), http://webarchive .nationalarchives.gov.uk/20130128112038/http://www.justice.gov.uk/news/newsrelease 080409b.htm.

51. See Ministry of Justice, Voting Rights of Convicted Prisoners Detained within the United Kingdom: Second Stage Consultation, Consultation Paper CP6/09 (April 8, 2009), 24.

52. 517 Parl. Deb., HC (6th ser.) (November 3, 2010), col. 921.

53. 520 Parl. Deb., HC (6th ser.) (December 20, 2010), col. 151WS.

54. 523 Parl. Deb., HC (6th ser.) (February 10, 2011), beginning at col. 493 ("Voting by Prisoners"), http://www.publications.parliament.uk/pa/cm201011/cmhansrd/cm110210/debtext /110210-0001.htm#11021059000001.

55. Ibid., col. 493.

56. Ibid., col. 506.

57. Ibid., col. 512.

58. Ibid.

59. Ibid., col. 572.

60. Ibid., col. 514.

61. Ibid., col. 584.

62. The Conservative Party Manifesto 2015, *Strong Leadership, A Clear Economic Plan, A Brighter, More Secure Future*, 60, https://www.conservatives.com/manifesto2015.

63. See The Conservative and Unionist Party Manifesto 2017, *Forward Together: Our Plan for a Stronger Britain and a Prosperous Future*, 42–43, 45, https://s3.eu-west-2.amazonaws.com /manifesto2017/Manifesto2017.pdf.

64. CM Res. CM/ResDH(2015)251 (December 9, 2015).

65. Action Plan: *Hirst (no. 2)* Group of Cases, COE Doc. DH-DD(2016)1201 (October 25, 2016) (emphasis added).

66. Ibid.

67. Thierry Delvigne v Commune de Lesparre Médoc and Préfet de la Gironde (October 6, 2015), CJEU Case C650/13.

68. YouGov—The Sun Survey (November 2, 2010), http://d25d2506sfb94s.cloudfront.net /today_uk_import/YG-Archives-Pol-Sun-PrisonersVoting-021110.pdf ; YouGov—Sunday Times Survey (February 10–11, 2011), 10, http://cdn.yougov.com/today_uk_import/YG-Archives-Pol -ST-results-11-130211.pdf; YouGov—Sunday Times Survey (November 22–23, 2012), 8, http:// d25d2506sfb94s.cloudfront.net/cumulus_uploads/document/lmlmhdqllh/YG-Archives-Pol-ST -results%20-%2023-251112.pdf; YouGov Survey Results (Cambridge Programme Survey (January 25–26, 2015), https://d25d2506sfb94s.cloudfront.net/cumulus_uploads/document/2ivk6cddde /Warr_Prison.pdf.

69. YouGov—Sunday Times Survey (February 10–11, 2011), 8–10, http://cdn.yougov.com /today_uk_import/YG-Archives-Pol-ST-results-11-130211.pdf,

70. The just-in-time introduction of the Voting Eligibility (Prisoners) Draft Bill in response to the ECtHR's order in *Greens and M.T.* qualifies at best as an instance of "technical compliance"; see Bates 2014, 518.

71. Joint Committee on Human Rights, Human Rights Judgments, 7th Rep. Sess. 2014–2015, March 11, 2015, 14.

72. See Interim Resolution CM/ResDH(2009)160 (December 3, 2009).

73. Quoted in Caird, *Prisoners' Voting Rights*, House of Commons Library Briefing Paper CBP 7461, 16.

Chapter 7

1. See, similarly, King 2015, 167, with regard to legislative remedies in response to declarations of incompatibility under the HRA: "[D]espite some lengthy delays and the possible exception of prisoner voting [. . .] there has been no case to date where the Government or Parliament affirmatively chose not to remedy incompatible legislation."

2. Hillebrecht 2014, 99.

3. See, e.g., Hamlin 2016; Gies 2016.

4. See the five judgments in *O.; W.; B.; R.;* and *H.* (Merits) (July 8, 1987), which are briefly discussed in the Appendix.

Chapter 8

1. Lambert Abdelgawad and Weber 2008, 123.

2. Gusy 2005, 158 (my translation of the term *Randkorrekturen*).

3. Donald and Leach 2016, 283, 280 (citing Andreas Voßkuhle, president of the Federal Constitutional Court, and Christian Tomuschat, respectively).

4. Ibid., 281.

5. Germany signed the ECHR on November 11, 1950, and ratified it on December 5, 1952. On July 5, 1955, Germany submitted its first declarations under Article 25 ECHR [1950] (accepting the Commission's competence to receive individual complaints) and Article 46 ECHR [1950] (accepting the Court's jurisdiction).

6. The Convention was ratified in accordance with Article 59 (2) of Germany's constitution, the Grundgesetz (GG), or Basic Law, https://www.gesetze-im-internet.de/englisch_gg/englisch _gg.pdf, and has the same formal status as the legal instrument through which it has been transformed into domestic law, that is, that of a federal statute.

7. See Schmalz 2007, 9–16; Lambert Abdelgawad and Weber 2008, 118.

8. See Article 31 GG: "Federal law shall take precedence over *Land* law"; Schmalz 2007, 9; Sauer 2005, 39.

9. Lambert Abdelgawad and Weber 2008, 119; Satzger and Pohl 2006, 695.

10. See Articles 20 (3) and 93 (4) lit. a GG, respectively.

11. For the distinction between strong and weak judicial review, see Tushnet 2008, chap. 2.

12. See sec. 31, Bundesverfassungsgerichtsgesetz (Federal Constitutional Court Act).

13. See Grabenwarter 2008, 18–19.

14. Klein 2014, 203n89 (references to the ECtHR in just 2–3 percent of all FCC cases between 2004 and 2012).

15. Lambert Abdelgawad and Weber 2008, 141; see also Kilian 2012, 121 (referring to the longtime "wallflower" existence of the ECHR in German law and public life).

16. Grabenwarter 2008, 19.

17. Mark Tushnet has conjectured that the "German Constitutional Court probably has been more influential around the world than the U.S. Supreme Court" (Tushnet 2008, 18).

18. Donald and Leach 2016, 293–294, 298–299.

19. Ibid., 281–284; Pabel 2016, 155, 175; Klein 2014, 211–212.

20. Donald and Leach 2016, 281, 284.

Chapter 9

1. All six required payment only, see *Axen, Teubner and Jossifov* (February 27, 2003) and CM Res. ResDH(2003)163; *Siebert* (March 23, 2006); *Becker* (December 14, 2006); *Berger* (June 14, 2007); *Lück* (May 15, 2008) and CM Res. CM/ResDH(2011)114 (September 14, 2011); *Kalantari* (October 11, 2001) and CM Res. ResDH(2002)154 (December 17, 2002).

2. Neither of the most recently accessed lists (dated April 6, 2017) of judgments and decisions with respect to which information on payment of either the principal, default interest, or both, was still being awaited, or where information was incomplete, includes any entry for Germany in which payment had not been made yet within the three-month deadline; the lists are available at http://www.coe.int/en/web/execution/payment-information.

3. The Court's largest award ever, made in the Yukos case—€1.9 billion, see OAO Neftyanaya Kompaniya Yukos v. Russia (Just Satisfaction) (July 31, 2014)—and the much smaller award of €90 million in the Cyprus interstate case—see Cyprus v. Turkey (Just Satisfaction) (May 12, 2014)—are outliers.

4. The highest just satisfaction amount awarded against Germany so far came to €93,315 (see *Storck* [June 16, 2005], paras. 172–183 and op. para. 10); the highest sum ratified as part of a friendly settlement was €115,000 (see *von Hannover* [Friendly Settlement] [July 28, 2005], para. 7); and the highest amount offered in a judgment by way of a unilateral declaration was €210,000; see *Althoff and Others* (Just Satisfaction) (September 27, 2012), para. 13.

5. As one official at the Council of Europe Secretariat noted, the determination of the frequency required for a series of individual violations to be considered a structural problem is "somewhat arbitrary." Pers. comm., official at Department for the Execution of Judgments of the European Court of Human Rights, Council of Europe, Strasbourg, September 24, 2007.

6. This assessment received partial support from a comparative study that found that in "comparison to most other European countries, whether having common law or civil law systems, the German [here: civil justice] system performs extremely well" (Zuckerman 1999, 31). In terms of efficiency, Zuckerman ranked Germany among the top three countries (together with Japan and the Netherlands), with the highest number of judges per capita among all EU members offered as a partial explanation; see ibid., 43, 32.

7. See appendices to CM Res. ResDH(2001)6 and ResDH(2001)7 (February 26, 2001) regarding the cases of *Pammel* and *Probstmeier* (both July 1, 1997), respectively. Five additional legal staff had been hired at the Federal Constitutional Court in 2000.

8. See *König* (Merits) (June 28, 1978) and CM Res. DH(80)2 (October 10, 1980); *Eckle* (Merits) (July 15, 1982) and CM Res. DH(84)5 (December 7, 1984); *Deumeland* (May 29, 1986) and CM Res. DH(87)6 (February 12, 1987); *Bock* (March 29, 1989) and CM Res. DH(89)25 (September 12, 1989); *Metzger* (May 31, 2001) and CM Res. ResDH(2002)101 (Oct. 21, 2002); *H.T.* (October 11, 2001) and CM Res. ResDH(2002)149 (December 17, 2002); *Mianowicz* (October 18, 2001) and CM Res. ResDH(2002)123 (October 21, 2002); *Janssen* (December 20, 2001) and CM Res. ResDH(2002)88 (July 22, 2002); *Bayrak* (December 20, 2001) and CM Res. ResDH(2002)122 (October 21, 2002); *Volkwein* (April 4, 2002) and CM Res. ResDH(2002)150 (December 17, 2002); *Thieme* (October 17, 2002) and CM Res. ResDH(2004)10 (February 24, 2004); *Gisela Müller* (October 6, 2005) and CM Res. CM/ResDH(2007)122 (October 31, 2007).

9. Supervision was closed on the basis of the earlier resolutions in *Probstmeier* and *Pammel*; see *Klein* (July 27, 2000) and CM Res. ResDH(2001)103 (July 23, 2001); *Becker* (September 26, 2002) and CM Res. ResDH(2003)127 (July 22, 2003); *Hesse-Anger* (February 6, 2003) and CM Res. ResDH(2004)6 (February 24, 2004); *Kind* (February 20, 2003) and CM Res. ResDH(2004)7 (February 24, 2004); *Niederböster* (February 27, 2003), *Trippel* (December 4, 2003), *Voggenreiter* (January 8, 2004), *Wimmer* (February 24, 2005), *Klasen* (October 5, 2006) and CM Res. CM/ResDH(2007)163 (December 19, 2007); *Kaemena and Thöneböhn* (January 22, 2009) and CM Res. CM/ResDH(2010)52 (June 3, 2010).

10. See *Freitag* (July 19, 2007) and CM Res. CM/ResDH(2011)113 (September 14, 2011).

11. In one case—*Deumeland*—the finding of a violation was considered sufficient just satisfaction, so not even payment was due; see CM Res. DH(87)6 (February 12, 1987).

12. Two judgments on excessively long proceedings—*Herbolzheimer* (July 31, 2003) and *Uhl* (February 10, 2005)—had been scheduled for a final resolution as late as December 2010 (see Annotated Agenda, 1100th CM Mtg. (November 30 and December 1–2, 2010), COE Doc. CM/Del/OJ/DH(2010)1100 sec. 6.2), before their supervision was continued as part of a new group of judicial delay cases.

13. See *K.-F.* (November 27, 1997) and CM Res. DH(98)88 (April 22, 1998); *Erdem* (July 5, 2001) and CM Res. ResDH(2002)87 (July 22, 2002); *Cevizovic* (July 29, 2004) and CM Res. CM/ResDH(2007)120 (October 31, 2007); *Epple* (March 24, 2005, rev. December 15, 2005) and CM Res. CM/ResDH(2007)7 (February 28, 2007); *Dzelili* (November 10, 2005) and CM Res. CM/ResDH(2011)115 (September 14, 2011).

14. See *Niemietz* (December 16, 1992) and CM Res. DH(93)24 (June 11, 1993); *Buck* (April 28, 2005) and CM Res. CM/ResDH(2007)80 (June 20, 2007).

15. See *Megyeri* (May 12, 1992) and CM Res. DH(92)62 (November 10, 1992).

16. See *Van Kück* (June 12, 2003) and CM Res. CM/ResDH(2011)112 (September 14, 2011).

17. In *Böhmer* (October 3, 2002), the applicant's probation had been revoked by the Hamburg Appeals Court on the basis of an in-depth analysis of the applicant's guilt, which was still at issue in other proceedings pending at the trial level, thus violating the presumption of innocence guaranteed by Article 6 (2) ECHR. The only meaningful remedy in this case was thus the nonexecution of the faulty suspension revocation decision, and indeed, on October 21, 2003, shortly after the ECtHR's judgment, the senior public prosecutor issued a legally binding order on the unenforceability of the relevant decision; see CM Res. CM/ResDH(2011)215 (December 2, 2011);.for discussion, see Seher 2006.

18. See *Yilmaz* (April 17, 2003), para. 48; *Keles* (October 27, 2005), para. 66.

19. See CM Res. CM/ResDH(2007)121 (*Keles*) and CM/ResDH(2007)125 (*Yilmaz*) (both October 31, 2007). Although the option to apply for short-term visas remained open during the exclusion period, in the case of *Yilmaz* the relevant administrative authority had refused such a permit in 2000; see CM/ResDH(2007)125 (*Yilmaz*). The FCC has affirmed the ECtHR's reasoning and the importance of taking into account the protection of family life under Article 8 ECHR in expulsion proceedings; see FCC, Order of May 10, 2007, case no. 2 BvR 304/07, paras. 32ff.

20. Several post-2010 judgments also found violations of Article 8 due to unjustified interference with parent-child relationships: *Tsikakis* (February 10, 2011) and *Kuppinger* (January 15, 2015) (failure of domestic courts to enforce father's contact rights against obstruction by the mother); *B.B. and F.B.* (March 14, 2013) (withdrawal of parental authority on the basis solely of uncorroborated allegations of violence against their children by their daughter); *Moog* (October 6, 2016) (suspension of contact rights for more than three years).

21. *Kutzner* (February 26, 2002), para. 17.

22. Ibid., paras. 72–74.

23. See CM Res. ResDH(2004)40 (July 20, 2004).

24. *Kutzner*, paras. 75, 76.

25. Jauernig 2004, 1599 (marginal no. 9).

26. There is, unfortunately, no public information on the specific regime, if any, under which the children subsequently lived with their parents.

27. See Annotated Agenda, 871st CM Mtg. (February 10–11, 2004), Doc. CM/Del/OJ/ OT(2004)871 (*s.n. Kutzner*).

28. *Kutzner*, para. 73.

29. Six of the seven children were fetched by officials from their school, kindergarten, or home, and the seventh, a newborn only seven days old, directly from the hospital. They were then put in four different foster homes, and all parental contact with them was prohibited; see *Haase* (April 8, 2004), paras. 12–15, 104.

30. Kielmansegg 2008, 278.

31. See Annotated Agenda, 928th CM Mtg. (June 6–7, 2005), Doc. CM/Del/OJ/ DH(2005)928 Vol. 1 (*s.n. Haase*); the final resolution followed six years later, see CM Res. CM/ ResDH(2011)213 (December 2, 2011).

32. See *Haase and Others* (dec.) (February 12, 2008).

33. See, e.g., Franziska Coesfeld and Sascha Balasko, "Tote Yaya: Prüfer rügen gleich zwei Jugendämter," *Hamburger Abendblatt* (January 31, 2014), 7, https://www.abendblatt.de/hamburg /article124402631/Tote-Yaya-Pruefer-ruegen-gleich-zwei-Jugendaemter.html; Ralf Wiegand, "Fall Chantal: Schwere Versäumnisse im Hamburger Jugendamt," *Süddeutsche Zeitung* (February 4, 2012), http://www.sueddeutsche.de/panorama/fall-chantal-schwere-versaeumnisse-im -hamburger-jugendamt-1.1275487; "Verhungerte Lea-Sophie: Schwere Vorwürfe gegen Jugendamt," *Spiegel Online* (January 10, 2008), http://www.spiegel.de/panorama/justiz/0,1518,527849 ,00.html; Julia Jüttner, "Fall Kevin: Chronik eines vermeidbaren Todes," *Spiegel Online* (October 12, 2006), http://www.spiegel.de/panorama/justiz/fall-kevin-chronik-eines-vermeidbaren -todes-a-442225.html.

34. See, e.g., Cornelia Bolesch, "Wenn die Jugendämter zu mächtig werden," *Süddeutsche Zeitung* (May 5, 2008), 6; Katrin Hummel, "Wegnehmen ist das Einfachste," *Frankfurter Allgemeine Zeitung* (March 15, 2008), 3; Sabine Rückert, "Der Verdacht," *Die Zeit* 26/2003 (June 18, 2003), 11; Michael Fröhlingsdorf, "Drei mal Vier ist Elf," *Der Spiegel* 47/2002 (November 18, 2002), 76–83.

35. In March 2007, a European Parliament delegation took up the issue with the German government; see Summary of Meeting with German Authorities Concerning the "Jugendamt-Petitions," http://www.europarl.europa.eu/meetdocs/2004_2009/documents/dv/668/668349 /668349en.pdf.   .

36. Three subsequent judgments implicating child care proceedings related primarily to their excessive length under Article 6 (1) ECHR; see *Siebert* (Friendly Settlement) (March 23, 2006); *Glesmann* (January 10, 2008, no violation); *Nanning* (October 12, 2007) (this judgment also found a violation of Article 8 due to a disproportionate denial of access to the applicant's daughter; because the daughter, born in 1984, had already come of age by the time of the judgment, substantive remedial measures were no longer necessary in this respect). For post-2010 judgments, see *Tsikakis* (February 10, 2011); *Kuppinger* (January 15, 2015); *B.B. and F.B.* (March 14, 2013); *Moog* (October 6, 2016).

37. *Görgülü* (February 26, 2004).

38. Supervision was ended in June 2008; for the final resolution, see CM/ResDH(2009)4 (January 9, 2009).

39. For the history preceding the battle in the courts, see Klein 2010, 43–54.

40. *Görgülü*, paras. 44–51.

41. Ibid., para. 64.

42. FCC, Order of October 14, 2004, case no. 2 BvR 1481/04; quotations are from the English version at http://www.bverfg.de/e/rs20041014_2bvr148104en.html.

43. FCC, Order of December 28, 2004, case no. 1 BvR 2790/04.

44. Kielmansegg 2008, 303 (my translation of *ideologisch überfrachtet*).

45. FCC, Order of June 10, 2005, case no. 1 BvR 2790/04, para. 38 (calling the Oberlandesgericht (OLG) Naumburg's behavior a "violation of the obligation to decide according to law and justice . . . outside of its jurisdiction" [my translation]).

46. See OLG Naumburg, Press Release 023/06 (November 23, 2006), http://www.asp.sachsen-anhalt.de/presseapp/data/olg/2006/023_2006.htm, and Lamprecht 2007. The proceedings were terminated because the judges' individual responsibility could not be ascertained due to the confidentiality of their deliberations; see Schulte-Kellinghaus and Cebulla 2010, 234; see also Mandla 2010.

47. For an overview of the various proceedings and decisions, see Klein 2010.

48. See CM Res. CM/ResDH(2009)4 (January 9, 2009).

49. "*Sicherlich sind die Verfahren in Sachen Görgülü kein Ruhmesblatt für die deutsche Justiz. Allerdings sind die Urteile, die nicht den gesetzlichen Vorgaben bzw. den Vorgaben des EGMR genügten, stets aufgehoben und korrigiert worden.*" Comment by Minister Zypries, November 5, 2007, quoted in Fall Görgülü, http://de.wikimannia.org/Fall_G%F6rg%Fcl%FC.

50. See Annotated Agenda 1007th CM Mtg. (October 15–17, 2007), Doc.CM/Del/OJ/DH(2007)1007, sec. 4.3 (*s.n. Görgülü*) (noting failure to schedule make-up visits for boycotted meetings).

51. Kielmansegg 2008, 301.

52. Mandla 2010, 283.

53. See, e.g., Müller and Richter 2008, 162–170; Schmalz 2007; Sauer 2005; Hartwig 2005; Breuer 2005; Cremer 2004; Hofmann 2004. The case also received significant coverage in the national media, with one study counting several hundred newspaper and magazine articles and releases by press agencies; most of these reportedly focused on the domestic proceedings, whereas the ECtHR's judgment was rarely mentioned; see Klein 2010, 349, 524ff.

54. For another decision denying binding force of ECtHR judgments on national courts, see Landgericht Mainz, Order of October 22, 1998, case no. 1 Qs 225/98, *Neue Juristische Wochenschrift* (1999), 1271.

55. FCC, Order of October 14, 2004, case no. 2 BvR 1481/04, para. 47, http://www.bverfg.de/e/rs20041014_2bvr148104en.html.

56. Ibid., paras. 57–58.

57. Ibid., para. 59.

58. See, e.g., "Das tut mir weh," Thomas Darnstädt, Dietmar Hipp and Markus Verbeet, interview with Luzius Wildhaber (president of the ECtHR), *Der Spiegel* 47, November 15, 2004, 50–54, http://magazin.spiegel.de/EpubDelivery/spiegel/pdf/36625709; Hartwig 2005, 869n3, 869n4.

59. *Vogt* (Merits) (September 26, 1995).

60. Ibid., para. 61.

61. *Glasenapp* (August 28, 1986); *Kosiek* (August 28, 1986).

62. See *Vogt* (Merits) (September 26, 1995), para. 44. One of course cannot fail to notice that the former two decisions had been handed down while the Cold War was ongoing and Germany had still been a divided "frontier" state, which might account for the fact that the Court was more accepting of Germany's policy then than in 1994, when the need to prevent communist infiltration appeared less acute. In any event, the Court's distinction between *Vogt* and the preceding cases did not convince everybody; see ibid., diss. op. of Judge Jambrek, no. 7 (noting that the distinction to mask the change in the Court's "judicial policy" was "not persuasive"); Krisch 1999, 263 (calling the distinction a "jurisprudential façade" behind which the Court sought to hide its about-face).

63. Quoted in *Vogt* (Merits) (September 26, 1995), paras. 26, 27.

64. Quoted in ibid., para. 30; for the historical background, see Monson 1984.

65. See *Vogt* (Merits) (September 26, 1995), para. 34, citing FCC, Order of May 22, 1975, case no. 2 BvL 13/73.

66. See especially the comprehensive comparative study by Böckenförde, Tomuschat, and Umbach 1981; see, further, Komitee für Grundrechte und Demokratie 1982; Monson 1984; Braunthal 1992.

67. Report of the Commission of Inquiry Appointed Under Article 26 of the Constitution of the International Labour Organization to Examine the Observance of the Discrimination (Employment and Occupation) Convention, 1958 (No. 111), by the Federal Republic of Germany (November/December 1985), *Official Bulletin* (ILO) 70 (1987), Series B, Suppl. 1.

68. *Vogt* (Merits) (September 26, 1995), para. 36.

69. Thurn 2007, 90. As a result, applicants were no longer automatically checked for membership in what were considered extremist organizations by way of a query with the Bundesamt für Verfassungsschutz (Federal Office for the Protection of the Constitution), but only if there were concrete indications.

70. Figures given in *Bundestags-Drucksache* 14/8083 (January 25, 2002), 1, and 17/8376 (January 18, 2012), 1. The Amnesty International case, concerning a cemetery gardener (!), is noted in WDR, "Stichtag: 19. Mai 2006—Vor 30 Jahren: Neue Richtlinien zum Radikalenerlass," http://www1.wdr.de/stichtag1570.html.

71. *Vogt* (Just Satisfaction) (September 2, 1996). The applicant had been readmitted to the civil service in 1991 after the government in the state of Lower Saxony had changed from the conservative CDU to the Social Democrats and Greens; see Dammann 2002, 8. Notably, Lower Saxony's prime minister at the time, future chancellor Gerhard Schröder, had been Ms. Vogt's legal counsel during domestic proceedings in the case; see "Radikalenerlass: Staatsknete fällig," *Focus* 37 (September 9, 1996), http://www.focus.de/politik/deutschland/radikalenerlass-staatsknete-faellig_aid_162075.html.

72. See CM Res. DH(97)12 (January 28, 1997).

73. See ibid. Only one Land has reportedly decided to enable a fresh review of past cases; see Dammann 2002, 13 (reporting that Baden-Württemberg opted for such an approach in 2000).

74. For the government's responses, see *Bundestags-Drucksache* 13/3853 (February 26, 1996), 14/8967 (May 6, 2002), 16/6210 (August 9, 2007), and 17/8667 (February 10, 2012).

75. See Dammann 2002, 11–12; Dammann 2004.

76. See only the cases reported at http://www.berufsverbote.de, a website devoted to the issue of "professional bans." The ECtHR has received related applications from time to time but so far has considered the domestic decisions justifiable and has declared them inadmissible

("manifestly ill-founded") as a result; see *Volkmer* (dec.) (November 22, 2001); *Otto* (dec.) (November 24. 2005); *Erdel* (dec.) (February 13, 2007); *Kern* (dec.) (May 29, 2007); *Lahr* (dec.) (July 1, 2007).

77. As noted in Dammann 2004, in rejecting as inadmissible eight follow-up applications triggered by the *Vogt* judgment (in 2000, 2002, and 2003), the ECtHR reaffirmed that there was no legal requirement to provide for a reopening of proceedings in these cases.

78. See Braunthal 1992, 51, 118.

79. Hanno Kühnert, "Zu spätes Recht ist Unrecht," *Die Zeit* 41 (October 6, 1995), 83 (my translation).

80. For a case in which the Court viewed the removal of a teacher from the civil service due to his former involvement in political activities in the German Democratic Republic as proportionate, see *Volkmer* (dec.) (November 22, 2001).

81. See *Pakelli* (April 25, 1983) and CM Res. DH(84)1 (January 26, 1984).

82. See *Barthold* (Merits) (March 25, 1985), *Barthold* (Just Satisfaction) (January 31, 1986), CM Res. DH(87)5 (February 12, 1987).

83. FCC, Order of October 11, 1985 (*Pakelli-Beschluss*), case no. 2 BvR 336/85. The FCC explicitly left open the question of the consequences, if any, following from ECtHR judgments if the Convention violation continued to have effects; see ibid., 290.

84. See Kieschke 2003, 156n188.

85. Which is why the amendment has been referred to as *lex Pakelli*, although that case had been decided sixteen years earlier, in 1983; see, e.g., OLG Stuttgart, Order of October 26, 1999, case no. 1 WS 157/99, discussed in *Neue Zeitschrift für Strafrecht—Rechtsprechungsreport* no. 8 (2000), 243–244.

86. See Entwurf eines Gesetzes zur Reform des Wiederaufnahmerechts (Draft Bill on Reforming the Law of Reopening Proceedings), *Bundestags-Drucksache* 12/6219 (November 23, 1993).

87. See Entwurf eines Gesetzes zur Reform des strafrechtlichen Wiederaufnahmerechts (Draft Bill on Reforming the Law of Reopening Criminal Proceedings), *Bundestags-Drucksache* 13/3594 (January 29, 1996).

88. Ibid., 5.

89. Bundestag, Verbatim Record of 98th Sess., April 18, 1996, 8793–8800.

90. *Bundestags-Drucksache* 13/3594 (January 29, 1996), 7.

91. See ibid., 3, 9.

92. See Beschlussempfehlung und Bericht des Rechtsausschusses zum Entwurf eines Gesetzes zur Reform des strafrechtlichen Wiederaufnahmeverfahrens (Recommendation for Decision and Report of the Legal Committee on the Draft Bill on Reforming the Law of Reopening Criminal Proceedings), *Bundestags-Drucksache* 13/10333 (April 1, 1998). Notably, a further proposal submitted by the party Bündnis 90/Die Grünen to allow reopening even on the basis of judgments against other states that touch upon equivalent issues in German law was rejected by representatives of both major parties; see ibid., 3.

93. See section 359, no. 6, Strafprozessordnung (*Code of Criminal Procedure*), introduced by Gesetz zur Reform des strafrechtlichen Wiederaufnahmerechts (Act on Reforming the Law of Reopening Criminal Proceedings) (July 9, 1998), *Bundesgesetzblatt* (Federal Law Gazette), part 1, no. 44 (1998), 1802. An English translation of the *Code of Criminal Procedure* is available at https://www.gesetze-im-internet.de/englisch_stpo/.

94. *P.S.* (December 20, 2001). The violation concerned the fact that the applicant had been precluded from cross-examining the victim of his alleged sexual abuse, an eight-year-old girl,

in the criminal proceedings against him on account of the potential effects this might have had on the girl's state of health.

95. See CM Res. ResDH(2005)27 (April 25, 2005).

96. *Stambuk* (October 17, 2002).

97. See CM Res. ResDH(2004)41 (July 20, 2004).

98. Recommendation R(2000)2 of the Committee of Ministers to Member States on the Re-Examination or Reopening of Certain Cases at Domestic Level Following Judgments of the European Court of Human Rights (adopted January 19, 2000).

99. By 2006, more than 80 percent of the ECHR parties allowed for the reopening of criminal proceedings and roughly 50 percent did so in civil and administrative proceedings; see Committee of Ministers 2006, section IV.2.

100. New sec. 580, no. 8, Zivilprozessordnung (*Code of Civil Procedure*), introduced by Zweites Gesetzes zur Modernisierung der Justiz (Second Act on Modernizing the Judiciary) (December 22, 2006, entry into force December 31, 2006), *Bundesgesetzblatt* (Federal Law Gazette) part 1, no. 66 (2006), 3416, 3421. An English version of the Code of Civil Procedure can be found at https://www.gesetze-im-internet.de/englisch_zpo/englisch_zpo.html.

101. See Entwurf eines Zweiten Gesetzes zur Modernisierung der Justiz (Draft Second Act on Modernizing the Judiciary), *Bundestags-Drucksache* 16/3038 (October 19, 2006), 39, 40. The administration's proposal passed the legal committee without changes, see *Bundestags-Drucksache* 16/3640 (November 29, 2006), 11. Note that prior to this legislative change, both the courts and academic commentators had largely been opposed to the analogical application in civil cases of the reopening provision in the *Code of Criminal Procedure*, which was seen as a decision for the legislature to make; see Schmalz 2007, 71.

102. *Storck* (June 16, 2005). The case addressed violations of Articles 5 (1) and 8 ECHR due both to the involuntary detention of the applicant, then a minor, in a closed psychiatric ward between 1977 and 1979 at the request of her father and the administration of medical treatment against her will, and to the Bremen Court of Appeal's failure in 2000 to award compensation because it considered the detention lawful.

103. *Schüth* (Merits) (September 23, 2010). The case revolved around the employment termination of a church organist and choirmaster as a result of what the Catholic Church, his employer, considered an extramarital affair (the applicant had separated from his wife and lived with a new partner, with whom he expected a child; when the parish learned about this, the applicant was being dismissed for adultery). The ECtHR found that the German labor courts, in affirming the lawfulness of his termination, had not properly weighed the interests of the applicant against the interests of his employer, and itself noted that the reopening of the proceedings would constitute an appropriate remedial measure; see *Schüth* (Just Satisfaction) (June 28, 2012), para. 17. Since the applicant's domestic labor proceedings had ended in 2000, however, with his constitutional complaint having been disallowed by the FCC in 2002, they fell under the express exclusion of the new reopening provision.

104. See sec. 35, Gesetz betreffend die Einführung der Zivilprozessordnung (Act Concerning the Introduction of the Code of Civil Procedure), introduced by Article 9 (2) of the Second Act on Modernizing the Judiciary, 10.

105. FCC, Order of August 13, 2013, case no. 2 BvR 1380/08.

106. See CM Res. CM/ResDH(2014)264 (December 4, 2014) (*Schüth*) and CM/ResDH(2007)123 (October 31, 2007) (*Storck*). The latter resolution also reports general measures intended to prevent unlawful involuntary committals of minors by their parents (including the

requirement of a court order) that were had already been adopted in 1979 (amended in 2000) and 1992, that is, so long before the ECtHR's judgment that they are clearly not responding to the shortcomings in the pre-reform regime identified by the Court. In any event, the finding of the Convention violation in 1977–79 appears to be essentially incidental to assessing the Court of Appeals failure to award compensation, and that aspect was effectively remedied by way of just satisfaction, justifying the placement of this case in this chapter rather than Chapter 10.

107. See secs. 78–79 and 95 Bundesverfassungsgerichtsgesetz; Schmalz 2007, 71.

108. See Doc. DH-DD(2014)1412E (November 19, 2014), 3.

109. *Gäfgen* (June 1, 2010), para. 15.

110. *Gäfgen* (June 30, 2008).

111. *Gäfgen* (June 1, 2010), para. 124. The Court also took issue with the fact that the deputy chief had subsequently been appointed chief of the Police Headquarters for Technology, Logistics and Administration; ibid., para. 125.

112. "Gäfgen erhält 3000 Euro Schadenersatz," *Frankfurter Allgemeine Zeitung* (October 10, 2012),   http://www.faz.net/aktuell/politik/inland/folterandrohung-gaefgen-erhaelt-3000-euro -schadenersatz-11921017.html.

113. See "Gäfgen darf 3000 Euro behalten," *Süddeutsche Zeitung* (September 3, 2013), http://www.sueddeutsche.de/panorama/entschaedigung-fuer-folter-kindsmoerder-gaefgen -darf-euro-behalten-1.1761425; "Entschädigung für Gäfgen noch vor Weihnachten," *Frankfurt Allgemeine Zeitung* (December 17, 2013), http://www.faz.net/aktuell/rhein-main/kindsmoerder -entschaedigung-fuer-gaefgen-noch-vor-weihnachten-12715260.html.

114. See CM Res. CM/ResDH(2014)289 (December 17, 2014); Doc. DH-DD(2014)1417E (November 20, 2014).

115. Donald and Leach 2016, 289–290.

116. See CM Res. CM/ResDH(2017)119 (April 19, 2017).

117. Convention on the Transfer of Sentenced Persons (March 21, 1983), ETS No. 112.

118. *Smith* and *Buijen* (both April 1, 2010).

119. *Buijen*, paras. 24–25, 31.

120. *Buijen* and *Smith*: Final Action Report, COE Doc. DH-DD(2017)326 (March, 20, 2017), 2.

121. The relevant provision is sec. 23, Einführungsgesetz zum Gerichtsverfassungsgesetz (Introductory Act to the Courts Constitution Act).

122. *Buijen* and *Smith*: Final Action Report, 5.

Chapter 10

1. See CM/ResDH(2013)244 (December 5, 2013) (*Rumpf* and seventy other cases), which includes a list of the judgments covered. Just satisfaction, when awarded, had been paid and sixty-six of the seventy-one domestic proceedings had been concluded by the time of the final resolution, with the remaining ones reportedly "being rapidly pursued." See Communication from Germany Concerning the *Rumpf* Group of Cases against Germany, Doc. DH-DD(2013)1234 (November 14, 2013).

2. As noted by Kielmansegg (2008, 284), two earlier judgments slated for the adoption of final resolutions as late as December 2010 were later rejoined with the other judgments of the *Rumpf* group of cases.

3. *Rumpf* (September 2, 2010), para. 70 (emphasis added).

4. Donald and Leach 2016, 291.

5. Ibid., para. 73. The judgment became final on December 2, 2011.

6. Ibid., para. 72.

7. *Sürmeli* (June 8, 2006), para. 99

8. Ibid., para. 100.

9. Brett 2009, 317.

10. FCC, Order of April 30, 2003, case no. 1 PBvU 1/02.

11. See Gesetz über die Rechtsbehelfe bei Verletzung des Anspruchs auf rechtliches Gehör (Act on Legal Remedies in Case of Violation of the Right of to be Heard by a Court) (December 9, 2004), *Bundesgesetzblatt* (Federal Law Gazette), part 1, no. 66 (2004), 3220.

12. See *Bundestags-Drucksache* 16/7655 (December 28, 2007), 1.

13. *Sürmeli* (June 8, 2006), para. 90.

14. *Bundestags-Drucksache* 16/7655 (December 28, 2007), 2, 4; Marx and Roderfeld 2012, 22; *Rumpf* (September 2, 2010), para. 33.

15. The draft bill was already noted in the *Rumpf* judgment, (September 2, 2010), paras. 33–34, 58, but the Court nonetheless applied the pilot judgment procedure because it remained uncertain if and when the bill would become law; ibid., para. 72.

16. See Gesetz über den Rechtsschutz bei überlangen Gerichtsverfahren und strafrechtlichen Ermittlungsverfahren (Act on Legal Redress for Excessive Length of Court Proceedings and of Criminal Investigation Proceedings) (November 24, 2011), *Bundesgesetzblatt* (Federal Law Gazette), part 1, no. 60 (2011), 2302.

17. Subject to some differences in comparison to ordinary courts; see Steinhorst 2013.

18. *Bundestags-Drucksache* 17/3802 (November 17, 2010), 20.

19. Ibid., 16.

20. Marx and Roderfeld 2012, 74, 89, 158 (concerning the FCC); Pietron 2016, 179–191 (calling the reprimand an ineffective "pseudo-remedy").

21. "The Court accepts that the Remedy Act was enacted to address the issue of excessive length of domestic proceedings in an effective and meaningful manner." *Taron* and *Garcia Cancio* (Decisions of May 29, 2012), paras. 40, 47, respectively.

22. Bundesrechtsanwaltskammer 2011, 5, para 6.

23. Marx and Roderfeld 2012, 76.

24. Ibid., 75, 76; Pietron 2016, 181–184; Deutscher Richterbund 2011, para. 5.

25. *Bundestags-Drucksache* 17/3802, (November 17, 2010), 20.

26. Marx and Roderfeld 2012, 75n244. Bundesrechtsanwaltskammer 2011, 8, para. 10.

27. Donald and Leach 2016, 290.

28. Bundesrechtsanwaltskammer 2011, 4, para. 4.

29. Deutscher Richterbund 2011, paras. 5, 2.

30. European Commission for Democracy through Law (Venice Commission) 2006, 18–22.

31. Kielmansegg 2008, 284.

32. *Elsholz* (July 13, 2000), para. 53.

33. *Hoffmann* (October 11, 2001), para. 60; *Sahin* and *Sommerfeld* (both July 8, 2003), para. 95, paras. 94, 98, respectively. The latter two cases had been referred to the Grand Chamber by the government after the chamber judgments had adopted the *Hoffmann* reasoning; the chamber judgments had been rendered together with the one in *Hoffmann* on October 11, 2001.

34. *Sommerfeld*, para. 93.

35. See Gesetz zur Reform des Kindschaftsrechts (Act to Reform the Law on Family Matters) (December 16, 1997), *Bundesgesetzblatt* (Federal Law Gazette), part 1, no. 84 (1997), 2942.

36. See CM Res. ResDH(2001)155 (December 17, 2001) (*Elsholz*); ResDH(2004)5 (February 24, 2004) (*Hoffmann*); CM/ResDH(2010)17 (March 4, 2010) (*Sahin, Sommerfeld*). The *Sommerfeld* case also involved discrimination with respect to the possibility of lodging certain appeals proceedings under former sec. 63a, Gesetz über die Angelegenheiten der freiwilligen Gerichtsbarkeit (Act on Non-Contentious Proceedings) to decisions denying access, available only to divorced fathers, but not unmarried ones; the provision was also repealed as part of the 1997 reform.

37. See, similarly, Kielmansegg 2008, 294.

38. See Greßmann 1998, 10–16; Entwurf eines Gesetzes zur Reform des Kindschaftsrechts (Draft Bill on Reforming the Law on Family Matters), *Bundestags-Drucksache* 13/4899 (June 13, 1996) and *Bundesrats-Drucksache* 180/96 (March 22, 1996), 56, 58–59, 103–104, 115.

39. FCC, Judgment of January 29, 2003, case no. 1 BvL 20/99.

40. *Zaunegger* (December 3, 2009), para. 63.

41. Gesetz zur Reform der elterlichen Sorge nicht miteinander verheirateter Eltern (Act to Reform Parental Custody of Parents Not Married to Each Other) (April 16, 2013, entry into force May 19, 2013), *Bundesgesetzblatt* (Federal Law Gazette), part 1, no. 18 (2013), 795.

42. FCC, Order of July 21, 2010, case no. 1 BvR 420/09.

43. Entwurf eines Gesetzes zur Reform der elterlichen Sorge nicht miteinander verheirateter Eltern (Draft Bill to Reform Parental Custody of Parents Not Married to Each Other), *Bundesrats-Drucksache* 465/12 (August 19, 2012), 1, 8–9.

44. See ibid., 10.

45. If the mother remains silent in response to a father's application or does not advance any plausible concerns, and if the court is not aware of any reasons arguing against joint custody, then the assumption is that joint custody is beneficial for the child and is to be awarded in a simplified procedure; ibid., 11.

46. See CM Res. CM/ResDH(2014)163 (September 25, 2014); Doc. DH-DD(2013)698E (June 19, 2013). As to individual measures, the applicant has had regular contact with his child while ECtHR proceedings were ongoing.

47. *Niedzwiecki* and *Okpisz* (both October 25, 2005).

48. FCC, Order of July 6, 2004, case nos. 1 BvL 4/97, 1 BvL 5/97, 1 BvL 6/97.

49. See Gesetz zur Anspruchsberechtigung von Ausländern wegen Kindergeld, Erziehungsgeld und Unterhaltsvorschuss (Act on Entitlement of Foreigners with Respect to Child Benefits, Child-Raising Benefits and Child Support Advance Payments) (December 13, 2006), *Bundesgesetzblatt* (Federal Law Gazette), part 1, no. 60 (2006), 2915. Supervision of the case was closed following the law's adoption; see CM Res. CM/ResDH(2011)111 (September 14, 2011).

50. Entwurf eines Gesetzes zur Anspruchsberechtigung von Ausländern wegen Kindergeld, Erziehungsgeld und Unterhaltsvorschuss (Draft Bill on Entitlement of Foreigners with Respect to Child Benefits, Child-Raising Benefits and Child Support Advance Payments), *Bundestags-Drucksache* 16/1368 (May 3, 2006), 8.

51. Ibid., 9–10.

52. Ibid., passim.

53. See *Niedzwiecki*, para. 33; *Okpisz*, para. 34.

54. *Brauer* (May 28, 2009), paras. 21–22, 24.

55. Ibid., para. 43. The position has been reaffirmed in *Mitzinger* (Merits) (February 9, 2017).

56. Zweites Gesetz zur erbrechtlichen Gleichstellung nichtehelicher Kinder, zur Änderung der Zivilprozessordnung und der Abgabenordnung (Second Act for Equal Inheritance Rights for Children Born Outside of Marriage and for Amending the Code of Civil Procedure and the Fiscal Code), *Bundesgesetzblatt* (Federal Law Gazette), part 1, no. 17 (2011), 615. The Committee of Ministers closed the case on the basis of this law; see CM/ResDH(2012)83 (June 6, 2012).

57. See Entwurf eines Zweiten Gesetzes zur erbrechtlichen Gleichstellung nichtehelicher Kinder (Draft Second Act for Equal Inheritance Rights for Children Born Outside of Marriage), *Bundestag-Drucksache* 17/3305 (October 14, 2010), 7–8.

58. Statement by Ingrid Hönlinger (Bündnis 90/Die Grünen), *Deutscher Bundestag—Plenarprotokoll* 17/93 (February 24, 2011), 10607-B.

59. Ibid., 10607-C.

60. *Anayo* (December 21, 2010).

61. Former MP Marina Schuster (Free Democratic Party), quoted in Donald and Leach 2016, 297.

62. Gesetz zur Stärkung der Rechte des leiblichen, nicht rechtlichen Vaters (Act to Strengthen the Legal Position of Biological, Non-legal Fathers) (July 4, 2013), *Bundesgesetzblatt* (Federal Law Gazette), part 1, no. 36 (2013), 2176.

63. This addresses the issue in *Schneider* (September 15, 2011), where the paternity of a man who had been in a longer-term relationship with a married woman that soon after the relationship ended bore a child had remained unclear. Under German law at the time, children born in wedlock were automatically considered the husband's children; the family had refused the applicant's request to establish paternity, and the courts had denied contact with the child. The ECtHR, by contrast, argued that the determination of what is in the best interest of the child always requires a case-by-case analysis—here, whether to grant access—even if biological descent was merely assumed and not proven.

64. Entwurf eines Gesetzes zur Stärkung der Rechte des leiblichen, nicht rechtlichen Vaters (Draft Bill to Strengthen the Legal Position of Biological, Non-legal Fathers), *Bundesrats-Drucksache* 666/12 (November 2, 2012), 1, 7.

65. Ibid., 8–9.

66. As favored by the opposition Green Party, see Statement by Ingrid Hönliger (Bündnis 90/Die Grünen), *Deutscher Bundestag—Plenarprotokoll* 17/237, April 25, 2013, 29847B-C.

67. See CM Res. CM/ResDH(2017)63 (February 22, 2017) and Communication from Germany Concerning the Cases of Anayo and Schneider against Germany, Final Action Report, Doc. DH-DD(2016)1431 (December 21, 2016).

68. Federal Court of Justice, Order of October 5, 2016, case no. XII ZB 180/15.

69. Ibid., para. 16.

70. Ibid., para. 35–36.

71. Ibid., paras. 52–60.

72. *Anayo*, para. 71.

73. *Luedicke, Belkacem and Koç* (Merits) (November 28, 1978); *Luedicke, Belkacem and Koç* (Just Satisfaction) (March 10, 1980).

74. For the relevant domestic law, see *Luedicke, Belkacem and Koç* (Merits), paras. 11–14.

75. *Luedicke, Belkacem and Koç* (Merits), paras. 38, 41.

76. See Kieschke 2003, 79–80.

77. *Luedicke, Belkacem and Koç* (Merits), para. 40.

78. See Entwurf eines Gesetzes zur Änderung der Bundesgebührenordnung für Rechtsanwälte (Draft Bill on Modifying the Federal Scale of Lawyers' Fees), *Bundestags-Drucksache* 8/3691 (February 22, 1980), 22, and *Bundesrats-Drucksache* 1979/637, 60, quoted in Kieschke 2003, 77.

79. See No. 1904, Kostenverzeichnis zum Gerichtskostengesetz (Schedule of Court Costs Act), introduced by Fünftes Gesetz zur Änderung der Bundesgebührenordnung für Rechtsanwälte (Fifth Act on Modifying the Federal Scale of Lawyers' Fees) (August 18, 1980), *Bundesgesetzblatt* (Federal Law Gazette), part 1, no. 51 (1980), 1503, 1506–1507.

80. See statement by the German agent before the Court, made on another occasion, in which she argued that "supervision by the Committee of Ministers as to whether the State concerned executed the judgment, must be limited to the concrete case decided by the Court. Future similar cases must be left out of consideration" (Maier 1988, 1042).

81. See Bartsch 1988 and CM Res. DH(83)4 (March 23, 1983).

82. Öztürk (Merits) (February 21, 1984); Öztürk (Just Satisfaction) (October 23, 1984); for a detailed discussion of the case and its execution, see Kieschke 2003, 94–118.

83. See Öztürk (Merits), para. 49.

84. Ibid., para. 53.

85. Six of the eighteen judges issued dissenting opinions; see ibid.

86. See *Lutz* (August 25, 1987), para. 53.

87. See *Akdogan* (Comm. rep.) (July 5, 1988); *Zengin* (Comm. rep.) (December 12, 1988).

88. See *Rajaratnam* (dec.) (July 13, 1987); *Karabulut* and *Cavusoglu* (decs.) (October 11, 1989); *Shanmukanathan* and *R.R.* (decs.) (July 13, 1990). The applications in these cases had been lodged between July 1985 and October 1988.

89. Kieschke 2003, 102–103, 113.

90. The amended text of the relevant provision, currently located at No. 9005 (4) Kostenverzeichnis zum Gerichtskostengesetz (Schedule of Court Costs Act), cites to sec. 464, lit. c and sec. 467 (2) of the Strafprozessordnung (*Code of Criminal Procedure*), which allow the imposition of court costs if culpably caused by the defendant through delays or in an otherwise unnecessary manner. This exception applies to criminal and misdemeanor proceedings alike.

91. *Garcia Alva*; *Lietzow*; *Schöps* (all February 13, 2001).

92. See Gesetz zur Änderung und Ergänzung des Strafverfahrensrechts (Act to Modify and Complement the Law of Criminal Procedure) (August 2, 2000), *Bundesgesetzblatt* (Federal Law Gazette), part 1, no. 38 (2000), 1253–1262; the Court had noted the legal reform in its judgments; see *Garcia Alva*, para.27; *Lietzow*, para. 32; *Schöps*, para. 33.

93. See sec. 147 (5), Strafprozessordnung (*Code of Criminal Procedure*).

94. See CM Res. ResDH(2003)2 (*Garcia Alva*); ResDH(2003)3 (*Lietzow*); ResDH(2003)4 (*Schöps*) (all adopted February 24, 2003).

95. The applications in these cases had been lodged on January 4, March 4, and July 4, 1994.

96. See Lamy v. Belgium (March 30, 1989), para. 29; Nikolova v. Bulgaria (March 25, 1999), para. 63. For the contentious discussions in Germany on the effect of the *Lamy* decision on the interpretation of the pre-reform sec. 147 (2), *Code of Criminal Procedure*, see Kettner 2002, 122–131. For the broader point of the equality of arms between defendant and prosecutor, see Sanchez-Reisse v. Switzerland (October 21, 1986), para. 51; Toth v. Austria (December 12, 1991), para. 84.

97. See Entwurf eines Gesetzes zur Änderung und Ergänzung des Strafverfahrensrechts (Draft Bill to Modify and Complement the Law of Criminal Procedure), *Bundesrats-Drucksache* 65/99 (February 5, 1999), 43–44, and *Bundestags-Drucksache* 14/1484 (August 16, 1999), 21–22.

98. Debates have arisen as to whether the right of access relates to the entire file or only those parts that are relevant for keeping the defendant apprised of the reasons for his or her detention; see Renzikowski 2004, 113–114; Kühne and Esser 2002, 390–392.

99. *Mooren* (July 9, 2009), paras. 124–125. The case also involved a violation of Article 5 (4) ECHR as a result of excessively lengthy appellate proceedings. This violation resulted from the specifics of the case, however, and did not require any general measures.

100. See Article 1, no. 10, lit. a and b, Gesetz zur Änderung des Untersuchungshaftrechts (Act to Modify the Law on Detention on Remand) (July 29, 2009), *Bundesgesetzblatt* (Federal Law Gazette), part 1, no. 48 (2009), 2274 (the latter modifying sec. 147 [7] of the *Code of Criminal Procedure* to expand the right of access to information to defendants without counsel).

101. See Entwurf eines Gesetzes zur Änderung des Untersuchungshaftrechts (Draft Bill to Modify the Law on Detention on Remand), *Bundestags-Drucksache* 16/11644 (January 21, 2009), 34.

102. See Beulke 2012, 75.

103. *von Hannover* (Merits) (June 24, 2004).

104. For a summary of the proceedings in the civil courts, see ibid., paras. 18–23, 27–38.

105. FCC, Judgment of December 12, 1999, case no. 1 BvR 653/96. For an analysis of the domestic legal situation prior to the ECtHR judgment, see Eckstein and Altenhofen 2006, 13–42.

106. *von Hannover* (Merits), para. 72.

107. Ibid., paras. 76–77.

108. See, e.g., Michael Hanfeld, "Europas Richter hebeln die Pressefreiheit aus," *Frankfurter Allgemeine Zeitung* (June 24, 2004), 46; Dieter Grimm, "Es trifft die Pressefunktion in ihrem Kern," *Frankfurter Allgemeine Zeitung* (July 14, 2004), 34; Michael Hanfeld, "Zwischen den Zeilen," *Frankfurter Allgemeine Zeitung* (September 1, 2004), 36; Dominik Cziesche et al., "Zwangsjacke für die Presse," *Der Spiegel* 35/2004 (August 23, 2004), 140–143.

109. See Hans Leyendecker, "Oh Caroline," *Süddeutsche Zeitung* (September 1, 2004), http://www.sueddeutsche.de/panorama/385/375194/text/.

110. See Sanderson 2004; Gersdorf 2005; Behnsen 2005; Prütting 2005; Starck 2005; Lenski 2005; Peters 2005; Barnes 2006; Nohlen 2006; Eckstein and Altenhofen 2006; Rudolf 2006; Hedigan 2007.

111. See letter from Verband Deutscher Zeitschriftenverleger (VDZ) to Chancellor Gerhard Schröder (Aug. 19, 2004), http://www.kanzlei-prof-schweizer.de/bibliothek/content /02647/index.html; VDZ, "Eine Niederlage für die Pressefreiheit" (September 1, 2004), http://www.vdz.de/nachricht/print/98/artikel/vdz-eine-niederlage-fuer-die-pressefreiheit/; Behnsen 2005, 239.

112. See Ansgar Graw and Christian Seel, "Bundesregierung akzeptiert Caroline-Urteil," *Die Welt* (September 2, 2004), http://www.welt.de/print-welt/article338012/Bundesregierung _akzeptiert_Caroline_Urteil.html.

113. See "Stellungnahme des Präsidenten des Bundesverfassungsgerichts zur Entscheidung der Bundesregierung im sogenannten Caroline-von-Hannover-Verfahren vor dem EGMR" (Statement by the President of the Federal Constitutional Court on the Decision by the Government in the so-called Caroline-von-Hannover proceedings before the ECtHR), Press Release No. 84/2004 (September 1, 2004).

114. See Institut für Urheber- und Medienrecht, "Caroline-Urteil: Verfassungsrichter bestätigt Haltung der Bundesregierung," News No. 2033 (October 12, 2004), http://www .urheberrecht.org/news/2033/.

115. See to this effect "Stellungnahme des Präsidenten des Bundesverfassungsgerichts," Press Release No. 84/2004 (September 1, 2004).

116. See Antwort der Bundesregierung auf die Kleine Anfrage der Abgeordneten Rainer Funke, weiterer Abgeordneter und der Fraktion der FDP (Drucksache 15/4079) (Reply by the Government to the Inquiry by Member of Parliament Rainer Funke, other Members of Parliament, and the Group of the FDP), *Bundestags-Drucksache* 15/4210 (November 12, 2004), 4; Comment by Christian Starck, in Prütting 2005, 49–50.

117. *von Hannover* (Just Satisfaction/Friendly Settlement) (July 28, 2005).

118. Haug 2011, 41–55, 225.

119. FCJ (Civil Panel VI), Judgment of March 6, 2007, case no. VI ZR 13/06, 9–10 (my translation). The case was one of several on the issue of celebrity photos decided the same day; see "Neue Entscheidungen zur Veröffentlichung von Bildern prominenter Personen," Press Release No. 34/2007 (March 6, 2007).

120. FCC, Order of February 26, 2008, case nos. 1 BvR 1602/07, 1 BvR 1606/07, 1 BvR 1626/07.

121. Ibid., paras. 81–82.

122. Ibid., paras. 62–64.

123. Ibid., paras. 104, 105 (my translation).

124. *von Hannover* (Merits), paras. 72–73.

125. See Messing 2007, 66, 84–86.

126. Quoted in *von Hannover (no. 2)* (February 7, 2012), para. 91.

127. VDZ, "Eine Niederlage für die Pressefreiheit," http://www.vdz.de/nachricht/print/98/artikel/vdz-eine-niederlage-fuer-die-pressefreiheit/.

128. *von Hannover (no. 2)* (February 7, 2012); *Axel Springer AG* (February 7, 2012); *von Hannover (no. 3)* (September 19, 2013); *Bohlen* and *Ernst August von Hanover* (both February 19, 2015) (both concerning the use of the applicants' names in advertising); *Kahn* (March 17, 2016).

129. These include (1) the contribution to a debate of general interest; (2) whether the person is a private person or a public figure; (3) the person's own prior conduct, (4) the content and modalities of a picture's and accompanying report's publication; and (5) the circumstances in which the pictures were taken; see *von Hannover* (no. 2), paras. 109–113.

130. *von Hannover (no. 2)* (February 7, 2012), paras. 124–126; see also *von Hannover (no. 3)* (September 19, 2013), para. 57.

131. While the Court found a violation of Article 10 ECHR in *Axel Springer AG* (February 7, 2012), due to disproportionate injunctions against the applicant company prohibiting reports on the arrest and conviction of a well-known TV persona, the other judgments resulted in findings of no violation.

132. *M.* (December 17, 2009).

133. Ibid., paras. 52–53.

134. Quoted in ibid., para. 32.

135. Ibid., paras. 100, 102, 103.

136. Ibid., paras. 133–137.

137. The preventive detention regime yielded a number of further judgments against Germany. Six of these paralleled the fact patterns in *M.*—*Kallweit*, *Mautes*, and *Schummer* (all January 13, 2011); *Jendrowiak* (April 14, 2011); *O.H.* (November 24, 2011); *Kronfeldner* (January 19, 2012). Three involved the related issue of the subsequent transferal into preventive detention of criminals who had to be released from mental health institutions because the mental incapacity

issues that had resulted in their committal no longer existed, even though the possibility of such a transferal had not been legally provided for at the time when they committed their offenses; see *K.* and *G.* (both June 7, 2012); *S.* (June 28, 2012). Two concerned the possibility to order preventive detention not only at the moment of initial sentencing, but also later, after the prison sentence had already been (mostly) served; see *B.* (April 19, 2012) and *Haidn* (January 13, 2011) (the violation here resulted from the application of state law in Bavaria). Last but not least, the judgment in *Glien* (November 28, 2013) concerned the fact, among other things, that the applicant had been preventively detained in a prison wing, rather than a clinic or mental health institution, without appropriate medical and therapeutic offerings for a person of unsound mind.

138. See Koalitionsvertrag zwischen CDU, CSU und FDP, 17. Legislaturperiode (Coalition Agreement between CDU, CSU and FDP, 17th Legislative Period), 107, https://www.bmi.bund .de/SharedDocs/Downloads/DE/Ministerium/koalitionsvertrag.pdf?__blob=publicationFile.

139. Gesetz zur Neuordnung des Rechts der Sicherungsverwahrung und zu begleitenden Regelungen (Act to Reform the Law on Preventive Detention and on Accompanying Provisions) (December 22, 2010), *Bundesgesetzblatt* (Federal Law Gazette), part 1, no. 68 (2010), 2300 (includes Gesetz zur Therapierung und Unterbringung psychisch gestörter Gewalttäter (Therapieunterbringungsgesetz, ThUG) (Act on Therapy and Detention of Mentally Disturbed Violent Offenders [Therapy Detention Act]).

140. See sec. 66 (1), no. 1, *Strafgesetzbuch* (*German Criminal Code*, English translation available at https://www.gesetze-im-internet.de/englisch_stgb/).

141. Remde 2012, 59. According to one author, for about forty-five persons in preventive detention in March 2010 (8.4 percent of the total), the previous convictions had been primarily for fraud and stealing; Kinzig 2011, 178.

142. See Kinzig 2011, 178; Koalitionsvertrag zwischen CDU, CSU und FDP, 107, https:// www.bmi.bund.de/SharedDocs/Downloads/DE/Ministerium/koalitionsvertrag.pdf?__blob= publicationFile.

143. See sec. 66a, *Strafgesetzbuch* (*German Criminal Code*).

144. See ibid., sec. 66b (introduced in 2004).

145. Ibid., sec. 66b, no. 2 (my translation).

146. *Bundestags-Drucksache* 17/3403 (October 26, 2010), 15. The limited effectiveness of the 2004 arrangement had partly to do with restrictive manner in which the courts reviewed requests by the prosecution for ordering retrospective preventive detention: Of fifty-five cases dealt with by the Federal Court of Justice, the highest criminal court, between May 2005 and May 2009, their lawfulness was upheld in only eleven instances (20 percent); see Alex 2010, 27ff.

147. *Bundestags-Drucksache* 17/3403 (October 26, 2010), 33.

148. Ibid., 16, 33.

149. Ibid., 19.

150. Ibid., 54 (my translation); see further Dittmann 2012; Nußstein 2011, 1196.

151. *Bundestags-Drucksache* 17/3403 (October 26, 2010), 54–55.

152. See, e.g., Kinzig 2011, 182; Mahler and Pfäfflin 2012; Schöch 2012, 51; de Tribolet-Hardy, Lehner, and Habermeyer 2015, 169.

153. The title of the article by de Tribolet-Hardy, Lehner, and Habermeyer (2015).

154. See Müller et al. (2011) (speaking, inter alia, of an "abuse of psychiatry" and the "dilution of psychiatric concepts" by the Therapy Detention Act).

155. Höffler and Stadtland 2012, 244.

156. FCC, Judgment of May 4, 2011, case nos. 2 BvR 2365/09, 2 BvR 740/10, 2 BvR 2333/08.

157. The government responded to the FCC's judgment demand for remedial legislation by adopting the Gesetz zur bundesrechtlichen Umsetzung des Abstandsgebotes im Recht der Sicherungsverwahrung (Act to Effect Implementation under Federal Law of the Distance Requirement in the Law Governing Preventive Detention) (December 5, 2012), *Bundesgesetzblatt* (Federal Law Gazette), part 1, no. 57 (2012), 2425. For commentary, see Renzikowski 2013.

158. As had been suggested by the ECtHR in *M.* (December 17, 2009), para. 103.

159. For an interesting analysis of the FCC's reaction to the ECtHR's decisions concerning preventive detention, characterized first as "heteronomy," then "self-assertion," and eventually "liberation," see Volkmann 2011.

160. See CM Res. CM/ResDH(2014)290 (December 17, 2014) and Doc. DH-DD(2014)1463 (December 1, 2014). Three further judgments dealing with preventive detention concerned individual violations limited to the case at issue: *Schönbrod* (November 24, 2011) (delay of more than nine months in replacing expired detention order); *Rangelov* (March 22, 2012) (no therapeutic offerings in view of applicant's future expulsion); *H.W.* (September 19, 2013) (delay in reviewing continuation of preventive detention and failure to obtain fresh expert opinion).

161. This aspect of the preventive detention regime has, in its revised form, been deemed Convention-compliant by the ECtHR, see *Müller* (dec.) (February 10, 2015).

162. *Glien* (November 28, 2013), para. 87.

163. Ibid., paras. 89, 92ff. (violation due to preventive detention in a prison).

164. *Bergmann* (January 7, 2016), para. 114; *Petschulies* (June 2, 2016), para. 78; *W.P.* (October 6, 2016), para. 61.

165. Alex 2010, 45–46, 79, 133–134; see also Donald and Leach 2016, 288.

166. Peglau 2016.

167. Giegerich 2014, 233.

168. Nußberger 2014, 170.

169. *Karlheinz Schmidt* (July 18, 1994).

170. See CM Res. DH(96)100 (March 22, 1996).

171. See FCC, Order of October 17, 1961, case no. 1 BvL 5/61 (affirming the relevant law's constitutionality).

172. FCC, Order of January 24, 1995, case no. 1 BvL 18/93 and others; references to the ECtHR's judgment can be found in paras. 33, 48, 61, 91, 93, 99, 100.

173. Note that in order to eliminate gender discrimination, fire service duties and fire service levies could have also been extended to women as well, but this was apparently not a politically feasible option.

174. *Herz* (June 12, 2003).

175. See FCC, Order of April 30, 1997, case no. 2 BvR 817/90 et al.; Order of May 10, 1998, case no. 2 BvR 978/97; Order of December 5, 2001, case no. 2 BvR 527/99 et al.

176. See *Herz*, paras. 39, 67; CM Res. CM/ResDH(2011)110 (September 14, 2011).

177. *Jalloh* (July 11, 2006).

178. Ibid., para. 33.

179. Lück 2008, 201–203; Donald and Leach 2016, 284.

180. The violation of Article 6 (1) was seen as sufficiently remedied by the direct effect of the Convention in Germany so that courts in the future would have to take into account the ECtHR's jurisprudence on this issue; see CM Res. CM/ResDH(2010)53 (June 3, 2010).

Chapter 11

1. See Papier 2006, 4 (record of execution of ECtHR judgments in Germany "look[s] comparatively good"); Müller and Gusy 2013, 43 ("Once a judgment is delivered, the judicial and administrative systems generally function effectively and provide a range of execution mechanisms"); Zimmermann 2001, 353 (Germany has "usually tried to bring German law into conformity with the Convention").

2. Müller and Gusy 2013, 28.

3. As a former FCC president has noted, the "openness towards international law has its effects only within the [. . .] framework of the Basic Law's democratic system under the rule of law," and he admonished the ECtHR to "resist the temptation of intervening too much in ruling on individual cases in the way a non-constitutional court of appeal would" (Papier 2006, 3).

4. Cf. Lambert Abdelgawad and Weber 2008, 137 ("In Germany, a certain tension, if not a conflict, appears to exist between the German judges, in particular the Federal Constitutional Court, and the ECtHR"), 158 (noting "conflicting and competitive aspects" between the FCC and ECtHR).

5. For an overview, see generally Council of Europe, Steering Committee of Human Rights (CDDH), Information Submitted by Member States with Regard to the Implementation of the Five Recommendations Mentioned in the Declaration Adopted by the Committee of Ministers at Its 114th Session (May 12, 2004), Doc. CDDH(2006)008 Addendum III Bil (April 7, 2006), 64 (on file with author).

6. See Entwurf eines Zweiten Gesetzes zur Modernisierung der Justiz (Draft Second Act on Modernizing the Judiciary), *Bundestags-Drucksache* 16/3038 (October 19, 2006), 40.

7. See *Baader, Meins, Meinhof, Grundmann* (Comm'n dec.) (May 30, 1975).

8. See *Streletz, Kessler and Krenz* (March 22, 2001).

9. See *Jahn and Others* (June 30, 2005).

10. See *von Maltzan and Others, von Zitzewitz and Others, MAN Ferrostaal and Alfred Töpfer Stiftung* (dec.) (March 2, 2005).

11. Dothan 2015; on different standards for different countries, see also Dembour 2006, 51.

12. Donald and Leach 2016, 301–302.

Conclusion

1. See Jordan et al. 2009, 30 (71 percent of 2,724 international relations scholars from ten countries participating in the 2008 Theory and Practice of International Relations (TRIP) survey characterized their research orientation as either rationalist, constructivist, or both). In the 2011 version of the survey, covering twenty countries and 3,464 respondents, the question was asked differently, with 7 percent declaring that they employ a rational choice framework in their research, 46 percent saying they use a rationalist, though not strictly rational choice, approach, and 47 percent responding that they do not assume the rationality of actors; 22 percent of respondents identified as constructivists; see Maliniak, Peterson, and Tierney 2012, 26–27.

2. Notably, the modal answer to the question of how best to characterize respondents' work in the 2008 TRIP survey was "both rationalist and constructivist" (29 percent); Jordan et al. 2009, 30.

3. Hillebrecht 2014, 42–43 (emphasis in the original).

4. Alter 2014, 335.

5. For a discussion, see, e.g., Martinsen 2015a, 24–34.

6. See, e.g., Ginsburg 2014.

7. Marmo 2008.

8. Krisch 2008. 185.

9. On Italy, see, e.g., von Staden 2009, 202–228; on France, see Krisch 2008, 191–196.

10. See, e.g., Martin 2013.

11. See, e.g., Helfer and Voeten 2014 for evidence as to this effect.

12. Chayes and Chayes 1991.

13. de Gaay Fortman 2011, 76.

BIBLIOGRAPHY

Note on Internet sources: All website URLs in this bibliography as well as those appearing in the endnotes of the preceding chapters have been checked and are current as of June 16, 2017.

Abdelal, Rawi, Yoshiko M. Herrera, Alastair Iain Johnston, and Rose McDermott. 2009a. "Introduction." In Rawi Abdelal, Yoshiko M. Herrera, Alastair Iain Johnston, and Rose McDermott, eds., *Measuring Identity: A Guide for Social Scientists*, 1–13. Cambridge: Cambridge University Press.

———. 2009b. "Identity as a Variable." In Rawi Abdelal, Yoshiko M. Herrera, Alastair Iain Johnston, and Rose McDermott, eds., *Measuring Identity: A Guide for Social Scientists*, 17–32. Cambridge: Cambridge University Press.

Alex, Michael. 2010. *Nachträgliche Sicherungsverwahrung—Ein rechtsstaatliches und kriminalpolitisches Debakel*. Holzkirchen: Felix-Verlag.

Allee, Todd L., and Paul K. Huth. 2006. "Legitimizing Dispute Settlement: International Legal Rulings as Domestic Political Cover." *American Political Science Review* 100 (2): 219–234.

Allen, Jonathan, ed. 2006. *Policing and the Criminal Justice System—Public Confidence and Perceptions: Findings from the 2004/05 British Crime Survey*. London: Research Development and Statistics Directorate, Home Office. http://webarchive.nationalarchives.gov.uk/20100405140447/http:/www.homeoffice.gov.uk/rds/pdfs06/rdsolr0706.pdf.

Alter, Karen J. 2014. *The New Terrain of International Law: Courts, Politics, Rights*. Princeton, N.J.: Princeton University Press.

———. 2009. *The European Court's Political Power: Selected Essays*. New York: Oxford University Press.

———. 2001. *Establishing the Supremacy of European Law: The Making of an International Rule of Law in Europe*. Oxford: Oxford University Press.

Alter, Karen J., Laurence R. Helfer, and Mikael Rask Madsen. 2016. "How Context Shapes the Authority of International Courts." *Law and Contemporary Problems* 79 (1): 1–36.

Anagnostou, Dia, ed. 2013. *The European Court of Human Rights: Implementing Strasbourg's Judgments on Domestic Policy*. Edinburgh: Edinburgh University Press.

Anagnostou, Dia, and Alina Mungiu-Pippidi. 2014. "Domestic Implementation of Human Rights Judgments in Europe: Legal Infrastructure and Government Effectiveness Matter." *European Journal of International Law* 25: 205–227.

Arnardóttir, Oddný Mjöll, and Antoine Buyse, eds. 2016. *Shifting Centres of Gravity in Human Rights Protection: Rethinking Relations between the ECHR, EU, and National Legal Orders*. London: Routledge.

Arnold, William, 2010. "The Supreme Court of the United Kingdom: 'Something Old' and 'Something New.'" *Commonwealth Law Bulletin* 36 (3): 443–451.

Arold, Nina-Louisa. 2007. *The Legal Culture of the European Court of Human Rights.* Leiden: Martinus Nijhoff.

Barak, Aharon. 2006. *The Judge in a Democracy.* Princeton, N.J.: Princeton University Press.

———. 2005. *Purposive Interpretation in Law.* Princeton, N.J.: Princeton University Press.

Barkhuysen, Tom, and Michiel L. van Emmerik. 2005. "A Comparative View on the Execution of Judgments of the European Court of Human Rights." In Theodora A. Christou and Juan Pablo Raymond, eds., *European Court of Human Rights: Remedies and Execution of Judgments,* 1–24. London: British Institute of International and Comparative Law.

Barnes, Robin D. 2006. "The Caroline Verdict: Protecting Individual Privacy Against Media Invasion as a Matter of Human Rights." *Penn State Law Review* 110 (3): 599–614.

Bartsch, Hans-Jürgen. 1988. "The Supervisory Function of the Committee of Ministers Under Article 54: A Postscript to Luedicke-Belkacem-Koç." In Franz Matscher and Herbert Petzold, eds., *Protecting Human Rights—The European Dimension: Studies in Honour of Gérard J. Wiarda,* 47–54. Cologne: Carl Heymanns.

Bates, Ed. 2015. "The UK and Strasbourg: A Strained Relationship—The Long View." In Katja S. Ziegler, Elizabeth Wicks, and Loveday Hodson, eds., *The UK and European Human Rights: A Strained Relationship?,* 39–69. Oxford: Hart.

———. 2014. "Analyzing the Prisoner Voting Saga and the British Challenge to Strasbourg." *Human Rights Law Review* 14: 503–540.

———. 2011. "The Birth of the European Convention on Human Rights—and the European Court of Human Rights." In Mikael Rask Madsen and Jonas Christofferson, eds., *The European Court of Human Rights Between Law and Politics,* 17–42. Oxford: Oxford University Press.

———. 2010. *The Evolution of the European Convention on Human Rights: From Its Inception to the Creation of a Permanent Court of Human Rights.* Oxford: Oxford University Press.

Baxter, J. D. 1986. "Privacy and the Maintenance of State Advantage." *Cambrian Law Review* 17: 10–26.

Beach, Derek J. 2005. "Why Governments Comply: An Integrative Compliance Model that Bridges the Gap Between Instrumental and Normative Models of Compliance." *Journal of European Public Policy* 12 (1): 113–142.

Behnsen, Alexander. 2005. "Das Recht auf Privatleben und die Pressefreiheit—Die Entscheidung des Europäischen Gerichtshofs für Menschenrechte in der Sache *Hannover ./. Deutschland.*" *Zeitschrift für ausländisches öffentliches Recht und Völkerrecht* 65: 239–255.

Belkin, Aaron and R. L. Evans. 2000. "The Effects of Including Gay and Lesbian Soldiers in the British Armed Forces: Appraising the Evidence." Center for the Study of Sexual Minorities in the Military, UC Santa Barbara, http://escholarship.org/uc/item/433055x9.

Berman, Paul Schiff. 2012. *Global Legal Pluralism: A Jurisprudence of Law Beyond Borders.* Cambridge: Cambridge University Press.

Besson, Samantha. 2008. "The Reception Process in Ireland and the United Kingdom." In Helen Keller and Alex Stone Sweet, eds., *A Europe of Rights: The Impact if the ECHR on National Legal Systems,* 31–106. Oxford: Oxford University Press.

Beulke, Werner. 2012. "Der Beitrag des Europäischen Gerichtshofs für Menschenrechte zur Entwicklung des deutschen Verfahrensrechts aus Sicht eines deutschen Strafverteidigers." In Armin Höland, ed., *Wirkungen der Rechtsprechung des Europäischen Gerichtshofs für Menschenrechte im deutschen Recht,* 71–82. Berlin: Berliner Wissenschafts-Verlag.

Birkinshaw, Patrick. 1983. "Legal Order and Prison Administration." *Northern Ireland Legal Quarterly* 34 (4): 269–291.

———. 1981. "The Closed Society—Complaints Mechanisms and Disciplinary Proceedings in Prison." *Northern Ireland Legal Quarterly* 32 (2): 117–157.

Blackburn, Robert, and Jörg Polakiewicz, eds. 2001. *Fundamental Rights in Europe: The ECHR and Its Member States, 1950–2000.* Oxford: Oxford University Press.

Böckenförde, Ernst-Wolfgang, Christian Tomuschat, and Dieter C. Umbach, eds. 1981. *Extremisten und öffentlicher Dienst: Rechtslage und Praxis des Zugangs zum und der Entlassung aus dem öffentlichen Dienst in Westeuropa, USA, Jugoslawien und der EG.* Baden-Baden: Nomos.

Bonner, David. 1979. "The Beginning of the End for Corporal Punishment?" *Modern Law Review* 42 (5): 580–586.

Bowling, Ben, and Coretta Phillips. 2007. "Disproportionate and Discriminatory: Reviewing the Evidence on Police Stop and Search." *Modern Law Review* 70 (6): 936–961.

Boyle, Elizabeth Heger, and Melissa Thompson. 2001. "National Politics and Resort to the European Commission on Human Rights." *Law and Society Review* 35 (2): 321–344.

Braunthal, Gerard. 1992. *Politische Loyalität und Öffentlicher Dienst: Der "Radikalenerlaß" von 1972 und die Folgen.* Marburg: Schüren.

Brennan, Geoffrey, Lina Eriksson, Robert E. Goodin, and Nicholas Southwood. 2013. *Explaining Norms.* Oxford: Oxford University Press.

Brett, Angela. 2009. *Verfahrensdauer bei Verfassungsbeschwerdeverfahren im Horizont der Rechtsprechung des Europäischen Gerichtshofs für Menschenrechte zu Art. 6 Abs. 1 S. 1 EMRK.* Berlin: Duncker und Humblot.

Breuer, Marten. 2005. "Karlsruhe und die Gretchenfrage: Wie hast Du's mit Straßburg?" *Neue Zeitschrift für Verwaltungsrecht* 24 (4): 412–414.

Brewster, Rachel. 2009a. "The Limits of Reputation on Compliance." *International Theory* 1 (2): 323–333.

———. 2009b. "Unpacking the State's Reputation." *Harvard International Law Journal* 50 (2): 231–269.

Bruinsma, Fred J. 2006. "Judicial Identities in the European Court of Human Rights." In Aukje van Hoek, Antoine Hol, Oswald Jansen, Peter Rijpkema, and Rob Widdershoven, eds., *Multilevel Governance in Enforcement and Adjudication*, 203–240. Antwerp: Intersentia.

Bueno de Mesquita, Bruce, George W. Downs, Alastair Smith, and Feryal Marie Cherif. 2005. "Thinking Inside the Box: A Closer Look at Democracy and Human Rights." *International Studies Quarterly* 49: 439–457.

Bundesrechtsanwaltskammer. 2011. "Stellungnahme der Bundesrechtsanwaltskammer zum Regierungsentwurf eines Gesetzes über den Rechtsschutz bei überlangen Gerichtsverfahren und strafrechtlichen Ermittlungsverfahren—BT-Drucks. 17/3802 v. 17.11.2010." BRAK-Stellungnahme-Nr. 18/2011 (March). http://www.brak.de/zur-rechtspolitik/stellungnahmen-pdf/stellungnahmen-deutschland/2011/maerz/stellungnahme-der-brak-2011-18.pdf.

Burgorgue-Larsen, Laurence, and Amaya Úbeda de Torres. 2011. *The Inter-American Court of Human Rights: Case Law and Commentary.* Trans. Rosalind Greenstein. Oxford: Oxford University Press.

Çalı, Başak. 2007. "The Limits of International Justice at the European Court of Human Rights: Between Legal Cosmopolitanism and 'a Society of States.'" In Marie-Bénédicte Dembour and Tobias Kelly, eds., *Paths to International Justice: Social and Legal Perspectives*, 111–133. Cambridge: Cambridge University Press.

Çalı, Başak, and Anne Koch. 2014. "Foxes Guarding the Foxes? The Peer Review of Human Rights Judgments by the Committee of Ministers of the Council of Europe." *Human Rights Law Review* 14: 301–325.

———. 2011. "The Motivational Landscape of Compliance: An Ideational Analysis of Human Rights Judgments in Europe." Working paper presented at the Political Science Colloquium, Graduate Institute Geneva, March 24, 2011.

Callaghan, John. 2005. "The Plan to Capture the British Labour Party and Its Paradoxical Results, 1947–91." *Journal of Contemporary History* 40 (4): 707–725.

Cameron, Iain. 1986. "Telephone Tapping and the Interception Communications Act 1985." *Northern Ireland Legal Quarterly* 37 (2): 126–150.

Cao, Xun, Brian Greenhill, and Aseem Prakash. 2012. "Where Is the Tipping Point? Bilateral Trade and the Diffusion of Human Rights." *British Journal of Political Science* 43: 133–156.

Cardenas, Sonia. 2007. *Conflict and Compliance: State Responses to International Human Rights Pressure*. Philadelphia: University of Pennsylvania Press.

Carey, Sabine. 2009. *Protest, Repression and Political Regimes: An Empirical Analysis of Latin America and Sub-Saharan Africa*. Abingdon: Routledge.

Carey, Sabine, and Steven C. Poe, eds. 2004. *Understanding Human Rights Violations: New Systematic Studies*. Aldershot: Ashgate.

Carruba, Clifford J., and Matthew J. Gabel. 2015. *International Courts and the Performance of International Agreements: A General Theory with Evidence from the European Union*. Cambridge: Cambridge University Press.

Carruba, Clifford J., Matthew J. Gabel, and Charles Hankla. 2012. "Understanding the Role of the European Court of Justice in European Integration." *American Political Science Review* 106 (1): 214–223.

———. 2008. "Judicial Behavior Under Political Constraints: Evidence from the European Court of Justice." *American Political Science Review* 102 (4): 435–452.

Carter, Barry E., and Phillip R. Trimble. 1995. *International Law*. 2nd ed. Boston: Little, Brown.

Chapman, Becca, Catriona Mirrlees-Black, and Claire Brawn. 2002. *Improving Public Attitudes to the Criminal Justice System: The Impact of Information*. Home Office Research Study 245. London: Research, Development and Statistics Directorate, Home Office. https://www.prisonlegalnews.org/media/publications/home_office_research_study_245_improving_public_attitudes_on_the_criminal_justice_system_2002.pdf.

Chayes, Abram, and Antonia Handler Chayes. 1995. *The New Sovereignty: Compliance with International Regulatory Agreements*. Cambridge, Mass.: Harvard University Press.

———. 1991. "Compliance Without Enforcement: State Behavior Under Regulatory Treaties." *Negotiation Journal* 7 (3): 311–330.

Checkel, Jeffrey T. 2005. "International Institutions and Socialization in Europe: Introduction and Framework." *International Organization* 59: 801–826.

———. 2001. "Why Comply? Social Leaning and European Identity Change." *International Organization* 55 (3): 553–588.

———. 1999. "Norms, Institutions, and National Identity in Contemporary Europe." *International Studies Quarterly* 43: 83–114.

———. 1997. "International Norms and Domestic Politics: Bridging the Rationalist–Constructivist Divide." *European Journal of International Relations* 3 (4): 473–495.

Choudhury, Tufyal, and Helen Fenwick. 2012. "The Impact of Counter-Terrorism Measures on Muslim Communities." In Helen Fenwick, ed., *Developments in Counter-Terrorist Measures and Uses of Technology*, 45–76. New York: Routledge.

Christoffersen, Jonas, and Mikael Rask Madsen. 2011. "Introduction: The European Court of Human Rights Between Law and Politics." In Jonas Christoffersen and Mikael Rask Madsen, eds., *The European Court of Human Rights Between Law and Politics*, 1–13. Oxford: Oxford University Press.

Churchill, R. R., and J. R. Young. 1992. "Compliance with Judgments of the European Court of Human Rights and Decisions of the Committee of Ministers: The Experience of the United Kingdom, 1975–1987." *British Yearbook of International Law* 62: 283–346.

Cichowski, Rachel A. 2011. "Civil Society and the European Court of Human Rights." In Jonas Christoffersen and Mikael Rask Madsen, eds., *The European Court of Human Rights Between Law and Politics*, 77–97. Oxford: Oxford University Press.

———. 2006. "Courts, Rights, and Democratic Participation." *Comparative Political Studies* 39 (1): 50–75.

Cohen, Stan, and Laurie Taylor. 1978. *Prison Secrets*. London: National Council for Civil Liberties and Radical Alternatives to Prison.

Cole, Jared P. 2014. *The Political Question Doctrine: Justiciability and the Separation of Powers.* Congressional Research Service Report (December 23).Washington, D.C.: Congressional Research Service. https://www.fas.org/sgp/crs/misc/R43834.pdf.

Colvin, Madeleine. 1998. *Under Surveillance: Covert Policing and Human Rights Standards.* London: JUSTICE.

Committee of Ministers. 2017a. *Supervision of the Execution of Judgments and Decisions of the European Court of Human Rights—2016: 10th Annual Report of the Committee of Ministers.* Strasbourg: Council of Europe.

———. 2017b. "Rules of the Committee of Ministers for the Supervision of the Execution of Judgments and of the Terms of Friendly Settlements (Adopted by the Committee of Ministers on 10 May 2006 at the 964th meeting of the Ministers' Deputies and amended on 18 January 2017 at the 1275th meeting of the Ministers' Deputies)." https://rm.coe.int/16806eebf0.

———. 2008. "Monitoring of the Payment of Sums Awarded by way of Just Satisfaction: An Overview of the Committee of Ministers' Present Practice." Memorandum prepared by the Department for the Execution of Judgments of the European Court of Human Rights. COE Doc. CM/Inf/DH(2008)7 final. https://search.coe.int/cm/Pages/result_details.aspx?ObjectId=09000016805af4ec.

———. 2006. Ensuring the Continued Effectiveness of the European Convention on Human Rights: The Implementation of the Reform Measures Adopted by the Committee of Ministers at its 114th Session (12 May 2004). COE Doc. CM(2006)39 final (May 12). https://wcd.coe.int/ViewDoc.jsp?Ref=CM(2006)39&Language=lanEnglish&Ver=final.

Conant, Lisa. 2002. *Justice Contained: Law and Politics in the European Union.* Ithaca, N.Y.: Cornell University Press.

Council of Europe. 2016. *Impact of the European Convention on Human Rights in States Parties: Selected Examples.* Strasbourg: Council of Europe.

———. 2004. *Applying and Supervising the ECHR—Guaranteeing the Effectiveness of the European Convention on Human Rights: Collected Texts.* Strasbourg: Council of Europe, Directorate General of Human Rights. https://www.coe.int/t/dghl/standardsetting/cddh/Publications/reformcollectedtexts_e.pdf.

————. 1984. *Collection of Resolutions Adopted by the Committee of Ministers in Application of Articles 32 and 54 of the European Convention for the Protection of Human Rights and Fundamental Freedoms, 1959–1983*. Strasbourg: Council of Europe.

————. 1975–1985. *Collected Edition of the "Travaux Préparatoires" of the European Convention on Human Rights—Recueil des Travaux Préparatoires de la Convention Européenne des Droits de l'Homme*. Vols. 1–8. The Hague: Martinus Nijhoff.

Council of the European Union. 2008. "Council Decision of 18 February 2008 on the Principles, Priorities and Conditions Contained in the Accession Partnership with the Republic of Turkey and Repealing Decision 2006/35/EC (2008/157/EC)." *Official Journal of the European Union* L51: 4–18.

Crawford, James. 2013. *State Responsibility: The General Part*. Cambridge: Cambridge University Press.

Cremer, Hans-Joachim. 2014. "Prescriptive Orders in the Operative Provisions of Judgments by the European Court of Human Rights: Beyond *res judicanda*?" In Anja Seibert-Fohr and Mark E. Villiger, eds., *Judgments of the European Court of Human Rights—Effects and Implementation*, 39–58. Baden-Baden: Nomos; Farnham, Surrey: Ashgate.

————. 2004. "Zur Bindungswirkung von EGMR-Urteilen: Anmerkung zum Görgülü-Beschluss des BVerfG vom 14.10.2004." *Europäische Grundrechte-Zeitschrift* 31: 683–700.

Dahl, Robert A. 2015. *On Demcracy*. 2nd ed., with a new preface and two new chapters by Ian Shapiro. New Haven, Conn.: Yale University Press.

————. 1992. "Democracy and Human Rights Under Different Conditions of Development." In Asbjørn Eide and Bernt Hagtvet, eds., *Human Rights in Perspective: A Global Assessment*, 235–251. Oxford: Blackwell.

Dai, Xinyuan. 2013. "The Compliance Gap and the 'Efficacy' of International Human Rights Institutions." In Thomas Risse, Stephen C. Ropp, and Kathryn Sikkink, eds., *The Persistent Power of Human Rights: From Commitment to Compliance*, 85–102. Cambridge: Cambridge University Press.

————. 2007. *International Institutions and National Policies*. Cambridge: Cambridge University Press.

————. 2005. "Why Comply? The Domestic Constituency Mechanism." *International Organization* 59 (2): 363–398.

Dammann, Klaus. 2004. "Kein Sieg der Menschenrechte." *Ossietzky* 2, http://www.sopos.org /aufsaetze/40322606b3371/1.phtml.

————. 2002. "Berufsverbote und Europäische Menschenrechtskonvention – rechtliche und politische Konsequenzen." http://www.berufsverbote.de/tl_files/docs/hh-dammann.doc.

Davenport, Christian. 1999. "Human Rights and the Democratic Proposition." *Journal of Conflict Resolution* 43 (1): 92–116.

Davenport, Christian, and David A. Armstrong II. 2004. "Democracy and the Violation of Human Rights: A Statistical Analysis from 1976 to 1996." *American Journal of Political Science* 48 (3): 538–554.

Davis, David. 2013. "Britan Must Defy the European Court of Human Rights on Prisoner Voting as Strasbourg Is Exceeding Its Authority." In Spyridon Flogaitis, Tom Zwart, and Julie Fraser, eds., *The European Court of Human Rights and Its Discontents: Turning Criticism into Strength*, 65–70. Cheltenham: Edward Elgar.

de Gaay Fortman, Bas. 2011. *Political Economy of Human Rights: Rights, Realities and Realization*. Abingdon: Routledge.

Deitelhoff, Nicole. 2009. "The Discursive Process of Legalization: Charting Islands of Persuasion in the ICC Case." *International Organization* 63 (1): 33–65.

———. 2006. *Überzeugung in der Politik: Grundzüge einer Diskurstheorie internationalen Regierens*. Frankfurt am Main: Suhrkamp.

Deitelhoff, Nicole, and Harald Müller. 2005. "Theoretical Paradise—Empirically Lost? Arguing with Habermas." *Review of International Studies* 31 (1): 167–179.

Dembour, Marie-Bénédicte. 2006. *Who Believes in Human Rights? Reflections on the European Convention*. Cambridge: Cambridge University Press.

de Tribolet-Hardy, Fanny, Chris Lehner, and Elmar Habermeyer. 2015. "Forensische Psychiatrie ohne Diagnosen: Begriff der psychischen Störung im Kontext der Sicherungsverwahrung." *Forensische Psychiatrie, Psychologie, Kriminologie* 9: 164–170.

Deutscher Richterbund. 2011. "Stellungnahme des DRB zur öffentlichen Anhörung des Rechtsausschusses des Dt. Bundestages am 23.3.2011 zum Gesetzentwurf der Bundesregierung für ein Gesetz über den Rechtsschutz bei überlangen Gerichtsverfahren und strafrechtlichen Ermittlungsverfahren." Stellungnahme Nr. 09/11 (March). http://www.drb.de /stellungnahmen/2011/ueberlange-gerichtsverfahren.html.

Dicey, Albert Venn. 1915. *Introduction to the Study of the Law of the Constitution*. 8th ed. London: Macmillan. First published in 1885.

Dickson, Brice. 2010. *The European Convention on Human Rights and the Conflict in Northern Ireland*. Oxford: Oxford University Press.

di Mambro, Louise. 2010. "The Supreme Court of the United Kingdom: Jurisdiction and Procedure." *Commonwealth Law Bulletin* 36 (3): 453–460.

Dittmann, Volker. 2012. "'Psychische Störung' im Therapieunterbringungsgesetz (ThUG) und im Urteil des Bundesverfassungsgerichts zur Sicherungsverwahrung vom 4. Mai 2011—Versuch einer Klärung." In Jürgen Müller, Norbert Nedopil, Nahlah Saimeh, Elmar Habermeyer, and Peter Falkai, eds., *Sicherungsverwahrung—wissenschaftliche Basis und Positionsbestimmung: Was folgt nach dem Urteil des Bundesverfassungsgerichts vom 04.05.2011?*, 27–42. Berlin: Medizinisch Wissenschaftliche Verlagsgesellschaft.

Donald, Alice, and Philip Leach. 2016. *Parliaments and the European Court of Human Rights*. Oxford: Oxford University Press.

Dothan, Shai. 2015. *Reputation and Judicial Tactics: A Theory of National and International Courts*. Cambridge: Cambridge University Press.

———. 2011. "Judicial Tactics in the European Court of Human Rights." *Chicago Journal of International Law* 12 (1): 115–142.

Downs, George W., and Michael A. Jones. 2002. "Reputation, Compliance, and International Law." *Journal of Legal Studies* 31: S95–S114.

Downs, George W., David M. Rocke, and Peter N. Barsoom. 1996. "Is the Good News About Compliance Good News About Cooperation?" *International Organization* 50 (3): 379–406.

Drzemczewski, Andrew Z. 1990. "The Work of the Council of Europe's Directorate of Human Rights." *Human Rights Law Journal* 11 (1–2): 89–117.

———. 1978. "A 'Non-Decision' by the Committee of Ministers Under Article 32 (1) of the European Convention on Human Rights: The East African Asians Cases." *Modern Law Review* 41 (3): 337–342.

Drzemczewski, Andrew Z., and Paul Tavernier. 1998. "L'exécution des "décisions" des instances internationales de contrôle dans le domaine des droits de l'homme." In Société Francaise pour le Droit International, *La Protection des Droits de l'Homme et l'Évolution du Droit International*, 197–270. Paris: Éditions A. Pedone.

Duranti, Marco, 2017. *The Conservative Human Rights Revolution: European Identity, Transnational Politics, and the Origins of the Europesn Convention*. Oxford: Oxford University Press.

Dworkin, Gerald. 1973. "The Younger Committee Report on Privacy." *Modern Law Review* 36 (4): 399–406.

Dworkin, Ronald. 1998. *Law's Empire*. Oxford: Hart. First published in 1986.

———. 1978. *Taking Rights Seriously*. Cambridge, Mass.: Harvard University Press.

Dwyer, Claire, and Anne-Marie McAlinden. 2015. "Crime and Criminal Justice in Northern Ireland: Conflict, Transition and the Legacy of the Past." In Anne-Marie McAlinden and Clare Dwyer, eds., *Criminal Justice in Transition: The Northern Ireland Context*, 3–25. Oxford: Hart.

Dwyer, Déirdre. 2005. "Rights Brought Home: A. and Others v. Secretary of State for the Home Dept [2004] UKHL 56." *Law Quarterly Review* 121: 359–364.

Dzehtsiarou, Kanstantsin, and Alan Green. 2011. "Legitimacy and the Future of the European Court of Human Rights: Critical Perspectives from Academia and Practitioners." *German Law Journal* 12 (10): 1707–1715.

Dzehtsiarou, Kanstantsin, Tobias Lock, Paul Johnson, Fiona de Londras, Alan Greene, and Ed Bates. 2015. "The Legal Implications of a Repeal of the Human Rights Act 1998 and Withdrawal from the European Convention on Human Rights." http://ssrn.com/abstract=2605487.

Eckstein, Daniel, and Chrstian W. Altenhofen. 2006. *Das "Caroline"-Urteil des Europäischen Gerichtshofs für Menschenrechte: Eine Untersuchung der Auswirkungen auf das Spannungsfeld zwischen Pressefreiheit und allgemeinem Persönlichkeitsrecht unter Berücksichtigung der Rechtsprechung des Bundesgerichtshofs und des Bundesverfassungsgerichts*. Nierstein: Iatros.

Eckstein, Harry. 1975. "Case Study and Theory in Political Science." In Fred I. Greenstein and Nelson W. Polsby, eds., *Handbook of Political Science*, vol. 7: *Strategies of Inquiry*, 79–137. Reading, Mass.: Addison-Wesley.

Edel, Frédéric. 2007. *The Length of Civil and Criminal Proceedings in the Case-Law of the European Court of Human Rights*. Human Rights Case Files No. 16. Strasbourg: Council of Europe Publishing.

English, Rosalind. 2001a. "Forensic Immunity Post-*Osman*." *Modern Law Review* 64: 300–308.

———. 2001b. "The Decline and Fall of Osman." *New Law Journal* 151: 973–975.

Erdman, Joanna N. 2003. "The Deficiency of Consensus in Human Rights Protection: A Case Study of *Goodwin v. United Kingdom* and *I. v. United Kingdom*." *Journal of Law and Equality* 2 (2): 318–347.

Erman, Eva. 2005. *Human Rights and Democracy: Discourse Theory and Global Rights Institutions*. Aldershot, Hampshire: Ashgate.

Etienne, Julien. 2011. "Compliance Theory: A Goal-Framing Approach." *Law and Policy* 33 (3): 305–333.

European Commission for Democracy through Law (Venice Commission). 2006. *Report on the Effectiveness of National Remedies in Respect of Excessive Length of Proceedings*. Study no. 316/ 2004, COE Doc. CDL-AD(2006)036rev. Strasbourg: Council of Europe.

European Court of Human Rights. 2014a. *Practical Guide on Admissibility Criteria*. 3rd ed. Strasbourg: Council of Europe. http://www.echr.coe.int/Documents/Admissibility_guide _ENG.pdf.

———. 2014b. *The ECHR in 50 Questions*. Strasbourg: Council of Europe. http://www.echr.coe .int/Documents/50Questions_ENG.pdf.

———. 2012a. *Research Report: The New Admissibility Criterion Under Article 35 (3) (b) of the Convention: Case-Law Principles Two Years On.* Strasbourg: Council of Europe. http://www .echr.coe.int/Documents/Research_report_admissibility_criterion_ENG.pdf.

———. 2012b. "Unilateral Declarations: Policy and Practice." http://www.echr.coe.int /Documents/Unilateral_declarations_ENG.pdf.

———. 2011. "The General Practice Followed by the Panel of the Grand Chamber When Deciding on Requests for Referral in Accordance with Article 43 of the Convention." http://www .echr.coe.int/Documents/Note_GC_ENG.pdf.

———. 2007. "Just Satisfaction Claims." Practice Direction Issued by the President of the Court. March 28. http://www.echr.coe.int/Documents/PD_satisfaction_claims_ENG.pdf.

European Human Rights Advocacy Centre. 2012. "Request for the Initiation of Infringement Proceedings by the Committee of Ministers in Relation to the Judgment of the European Court of Human Rights in *Isayeva v Russia* (No. 57950/00, 24 February 2005)." COE Doc. DH-DD(2012)730E (August 22).

Ewing, Keith D., and Conor A. Gearty. 1990. *Freedom Under Thatcher: Civil Liberties in Modern Britain.* Oxford: Clarendon Press.

Farran, Sue. 1996. *The UK Before the European Court of Human Rights: Case Law and Commentary.* London: Blackstone Press.

Fatima, Shaheed. 2005. *Using International Law in Domestic Courts.* Oxford: Hart.

Fearon, James, and Alexander Wendt. 2002. "Rationalism v. Constructivism: A Skeptical View." In Walter Carlsnaes, Thomas Risse, and Beth A. Simmons, eds., *Handbook of International Relations*, 52–72. London: Sage.

Feldman, David. 2002. *Civil Liberties and Human Rights in England and Wales.* 2nd ed. Oxford: Oxford University Press.

Fenwick, Helen. 2007. *Civil Liberties and Human Rights.* 4th ed. Abingdon: Routledge-Cavendish.

———. 2001. "Covert Surveillance Under the Regulation of Investigatory Powers Act 2000, Part II." *Journal of Criminal Law* 65: 521–536.

———. 2000. *Civil Rights: New Labour, Freedom and the Human Rights Act.* Harlow: Longman.

Finnemore, Martha, and Kathryn Sikkink. 1998. "International Norm Dynamics and Political Change." *International Organization* 52 (4): 887–917.

Finnie, Wilson. 1991. "Anti-terrorist Legislation and the European Convention on Human Rights." *Modern Law Review* 54: 288–293.

Fisher, Roger. 1981. *Improving Compliance with International Law.* Charlottesville: University Press of Virginia.

Flauss, Jean-François. 1988. "La Pratique du Comité des Ministres du Conseil de l'Europe au Titre de l'Article 54 de la Convention Européenne des Droits de L'Homme (1985–1988)." *Annuaire Français de Droit International* 34: 408–423.

Flogaitis, Spyridon, Tom Zwart, and Julie Fraser, eds. 2013. *The European Court of Human Rights and Its Discontents: Turning Criticism into Strength.* Cheltenham: Edward Elgar.

Foster, Steven. 2006. *The Judiciary, Civil Liberties and Human Rights.* Edinburgh: Edinburgh University Press.

Franck, Thomas M. 1992. *Political Questions, Judicial Answers: Does the Rule of Law Apply to Foreign Affairs?* Princeton, N.J.: Princeton University Press.

Galanter, Mark. 1983. "The Radiating Effects of Courts." In Keith O. Boyum and Lynn Mather, eds., *Empirical Theories About Courts*, 117–142. New York: Longman.

Gearty, Conor A. 2013. *Liberty and Security*. Cambridge: Polity.

———. 2002. "Osman Unravels." *Modern Law Review* 65 (1): 87–95.

———. 2001. "Unraveling *Osman*." *Modern Law Review* 64 (2): 159–190.

———. 1997. "The United Kingdom." In Conor A. Gearty, ed., *European Civil Liberties and the European Convention on Human Rights: A Comparative Study*, 53–103. The Hague: Martinus Nijhoff.

Geisinger, Alex, and Michael Ashley Stein. 2008. "Rational Choice, Reputation, and Human Rights Treaties." *Michigan Law Review* 106: 1129–1142.

———. 2007. "A Theory of Expressive International Law." *Vanderbilt Law Review* 60: 77–131.

Gerards, Janneke, and Joseph Fleuren, eds. 2014. *Implementation of the European Convention on Human Rights and of the Judgments of the ECtHR in National Case-Law: A Comparative Analysis*. Cambridge: Intersentia.

Gersdorf, Hubertus. 2005. "Caroline-Urteil des EGMR: Bedrohung der nationalen Medienordnung." *Archiv für Presserecht—Zeitschrift für Medien- und Kommunikationsrecht* 3/2005: 221–227.

Ghandhi, S. 1983. "Birching in the Isle of Man." *Modern Law Review* 46 (4): 513–517.

Giegerich, Thomas. 2014. "The Struggle by the German Courts and Legislature to Transpose the Strasbourg Case Law on Preventive Detention into German Law." In Anja Seibert-Fohr and Mark E. Villiger, eds., *Judgments of the European Court of Human Rights—Effects and Implementation*, 207–236. Baden-Baden: Nomos.

Gies, Lieve. 2015. "Human Rights, the British Press and the Deserving Claimant." In Katja S. Ziegler, Elizabeth Wicks, and Loveday Hodson, eds., *The UK and European Human Rights: A Strained Relationship?*, 473–492. Oxford: Hart.

Giliker, Paula. 2000. "*Osman* and Police Immunity in the English Law of Torts." *Legal Studies* 20: 372–392.

Ginsburg, Tom. 2014. "Political Constraints on International Courts." In Cesare P. R. Romano, Karen J. Alter, and Yuval Shany, eds., *The Oxford Handbook of International Adjudication*, 483–502. Oxford: Oxford University Press.

Gionnopoulos, Christos. 2015. "Considerations on Protocol No. 16: Can the New Advisory Competence of the European Court of Human Rights Breathe New Life into the European Convention on Human Rights?" *German Law Journal* 16 (2): 337–350.

Goldhaber, Michael D. 2007. *A People's History of the European Court of Human Rights*. New Brunswick, N.J. : Rutgers University Press.

Goodman, Ryan, and Derek Jinks. 2013. *Socializing States: Promoting Human Rights Through International Law*. Oxford: Oxford University Press.

———. 2004. "How to Influence States: Socialization and International Human Rights Law." *Duke Law Journal* 54 (3): 621–703.

Gostin, Lawrence O. 1982. "Human Rights, Judicial Review and the Mentally Disordered Offender." *Criminal Law Review*: 779–793.

Grabenwarter, Christoph. 2008. *Europäische Menschenrechtskonvention*. 3rd ed. Munich: C. H. Beck.

Greer, Steven. 2006. *The European Convention on Human Rights: Achievements, Problems and Prospects*. Cambridge: Cambridge University Press.

Greßmann, Michael. 1998. *Neues Kindschaftsrecht*. Bielefeld: Gieseking.

Grewal, Sharanbir, and Erik Voeten. 2015. "Are New Democracies Better Human Rights Compliers?" *International Organization* 69: 497–518.

Gusy, Christoph. 2005. "Die Rezeption der EMRK in Deutschland." In Constance Grewe and Christoph Gusy, eds., *Menschenrechte in Bewährung: Die Rezeption der Europäischen Menschenrechtskonvention in Frankreich und Deutschland im Vergleich*, 129–159. Baden-Baden: Nomos.

Guzman, Andrew. 2008. *How International Law Works: A Rational Choice Theory*. Oxford: Oxford University Press.

Hafner-Burton, Emilie. 2013. *Making Human Rights a Reality*. Princeton, N.J.: Princeton University Press.

———. 2009. *Forced to Be Good: Why Trade Agreements Boost Human Rights*. Ithaca, N.Y.: Cornell University Press.

———. 2005. "Trading Human Rights: How Preferential Trade Agreements Influence Government Repression." *International Organization* 59 (3): 593–629.

Hafner-Burton, Emilie, and Kiyoteru Tsutsui. 2005. "Human Rights in a Globalizing World: The Paradox of Empty Promises." *American Journal of Sociology* 110: 1373–411.

Hamlin, Rebecca. 2016. "'Foreign Criminals,' the Human Rights Act, and the New Constitutional Politics of the United Kingdom." *Journal of Law and Courts* 4 (2): 437–461.

Hanks, Peter. 1988. "National Security—A Political Concept." *Monash University Law Review* 14: 114–133.

Hansen, Victor. 2013. "The Impact of Military Justice Reforms on the Law of Armed Conflict: How to Avoid Unintended Consequences." *Michigan State International Law Review* 21 (2): 237–272.

Harlow, Carol. 2004. "Damages and Human Rights." *New Zealand Law Review*: 429–450.

Harmsen, Robert. 2011. "The Reform of the Convention System: Institutional Restructuring and the (Geo-)Politics of Human Rights." In Jonas Christoffersen and Mikael Rask Madsen, eds., *The European Court of Human Rights Between Law and Politics*, 119–143. Oxford: Oxford University Press.

———. 2001. "The European Convention on Human Rights after Enlargement." *International Journal of Human Rights* 5 (4): 18–43.

Harris, David J., Michael O'Boyle, and Colin Warbrick. 1995. *Law of the European Convention on Human Rights*. London: Butterworths.

Hart, H.L.A. 1994. *The Concept of Law*. 2nd ed. Oxford: Oxford University Press.

Hartwig, Matthias. 2005. "Much Ado About Human Rights: The Federal Constitutional Court Confronts the European Court of Human Rights." *German Law Journal* 6 (5): 869–894.

Hathaway, Oona A. 2002. "Do Human Rights Treaties Make a Difference?" *Yale Law Journal* 118: 1935–2042.

Haug., Thomas. 2011. *Bildberichterstattung über Prominente. Unter besonderer Berücksichtigung der Zulässigkeit der gerichtlichen Beurteilung des Informationswertes von Medienberichten*. Baden-Baden: Nomos.

Hawkins, Darren, and Wade Jacoby. 2010. "Partial Compliance: A Comparison of the European and Inter-American Courts for Human Rights." *Journal of International Law and International Relations* 6: 35–85.

———. 2008. "Agent Permeability, Principal Delegation and the European Court of Human Rights." *Review of International Organizations* 3: 1–28.

———. 2006. "How Agents Matter." In Darren G. Hawkins, David A. Lake, Daniel L. Nielson, and Michael J. Tierney, eds., *Delegation and Agency in International Organizations*, 199–228. Cambridge: Cambridge University Press.

Hedigan, John. 2007. "The Princess, the Press and Privacy: Observations on Caroline von Han-nover v. Germany." In Lucius Caflisch, Johan Callewaert, Roderick Liddell, Paul Mahone, and Mark Villiger, eds., *Liber Amicorum Luzius Wildhaber—Human Rights—Strasbourg Views / Droits de l'homme—Regards de Strasbourg*, 193–205. Kehl: N. P. Engel.

Heinze, Eric. 2001. "Sexual Orientation and International Law: A Study in the Manufacture of Cross-Cultural 'Sensitivity.'" *Michigan Journal of International Law* 22: 283–309.

Held, David. 2006. *Models of Democracy*. 3rd ed. Stanford, Calif.: Stanford University Press.

Helfer, Laurence R. 2014a. "Effectiveness of International Adjudicators." In Cesare P. R. Romano, Karen J. Alter, and Yuval Shany, eds., *The Oxford Handbook of International Adjudication*, 464–482. Oxford: Oxford University Press.

———. 2014b. "The Successes of and Challenges for the European Court, Seen from the Out-side." In *Conference on the Long-Term Future of the European Court of Human Rights: Pro-ceedings, Oslo, 7–8 April/avril 2014*, COE Doc H/Inf (2014)1, 38–42. Strasbourg: Council of Europe.

———. 2008. "Redesigning the European Court of Human Rights: Embeddedness as a Deep Structural Principle of the European Human Rights Regime." *European Journal of Interna-tional Law* 19 (1): 125–159.

Helfer, Laurence R., and Anne-Marie Slaughter. 2005. "Why States Create International Tribu-nals: A Response to Professors Posner and Yoo." *California Law Review* 93 (3): 899–956.

———. 1997. "Toward a Theory of Effective Supranational Adjudication." *Yale Law Journal* 107: 272–391.

Helfer, Laurence R., and Erik Voeten. 2014. "International Courts as Agents of Legal Change: Evidence from LGBT Rights in Europe." *International Organization* 68 (1): 77–110.

Henderson, Conway W. 1993 "Population Pressures and Political Repression." *Social Science Quarterly* 74 (2): 322–333.

———. 1991. "Conditions Affecting the Use of Political Repression." *Journal of Conflict Resolu-tion* 35 (1): 120–142.

Henkin, Louis. 1990. "International Law: Politics, Values and Functions." In *Collected Courses of the Hague Academy of International Law* 216, 9–416. Dordrecht: Martinus Nijhoff.

Higgins, Rosalyn. 1978. "The Execution of the Decisions of Organs Under the European Con-vention on Human Rights." *Revue Hellénique de Droit International* 31 (1): 1–40.

Hill, Michael, and Peter Hupe. 2002. *Implementing Public Policy: Governance in Theory and Practice*. London: Sage.

Hillebrecht, Courtney. 2014. *Domestic Politics and International Human Rights Tribunals: The Problem of Compliance*. New York: Cambridge University Press.

———. 2009. "Rethinking Compliance: The Challenges and Prospects of Measuring Compli-ance with International Human Rights Tribunals." *Journal of Human Rights Practice* 1 (3): 362–379.

Hodson, Loveday. 2011. *NGOs and the Struggle for Human Rights in Europe*. Oxford: Hart.

Höffler, Katrin, and Cornelis Stadtland. 2012. "Mad or Bad? Der Begriff 'psychische Störung' des ThUG im Lichte der Rechtsprechung des BVerfG und des EGMR." *Strafverteidiger* 32 (4): 239–246.

Hoffman, David, and John Rowe. 2013. *Human Rights in the UK: An Introduction to the Human Rights Act 1998*. 4th ed. Harlow: Pearson Longman.

Hoffmann, Rt. Hon. Lord. 1999. "Human Rights and the House of Lords." *Modern Law Review* 62: 159–166.

Hofmann, Rainer. 2004. "The German Federal Constitutional Court and Public International Law: New Decisions, New Approaches?" *German Yearbook of International Law* 47: 9–38.

Hoggett, Brenda. 1983. "The Mental Health Act 1983." *Public Law* (Summer): 172–190.

Hope, Daniel. 2009. "Law Lords in Parliament." In Louis Blom-Cooper, Brice Dickson, and Gavin Drewry, eds., *The Judicial House of Lords 1876–2009*, 164–177. Oxford: Oxford University Press.

Hoyano, Laura C. H. 1999. "Policing Flawed Police Investigations: Unravelling the Blanket." *Modern Law Review* 62: 912–936.

———. 1998. *Using Human Rights Law in English Courts*. Oxford: Hart.

Howard, Robert M., and Henry F. Carey. 2004. "Is an Independent Judiciary Necessary for Democracy?" *Judicature* 87 (6): 284–290.

Howse, Robert, and Ruti Teitel. 2010. "Beyond Compliance: Rethinking Why International Law Really Matters." *Global Policy* 1 (2): 127–136.

Huneeus, Alexandra. 2014. "Compliance with Judgments and Decisions." In Cesare P. R. Romano, Karen J. Alter, and Yuval Shany, eds., *The Oxford Handbook of International Adjudication*, 437–463. Oxford: Oxford University Press.

———. 2011. "Courts Resisting Courts: Lessons from the Inter-American Court's Struggle to Enforce Human Rights." *Cornell International Law Journal* 44: 493–533.

Ichim, Octavian. 2015. *Just Satisfaction Under the European Convention on Human Rights*. Cambridge: Cambridge University Press.

Ignatieff, Michael, ed. 2005. *American Exceptionalism and Human Rights*. Princeton, N.J.: Princeton University Press.

Jackson, Donald W. 1997. *The United Kingdom Confronts the European Convention on Human Rights*. Gainesville: University Press of Florida.

Jacobson, Harold K., and Edith Brown Weiss. 1998. "A Framework for Analysis." In Edith Brown Weiss and Harold Jacobson, eds., *Engaging Countries: Strengthening Compliance with International Environmental Accords*, 1–18. Cambridge, Mass.: MIT Press.

Janis, Mark W. 2000. "The Efficacy of Strasbourg Law." *Connecticut Journal of International Law* 15: 39–46.

Janis, Mark W, Richard S. Kay, and Anthony W. Bradley. 2008. *European Human Rights Law: Texts and Materials*. 3rd ed. Oxford: Oxford University Press.

Jauernig, Othmar. 2004. *Bürgerliches Gesetzbuch: Kommentar*. 11th ed. Munich: C. H. Beck.

Jepperson, Ronald L., Alexander Wendt, and Peter J. Katzenstein. 1996. "Norms, Identity, and Culture in National Security." In Peter J. Katzenstein, ed., *The Culture of National Security: Norms and Identity in World Politics*, 33–75. New York: Columbia University Press.

Johnson, Paul. 2016. *Going to Strasbourg: An Oral History of Sexual Orientation Discrimination and the European Convention on Human Rights*. Oxford: Oxford University Press.

Jönsson, Christer, and Jonas Tallberg. 1998. "Compliance and Post-Agreement Bargaining." *European Journal of International Relations* 4 (4): 371–408.

Jordan, Richard, Daniel Maliniak, Amy Oakes, Susan Peterson, and Michael J. Tierney. 2009. One Discipline or Many? TRIP Survey of International Relations Faculty in Ten Countries. Teaching, Research, and International Policy Project Final Report. Available at https://www.wm.edu/offices/itpir/_documents/trip/final_trip_report_2009.pdf.

Kapiszewski, Diana, and Matthew M. Taylor. 2013. "Compliance: Conceptualizing, Measuring and Explaining Adherence to Judicial Rulings." *Law and Social Inquiry* 38 (4): 803–835.

Katzenstein, Peter J. 1996. "Introduction: Alternative Perspectives on National Security." In Peter J. Katzenstein, ed., *The Culture of National Security: Norms and Identity in World Politics*, 1–32. New York: Columbia University Press.

Katzenstein, Peter J., Robert O. Keohane, and Stephen D. Krasner. 1998. "*International Organization* and the Study of World Politics." *International Organization* 52 (4): 645–685.

Keating, Heather. 2006. "Protecting or Punishing Children: Physical Punishment, Human Rights and English Law Reform." *Legal Studies* 26 (3): 394–413.

Keith, Linda Camp. 1999. "The United Nations International Covenant on Civil and Political Rights: Does It Make a Difference in Human Rights Behavior?" *Journal of Peace Research* 36: 95–118.

Keller, Helen, Magdalena Forowicz, and Lorenz Engi. 2010. *Friendly Settlements Before the European Court of Human Rights: Theory and Practice*. Oxford: Oxford University Press.

Keller, Helen, and Cedric Marti. 2016. "Reconceptualizing Implementation: The Judicialization of the Execution of the European Court of Human Rights' Judgments." *European Journal of International Law* 26 (4): 829–850.

Keller, Helen, and Alex Stone Sweet, eds. 2008. *A Europe of Rights: The Impact of the ECHR on National Legal Systems*. Oxford: Oxford University Press.

Kelsen, Hans. 1950. *The Law of the United Nations: A Critical Analysis of Its Fundamental Problems*. London: Stevens and Sons.

Keohane, Robert O. 2000. "Ideas Part-Way Down." *Review of International Studies* 26: 125–130.

———. 1984. *After Hegemony: Cooperation and Discord in the World Political Economy*. Princeton, N.J.: Princeton University Press.

Kermode, David. 2001. "Constitutional Development and Public Policy, 1900–1979." In John Belchem, ed., *A New History of the Isle of Man*. Vol. 5, *The Modern Period 1830–1999*, 94–184. Liverpool: Liverpool University Press.

Kettner, Peter. 2002. *Der Informationsvorsprung der Staatsanwaltschaft im Ermittlungsverfahren: Untersuchung anhand des Akteneinsichtsrechts und des Verhältnisses zur Öffentlichkeit*. Berlin: TENEA Verlag für Medien.

Kielmansegg, Sebastian Graf. 2008. "Jenseits von Karlsruhe: Das deutsche Familienrecht in der Straßburger Rechtsprechung." *Archiv des Völkerrechts* 46: 273–308.

Kieschke, Olaf. 2003. *Die Praxis des Europäischen Gerichtshofs für Menschenrechte und ihre Auswirkungen auf das deutsche Strafverfahrensrecht: Eine Bestandsaufnahme am Beispiel ausgewählter Entscheidungen des EGMR gegen die Bundesrepublik Deutschland*. Berlin: Duncker und Humblot.

Kilian, Michael. 2012. "Der Einfluss der Europäischen Menschenrechtskonvention auf die deutsche Verfassungsrechtsprechung." In Armin Höland, ed., *Wirkungen der Rechtsprechung des Europäischen Gerichtshofs für Menschenrechte im deutschen Recht*, 119–146. Berlin: Berliner Wissenschafts-Verlag.

King, Gary, Robert O. Keohane, and Sidney Verba. 1994. *Designing Social Inquiry: Scientific Inference in Qualitative Research*. Princeton, N.J.: Princeton University Press.

King, Jeff. 2015. "Parliament's Role Following Declarations of Incompatibility Under the Human Rights Act." In Murray Hunt, Hayley J. Hooper, and Paul Yowell, eds., *Parliaments and Human Rights: Redressing the Democratic Deficit*, 165–193. Oxford: Hart.

Kingsbury, Benedict. 1998. "The Concept of Compliance as a Function of Competing Conceptions of International Law." *Michigan Journal of International Law* 19: 345–372.

Kingscote, Geoffrey. 2001. "Have Human Rights Principles Eroded Local Authority Immunity?" *New Law Journal* 151: 844–845.

Kinley, David. 1993. *The European Convention on Human Rights: Compliance Without Incorporation*. Aldershot: Dartmouth.

Kinzig, Jörg. 2011. "Die Neuordnung des Rechts der Sicherungsverwahrung." *Neue Juristische Wochenschrift* 2011 (4): 177–182.

Klein, Eckart. 2014. "Germany." In Janneke Gerards and Joseph Fleuren, eds., *Implementation of the European Convention on Human Rights and of the Judgments of the ECtHR in National Case-Law: A Comparative Analysis*, 185–216. Cambridge: Intersentia.

Klein, Karen. 2010. *Der Fall Görgülü: Ein Sorgerechtsstreit schreibt Rechtsgeschichte*. St. Ingbert: Röhrig Universitätsverlag.

Klerk, Yvonne S. 1998. "Supervision of the Execution of the Judgments of the European Court of Human Rights: The Committee of Ministers' Role Under Article 54 of the European Convention on Human Rights." *Netherlands Law Review* 45: 65–86.

Klug. Francesca. 2000. *Values for a Godless Age: The Story of the UK's New Bill of Human Rights*. London: Penguin.

Koh, Harold H. 1999. "How is International Human Rights Law Enforced?" *Indiana Law Journal* 74: 1397–1417.

———. 1998. "The 1998 Frankel Lecture: Bringing International Law Home." *Houston Law Review* 35: 628–681.

Komitee für Grundrechte und Demokratie, ed. 1982. *Ohne Zweifel für den Staat: Die Praxis zehn Jahre nach dem Radikalenerlaß*. Hamburg: Rowohlt.

Krisch, Daniel J. 1999. "*Vogt v. Germany*: The European Court of Human Rights Expands the Scope of Articles 10 and 11 of the European Convention on Human Rights to Include the Political Activities of Civil Servants." *Connecticut Journal of International Law* 14: 237–265.

Krisch, Nico. 2010. *Beyond Constitutionalism: The Pluralist Structure of Postnational Law*. Oxford: Oxford University Press.

———. 2008. "The Open Architecture of European Human Rights Law." *Modern Law Review* 71 (2): 183–216.

Kühne, H.-H., and R. Esser. 2002. "Die Rechtsprechung des Europäischen Gerichtshofes für Menschenrechte (EGMR) zur Untersuchungshaft: Ein Bericht über die Entwicklungen in den Jahren 2000 und 2001." *Strafverteidiger* 22 (7): 383–393.

Kurban, Dilek. 2016. "Forsaking Individual Justice: The Implications of the European Court of Human Rights' Pilot Judgment Procedure for Victims of Gross and Systematic Violations." *Human Rights Law Review* 16 (4): 731–769.

Kutz, Christopher L. 1994. "Just Disagreement: Indeterminacy and Rationality in the Rule of Law." *Yale Law Journal* 103: 997–1030.

Laffranque, Julia. 2014. "Can't Get Just Satisfaction." In Anja Seibert-Fohr and Mark E. Villiger, eds., *Judgments of the European Court of Human Rights—Effects and Implementation*, 75–114. Baden-Baden: Nomos.

Lambert Abdelgawad, Elisabeth. 2016. "The Economic Crisis and the Evolution of the System Based on the ECHR: Is There Any Correlation?" *European Law Journal* 22 (1): 74–91.

———. 2014. "Is There a Need to Advance the Jurisprudence of the European Court of Human Rights with Regard to the Award of Damages?" In Anja Seibert-Fohr and Mark E. Villiger, eds., *Judgments of the European Court of Human Rights—Effects and Implementation*, 115–136. Baden-Baden: Nomos.

———. 2008. *The Execution of the Judgments of the European Court of Human Rights*. 2nd ed. Strasbourg: Council of Europe Publishing.

———. 2002. *The Execution of the Judgments of the European Court of Human Rights*. Strasbourg: Council of Europe Publishing.

Lambert Abdelgawad, Elisabeth, and Anne Weber. 2008. "The Reception Process in France and Germany." In Helen Keller and Alec Stone Sweet, eds., *A Europe of Rights: The Impact of the ECHR on National Legal Systems*, 107–159. Oxford: Oxford University Press.

Lamprecht, Rolf. 2007. "Wenn der Rechtsstaat seine Unschuld verliert." *Neue Juristische Wochenschrift* 38: 2744–2746.

Lamprecht, Sarah. 2015. "Reforms to Lessen the Influence of the European Court of Human Rights: A Successful Strategy?" *European Public Law* 21 (2): 257–284.

Landman, Todd. 2005. *Protecting Human Rights*. Washington, D.C.: Georgetown University Press.

Laws, John. 2014. "Are Human Rights Undemocratic?" In Anja Seibert-Fohr and Mark E. Villiger, eds., *Judgments of the European Court of Human Rights—Effects and Implementation*, 187–192. Baden-Baden: Nomos.

Lawther, Cheryl. 2015. "Criminal Justice, Truth Recovery and Dealing with the Past in Northern Ireland." In Anne-Marie McAlinden and Clare Dwyer, eds., *Criminal Justice in Transition: The Northern Ireland Context*, 27–45. Oxford: Hart.

Leach, Philip. 2013. "No Longer Offering Fine Mantras to a Parched Child? The European Court's Developing Approach to Remedies." In Andreas Føllesdal, Birgit Peters, and Geir Ulfstein, eds., *Constituting Europe: The European Court of Human Rights in a National, European and Global Context*, 142–180. Cambridge: Cambridge University Press.

———. 2011. *Taking a Case to the European Court of Human Rights*. 3rd ed. Oxford: Oxford University Press.

Leach, Philip, Helen Hardman, Svetlana Stephenson, and Brad K. Blitz. 2010. *Responding to Systemic Human Rights Violations: An Analysis of "Pilot Judgments" of the European Court of Human Rights and Their Impact at the National Level*. Antwerp: Intersentia.

Leeb, David. 2001. *Die innerstaatliche Umsetzung der Feststellungsurteile des Europäischen Gerichtshofes für Menschenrechte im entschiedenen Fall*. Linz: Universitätsverlag Rudolf Trauner.

Lenski, Sophie-Charlotte. 2005. "Der Persönlichkeitsschutz Prominenter unter EMRK und Grundgesetz." *Neue Zeitschrift für Verwaltungsrecht* 1/2005: 51–53.

Leuprecht, Peter. 1993. "The Execution of Judgments and Decisions." In Ronald St. John Macdonald, Franz Matscher, and Herbert Petzold, eds., *The European System for the Protection of Human Rights*, 791–800. Dordrecht: Martinus Nijhoff.

———. 1988. "The Protection of Human Rights by Political Bodies: The Example of the Committee of Ministers of the Council of Europe." In Manfred Nowak, Dorothea Steurer, and Hannes Tretter, eds., *Fortschritt im Bewußtsein der Menschenrechte—Progress in the Spirit of Human Rights: Festschrift für Felix Ermacora*, 95–108. Kehl am Rhein: N. P. Engel.

Lillard, Monique C. 2005. "McGoliath v. David: The European Court of Human Rights Recent 'Equality of Arms' Decision." *German Law Journal* 6 (5): 895–907.

Lillich, Richard B. 1991. "The Soering Case." *American Journal of International Law* 85 (1): 128–149.

Linz, Juan L. 1992. "Types of Political Regimes and Respect for Human Rights: Historical and Cross-National Perspectives." In Asbjørn Eide and Bernt Hagtvet, eds., *Human Rights in Perspective: A Global Assessment*, 177–222. Oxford: Blackwell.

Lloyd, Ian J. 1986. "The Interception of Communications Act 1985." *Modern Law Review* 49: 86–95.

Lohmann, Susanne. 1993. "A Signaling Model of Informative and Manipulative Political Action." *American Political Science Review* 87 (2): 319–333.

Lord Lester of Herne Hill. 1998. "U.K. Acceptance of the Strasbourg Jurisdiction: What Really Went on in Whitehall in 1965." *Public Law* 237–253.

Lovat, Henry, and Yuval Shany. 2014. "The European Court of Human Rights." In Yuval Shany, *Assessing the Effectiveness of International Courts*, 253–276. Oxford: Oxford University Press.

Lück, Simon A. 2008. "Die Auswirkungen des EGMR-Urteils vom 11. Juni 2006 zum zwangsweisen Brechmitteleinsatz auf die deutsche Strafverfolgung." *Kritische Justiz* 41 (2): 198–203.

Lunney, Mark. 1999. "A Tort Lawyer's View of *Osman v United Kingdom*." *King's College Law Journal* 10: 238–247.

Lupu, Yonatan, and Eric Voeten. 2012. "Precedent on International Courts: A Network Analysis of Case Citations by the European Court of Human Rights." *British Journal of Political Science* 42: 413–439.

Macdonald, Ronald St. John. 1999. "Supervision of the Execution of the Judgments of the European Court of Human Rights." In René-Jean Dupuy, ed., *Mélanges en l'honneur de Nicolas Valticos: Droit et justice*, 417–437. Paris: Éditions A. Pedone.

Mackenzie, Ruth, Cesare Romano, and Yuval Shany. 2010. *The Manual on International Courts and Tribunals.* 2nd ed. Oxford: Oxford University Press.

MacMullen, Andrew. 2004. "Intergovernmental Functionalism? The Council of Europe in European Integration." *European Integration* 26 (4): 405–429.

Madsen, Mikael Rask. 2016. "The Challenging Authority of the European Court of Human Rights: From Cold War Legal Diplomacy to the Brighton Declaration and Backlash." *Law and Contemporary Problems* 79 (1): 141–178.

———. 2011. "The Protracted Institutionalization of the Strasbourg Court: From Legal Diplomacy to Integrationist Jurisprudence." In Jonas Christofferson and Mikael Rask Madsen, eds., *The European Court of Human Rights Between Law and Politics*, 43–60. Oxford: Oxford University Press.

———. 2007. "From Cold War Instrument to Supreme European Court: The European Court of Human Rights at the Crossroads of International and National Law and Politics." *Law and Social Inquiry* 32 (1): 137–159.

Mahler, John, and Friedemann Pfafflin. 2012. "Die psychische Störung im ThUG." *Recht und Psychiatrie* 30 (3): 130–137.

Mahoney, Paul. 2002. "New Challenges for the European Court of Human Rights Resulting from the Expanding Case Load and Membership." *Pennsylvania State International Law Review* 21: 101–114.

Maier, Ingrid. 1988. Intervention Relating to Report on "Responsibilities of the Organs of the European Convention, including the Committee of Ministers." In *Proceedings of the Sixth International Colloquy About the European Convention on Human Rights*, 1040–1048. Dordrecht: Martinus Nijhoff.

Maliniak, Daniel, Susan Peterson, and Michael J. Tierney. 2012. *Trip Around the World: Teaching, Research, and Policy Views of International Relations Faculty in 20 Countries.* Williamsburg, Va.: TRIP Project, College of William and Mary. https://www.wm.edu/offices/itpir/_documents/trip/trip_around_the_world_2011.pdf.

Mandla, Christoph. 2010. "Über die vermeintliche Verfolgung Unschuldiger—Vom untauglichen Versuch einer Reinwaschung, Erwiderung zu Cebulla und Schulte-Kellinghaus." *Betrifft Justiz* 102: 279–286.

March, James G., and Johan P. Olsen. 2008. "The Logic of Appropriateness." In Michael Moran, Martin Rein, and Robert E. Goodin, eds., *The Oxford Handbook of Public Policy*, 689–708. Oxford: Oxford University Press.

———. 1998. "The Institutional Dynamics of International Political Orders." *International Organization* 52 (4): 943–969.

Marks, Susan. 1995. "Civil Liberties at the Margin: The UK Derogation and the European Court of Human Rights." *Oxford Journal of Legal Studies* 15 (1): 69–95.

Marmo, Marinella. 2008. "The Execution of Judgments of the European Court of Human Rights—A Political Battle." *Maastricht Journal of European and Comparative Law* 15: 235–258.

Marshall, Monty G., Ted Robert Gurr, and Keith Jaggers. 2017. *Polity IV Project—Political Regime Characteristics and Transitions, 1800–2016: Dataset Users' Manual.* Vienna, Va.: Center for Systemic Peace. http://www.systemicpeace.org/inscr/p4manualv2016.pdf.

Marston, Geoffrey. 1993. "The United Kingdom's Part in the Preparation of the European Convention on Human Rights, 1950." *International and Comparative Law Quarterly* 42: 796–826.

Martin, Lisa. 2013. "Against Compliance." In Jeffrey L. Dunoff and Mark. A. Pollack, eds., *Interdisciplinary Perspectives on International Law and International Relations: The State of the Art*, 591–610. Cambridge: Cambridge University Press.

Martinsen, Dorte Sindbjerg. 2015a. *An Ever More Powerful Court? The Political Constraints of Legal Integration in the European Union.* Oxford: Oxford University Press.

———. 2015b. "Judicial Influence on Policy Outputs? The Political Constraints of Legal Integration in the European Union." *Comparative Political Studies* 48 (12): 1612–1660.

Marx, Martin, and Werner Roderfeld. 2012. *Rechtsschutz bei überlangen Gerichts- und Ermittlungsverfahren: Handkommentar.* Baden-Baden: Nomos.

McAlinden, Anne-Marie, and Clare Dwyer, eds. 2015. *Criminal Justice in Transition: The Northern Ireland Context.* Oxford: Hart.

McCann, Michael. 2006. "Law and Social Movements: Contemporary Perspectives." *Annual Review of Law and Social Science* 2: 17–38.

———. 1998. "How Does Law Matter for Social Movements?" In Bryant G. Garth and Austin Sarat, eds., *How Does Law Matter?*, 76–108. Evanston, Ill.: Northwestern University Press.

McCoubrey, H. 1997. "Due Process and British Courts Martial: A Commentary upon the Findlay Case." *Journal of Armed Conflict Law* 2: 83–89.

Mercer, Jonathan. 1996. *Reputation and International Politics.* Ithaca, N.Y.: Cornell University Press.

Merrills, J. G. 2011. *International Dispute Settlement.* 5th ed. Cambridge: Cambridge University Press.

Messing, Volker. 2007. *Das Caroline-Urteil: Auswirkungen der Entscheidung des Europäischen Gerichtshofs für Menschenrechte auf die deutsche Presse.* Saarbrücken: VDM—Verlag Dr. Müller.

Mitchell, Ronald B. 2007. "Compliance Theory: Compliance, Effectiveness, and Behavioural Change in International Environmental Law." In Daniel Bodansky, Jutta Brunnée, and Ellen Hey, eds., *The Oxford Handbook of International Environmental Law*, 893–921. Oxford: Oxford University Press.

———. 1994. *Intentional Oil Pollution at Sea: Environmental Policy and Treaty Compliance.* Cambridge, Mass.: MIT Press.

Mitchell, Sara McLaughlin, and Paul R. Hensel. 2007. "International Institutions and Compliance with Agreements." *American Journal of Political Science* 51 (4): 721–737.

Mole, Nuala, and Catharina Harby. 2006. *The Right to a Fair Trial: A Guide to the Implementation of Article 6 of the European Convention on Human Rights.* Human Rights Handbook No. 3. 2nd ed. Strasbourg: Council of Europe.

Monson, Robert A. 1984. "Political Toleration Versus Militant Democracy: The Case of Germany." *German Studies Review* 7 (2): 301–324.

Monti, G. 1999. "*Osman v UK*—Transforming English Negligence Law into French Administrative Law?" *International and Comparative Law Quarterly* 48: 757–778.

Moore, David W. 2006. "Death Penalty Gets Less Support From Britons, Canadians Than Americans." Gallup News Service (February 20). http://www.gallup.com/poll/21544/death-penalty-gets-less-support-from-britons-canadians-than-americans.aspx.

Moravcsik, Andrew. 2000. "The Origins of International Human Rights Regimes: Democratic Delegation in Postwar Europe." *International Organization* 54 (2): 217–252.

———. 1995. "Explaining International Human Rights Regimes: Liberal Theory and Western Europe." *European Journal of International Relations* 1 (2): 157–189.

———. 1993. "Introduction: Integrating International and Domestic Theories of International Bargaining." In Peter B. Evans, Harold K. Jacobson, and Robert D. Putnam, eds., *Double-Edged Diplomacy: International Bargaining and Domestic Politics*, 3–42. Berkeley: University of California Press.

Morrow, James D. 2007. "When Do States Follow the Laws of War?" *American Political Science Review* 101 (3): 559–572.

Motoc, Ulia, and Ineta Ziemele, eds. 2016. *The Impact of the ECHR on Democratic Change in Central and Eastern Europe: Judicial Perspectives.* Cambridge: Cambridge University Press.

Mowbray, Alastair. 2012. *Cases, Materials, and Commentary on the European Convention on Human Rights.* 3rd ed. Oxford: Oxford University Press.

Müller, Felix, and Tobias Richter. 2008. "Report on the *Bundesverfassungsgericht's* (Federal Constitutional Court) Jurisprudence in 2005/2006." *German Law Journal* 9 (2): 161–194.

Müller, Jürgen, Norbert Nedopil, Nahlah Saimeh, Elmar Habermeyer, and Peter Falkai. 2011. "Stellungnahme der Deutschen Gesellschaft für Psychiatrie, Psychotherapie und Nervenheilkunde (DGPPN) zum Therapieunterbringungsgesetz—ThUG." *Forensische Psychiatrie, Psychologie, Kriminologie* 5: 116–118.

Müller, Sebastian, and Christoph Gusy. 2013. "The Interrelationship Between Domestic Judicial Mechanisms and the Strasbourg Court Rulings in Germany." In Dia Anagnostou, ed., *The European Court of Human Rights: Implementing Strasbourg's Judgments on Domestic Policy*, 27–48. Edinburgh: Edinburgh University Press.

Murdoch, Jim. 1997. "Scotland and the European Convention." In Brice Dickson, ed., *Human Rights and the European Convention: The Effects of the Convention on the United Kingdom and Ireland*, 113–142. London: Sweet and Maxell.

Neumayer, Eric. 2005. "Do International Human Rights Treaties Improve Respect for Human Rights?" *Journal of Conflict Resolution* 49 (6): 925–953.

Neyer, Jürgen, and Dieter Wolf. 2005. "The Analysis of Compliance with International Rules: Definitions, Variables, and Methodology." In Michael Zürn and Christian Joerges, eds., *Law and Governance in Postnational Europe: Compliance Beyond the Nation-State*, 40–64. Cambridge: Cambridge University Press.

Nobes, Gavin, and Marjorie Smith. 1997. "Physical Punishment of Children in Two-parent Families." *Clinical Child Psychology and Psychiatry* 2 (2): 271–281.

Nohlen, Nicolas. 2006. "Von Hannover v. Germany." *American Journal of International Law* 100: 196–201.

Nußberger, Angelika. 2014. "Subsidiarity in the Control of Decisions Based on Proportionality: An Analysis of the Basis of the Implementation of ECtHR Judgments into German Law." In Anja Seibert-Fohr and Mark E. Villiger, eds., *Judgments of the European Court of Human Rights—Effects and Implementation*, 165–185. Baden-Baden: Nomos.

Nußstein, Karl. 2011. "Das Therapieunterbringungsgesetz—Erste Erfahrungen aus der Praxis." *Neue Juristische Wochenschrift* 17: 1194–1197.

O'Boyle, Michael P. 1977. "Emergency Situations and the Protection of Human Rights: A Model Derogation Clause for a Northern Ireland Bill of Rights." *Northern Ireland Law Quarterly* 28: 160–187.

Oomen, B. M. 2016. "A Serious Case of Strasbourg-Bashing? An Evaluation of the Debates on the Legitimacy of the European Court of Human Rights in the Netherlands." *International Journal of Human Rights* 20 (3): 407–425.

Open Society Justice Initiative. 2013. *From Rights to Remedies: Structures and Strategies for Implementing International Human Rights Decisions.* New York: Open Society Foundations.

———. 2010. *From Judgment to Justice: Implementing International and Regional Human Rights Decisions.* New York: Open Society Foundations.

Pabel, Katharina. 2016. "Germany: The Long Way of Integrating the Strasbourg Perspective into the Protection of Fundamental Rights." In Patricia Popelier, Sarah Lambrecht, and Koen Lemmens, eds., *Criticism of the European Court of Human Rights—Shifting the Convention System: Counter-Dynamics at the National and EU Level*, 155–175. Cambridge: Intersentia.

Padfield, Nicola. 2002. *Beyond the Tariff: Human Rights and the Release of Life Sentence Prisoners.* Cullompton, Devon: Willan Publishing.

Palmer, Stephanie. 1994. "Redefining the Meaning of Life: The Early Release of Life Prisoners." *Cambridge Law Journal* 53 (3): 480–491.

Papier, Hans-Jürgen. 2006. "Execution and Effects of the Judgments of the European Court of Human Rights from the Perspective of German National Courts." *Human Rights Law Journal* 27 (1–4): 1–4.

Parliamentary Assembly of the Council of Europe. 2015. *Implementation of Judgments of the European Court of Human Rights.* Committee on Legal Affairs and Human Rights. Rapporteur: Klaas de Vries. PACE Doc. 13864 (September 9). http://assembly.coe.int/nw/xml/XRef/Xref-DocDetails-EN.asp?FileID=22005&lang=EN.

Pasqualucci, Jo M. 2013. *The Practice and Procedure of the Inter-American Court of Human Rights.* 2nd ed. Cambridge: Cambridge University Press.

Paulson, Colter. 2004. "Compliance with Final Judgments of the International Court of Justice Since 1987." *American Journal of International Law* 98: 434–461.

Peay, Jill. 1982. "Mental Health Review Tribunals and the Mental Health (Amendment) Act." *Criminal Law Review*: 794–808.

Peglau, Jens. 2016. "Die Sicherungsverwahrung im 'Dialog' zwischen EGMR und BVerfG." *Juristische Rundschau* 2016 (9), 491–498.

Peters, Anne. 2005. "Die Causa Caroline: Kampf der Gerichte." *Betrifft Justiz* 83: 160–168.

Phillips, Barry. 1994. "The Case for Corporal Punishment in the United Kingdom: Beaten into Submission in Europe?" *International and Comparative Law Quarterly* 43: 153–163.

Pietron, Danielle. 2016. *Die Effektivität des Rechtsschutzes gegen überlange Verfahren*. Hamburg: Verlag Dr. Kovač.

Poe, Steven C., and C. Neal Tate. 1994. "Repression of Human Rights to Personal Integrity in the 1980s: A Global Analysis." *American Political Science Review* 88: 853–872.

Poe, Steven C., C. Neal Tate, and Linda Camp Keith. 1999. "Repression of the Human Right to Personal Integrity Revisited: A Global Cross-National Study Covering the Years 1976–1993." *International Studies Quarterly* 43 (2): 291–313.

Polakiewicz, Jörg G. 1993. *Die Verpflichtungen der Staaten aus den Urteilen des Europäischen Gerichtshofs für Menschenrecht*. Berlin: Springer-Verlag.

Popelier, Patricia, Sarah Lambrecht, and Koen Lemmens, eds. 2016. *Criticism of the European Court of Human Rights—Shifting the Convention System: Counter-Dynamics at the National and EU Level*. Cambridge: Intersentia.

Posner, Eric A., and John C. Yoo. 2005. "Judicial Independence in International Tribunals." *California Law Review* 93 (1): 1–74.

Pressman, Jeffrey L., and Aaron Wildavsky. 1984. *Implementation: How Great Expectations in Washington Are Dashed in Oakland; or, Why It's Amazing That Federal Programs Work At All, This Being a Saga of the Economic Development Administration As Told by Two Sympathetic Observers Who Seek to Build Morals on a Foundation of Ruined Hopes*. 3rd rev. ed. Berkeley: University of California Press.

Prütting, Hanns, ed. 2005. *Das Caroline-Urteil des EGMR und die Rechtsprechung des Bundesverfassungsgerichts*. Munich: C. H. Beck.

Pülzl, Helga, and Oliver Treib. 2007. "Implementing Public Policy." In Frank Fischer, Gerald J. Milller, and Mara S. Sidney, eds., *Handbook of Public Policy Analysis: Theory, Politics, and Methods*, 89–107. Boca Raton: CRC Press.

Pustorino, Pietro. 2016. "Russian Constitutional Court and the execution 'à la carte' of ECtHR Judgments." *Questions of International Law* 32: 5–18. http://www.qil-qdi.org/russian-constitutional-court-execution-la-carte-ecthr-judgments/.

Putnam, Robert D. 1988. "Diplomacy and Domestic Politics: The Logic of Two-Level Games." *International Organization* 42 (3): 427–460.

Rains, Robert E. 2005. "Legal Recognition of Gender Change for Transsexual Persons in the United Kingdom: The Human Rights Act 1998 and 'Compatibility' with European Human Rights Law." *Georgia Journal of International and Comparative Law* 33: 333–414.

Raustiala, Kal. 2000. "Compliance and Effectiveness in International Regulatory Cooperation." *Case Western Reserve Journal of International Law* 32: 387–440.

Raustiala, Kal, and Anne-Marie Slaughter. 2002. "International Law, International Relations and Compliance." In Walter Carlsnaes, Thomas Risse, and Beth A. Simmons, eds., *Handbook of International Relations*, 538–558. London: Sage.

Rayside, David. 1998. *On the Fringe: Gays and Lesbians in Politics*. Ithaca, N.Y.: Cornell University Press.

Raz, Joseph. 1975. *Practical Reason and Norms*. Oxford: Oxford Univesity Press.

Reenock, Christopher, Jeffrey K. Staton, and Marius Radean. 2014. "Legal Institutions and Democratic Survival." *Journal of Politics* 75 (2): 491–505.

Remde, Carina. 2012. *Die Zukunft präventiven Freiheitsentzugs vor dem Hintergrund der EMRK*. Hamburg: Verlag Dr. Kovač.

Renzikowski, Joachim. 2013. "Abstand halten!—Die Neuregelung der Sicherungsverwahrung." *Neue Juristische Wochenschrift* 23: 1633–1696.

———. 2004. "Fair Trial als Waffengleichheit—adversatorische Elemente im Strafprozess?" In Joachim Renzikowski, ed., *Die EMRK im Privat-, Straf- und Öffentlichen Recht: Grundlagen einer europäischen Rechtskultur*, 97–122. Baden-Baden: Nomos.

Ress, Georg. 1995. "Article 54." In Louis-Edmond Pettiti, Emmanuel Decaux, and Pierre-Henri Imbert, eds., *La Convention européenne des droits de l'homme: Commentaire article par article*, 857–869. Paris: Economica.

Risse, Thomas. 2000. "Let's Argue! Communicative Action in World Politics." *International Organization* 54 (1): 1–39.

Risse, Thomas, Stephen C. Ropp, and Kathryn Sikkink, eds. 2013. *The Persistent Power of Human Rights: From Commitment to Compliance*. Cambridge: Cambridge University Press.

———. 1999. *The Power of Human Rights: International Norms and Domestic Change*. Cambridge: Cambridge University Press.

Risse, Thomas, and Kathryn Sikkink. 1999. "The Socialization of International Human Rights Norms into Domestic Practices: Introduction." In Thomas Risse, Stephen C. Ropp, and Kathryn Sikkink, eds., *The Power of Human Rights: International Norms and Domestic Change*, 1–38. Cambridge: Cambridge University Press.

Risse-Kappen, Thomas. 1995. "Democratic Peace—Warlike Democracies? A Social Constructivist Interpretation of the Liberal Argument." *European Journal of International Relations* 1 (4): 491–517.

Roberts, Julian V., Loretta J. Stalans, David Indermaur, and Mike Hough. 2003. *Penal Populism and Public Opinion: Lessons from Five Countries*. Oxford: Oxford University Press.

Robertson, Arthur H., ed. 1973. *Privacy and Human Rights: Reports and Communications Presented at the Third International Colloquy About the European Convention on Human Rights, Organized by the Belgian Universities and the Council of Europe, with the Support of the Belgian Government, Brussels, 30 September–3 October 1970*. Manchester: Manchester University Press.

———. 1950. "The European Convention for the Protection of Human Rights." *British Yearbook of International Law* 27: 145–163.

Romano, Cesare P. R. 2011. "A Taxonomy of International Rule of Law Institutions." *Journal of International Dispute Settlement* 2 (1): 241–277.

———. 1999. "The Proliferation of International Judicial Bodies: The Pieces of the Puzzle." *NYU Journal of International Law and Politics* 31: 709–751.

Rowe, Peter. 2003. "A New Court to Protect Human Rights in the Armed Forces of the UK: The Summary Appeal Court." *Journal of Conflict and Security Law* 8 (1): 201–215.

Rowlinson, Simon P. 2002. "The British System of Military Justice." *Air Force Law Review* 52: 17–52.

Rudolf, Beate. 2006. "Council of Europe: von Hannover v. Germany." *International Journal of Constitutional Law* 4 (3): 533–539.

———. 2003. "European Court of Human Rights: Legal Status of Postoperative Transsexuals." *International Journal of Constitutional Law* 1: 716–721.

Ruggie, John Gerard. 1998. "What Makes the World Hang Together? Neo-utilitarianism and the Social Constructivist Challenge." *International Organization* 52 (4): 855–885.

Ryssdal, Rolv. 1996. "The Enforcement System Set Up Under the European Convention on Human Rights." In Mielle K. Bulterman and Martin Kuijer, eds., *Compliance with Judgments of International Courts*, 49–69. The Hague: Martinus Nijhoff.

Sanderson, M. A. 2004. "Is *von Hannover v. Germany* a Step Backward for the Substantive Analysis of Speech and Privacy Interests?" *European Human Rights Law Review* 9 (6): 631–644.

Satzger, Helmut, and Tobias Pohl. 2006. "The German Constitutional Court and the European Arrest Warrant: 'Cryptic Signals' from Karlsruhe." *Journal of International Criminal Justice* 4: 686–701.

Sauer, Heiko. 2005. "Die neue Schlagkraft der gemeineuropäischen Grundrechtsjudikatur: Zur Bindung deutscher Gerichte an die Entscheidungen des Europäischen Gerichtshofs für Menschenrechte." *Zeitschrift für ausländisches öffentliches Recht und Völkerrecht* 65: 35–69.

Sauvain, Stephen J. 1975. "The Report of the Committee on Contempt of Court." *Modern Law Review* 38 (3): 311–314.

Schmalz, Nikolaus. 2007. *Die Rechtsfolgen eines Verstoßes gegen die Europäische Menschenrechtskonvention für die Bundesrepublik Deutschland.* Frankfurt am Main: Peter Lang.

Schmidt, Susanne K. 2014. "Judicial Europeanisation: The Case of *Zambrano* in Ireland." *West European Politics* 37 (4): 769–785.

Schöch, Heinz. 2012. "Sicherungsverwahrung im Übergang." *Neue Kriminalpolitik* 24 (2): 47–54.

Schulte-Kellinghaus, Thomas, and Mario Cebulla. 2010. "Richterliche Unabhängigkeit als Rechtsbeugung." *Betrifft Justiz* 101: 230–235.

Seher, Gerhard. 2006. "Bewährungswiderruf wegen Begehung einer neuen Straftat: Konsequenzen aus der Rechtsprechung des EGMR zur Unschuldsvermutung." *Zeitschrift für die gesamte Strafrechtswissenschaft* 118 (1): 101–158.

Shany, Yuval. 2014. *Assessing the Effectiveness of International Courts.* Oxford: Oxford Univeryity Press.

———. 2013. "The Effectiveness of the Human Rights Committee and the Treaty Body Reform." In Marten Breuer et al., eds., *Der Staat im Recht: Festschrift für Eckart Klein zum 70. Geburtstag,* 1307–1323. Berlin: Duncker und Humblot.

———. 2012. "Assessing the Effectiveness of International Courts: A Goal-Based Approach." *American Journal of International Law* 106 (2): 225–270.

Shapiro, Martin. 1981. *Courts: A Comparative Political Analysis.* Chicago: University of Chicago Press.

Shircore, Mandy. 2006. "Police Liability for Negligent Investigations: When Will a Duty of Care Arise?" *Deakin Law Review* 11 (1): 33–62.

Sicilianos, Linos-Alexander. 2014. "The Role of the European Court of Human Rights in the Execution of Its Own Judgments: Reflections on Article 46 ECHR." In Anja Seibert-Fohr and Mark E. Villiger, eds., *Judgments of the European Court of Human Rights—Effects and Implementation,* 285–315. Baden-Baden: Nomos.

Simmons, Beth A. 2009. *Mobilizing for Human Rights: International Law in Domestic Politics.* Cambridge: Cambridge University Press.

———. 2002. "Capacity, Commitment, and Compliance: International Institutions and Territorial Disputes." *Journal of Conflict Resolution* 46 (6): 829–856.

Simpson, Alfred W. B. 2001. *Human Rights and the End of Empire: Britain and the Genesis of the European Convention.* Oxford: Oxford University Press.

Smirnova, Maria. 2015. "Russian Constitutional Court Affirms Russian Constitution's Supremacy over ECtHR Decisions." EJIL *Talk!* (blog), July 15. http://www.ejiltalk.org/russian-constitutional-court-affirms-russian-constitutions-supremacy-over-ecthr-decisions/.

Starck, Christian. 2005. "Das Caroline-Urteil des EGMR und seine verfassungsrechtlichen Konsequenzen." In Hanns Prütting, ed., *Das Caroline-Urteil des EGMR und die Rechtsprechung des Bundesverfassungsgerichts,* 23–36. Munich: C. H. Beck.

Steering Committee for Human Rights. 2015. "CDDH Report on the Longer-Term Future of the System of the European Convention on Human Rights." COE Doc. CDDH(2015)R84 Addendum I (December 11). https://www.coe.int/t/dghl/standardsetting/cddh/reformechr /CDDH(2015)R84_Addendum%20I_EN-Final.pdf.

———. 2012. "CDDH Final Report on Measures Requiring Amendment of the European Convention on Human Rights." COE Doc. CDDH(2012)R74 Addendum 1 (February 15). http://www.coe.int/t/dgi/brighton-conference/Documents/CDDH-amendment-measures -report_en.pdf.

Steinhorst, Lars. 2013. "Rechtsschutz bei überlangen Gerichtsverfahren vor dem Bundesverfassungsgericht." In Carola Schulze und Wladimir I. Fadeev, eds., *Verfassungsgerichtsbarkeit in der Russischen Föderation und in der Bundesrepublik Deutschland: Rundtischgespräch an der Moskauer Staatlichen Juristischen Kutafin-Universität am 9. und 10. Oktober 2012*, 93–105. Potsdam: Universitätsverlag.

Stone Sweet, Alec. 2004. *The Judicial Construction of Europe*. Oxford: Oxford University Press.

Stone Sweet, Alec, and Thomas L. Brunell. 2012. "The European Court of Justice, State Noncompliance, and the Politics of Override." *American Political Science Review* 106 (1): 204–213.

Stone Sweet, Alec, and Hellen Keller. 2008. "The Reception of the ECHR in National Legal Orders." In Helen Keller and Alec Stone Sweet, eds., *A Europe of Rights: The Impact of the ECHR on National Legal Systems*, 3–28. Oxford: Oxford University Press.

Sundberg, Fredrik G. E. 2004. "Le contrôle de l'exécution des arrêts de la Cour européenne des Droits de l'homme." In *Libertés, Justice, Tolérance: Mélanges en hommage au Doyen Gérard Cohen-Jonathan*, vol. 2, 1515–1535. Brussels: Bruylant.

———. 2001. "Control of the Execution of Decisions Under the ECHR: Some Remarks on the Committee of Ministers' Control of the Proper Implementation of Decisions Finding Violations of the Convention." In Gudmundur Alfredsson, Jonas Grimheden, Bertram G. Ramcharan, and Alfred de Zayas, eds., *International Human Rights Monitoring Mechanisms: Essays in Honour of Jakob Th. Möller*, 561–585. The Hague: Martinus Nijhoff.

Sunstein, Cass R. 1994. *Legal Reasoning and Political Conflict*. New York: Oxford University Press.

Tamanaha, Brian Z. 2004. *On the Rule of Law: History, Politics, Theory*. Cambridge: Cambridge University Press.

Taylor, Nick. 2002. "State Surveillance and the Right to Privacy." *Surveillance and Society* 1 (1): 66–85.

Taylor, Nick, and Clive Walker. 1996. "Bugs in the System." *Journal of Comparative Law* 1: 105–124.

Tettenborn, A. M. 1981. "The Contempt of Court Bill: Some Problems." *Solicitors' Journal* 125: 123–124.

Thurn, John Philipp. 2007. "Angst vor kommunistischen BriefträgerInnen: Zur Geschichte und Gegenwart der Berufsverbote." *Forum Recht* (October 24), http://www.linksnet.de/de /artikel/20835.

Tilly, Charles. 1999. "From Interactions to Outcomes in Social Movements." In Marco Giugni, Doug McAdam, and Charles Tilly, eds., *How Social Movements Matter*, 253–270. Minneapolis: University of Minnesota Press.

Tilly, Charles, and Sidney Tarrow. 2007. *Contentious Politics*. Boulder, Colo.: Paradigm Publishers.

Tomkins, Adam. 1995. "The Committee of Ministers: Its Roles Under the European Convention on Human Rights." *European Human Rights Law Review* 1: 49–62.

Tomz, Michael. 2007. *Reputation and International Cooperation: Sovereign Debt Across Three Centuries*. Princeton, N.J.: Princeton University Press.

Tushnet, Mark. 2008. *Weak Courts, Strong Rights: Judicial Review and Social Welfare Rights in Comparative Constitutional Law*, Princeton, N.J.: Princeton University Press.

Ulbert, Cornelia, and Thomas Risse. 2005. "Deliberatively Changing the Discourse: What Does Make Arguing Effective?" *Acta Politica* 40 (3): 351–367.

Venzke, Ingo. 2012. *How Interpretation Makes International Law: On Semantic Change and Normative Twists*. Oxford: Oxford University Press.

Vick, Douglas W. 2002. "The Human Rights Act and the British Constitution." *Texas International Law Journal* 37: 329–372.

Victor, David G., Kal Raustiala, and Eugene B. Skolnikoff. 1998. "Introduction and Overview." In David G. Victor, Kal Raustiala, and Eugene B. Skolnikoff, eds., *The Implementation and Effectiveness of International Environmental Commitments: Theory and Practice*, 1–46. Cambridge, Mass.: MIT Press.

Viljoen, Frans, and Lirette Louw. 2007. "State Compliance with the Recommendations of the African Commission on Human and Peoples' Rights, 1994-2004." *American Journal of International Law* 101 (1): 1–34.

Voeten, Eric. 2014. "Domestic Implementation if European Court of Human Rights Judgments: Legal Infrastructure and Government Effectiveness Matter: A Reply to Dia Anagnostou and Alina Mungiu-Pippidi." *European Journal of International Law* 25 (1): 229–238.

———. 2011. "Politics, Judicial Behaviour, and Institutional Design." In Jonas Christofferson and Mikael Rask Madsen, eds., *The European Court of Human Rights Between Law and Politics*, 61–76. Oxford: Oxford University Press.

———. 2008. "The Impartiality of International Judges: Evidence from the European Court of Human Rights." *American Political Science Review* 102 (4): 417–433.

———. 2007. "The Politics of International Judicial Appointments: Evidence from the European Court of Human Rights." *International Organization* 61 (4): 669–701.

Vogiatzis, Nikos. 2016. "The Admissibility Criterion Under Article 35(3)(b) ECHR: A 'Significant Disadvantage' to Human Rights Protection?" *International and Comparative Law Quarterly* 65 (1): 185–211.

Voland, Thomas, and Britta Schiebel. 2017. "Advisory Opinions of the European Court of Human Rights: Unbalancing the System of Human Rights Protection in Europe?" *Human Rights Law Review* 17 (1): 73–95.

Volcansek, Mary L. 1986. *Judicial Politics in Europe: An Impact Analysis*. New York: Peter Lang.

Volkmann, Uwe. 2011. "Fremdbestimmung—Selbstbehauptung—Befreiung: Das BVerfG in der Frage der Sicherungsverwahrung." *Juristen-Zeitung* 66: 835–842.

von Bogdandy, Armin, and Ingo Venzke. 2013. "On the Functions of International Courts: An Appraisal in Light of Their Burgeoning Public Authority." *Leiden Journal of International Law* 26: 49–72.

von Staden, Andreas. 2016a. "The Political Economy of the Non-enforcement of International Human Rights Pronouncements by States." In Alberta Fabbricotti, ed., *The Political Economy of International Law*, 230–257. Cheltenham: Edward Elgar.

———. 2016b. "Ineffektivität als Legitimitätsproblem: Die Befolgung der 'Auffassungen' der Ausschüsse der UN-Menschenrechtsverträge in Individualbeschwerdeverfahren." *Kritische Justiz* 49: 453–467.

———. 2009. "Shaping Human Rights Policy in Europe: Assessing and Explaining Compliance with the Judgments of the European Court of Human Rights." PhD diss., Princeton University.

———. 2007. "Assessing the Impact of the Judgments of the European Court of Human Rights on Domestic Human Rights Policies." Paper prepared for the 2007 Annual Meeting of the American Political Science Association, Chicago, Ill., August 30–September 2.

Wadham, John, Helen Mountfield, Anna Edmundson, and Caoilfhionn Gallagher. 2007. *Blackstone's Guide to the Human Rights Act 1998.* 4th ed. Oxford: Oxford University Press.

Walsh, Dermot P.J. 1982. "Arrest and Interrogation: Northern Ireland 1981." *Journal of Law and Society* 9 (1): 37–62.

Warbrick, Colin. 1991. "Expansion of Rights Protected by the European Convention on Human Rights." In W. E. Butler, ed., *Control over Compliance with International Law*, 139–151. Dordrecht: Martinus Nijhoff.

———. 1990. "Coherence and the European Court of Human Rights: The Adjudicative Background to the Soering Case." *Michigan Journal of International Law* 11: 1073–1096.

Weiler, Joseph H. H. 1991. "The Transformation of Europe." *Yale Law Journal* 100: 2403–2483.

Weir, Tony. 1999. "Down Hill—All the Way?" *Cambridge Law Journal* 58: 4–7.

White, Robin C. A., and Clare Ovey. 2010. *Jacobs, White and Ovey: The European Convention on Human Rights.* 5th ed. Oxford: Oxford University Press.

Wicks, Elizabeth. 2005. "Taking Account of Strasbourg? The British Judiciary's Approach to Interpreting Convention Rights." *European Public Law* 11 (3): 405–428.

———. 2000. "The United Kingdom Government's Perceptions of the European Convention on Human Rights at the Time of Entry." *Public Law* (Autumn): 438–455.

Wildhaber, Luzius. 2000. Letter of 28 March 2000 from Mr. Luzius Wildhaber, President of the European Court of Human Rights, to Mr. Gunnar Jansson, Chairperson of the Committee on Legal Affairs and Human Rights. In Parliamentary Assembly of the Council of Europe, Committee on Legal Affairs and Human Rights, *Execution of Judgments of the European Court of Human Rights*, Rapporteur: Erik Jurgens, PACE Doc. 8808 (July 12, 2000), appendix 2. https://assembly.coe.int/nw/xml/XRef/X2H-Xref-ViewHTML.asp?FileID=9013&lang=EN.

Williams, Jane. 2007. "Incorporating Children's Rights: The Divergence in Law and Policy." *Legal Studies* 27 (2): 261–287.

Young, James. 1981. "The Contempt of Court Act 1981." *British Journal of Law and Society* 8 (2): 243–255.

Young, Oran R. 1979. *Compliance and Public Authority: A Theory with International Applications.* Baltimore: Johns Hopkins University Press.

Young, Oran R., and Marc A. Levy (with the assistance of Gail Osherenko). 1999. "The Effectiveness of International Environmental Regimes." In Oran Young, ed., *The Effectiveness of International Environmental Regimes: Causal Connections and Behavioral Mechanisms*, 1–31. Cambridge, Mass.: MIT Press.

Ziegler, Katja S., Elizabeth Wicks, and Loveday Hodson, eds. 2015. *The UK and European Human Rights: A Strained Relationship?* Oxford: Hart.

Zimmermann, Andreas. 2001. "Germany." In Robert Blackburn and Jörg Polakiewicz, eds. *Fundamental Rights in Europe: The ECHR and Its Member States, 1950–2000*, 335–354. Oxford: Oxford University Press.

Zorn, Christopher, and Steven R. van Winkle. 2001. "Government Responses to the European Court of Human Rights." Paper prepared for the conference On the Effects of and Responses to Globalization, Boğaziçi University, Istanbul, Turkey, May 31–June 1.

———. 2000. "Explaining Compliance with the European Court of Human Rights." Paper prepared for the Annual Meeting of the Midwest Political Science Association, Chicago, Ill., April 27–30.

Zuckerman, Adrian A. S. 1999. "Justice in Crisis: Comparative Dimensions of Civil Procedure." In Adrian A. S. Zuckerman, ed., *Civil Justice in Crisis: Comparative Perspectives of Civil Procedure*, 3–52. Oxford: Oxford University Press.

Zürn, Michael. 2005. "Introduction: Law and Compliance at Different Levels." In Michael Zürn and Christian Joerges, eds., *Law and Governance in Postnational Europe: Compliance Beyond the Nation-State*, 1–39. Cambridge: Cambridge University Press.

Zürn, Michael, and Christian Joerges, eds. 2005. *Law and Governance in Postnational Europe: Compliance beyond the Nation-State*. Cambridge: Cambridge University Press.

INDEX

AIRE Center (NGO), 140, 143
Alter, Karen, 207, 253n103
Amnesty International, 82, 166

Barak, Aharon, 35
Basic Law (*Grundgesetz*), 150, 151, 165, 168, 170, 180, 196, 197, 199
Biometric data, 132–35
Blair, Tony, 69, 89, 90, 137, 268n68
Brexit, 67, 71, 72, 139
Brighton Declaration, 2, 19
British Irish Human Rights Watch (NGO), 131
Brown, Gordon, 71
Brussels Declaration, 2, 19
Bundestag, 150, 152

Cameron, David, 71, 135, 137, 138
Checkel, Jeffrey, 29, 254n139
Committee of Ministers: backlog of cases under supervision and, 3; compliance threshold and, 36; enforcement by, 45, 48; final resolutions as proxy for compliance, 17–20; interim resolutions and, 18, 48, 79, 108, 139, 234, 240; non-compliance proceedings and, 16–17, 132; peer pressure and, 7, 141; quasi-judicial decision-making authority of, 11, 68, 128, 244n59, 263n19; supervision of judgments and decisions, 3, 5, 12, 22, 31, 36, 60, 246n89, 247n111, 247n117, 255n141, 301n80
Compliance: broad, 16, 53, 54, 55, 56, 58, 59, 70, 87, 88, 100, 101, 106, 144, 145, 190, 206, 224; causality and, 32, 33, 210–11; culture of, 43, 44, 149; data set, 5, 17, 20–22, 27, 77, 135, 171, 243n43, 247n111; definition of, 30; depth of, 5, 27, 38, 56, 68, 82, 100, 203, 215; effectiveness and,

32–34, 210, 250n43; 250n44; enforcement and, 3, 7, 29, 30, 44, 45, 46, 48, 56–57, 58, 59, 64, 79, 85, 143–44, 145, 202, 206, 207, 212, 249n24, 256n161, 256n162; first-order, 3, 9, 17, 36, 83; habitual, 40, 43, 50, 115, 187; "how" of, 7, 51, 53, 59, 62, 204, 205; hybrid constructivist-rationalist theory of, 27, 30, 205, 207; minimalist, 7, 40, 54, 68, 72, 84, 87, 99, 100, 106, 120, 124, 125, 132, 144, 145, 212, 213; mobilization and, 28, 52, 57, 58–59; partial, 4, 5, 31, 45; reciprocity and, 28, 45, 46; reputation and, 4, 28, 46–48, 254n132; reservation costs and, 45, 141, 206; retaliation and, 28, 45; second-order, 3, 9, 17, 29, 36, 50; state of, 5, 17, 20, 22–26, 27, 243n43; "why" of, 5, 7, 205. *See also* Execution of judgments; rational choice within normative constraints
Conant, Lisa, 52, 57, 58, 249n15
Congress of Europe, 10
Constitutional Reform Act, 70
Corporal punishment and disciplining, 88–91, 263n9
Council of Europe: enforcement and, 6, 45; enlargement of, 1, 10, 12, 22; Statute of the, 41, 45
Court of Justice of the European Union, 9, 10, 13, 42, 43, 52, 57, 139, 207, 151, 242n26

Dai, Xinyuan, 57–58
Death penalty, 81–84, 85, 118,
Democracy: compliance and, 24, 25; human rights protection and, 7, 40–41, 43, 48, 49; liberal, 6, 39, 40–41, 43, 44, 48, 49
Department for the Execution of the Judgments of the ECtHR, 19

ACKNOWLEDGMENTS

This book has been long in the making. It has its roots in 2005 when I began research for it at Princeton University, at a time when there was very little political science literature on the European Convention and Court of Human Rights in general, and even less on second-order compliance with the Court's judgments. Elements of the book's arguments were first presented at the 2007 Annual Meeting of the American Political Science Association and a first version of the full study, covering the Court's output up to the year 2005, was completed in 2009. For a number of reasons, repeated delays unfortunately intervened during rewriting and preparing the manuscript for publication. This necessitated, among other things, the recurrent and time-consuming task of broadening and updating both the overall data set and the case studies in order to have the manuscript reflect the quantitative growth in the Court's output as well as the more recent developments with respect to the judgments' execution. Despite these delays, I believe that the book's arguments remain highly topical to understanding the patterns of compliance with the Court's judgments, and none of the studies on the Court that have appeared in the meantime have rendered them any less relevant or nugatory.

Several people that helped this project along deserve mention and gratitude. While at Princeton, Anne-Marie Slaughter, Robert O. Keohane, Andrew Moravcsik, and William Burke-White provided first-rate guidance that considerably improved the overall quality of the work. I am deeply grateful for the time they took to discuss the project with me and for the always constructive input they provided. In 2007, financed in part by a research grant from Princeton's Niehaus Center for Globalization and Governance, I had the opportunity to observe the workings of the Council of Europe from the inside during a four-week research visit to the Department for the Execution of Judgments of the European Court of Human Rights. Thanks at the Council go to Elena Malagoni, Frederik Sundberg, and other members of the staff for their hospitality and willingness to frankly discuss various aspects of the execution of the Court's judgments. I would also like to express gratitude to the American Political Science Association's Human Rights Section which provided encouragement along the way by awarding me two of its prizes in 2008 and 2010 for earlier work related to this book. At the University of Pennsylvania Press, I thank Peter Agree for his consistently good spirits and for smoothly guiding me through the publication process. Special kudos go to the Press's editorial staff for the excellent work in improving the overall clarity of the manuscript and to the three anonymous reviewers for offering very valuable feedback on earlier versions of the manuscript. At the University of Hamburg, I thank Julia Kühn for providing able research assistance during the final updating of the data set.

The biggest gratitude of all, however, goes to my family for their endurance with respect to this project: To Eva, who has been part of it from the beginning and has supported me in all ways imaginable during the highs and lows that come with writing and revising a book manuscript, and to our two sons, Julian and Lukas, who too often saw their dad disappear into the upstairs study, rather than play with them. I could not have finished this book without their encouragement, understanding, and love, and dedicate it to them.